SEACOAST AND UPLAND:
A New England Anthology

SEACOAST AND UPLAND:
A New England Anthology

Perry D. Westbrook

South Brunswick and New York: A. S. Barnes and Company
London: Thomas Yoseloff Ltd

A. S. Barnes and Co., Inc.
Cranbury, New Jersey 08512

Thomas Yoseloff Ltd
108 New Bond Street
London W1Y OQX, England

ISBN 0-498-01032-5
Printed in the United States of America

Acknowledgments

HARCOURT BRACE JOVANOVICH—for "Old Man Warner," by Dorothy Canfield. Copyright, 1923, by Harcourt Brace Jovanovich, Inc.; copyright, 1951, by Dorothy Canfield Fisher. Reprinted from A HARVEST OF STORIES by Dorothy Canfield by permission of Harcourt Brace Jovanovich, Inc.

HARVARD UNIVERSITY PRESS—for poems by Emily Dickinson, the first lines of which and the numbers of which in Thomas H. Johnson, Editor, THE POEMS OF EMILY DICKINSON are as follows: "These are the days when Birds come back" (#130). "I cautious, scanned my little life" (#178), "I shall know why" (#193), "There's a certain Slant of Light" (#258), "The Robin's my Criterion for Tune" (#285), "I went to Heaven" (#374), "There's been a Death, in the Opposite House" (#389), "I'm sorry for the Dead—Today" (#529), "I asked no other thing" (#621), "Soil of Flint, if steady tilled" (#681), "After a hundred years" (#1147), "The Butterfly's Assumption Gown" (#1244), "There is a solitude of space" (#1695). Reprinted by permission of the publishers and the Trustees of Amherst College from Thomas H. Johnson, Editor, THE POEMS OF EMILY DICKINSON, Cambridge, Mass.: The Belknap Press of Harvard University Press, Copyright, 1951, 1955, by The President and Fellows of Harvard College.

HOLT, RINEHART AND WINSTON, INC.—for "The Black Cottage" and "A Servant to Servants" by Robert Frost. From THE POETRY OF ROBERT FROST edited by Edward Connery Lathem. Copyright 1930, 1934, 1939, © 1969 by Holt, Rinehart and Winston, Inc. Copyright © 1958, 1962 by Robert Frost. Copyright © 1967 by Lesley Frost Ballantine. Reprinted by permission of Holt, Rinehart and Winston, Inc.

Contents

Introduction

The purpose of this anthology is to provide examples of the literary expression of rural and coastal New England from approximately 1800 to the middle of our own century. For the most part, the selections are factual or fictional narratives, either in prose or in verse, presenting New England scenes and people and written by men and women who had either lived the life they have described or, like Charles W. Eliot, had an intimate knowledge of it. Accounts of urban existence are excluded, as are most city-bred writers. We are interested in the voices of the backcountry and of the remote reaches of the coast. These voices have been numerous, and many of the earlier ones have gone unheard by later generations. Yet they are eminently worth listening to, for they speak to us from the past of a region of which the people and culture have long ago spread across the northern half of the United States.

There were and are, of course, two New Englands: that of Boston and several other large cities and university or college towns, and that of the villages and farmlands. The influence of both upon the nation and upon each other has been beyond measurement. For over a century the New England of the cities and universities provided the greater part of America's leaders and mentors in literature, education, theology, social and natural science, and technology. Yet, sustaining this contribution by supplying much of the talent that produced it were the scores of remote townships which Henry Ward Beecher, writing a century ago, aptly described as the "brood comb" of New England. The emigrants from New England to the West were mainly from the rural areas, and they carried with them their village way of life.

The nineteenth century witnessed an intense and enduring nationwide interest in New England culture and history, and New Englanders themselves were second to none in their eagerness to examine their institutions and customs and reveal whatever distinctive qualities, even the not so admirable ones, they came upon.

Just as Irish nationalists sought the uncorrupted roots of their culture in the Aran Islands, so native New Englanders and other Americans resorted to the backcountry of the region, where— again in Henry Ward Beecher's words—"the manners, morals, customs and religion of the fathers" still remained. Thus Sarah Orne Jewett devoted herself to writing about Maine villagers in the complete faith that she was recording that which was most authentic and most significant and best in American life. In the Preface to *Deephaven,* her first book, she quoted from George Sand's *Légendes Rustiques:* "The countryman is, so to speak, the only historian of prehistoric times that we have. Honor and intellectual profit to those who consecrate themselves to each hamlet's marvelous traditions, which when assembled and classi- fied, compared among themselves and minutely examined, may cast much light on the profound darkness of primitive ages." Not all the authors represented in this volume shared Miss Jewett's seriousness of purpose; many of them exhibit the ironi- cal humor that is a basic element in the Yankee character; but, sons and daughters of the Puritans that they were, none of them shirked a writer's responsibility, as they conceived it, of present- ing the truth, each to the best of his ability.

The truth about New England was frequently creditable and inspiring, but by no means always. Much of the nineteenth cen- tury was a period of decline and demoralization for the region, especially in areas far fom the cities. Poverty plagued the coun- tryside and rural degeneracy was endemic. The terrible picture of hill people in the Berkshires that Edith Wharton gives us in her novel *Summer* could be documented by a score of sociological studies appearing in American periodicals, including the *Atlantic Monthly,* in the 1890s and early 1900s. Though Mrs. Wharton's starkness was seldom equaled, these deplorable conditions are reflected in stories by many other writers, for example, in Mary E. Wilkins Freeman's "Sister Liddy" and the usually cheerful Rowland Robinson's "The Purification of Cornbury." But gen- erally, with the country folk of these and other authors, tradi- tional strengths prevail over adversity and render the most unpromising existence worthwhile in terms of individual dignity and fulfillment.

If there is one premise shared by all the authors in this volume, it is the Puritan one that life on this earth is of the utmost sig- nificance. To the strict Puritan, of course, existence is the time during which each immortal soul, in accordance with God's decree of election but through the instrumentality of each individual's human will, wins or fails to win the divine grace that will save it from eternal hellfire and consign it to everlasting bliss in heaven. Though in the nineteenth century the harshness of the old religion was softened by such philosophical and theological movements as Transcendentalism and Unitarianism, no such influence went very far, or was intended to, in undermining the traditional sense of the seriousness of life, the Puritan devotion to duty, and the Calvinistic overdevelopment of conscience. Indeed, in the hinterland orthodox Calvinism remained dominant, though certain evangelical and emotional sects, like Adventism and Methodism, were making significant inroads. The difference between the religious climate in the backcountry and that in older and more sophisticated sections is illustrated, in this volume, in Rose Terry Cooke's "Mrs. Flint's Married Experience," which depicts orthodoxy in full sway, and in the excerpt from Harriet Beecher Stowe's *The Minister's Wooing,* which records the revolt of an educated Newport woman against the inhumanities of traditional Calvinism. By the end of the century, Mary E. Wilkins Freeman in stories like "A Conflict Ended" depicted village Calvinism as vestigial, not a conviction but a state of mind characterized by a crabbed stubbornness and a warped will. Here individualism had gone to seed, and religious faith was reduced to neurosis.

Something should be said about the history and the social and economic trends in the hill country and the remote coastal areas of New England during the period covered by this anthology. Extensive settlement of these regions did not occur until after the Revolution, when the older towns had become critically overpopulated. The migration that occurred has been likened to the swarming of a hive. In this collection, Seth Hubbell's narrative of his journey northward from Long Island Sound and his settling his family in Vermont gives us an idea of the physical hardships as well as of the motivation involved in such movements of population. Seth Hubbell was only one of tens of thousands of such emigrants who founded scores of new towns throughout the northern and western parts of New England. They cleared away the forests; they piled stones from the fields into fences sometimes six or ten feet wide. Under their axes and ploughs high hilltops and steep mountainsides were converted into meadow and pasture. By 1830 many a county and township attained populations much larger than they possess at present. In addition to their huge capacity for work—their greatest asset

—the settlers brought with them their religious convictions, their traditional respect for education, and their town-meeting form of government. The church, the schoolhouse, and the town hall are to be found on almost every New England village green. The presence and influence of religion is discernible in various selections in this volume. The town meeting, however, has been singled out for special attention because it is so fundamental an institution in New England rural life. In a selection from Emerson it is described somewhat idealistically as it existed in its pristine form in eastern Massachusetts. In a piece by Rowland Robinson it is presented, rather humorously, as it functioned in a newly settled backcountry township. In an account by the editor of this anthology it appears in action as it persists on a Maine island at the present time.

The newly settled regions flourished only briefly. Before the middle of the nineteenth century decline had set in. Much of the land that had been cleared had proved to be ill suited to farming, especially on more than a self-sufficiency scale. The opening of the West by the Erie Canal in 1825 and later by the railroads, the California Gold Rush, and the lure of the manufacturing cities down country set up a serious population drain. The Civil War accelerated the process by its call for men of military age, many of whom either were killed or settled elsewhere when peace came, so that during the postwar decades the region was disproportionately populated by the elderly and by spinsters. Before the end of the century large segments of the countryside were returning to forest, farmhouses and barns were collapsing into their cellar holes, and whole communities were becoming ghost towns. Today among New England's mountains and along her shores silent evidences of this vanished population may be found —networks of stone walls, overgrown home-burying plots, cellar holes with a lilac bush or gnarled apple tree testifying that here was once a family's home. The abandoned farm became so much a part of the New England scene that no writer wishing to catch the mood of the region could ignore it. It is the subject of several of Robinson's and Frost's best poems. Sarah Orne Jewett's "The Gray Man," included in this volume, captures in prose the poignant sense of loneliness and hopelessness evoked by a deserted hill farm. "The stories of strange lives have been whispered to the earth, their thoughts have burnt themselves into the cold rocks." No one acquainted with the New England countryside can fail to be moved by these words of Miss Jewett's.

The history of the coast closely parallels that of the backcountry. The immigrants from the Southern New England litoral established communities or solitary homesteads on the most distant of the rocky islands and on the shores of the most inaccessible coves of the Maine coast. Here flourished a population of farmer-fishermen, men that tilled the sparse soil in the brief, foggy summers, and in other seasons fished or, accompanied sometimes by their families, sailed schooners or larger vessels in the coastwise and foreign trade. A more versatile or self-reliant people would be hard to imagine—men and women who had acquaintance with faraway lands but were deeply rooted in their own Maine townships. But this way of life, like that of the farming areas, underwent far-reaching change. Here, also, the lure of the cities, the opening of the West, the Civil War took their toll of the population. In addition, the coming of the steamship, the abandonment of small ports unable to accommodate vessels of deep draft, the concentration of the fishing industry in several ports like Gloucester and Boston wrecked the coastal economy. The one-time farmer-fisherman slowly gave up his farming and confined his fishing to lobstering and herring seining. Of these remarkable people, both in their prosperity and in their decline, Sarah Orne Jewett and Mary Ellen Chase, each in her generation, are the literary voices.

History, sociology, and economics are not all of life. There are other equally important and perhaps more fascinating things, such as the beauty and strangeness and occasional frightfulness of nature and of human character. To these the New England rural and coastal writers gave their chief attention, for they were artists first and social historians secondarily and perhaps unconsciously. The main preoccupation of artists must always be the aspects of outward nature and the souls and actions of individual men and women rather than of societies.

In the selection of material for this anthology the focus has been on lesser-known writers or relatively unfamiliar work by well-known figures. Much of what is included is obtainable only with difficulty elsewhere, but nothing has been included that is without either real literary merit or exceptional regional significance or, preferably, both. The arrangement of the selections is in accordance with their authors' birth dates. Though this is doubtless somewhat arbitrary, it does serve to give some indication of the points of view of different generations.

SEACOAST AND UPLAND:
A New England Anthology

Seth Hubbell

Seth Hubbell (1759–1832), a native of Connecticut, tells, in the following selection, the story of his journey to northern Vermont and of his establishing himself and family there. Here we have a detailed account of the first step in the conversion of a wilderness into a community—a rather typical experience of a typical settler. Most remarkable is Seth's wonder at his endurance and ability to survive. His suggestion that he was under a providence reflects the Calvinistic religious climate in which he lived: his own perseverance and indestructible will were God's instruments in accomplishing His purpose. Hubbell's Narrative, though completed by 1824, was apparently not published before 1827, the date of the text reprinted here without revision.

A Narrative of the Sufferings of Seth Hubbell and Family, in His Beginning a Settlement in the Town of Wolcott, in the State of Vermont

This narrative was written for the private use and gratification of the sufferer, with no intention of its ever appearing before the public, but certain reasons connected with his present circumstances have induced him (by the advice of his friends) to commit it to the press. It is a simple narration of real facts, the most of which many living witnesses can now attest to. The learned reader will excuse the many imperfections in this little work: the writer not being bred to literary knowledge, is sensible of his inability to entertain the curious: but if his plain and simple dress can reach the sympathy of the feeling heart, it may be gratifying to some. It may also serve to still the murmurings of those who are commencing settlements in the neighborhood of plenty, and teach them to be reconciled to their better fate, and duly appreciate the privileges they enjoy, resulting from the toils of the suffering few who broke the way into the wilderness.

In the latter part of February, 1789, I set out from the town of Norwalk, in Connecticut, on my journey for Wolcott, to commence a settlement and make that my residence; family consisting of my wife and five children, they all being girls, the eldest nine or ten years old. My team was a yoke of oxen and a horse. After I had proceeded on my journey to within about one hundred miles of Wolcott, one of my oxen failed; but I however kept him yoked with the other till about noon each day; then turned him before, and took his end of the yoke myself, and proceeded on in that manner with my load to about fourteen miles of my journey's end, when I could get the sick ox no further, and was forced to leave him with Thomas W. Connel, in Johnson; but he had neither hay nor grain for him. I then proceeded on with some help to Esq. McDaniel's in Hydepark: this brought me to about eight miles of Wolcott, and to the end of the road. It was now about the 20th of March; the snow not far from four feet deep; no hay to be had for my team, and no way for them to subsist but by browse. As my sick ox at McConnel's could not be kept on browse, I interceded with a man in Cambridge for a little hay to keep him alive, which I backed, a bundle at a time, five miles, for about ten days, when the ox died. On the 9th of April I set out from Esq. McDaniel's, his being the last house, for my intended residence in Wolcott, with my wife and two eldest children. We had eight miles to travel on snowshoes, by marked trees—no road being cut: my wife had to try this new mode of traveling, and she performed the journey remarkably well. The path had been so trodden by snowshoes as to bear up the children. Esq. Taylor, with his wife and two small children, who moved on with me, had gone on the day before. We were the first families in Wolcott: in Hydepark there had two families wintered the year before. To the east of us it was eighteen miles to inhabitants, and no road but marked trees: to the south about twenty, where there was infant settlements, but no communication with us; and to the north, it was almost indefinite, or to the regions of Canada.

I had now got to the end of my journey, and I may say almost to the end of my property, for I had not a mouthful of meat or kernel of grain for my family, nor had I a cent of money to buy with, or property that I could apply to that purpose. I however had the good luck to catch a saple. The skin I carried fifty miles, and exchanged for half a bushel of wheat, and backed it home. We had now lived three weeks without bread; though in the time I had bought a moose of an Indian, which I paid for by selling the shirt off my back, and backed the meat five miles, which answered to subsist upon. I would here remark that it was my fate to move on my family at that memorable time called the "scarce season," which was generally felt through the state, especially in the northern parts in the infant settlements: no grain or provision of any kind, of consequence, was to be had on the river Lamoille. I had to go into New-Hampshire, sixty miles, for the little I had for my family, till harvest, and this was so scanty a pittance that we were under the painful necessity of allowancing the children till we had a supply. The three remaining children that I left in Hydepark, I brought one at a time on my back on snowshoes, as also the whole of my goods.

I moved from Connecticut with the expectation of having fifty acres of land given me when I came on, but this I was disappointed of, and was under the necessity soon after I came on of selling a yoke of oxen and a horse to buy the land I now live on, which reduced my stock to but one cow; and this I had the misfortune to lose the next winter. That left me wholly destitute of a single hoof of a creature: of course the second summer I had to support my family without a cow. I would here notice that I spent the summer before I moved, in Wolcott, in making preparation for a settlement, which, however, was of no avail to me, and I lost the summer; and to forward my intended preparation, I brought on a yoke of oxen, and left them, when I returned in the fall, with a man in Johnson, to keep through the winter, on certain conditions; but when I came on in the spring, one of them was dead, and this yoke of oxen that I put off for my land was made of the two surviving ones. But to proceed, in the fall I had the good fortune to purchase another cow; but my misfortunes still continued, for in the June following she was killed by a singular accident. Again I was left without a cow, and here I was again frustrated in my calculations: this last cow left a fine heifer calf that in the next fall I lost by being choaked. Soon after I arrived, I took two cows to double in four years. I had one of my own besides, which died in calving. In June following, one of those taken to double, was killed while fighting; the other was found dead in the yard; both of which I had to replace. In the same spring, one of my neighbour's oxen hooked a bull of two years old, which caused his death soon after. Here I was left destitute—no money to buy, or article to traffic for one; but there was a door opened. I was informed that a merchant in Haverhill was buying snakeroot and sicily. This was a new kind of traffic that I had no great faith in; but I thought to improve every means or semblance of means in my power. Accordingly, with the help of my two oldest girls, I dug and dried a horse-load, and carried this new commodity to the merchant; but this was like most hearsay reports of fine markets, always a little way a-head, for he knew nothing about this strange article, and would not even venture to make an offer; but after a long conference I importuned with the good merchant to give me a three year old heifer for my roots, on certain conditions too tedious to mention. I drove her home, and with joy she was welcomed to my habitation, and it has been my good fortune to have a cow ever since. Though my faith was weak, yet being vigilant and persevering, I obtained the object, and the wilderness produced me a cow.

When I came into Wolcott my farming tools consisted of one axe and an old hoe. The first year I cleared about two acres, wholly without any team, and being short of provision was obliged to work the chief of the time till harvest with scarce a sufficiency to support nature. My work was chiefly by the river. When too faint to labor, for want of food, I used to take a fish from the river, broil it on the coals, and eat it without bread or salt, and then to my work again. This was my common practice the first year till harvest. I could not get a single potatoe to plant the first season, so scarce was this article. I then thought if I could but get enough of this valuable production to eat I would never complain. I rarely see this article cooked, but the thought strikes my mind; in fact to this day I have a great veneration for this precious root. I planted that which I cleared in season with corn; and an early frost ruined the crop, so that I raised nothing the first year: had again to buy my provision. My seed corn, about eight quarts, cost me two and a half yards of whitened linen, yard wide, and this I had to go twenty miles after. Though this may be called extortion, it was a solitary instance of the kind;

all were friendly and ready to assist me in my known distress, as far as they had ability. An uncommon degree of sympathy pervaded all the new settlers, and I believe this man heartily repented the act, for he was by no means indigent, and was many times reminded of it by way of reproof.

My scanty supply of bread-corn made it necessary to improve the first fruits of harvest at Lake Champlain, to alleviate our distress, it being earlier than with us. Accordingly, on the last days of July or first of August, I took my sickle, and set out for the Lake, a distance of better than forty miles. When I had got there, I found their grain was not ripe enough to begin upon; but was informed that on the Grand-Isle they had began their harvest. I was determined to go on, but had nothing to pay my passage. I finally hired a man to carry me over from Georgia for the small compensation of a case and two lances that I happened to have with me; but when I had got on to the Island, I found I was still too early. There was no grain ripe here, but I found the most forward I could, plead my necessity, and stayed by the owner till I got one and a half bushel of wheat, and worked for him to pay for it: it was quite green; I dried it and set out for home; but my haste to get back prevented my drying it sufficiently. I found a boat bound for Mansfield's mills, on the river Lamoille, and got my grain on board, and had it bro't there free from expense. I got it ground or rather mashed, for it was too damp to make meal. I here hired my meal carried on to Cambridge borough for my sickle, and there got it ground the second time, but it was still far from good meal. From the Borough I was so fortunate as to get it home on a horse. I was a fortnight on this tour. My wife was fearful some accident had happened, and sent a man in pursuit of me, who met me on my way home. I left my family without bread or meal, and was welcomed home with tears: my wife baked a cake, and my children again tasted bread.

I had the good fortune to buy on trust, the winter after I lost my corn, of a man in Cambridge, twenty-four miles from home, twelve bushels of corn, and one of wheat. This, by the assistance of some kind friends, I got to Esq. McDaniel's. I also procured by digging on shares in Hydepark, twelve or thirteen bushels of potatoes. This grain and potatoes I carried eight miles on my back. My common practice was one half bushel of meal, and one half bushel of potatoes at a load.

The singular incidents that took place in getting this grain on, though tedious to mention, may be worthy of notice. Soon after I set out from home, sometime in the month of March; it began to rain, and was a very rainy day and night. The Lamoille was raised—the ice became rotten and dangerous crossing—many of the small streams were broken up. The man of whom I purchased the grain was so good as to take his team and carry it to the mill. The owner of the mill asked me how I expected to get my meal home. I answered him as the case really was, that I knew not. The feeling man then offered me his oxen and sled to carry it to the Park, and I thankfully accepted his kind offer. He then turned to the miller, and directed him to grind my grist toll free. While at the mill a man requested me to bring a half hogshead tub on my sled up to Johnson. By permission of the owner of the oxen, he put the tub on the sled, and it was a Providential circumstance; for when I came to Brewster's branch, a wild stream, I found it broken up, run rapid and deep. At first I was perplexed what to do. To go across with my bags on the sled would ruin my meal; I soon thought of the tub; this held about half of my bags; the other half I left on the shore, and proceeded into the branch and crossed with safety. Though I was wet nearly to my middle, I unloaded the tub and returned into the branch, holding the tub on the sled, but the stream was so rapid, the tub being empty, that in spite of all my exertions I was washed off the sled and carried down the stream, holding on to the tub, for this I knew was my only alternative to get across my load. At length I succeeded in getting the tub to the shore, though I was washed down the stream more than twenty rods, sometimes up to my armpits in the water, and how I kept the tub from filling in this hasty struggle, I know not, but so it was. The oxen, though turned towards home, happily for me, when they had got across the stream, stopt in the path, till I came up with the tub. I then put in the other half of my load, and succeeded in getting the whole across the branch, and travelled on about three miles and put up for the night. Wet as I was, and at that season of the year, it is easy to conceive my uncomfortable situation, for the thaw was over, and it was chilly and cold. In the morning I proceeded for home—came to the river: not being sensible how weak the ice was, I attempted to cross, but here a scene ensued that I can never forget. When about half across the river, I perceived the ice settling under my oxen. I jumped on to the tongue of my sled, and hastened to the oxen's heads, and pulled out the pin that held the yoke. By this time the oxen were sunk to their knees in water.

I then sprang to the sled, and drawed it back to the shore, without the least difficulty, notwithstanding the load, and returned to my oxen. By this time they had broken a considerable path in the ice, and were struggling to get out. I could do nothing but stand and see them swim round—sometimes they would be nearly out of sight, nothing scarcely but their horns to be seen; they would then rise and struggle to extricate themselves from their perilous situation. I called for help in vain; & to fly for assistance would have been imprudent and fatal. Notwithstanding my unhappy situation, and the manner by which I came by the oxen, &c. I was not terrified in the least—I felt calm and composed;—at length the oxen swam up to where I stood and laid their heads on the ice at my feet. I immediately took the yoke from off their necks; they lay still till the act was performed, and then returned to swimming as before. By this time they had made an opening in the ice as much as two rods across. One of them finally swam to the downstream side, and in an instant, as if lifted out of the water, he was on his side on the ice, and got up and walked off; the other swam to the same place and was out in the same way. I stood on the opposite side of the opening, and saw with astonishment every movement. I then thought, and the impression is still on my mind, that they were helped out by supernatural means; most certainly no natural cause could produce an effect like this: that a heavy ox six and a half feet in girth, can of his own natural strength heave himself out of the water on his side on the ice, is too extraordinary to reconcile to a natural cause;—that in the course of Divine Providence events do take place out of the common course of nature, that our strongest reasoning cannot comprehend, is impious to deny: though we acknowledge the many chimeras of superstition, ignorance and barbarism in the world; and when we are eye witnesses to such events, it is not for us to doubt, but to believe and tremble. Others have a right to doubt my testimony: but in this instance, for me to doubt would be perjury to my own conscience, and I may add ingratitude to my Divine Benefactor. In fact a signal Providence seemed to direct the path for me to pursue to procure this grain. Though I was doomed to encounter perils, to suffer fatigue and toil, there was a way provided for me to obtain the object in view. In the first onset I accidentally fell in with the man of whom I purchased at the Park. I found he had grain to sell. I requested of him this small supply on trust: we were strangers to each other—a peculiar friend of mine, happening to be by, volunteered his word for the pay. I knew not where nor how to get the money, but necessity drove me to make the purchase, and in the course of the winter I was so fortunate as to catch saple enough to pay the debt by the time it was due. Though I hazarded my word, it was in a good cause—it was for the relief of my family, and so it terminated. But to return,

I had now gone to the extent of my abilities for bread corn, but was destitute of meat; and beef and pork were scarcer in those times. Accordingly I had to have recourse to wild meat for a substitute, and had the good luck to purchase a moose of a hunter; and the meat of two more I brought in on shares—had the one for bringing in the other. These two were uncommonly large—were judged to weigh seven hundred weight each. The meat of these three moose I brought in on my back, together with the large bones and heads. I backed them five or six miles over rough land, cut up by sharp ridges and deep hollows, and interspersed with underbrush and windfalls, which made it impracticable to pass with a hand sled, which, could I have used, would much eased my labor. A more laborious task was this than that of bringing my meal, &c. from the Park.

My practice was to carry my loads in a bag, to tie the ends of the bag so nigh that I could but comfortably get my head through, so that the weight of my load would rest on my shoulders. I often had to encounter this hardship in the time of a thaw, which made the task more severe, especially in the latter part of winter and fore part of the spring, when the snow became coarse and harsh, and will not so readily support the snowshoe. My hold would often fail without any previous notice to guard against it—perhaps slide under a log or catch in a bush and pitch me into the snow with my load about my neck. I have repeatedly had to struggle in this situation for some time to extricate myself from my load, it being impossible to get up with my load on. Those who are acquainted with this kind of burden may form an idea of what I had to encounter—the great difficulty of carrying a load on snowshoes in the time of a thaw, is one of those kinds of fatigue that it is hard to describe, nor can be conceived but by experience. It is wearisome at such times to travel without a load; but with one, especially at this late season, it is intolerable: but thaw or freeze my necessities obliged me to be at my task, and still to keep up my burthen. I had to draw my firewood through the winter on a hand sled: in fact, my snowshoes were constantly hung to my feet.

Being destitute of team for four or five years, and without farming tools, I had to labor under great embarrassments: my grain I hoed in the three first years. After I raised a sufficiency for my family, I had to carry it twelve miles to mill on my back, for the three first years: this I had constantly to do once a week. My common load was one bushel, and generally carried it eight miles before I stopped to rest. My wife at one time sold her shirt to purchase a moose hide which I was obliged to carry thirty miles on my back, and sold it for a bushel of corn, and bro't the corn home in the same way.

For a specimen of the hardships those have often to encounter who move into the wilderness, I will give the following, that took place the winter after I came on: We had a remarkable snow, the first of consequence, that fell; it was full two feet deep. Our communication was with the inhabitants of Hydepark, and it was necessary for us to keep the road, or rather path, so that we could travel; we were apprehensive of danger, if we did not immediately tread a path through this snow. I was about out of meal, and had previously left a bushel at a deserted house about five miles on the way. I agreed with Esq. Taylor, he being the only inhabitant with me, to start the next day on the proposed tour. We accordingly started before sunrise; the snow was light, and we sunk deep into it. By the middle of the day it give some, which made it still worse; our snowshoes loaded at every step; we had to use nearly our whole strength to extricate the loaded shoe from its hold. It seemed that our hip joints would be drawn from their sockets. We were soon worried—could go but a few steps without stopping: our fatigue and toil become almost insupportable—were obliged often to sit down and rest, and were several times on the point of giving up the pursuit, and stop for the night, but this must have been fatal, as we had no axe to cut wood for a fire; our blood was heated, and we must have chilled. We finally, at about dusk, reached the deserted house, but was in effect exhausted. It seemed we could not have reached this house had it been twenty rods further: so terrible is the toil to travel through deep snow, that no one can have a sense of it till taught by experience. This day's journey is often on my mind; in my many hard struggles it was one of the severest. We struck up a fire and gathered some fuel that lay about the house, and after we had recovered strength, I baked a cake of my meal. We then lay down on some hewn planks, and slept sound till morning. It froze at night; the track we had made rendered it quite feasible travelling. The next day I returned home with my bushel of meal.

Another perilous tour I will mention, that occurred this winter. It was time to bring on another load of meal from Esq. Mc-Daniels. I proposed in my mind to go early the next morning. There had been a thaw, and in the time of the thaw a man had driven a yoke of oxen from Cabot, and went down on my path, and trod it up. The night was clear—the moon shone bright, and it was remarkably cold. I awoke, supposing it nearly day, and sat out, not being sensible of the cold, and being thinly clad I soon found I was in danger of freezing, and began to run, jump, and thrash my hands, &c. The path being full of holes, and a light snow had just fallen that filled them up, I often fell, and was in danger of breaking my limbs, &c. The cold seemed to increase, and I was forced to exert my utmost strength to keep from freezing: my limbs became numb before I got through, though I ran about every step of the eight miles, and when I got to McDaniel's the cocks crowed for day. I was surprised upon coming to the fire to find that the bottoms of my mockasins and stockings were cut and worn through, the bottoms of my feet being entirely bare, having cut them by the holes in the path, but notwithstanding the severity of the frost, I was preserved, not being frozen in any part. Had I broken a limb, or but slightly spraint a joint, which I was in imminent danger of doing, I must have perished on the way, as a few minutes of respite must have been fatal.

In the early part of my residence in Wolcott, by some means I obtained knowledge of their being beaver on a small stream in Hardwick; and desirous to improve every means in my power for the support of my family, and to retrieve my circumstances, I determined on a tour to try my fortune at beaver hunting. Accordingly, late in the fall, I set out in company with my neighbor Taylor on the intended enterprise. We took what was called the Coos road, which was nothing more than marked trees: in about seven miles we reached the stream, and proceeded up it about three miles farther, and searched for beaver, but were soon convinced that they had left the ground. We, however, set a few traps. Soon after we started it began to rain, and before night the rain turned into a moist snow that melted on us as fast as it fell. Before we reached the hunting ground, we were wet to our skins; night soon came on—we found it necessary to camp (as the hunters use the term); with difficulty we struck up a fire, but our fuel was poor, chiefly green timber—the storm increased—

the snow continued moist; our bad accommodations grew worse and worse; our fire was not sufficient to warm us and much less to dry us; we dared not attempt to lay down, but continued on our feet through the night, feeding our fire and endeavoring to warm our shivering limbs. This is a memorable night to me; the most distressing I ever experienced; we anxiously looked for day. At length the dawn appeared, but it was a dismal and a dreary scene. The moist snow had adhered to every thing in its way; the trees and underwood were remarkably loaded, were completely hid from sight—nothing to be seen but snow, and nothing to be heard but the cracking of the bended boughs under the enormous weight, we could scarcely see a rod at noon day. When light enough to travel, we set out for home, and finding it not safe to leave the stream for fear of getting bewildered and lost, we followed it back; it was lined the chief of the way with beaver meadow, covered with a thick growth of alders; we had no way to get through them but for one to go forward and beat off the snow with a heavy stick. We thus proceeded, though very slowly, down the stream to the Coos road, and worried through the ten miles home at the dusk of the evening, nearly exhausted by fatigue, wet and cold, for it began to freeze in the morning; our clothes were frozen stiff on our backs; when I pulled off my great coat it was so stiff as to stand up on the floor. In order to save our traps we had to make another trip, and one solitary muskrat made up our compensation for this hunting tour.

A painful circumstance respecting my family I must here mention. In the year 1806, we were visited with sickness that was uncommonly distressing, five being taken down at the same time, and several dangerously ill. In this sickness I lost my wife, the partner of my darkest days, who bore her share of our misfortunes with becoming fortitude. I also lost a daughter at the same time, and another was bedrid about six months, and unable to perform the least labour for more than a year. This grievous calamity involved me in debts that terminated in the loss of my farm, my little all; but by the indulgence of feeling relatives I am still permitted to stay on it. Though I have been doomed to hard fortune I have been blest with a numerous offspring; have had by my two wives seventeen children, thirteen of them daughters; have had fifty-one grand-children, and six great-grand-children, making my posterity seventy-four souls.

I have here given but a sketch of my most important sufferings. The experienced farmer will readily discover, that under the many embarrassments I had to encounter, I must make but slow progress in clearing land; no soul to help me, no funds to go to: raw and inexperienced in this kind of labor, though future wants pressed the necessity of constant application to this business, a great portion of my time was unavoidably taken up in pursuit of sustenance for my family; however reluctant to leave my labor, the support of nature must be attended to, the calls of hunger cannot be dispensed with. I have now to remark, that at this present time, my almost three score years and ten, I feel the want of those forced exertions of bodily strength that were spent in those perils and fatigues, and have worn down my constitution, to support my decaying nature.

When I reflect on those past events, the fatigue and toil I had to encounter, the dark scenes I had to pass through, I am struck with wonder and astonishment at the fortitude and presence of mind that I then had to bear me up under them. Not once was I discouraged or disheartened: I exercised all my powers of body and mind to do the best I could, and left the effect for future events to decide, without embarrassing my mind with imaginary evils. I could lay down at night, forgetting my troubles, and sleep composed and calm as a child; I did in reality experience the just proverb of the wise man, that "the sleep of the laboring man is sweet, whether he eat little or much." Nor can I close my tale of sufferings without rendering my feeble tribute of thanks and praise to my benign Benefactor, who supplies the wants of the needy and relieves the distressed, that in his wise Providence has assisted my natural strength both of body and of mind to endure those scenes of distress and toil.

COUNTY OF ORLEANS, *Nov'r.* 1824.

The undersigned, having read in manuscript the foregoing narrative, and having lived in habits of intimacy with, and in the neighborhood of Seth Hubbell at the time of his sufferings, we are free to inform the public, that we have no doubt but his statements are, in substance, correct. Many of the circumstances herein narrated we were at the time personally knowing to, and are sensible more might be added without exaggeration, in many instances wherein he suffered.

THOMAS TAYLOR, *Justice of Peace.*
DARIUS FITCH, *J. of Peace.*
JOHN McDANIEL, *J. P.*
JESSE WHITNEY, *J. P.*

Ralph Waldo Emerson

Ralph Waldo Emerson (1803-1882), one of America's greatest literary figures, was born in Boston and educated at Harvard. From 1835 to his death he lived in Concord, the home of his ancestors. The "Historical Discourse" of which a part is given here was delivered as a lecture in 1835. Because it is an analysis of the self-government of a prototypal New England village, it is appropriate that its position be near the beginning of this collection. Emerson's enthusiasm for the town meeting reflects a mood common in the last century among students of New England culture. The following excerpt from the "Historical Discourse" is based on the text as found in Volume XI of The Works of Ralph Waldo Emerson *(1883).*

Historical Discourse

FELLOW CITIZENS:

The town of Concord begins, this day, the third century of its history. By a common consent, the people of New England, for a few years past, as the second centennial anniversary of each of its early settlements arrived, have seen fit to observe the day. You have thought it becoming to commemorate the planting of the first inland town. The sentiment is just, and the practice is wise. Our ears shall not be deaf to the voice of time. We will review the deeds of our fathers, and pass that just verdict on them we expect from posterity on our own.

And yet, in the eternity of nature, how recent our antiquities appear! The imagination is impatient of a cycle so short. Who can tell how many thousand years, every day, the clouds have shaded these fields with their purple awning? The river, by whose banks most of us were born, every winter, for ages, has spread its crust of ice over the great meadows which, in ages, it had formed. But the little society of men who now, for a few years, fish in this river, plough the fields it washes, mow the grass and reap the corn, shortly shall hurry from its banks as did their forefathers. "Man's life," said the Witan to the Saxon king, "is the sparrow that enters at a window, flutters round the house, and flies out at another, and none knoweth whence he came, or whither he goes." The more reason that we should give to our being what permanence we can;—that we should recall the Past, and expect the Future.

Yet the race survives whilst the individual dies. In the country, without any interference of the law, the agricultural life favors the permanence of families. Here are still around me the lineal descendants of the first settlers of this town. Here is Blood, Flint, Willard, Meriam, Wood, Hosmer, Barrett, Wheeler, Jones, Brown, Buttrick, Brooks, Stow, Hoar, Heywood, Hunt, Miles,— the names of the inhabitants for the first thirty years; and the family is in many cases represented, when the name is not. If the name of Bulkeley is wanting, the honor you have done me this day, in making me your organ, testifies your persevering kindness to his blood.

I shall not be expected, on this occasion, to repeat the details of that oppression which drove our fathers out hither. Yet the town of Concord was settled by a party of non-conformists, immediately from Great Britain. The best friend the Massachusetts colony had, though much against his will, was Archbishop Laud in England. In consequence of his famous proclamation setting up certain novelties in the rites of public worship, fifty godly ministers were suspended for contumacy, in the course of two years and a half. Hindered from speaking, some of these dared to print the reasons of their dissent, and were punished with imprisonment or mutilation.[1] This severity brought some of the best men in England to overcome that natural repugnance to emigration which holds the serious and moderate of every nation to their own soil. Among the silenced clergymen was a distin-

---

1. Neal's *History of New England,* vol. i. p. 132. [All footnotes are Emerson's.]

guished minister of Woodhill, in Bedfordshire, Rev. Peter Bulkeley, descended from a noble family, honored for his own virtues,
his learning and gifts as a preacher, and adding to his influence
the weight of a large estate.[2] Persecution readily knits friendship
between its victims. Mr. Bulkeley having turned his estate into
money and set his face towards New England, was easily able to
persuade a good number of planters to join him. They arrived in
Boston in 1634.[3] Probably there had been a previous correspondence with Governor Winthrop, and an agreement that they
should settle at Musketaquid. With them joined Mr. Simon Willard, a merchant from Kent in England. They petitioned the
General Court for a grant of a township, and on the 2d of September, 1635, corresponding in New Style to 12th September,
two hundred years ago this day, leave to begin a plantation at
Musketaquid was given to Peter Bulkeley, Simon Willard, and
about twelve families more. A month later, Rev. John Jones
and a large number of settlers destined for the new town arrived
in Boston.[4]

The grant of the General Court was but a preliminary step.
The green meadows of Musketaquid or *Grassy Brook* were far
up in the woods, not to be reached without a painful and dangerous journey through an uninterrupted wilderness. They could
cross the Massachusetts or Charles river, by the ferry at New-
town; they could go up the river as far as Watertown. But the
Indian paths leading up and down the country were a foot broad.
They must then plunge into the thicket, and with their axes cut
a road for their teams, with their women and children and their
household stuff, forced to make long circuits too, to avoid hills
and swamps. Edward Johnson of Woburn has described in an
affecting narrative their labors by the way. "Sometimes passing
through thickets where their hands are forced to make way for
their bodies' passage, and their feet clambering over the crossed
trees, which when they missed, they sunk into an uncertain bottom
in water, and wade up to their knees, tumbling sometimes higher,
sometimes lower. At the end of this, they meet a scorching plain,
yet not so plain but that the ragged bushes scratch their legs
foully, even to wearing their stockings to their bare skin in two
or three hours. Some of them, having no leggins, have had the
blood trickle down at every step. And in time of summer, the

---

2. Neal's *History of New England,* vol. i. p. 321.
3. Shattuck's *History of Concord,* p. 158.
4. Shattuck, p. 5.

sun casts such a reflecting heat from the sweet fern, whose scent is very strong, that some nearly fainted." They slept on the rocks, wherever the night found them. Much time was lost in travelling they knew not whither, when the sun was hidden by clouds; for "their compass miscarried in crowding through the bushes," and the Indian paths, once lost, they did not easily find.

Johnson, relating undoubtedly what he had himself heard from the pilgrims, intimates that they consumed many days in exploring the country, to select the best place for the town. Their first temporary accommodation was rude enough. "After they have found a place of abode, they burrow themselves in the earth for their first shelter, under a hill-side, and casting the soil aloft upon timbers, they make a fire against the earth, at the highest side. And thus these poor servants of Christ provide shelter for themselves, their wives and little ones, keeping off the short showers from their lodgings, but the long rains penetrate through, to their great disturbance in the night season. Yet in these poor wigwams they sing psalms, pray and praise their God, till they can provide them houses, which they could not ordinarily, till the earth, by the Lord's blessing, brought forth bread to feed them. This they attain with sore travail, every one that can lift a hoe to strike into the earth, standing stoutly to his labors, and tearing up the roots and bushes from the ground, which, the first year, yielded them a lean crop, till the sod of the earth was rotten, and therefore they were forced to cut their bread very thin for a long season. But the Lord is pleased to provide for them great store of fish in the spring time, and especially, alewives, about the bigness of a herring."[5] These served them also for manure. For flesh, they looked not for any, in those times, unless they could barter with the Indians for venison and raccoons. "Indian corn, even the coarsest, made as pleasant meal as rice."[6] All kinds of garden fruits grew well, "and let no man," writes our pious chronicler, in another place, "make a jest of pumpkins, for with this fruit the Lord was pleased to feed his people until their corn and cattle were increased."[7]

The great cost of cattle, and the sickening of their cattle upon such wild fodder as was never cut before; the loss of their sheep and swine by wolves; the sufferings of the people in the great

5. Johnson's *Wonder-Working Providence,* chap. xxxv. I have abridged and slightly altered some sentences.
6. Mourt, *Beginning of Plymouth,* 1621, p. 60.
7. Johnson, p. 56.

snows and cold soon following; and the fear of the Pequots; are the other disasters enumerated by the historian.

The hardships of the journey and of the first encampment, are certainly related by their contemporary with some air of romance, yet they can scarcely be exaggerated. A march of a number of families with their stuff, through twenty miles of unknown forest, from a little rising town that had not much to spare, to an Indian town in the wilderness that had nothing, must be laborious to all, and for those who were new to the country and bred in softness, a formidable adventure. But the pilgrims had the preparation of an armed mind, better than any hardihood of body. And the rough welcome which the new land gave them was a fit introduction to the life they must lead in it.

But what was their reception at Musketaquid? This was an old village of the Massachusetts Indians. Tahattawan, the Sachem, with Waban his son-in-law, lived near Nashawtuck, now Lee's Hill.[8] Their tribe, once numerous, the epidemic had reduced. Here they planted, hunted and fished. The moose was still trotting in the country, and of his sinews they made their bowstring. Of the pith elder, that still grows beside our brooks, they made their arrow. Of the Indian Hemp they spun their nets and lines for summer angling, and, in winter, they sat around holes in the ice, catching salmon, pickerel, breams and perch, with which our river abounded.[9] Their physical powers, as our fathers found them, and before yet the English alcohol had proved more fatal to them than the English sword, astonished the white men.[10] Their sight was so excellent, that, standing on the sea shore, they often told of the coming of a ship at sea, sooner by one hour, yea, two hours sail, than any Englishman that stood by, on purpose to look out.[11] Roger Williams affirms that he has known them run between eighty and a hundred miles in a summer's day, and back again within two days. A little pounded parched corn or nocake sufficed them on the march. To his bodily perfection, the wild man added some noble traits of character. He was open as a child to kindness and justice. Many instances of his humanity were known to the Englishmen who suffered in the woods from sickness or cold. "When you came over the morning waters," said one of the Sachems, "we took you into our arms. We fed

8. Shattuck, p. 3.
9. Josselyn's *Voyages to New England,* 1638.
10. Hutchinson's *History of Massachusetts,* vol. i. chap. 6.
11. Thomas Morton; *New England Canaan,* p. 47.

you with our best meat. Never went white man cold and hungry from Indian wigwam."

The faithful dealing and brave good-will, which, during the life of the friendly Massasoit, they uniformly experienced at Plymouth and at Boston, went to their hearts. So that the peace was made, and the ear of the savage already secured, before the pilgrims arrived at his seat of Musketaquid, to treat with him for his lands.

It is said that the covenant made with the Indians by Mr. Bulkeley and Major Willard, was made under a great oak, formerly standing near the site of the Middlesex Hotel.[12] Our Records affirm that Squaw Sachem, Tahattawan, and Nimrod did sell a tract of six miles square to the English, receiving for the same, some fathoms of Wampumpeag, hatchets, hoes, knives, cotton cloth and shirts. Wibbacowet, the husband of Squaw Sachem, received a suit of cloth, a hat, a white linen band, shoes, stockings and a great coat; and, in conclusion, the said Indians declared themselves satisfied, and told the Englishmen they were welcome. And after the bargain was concluded, Mr. Simon Willard, pointing to the four corners of the world, declared that they had bought three miles from that place, east, west, north and south.[13]

The Puritans, to keep the remembrance of their unity one with another, and of their peaceful compact with the Indians, named their forest settlement CONCORD. They proceeded to build, under the shelter of the hill that extends for a mile along the north side of the Boston road, their first dwellings. The labors of a new plantation were paid by its excitements. I seem to see them, with their pious pastor, addressing themselves to the work of clearing the land. Natives of another hemisphere, they beheld, with curiosity, all the pleasing features of the American forest. The landscape before them was fair, if it was strange and rude. The little flower which at this season stars our woods and roadsides with its profuse blooms, might attract even eyes as stern as theirs with its humble beauty. The useful pine lifted its cones into the frosty air. The maple which is already making the forest gay with its orange hues, reddened over those houseless men. The majestic summits of Wachusett and Monadnoc towering in the horizon, invited the steps of adventure westward.

As the season grew later, they felt its inconveniences. "Many

_____

12. Shattuck, p. 6.
13. Depositions taken in 1684, and copied in the first volume of the Town Records.

were forced to go barefoot and bareleg, and some in time of frost and snow, yet were they more healthy than now they are."[14] The land was low but healthy; and if, in common with all the settlements, they found the air of America very cold, they might say with Higginson, after his description of the other elements, that "New England may boast of the element of fire, more than all the rest; for all Europe is not able to afford to make so great fires as New England. A poor servant, that is to possess but fifty acres, may afford to give more wood for fire as good as the world yields, than many noblemen in England."[15] Many were their wants, but more their privileges. The light struggled in through windows of oiled paper,[16] but they read the word of God by it. They were fain to make use of their knees for a table, but their limbs were their own. Hard labor and spare diet they had, and off wooden trenchers, but they had peace and freedom, and the wailing of the tempest in the woods sounded kindlier in their ear than the smooth voice of the prelates, at home, in England. "There is no people," said their pastor to his little flock of exiles, "but will strive to excel in something. What can we excel in, if not in holiness? If we look to number, we are the fewest; if to strength, we are the weakest; if to wealth and riches, we are the poorest of all the people of God through the whole world. We cannot excel nor so much as equal other people in these things; and if we come short in grace and holiness too, we are the most despicable people under heaven. Strive we, therefore, herein to excel, and suffer not this crown to be taken away from us."[17] The sermon fell into good and tender hearts; the people conspired with their teacher. Their religion was sweetness and peace amidst toil and tears. And, as we are informed, "the edge of their appetite was greater to spiritual duties at their first coming, in time of wants, than afterwards."

The original Town Records, for the first thirty years, are lost. We have records of marriages and deaths, beginning nineteen years after the settlement; and copies of some of the doings of the town in regard to territory, of the same date. But the original distribution of the land, or an account of the principles on which it was divided, are not preserved. Agreeably to the custom of the times, a large portion was reserved to the public, and it

---

14. Johnson.
15. *New England's Plantation.*
16. E. W.'s Letter in Mourt, 1621.
17. Peter Bulkeley's *Gospel Covenant; Preached at Concord in N. E.* 2d Edition; London, 1651, p. 432.

appears from a petition of some new comers, in 1643, that a part had been divided among the first settlers without price, on the single condition of improving it.[18] Other portions seem to have been successively divided off and granted to individuals, at the rate of sixpence or a shilling an acre. But, in the first years, the land would not pay the necessary public charges, and they seem to have fallen heavily on the few wealthy planters. Mr. Bulkeley, by his generosity, spent his estate, and, doubtless in consideration of his charges, the General Court, in 1639, granted him 300 acres towards Cambridge; and to Mr. Spencer, probably for the like reason, 300 acres by the Alewife River. In 1638, 1200 acres were granted to Governor Winthrop, and 1000 to Thomas Dudley of the lands adjacent to the town, and Governor Winthrop selected as a building spot the land near the house of Capt. Humphrey Hunt.[19] The first record now remaining is that of a reservation of land for the minister, and the appropriation of new lands as commons or pastures to some poor men. At the same date, in 1654, the town having divided itself into three districts, called the North, South and East quarters, Ordered, "that the North quarter are to keep and maintain all their highways and bridges over the great river, in their quarter, and, in respect of the greatness of their charge thereabout, and in regard of the ease of the East quarter above the rest, in their highways, they are to allow the North quarter £3."[20]

Fellow Citizens, this first recorded political act of our fathers, this tax assessed on its inhabitants by a town, is the most important event in their civil history, implying, as it does, the exercise of a sovereign power, and connected with all the immunities and powers of a corporate town in Massachusetts. The greater speed and success that distinguish the planting of the human race in this country, over all other plantations in history, owe themselves mainly to the new subdivisions of the State into small corporations of land and power. It is vain to look for the inventor. No man made them. Each of the parts of that perfect structure grew out of the necessities of an instant occasion. The germ was formed in England. The charter gave to the freemen of the Company of Massachusetts Bay, the election of the Governor and Council of Assistants. It moreover gave them the power of prescribing the manner in which freemen should be elected; and

---

18. See the Petition in Shattuck, p. 14.
19. Shattuck, p. 14.
20. Town Records; Shattuck, p. 34.

ordered that all fundamental laws should be enacted by the free-men of the colony. But the Company removed to New England; more than one hundred freemen were admitted the first year, and it was found inconvenient to assemble them all.[21] And when, presently, the design of the colony began to fulfill itself, by the settlement of new plantations in the vicinity of Boston, and par-ties, with grants of land, straggled into the country to truck with the Indians and to clear the land for their own benefit, the Gov-ernor and freemen in Boston found it neither desirable nor pos-sible to control the trade and practices of these farmers. What could the body of freemen, meeting four times a year, at Boston, do for the daily wants of the planters at Musketaquid? The wolf was to be killed; the Indian to be watched and resisted; wells to be dug; the forest to be felled; pastures to be cleared; corn to be raised; roads to be cut; town and farm lines to be run. These things must be done, govern who might. The nature of man and his condition in the world, for the first time within the period of certain history, controlled the formation of the State. The necessity of the colonists wrote the law. Their wants, their poverty, their manifest convenience made them bold to ask of the Governor and of the General Court, immunities, and, to certain purposes, sovereign powers. The townsmen's words were heard and weighed, for all knew that it was a petitioner that could not be slighted; it was the river, or the winter, or famine, or the Pequots, that spoke through them to the Governor and Council of Massachusetts Bay. Instructed by necessity, each little company organized itself after the pattern of the larger town, by appointing its constable, and other petty half-military officers. As early as 1633,[22] the office of townsman or *selectman* appears, who seems first to have been appointed by the General Court, as here, at Concord, in 1639. In 1635, the Court say, "whereas particular towns have many things which concern only them-selves, it is Ordered, that the freemen of every town shall have power to dispose of their own lands, and woods, and choose their own particular officers."[23] This pointed chiefly at the office of constable, but they soon chose their own selectmen, and very early assessed taxes; a power at first resisted,[24] but speedily con-firmed to them.

---

21. Bancroft; *History of the United States,* vol. i. p. 389.
22. Savage's *Winthrop,* vol. i. p. 114.
23. Colony Records, vol. i.
24. See Hutchinson's *Collection,* p. 287.

Meantime, to this paramount necessity, a milder and more pleasing influence was joined. I esteem it the happiness of this country, that its settlers, whilst they were exploring their granted and natural rights and determining the power of the magistrate, were united by personal affection. Members of a church before whose searching covenant all rank was abolished, they stood in awe of each other, as religious men. They bore to John Winthrop, the Governor, a grave but hearty kindness. For the first time, men examined the powers of the chief whom they loved and revered. For the first time, the ideal social compact was real. The bands of love and reverence held fast the little state, whilst they untied the great cords of authority to examine their soundness and learn on what wheels they ran. They were to settle the internal constitution of the towns, and, at the same time, their power in the commonwealth. The Governor conspires with them in limiting his claims to their obedience, and values much more their love than his chartered authority. The disputes between that forbearing man and the deputies are like the quarrels of girls, so much do they turn upon complaints of unkindness, and end in such loving reconciliations. It was on doubts concerning their own power, that, in 1634, a committee repaired to him for counsel, and he advised, seeing the freemen were grown so numerous, to send deputies from every town once in a year to revise the laws and to assess all monies.[25] And the General Court, thus constituted, only needed to go into separate session from the council, as they did in 1644,[26] to become essentially the same assembly they are this day.

By this course of events, Concord and the other plantations found themselves separate and independent of Boston, with certain rights of their own, which, what they were, time alone could fully determine; enjoying, at the same time, a strict and loving fellowship with Boston, and sure of advice and aid, on every emergency. Their powers were speedily settled by obvious convenience, and the towns learned to exercise a sovereignty in the laying of taxes; in the choice of their deputy to the house of representatives; in the disposal of the town lands; in the care of public worship, the school and the poor; and, what seemed of at least equal importance, to exercise the right of expressing an opinion on every question before the country. In a town-meeting, the great secret of political science was uncovered, and the prob-

25. Winthrop's *Journal*, vol. i. pp. 128, 129, and the Editor's Note.
26. Winthrop's *Journal*, vol. ii. p. 160.

lem solved, how to give every individual his fair weight in the government, without any disorder from numbers. In a town-meeting, the roots of society were reached. Here the rich gave counsel, but the poor also; and moreover, the just and the unjust. He is ill-informed who expects, on running down the town records for two hundred years, to find a church of saints, a metropolis of patriots, enacting wholesome and creditable laws. The constitution of the towns forbid it. In this open democracy, every opinion had utterance; every objection, every fact, every acre of land, every bushel of rye, its entire weight. The moderator was the passive mouth-piece, and the vote of the town, like the vane on the turret overhead, free for every wind to turn, and always turned by the last and strongest breath. In these assemblies, the public weal, the call of interest, duty, religion, were heard; and every local feeling, every private grudge, every suggestion of petulance and ignorance, were not less faithfully produced. Wrath and love came up to town-meeting in company. By the law of 1641, every man,—freeman or not,—inhabitant or not, —might introduce any business into a public meeting. Not a complaint occurs in all the volumes of our Records, of any inhabitant being hindered from speaking, or suffering from any violence or usurpation of any class. The negative ballot of a ten shilling freeholder was as fatal as that of the honored owner of Blood's Farms or Willard's Purchase. A man felt himself at liberty to exhibit, at town-meeting, feelings and actions that he would have been ashamed of anywhere but amongst his neighbors. Individual protests are frequent. Peter Wright [1705] desired his dissent might be recorded from the town's grant to John Shepard.[27] In 1795, several town-meetings are called, upon the compensation to be made to a few proprietors for land taken in making a bridle road; and one of them demanding large damages, many offers were made him in town-meeting, and refused; "which the town thought very unreasonable." The matters there debated are such as to invite very small considerations. The ill-spelled pages of the town records contain the result. I shall be excused for confessing that I have set a value upon any symptom of meanness and private pique which I have met with in these antique books, as proof that justice was done; that if the results of our history are approved as wise and good, it was yet a free strife; if the good counsel prevailed, the sneaking coun-

---

27. Concord Town Records.

sel did not fail to be suggested; freedom and virtue, if they triumphed, triumphed in a fair field. And so be it an everlasting testimony for them, and so much ground of assurance of man's capacity for self-government.

It is the consequence of this institution that not a school-house, a public pew, a bridge, a pound, a mill-dam, hath been set up, or pulled down, or altered, or bought, or sold, without the whole population of this town having a voice in the affair. A general contentment is the result. And the people truly feel that they are lords of the soil. In every winding road, in every stone fence, in the smokes of the poor-house chimney, in the clock on the church, they read their own power, and consider, at leisure, the wisdom and error of their judgments.

The British government has recently presented to the several public libraries of this country, copies of the splendid edition of the Domesday Book, and other ancient public Records of England. I cannot but think that it would be a suitable acknowledgment of this national munificence, if the records of one of our towns,—of this town, for example,—should be printed, and presented to the governments of Europe; to the English nation, as a thank-offering, and as a certificate of the progress of the Saxon race; to the continental nations as a lesson of humanity and love. Tell them, the Union has twenty-four States, and Massachusetts is one. Tell them, Massachusetts has three hundred towns, and Concord is one; that in Concord are five hundred rateable polls, and every one has an equal vote.

Nathaniel Hawthorne

Nathaniel Hawthorne (1804-1864), a native of Salem, is not primarily a writer about village or country life, though long periods of residence in Raymond, Maine, and Lenox and Concord, Massachusetts, gave him a firsthand knowledge of rural New England. "Chippings with a Chisel" is included here because it so effectively describes a New England graveyard and presents us with a portrait of one of the itinerant stonecutters who used to travel from town to town in the last century. Hawthorne gathered the material for this sketch during an actual month-long visit that he made to Martha's Vineyard in the 1830s. In two matters of detail, however, he is in error. As we now know, there is no reason to assume that the more skillfully carved stones in Edgartown Cemetery were imported from England. Many stones remarkable for their workmanship were produced in mainland New England in the Colonial period and later, and some of them were brought to Martha's Vineyard. Secondly, Mr. Wigglesworth in the story would scarcely have been carving a death's head at so late a date. Death's heads went out of fashion as funerary decorations shortly after 1750 and seldom, if ever, occurred after 1800. They were supplanted by the weeping willows and other devices that Hawthorne describes.

"Chippings with a Chisel" was first published in The Democratic Review *in 1838 and was included in the second edition of* Twice Told Tales *(1842). The text in this anthology is from* The Complete Works of Nathaniel Hawthorne, *Volume I, 1882.*

Chippings with a Chisel

Passing a summer, several years since, at Edgartown, on the island of Martha's Vineyard, I became acquainted with a certain carver of tombstones, who had travelled and voyaged thither from the interior of Massachusetts, in search of professional employment. The speculation had turned out so successful that my friend expected to transmute slate and marble into silver and gold, to the amount of at least a thousand dollars, during the few months of his sojourn at Nantucket and the Vineyard. The secluded life, and the simple and primitive spirit which still characterizes the inhabitants of those islands, especially of Martha's Vineyard, insure their dead friends a longer and dearer remembrance than the daily novelty and revolving bustle of the world can elsewhere afford to beings of the past. Yet while every family is anxious to erect a memorial to its departed members, the untainted breath of ocean bestows such health and length of days upon the people of the isles, as would cause a melancholy dearth of business to a resident artist in that line. His own monument, recording his death by starvation, would probably be an early specimen of his skill. Gravestones, therefore, have generally been an article of imported merchandise.

In my walks through the burial-ground of Edgartown—where the dead have lain so long that the soil, once enriched by their decay, has returned to its original barrenness—in that ancient burial-ground I noticed much variety of monumental sculpture. The elder stones, dated a century back or more, have borders elaborately carved with flowers, and are adorned with a multiplicity of death's heads, cross-bones, scythes, hour-glasses, and other lugubrious emblems of mortality, with here and there a winged cherub to direct the mourner's spirit upward. These productions of Gothic taste must have been quite beyond the colonial skill of the day, and were probably carved in London, and brought across the ocean to commemorate the defunct worthies of this lonely isle. The more recent monuments are mere slabs of slate, in the ordinary style, without any super-

fluous flourishes to set off the bald inscriptions. But others—
and those far the most impressive both to my taste and feelings
—were roughly hewn from the gray rocks of the island, evidently
by the unskilled hands of surviving friends and relatives. On
some there were merely the initials of a name; some were inscribed with misspelt prose or rhyme, in deep letters, which the
moss and wintry rain of many years had not been able to obliter-
ate. These, these were graves where loved ones slept! It is an old
theme of satire, the falsehood and vanity of monumental eulo-
gies; but when affection and sorrow grave the letters with their
own painful labor, then we may be sure that they copy from the
record on their hearts.

My acquaintance, the sculptor,—he may share that title with
Greenough, since the dauber of signs is a painter as well as
Raphael,—had found a ready market for all his blank slabs of
marble, and full occupation in lettering and ornamenting them.
He was an elderly man, a descendant of the old Puritan family
of Wigglesworth, with a certain simplicity and singleness both
of heart and mind, which, methinks, is more rarely found among
us Yankees than in any other community of people. In spite of
his gray head and wrinkled brow, he was quite like a child in all
matters save what had some reference to his own business; he
seemed, unless my fancy misled me, to view mankind in no other
relation than as people in want of tombstones; and his literary
attainments evidently comprehended very little, either of prose
or poetry, which had not, at one time or other, been inscribed
on slate or marble. His sole task and office among the immortal
pilgrims of the tomb—the duty for which Providence had sent
the old man into the world as it were with a chisel in his hand—
was to label the dead bodies, lest their names should be forgotten
at the resurrection. Yet he had not failed, within a narrow scope,
to gather a few sprigs of earthly, and more than earthly, wisdom,
—the harvest of many a grave.

And lugubrious as his calling might appear, he was as cheerful
an old soul as health and integrity and lack of care could make
him, and used to set to work upon one sorrowful inscription or
another with that sort of spirit which impels a man to sing at
his labor. On the whole I found Mr. Wigglesworth an entertaining, and often instructive, if not an interesting, character; and
partly for the charm of his society, and still more because his
work has an invariable attraction for "man that is born of
woman," I was accustomed to spend some hours a day at his

workshop. The quaintness of his remarks, and their not infrequent truth—a truth condensed and pointed by the limited sphere
of his view—gave a raciness to his talk, which mere worldliness
and general cultivation would at once have destroyed.

Sometimes we would discuss the respective merits of the
various qualities of marble, numerous slabs of which were resting
against the walls of the shop; or sometimes an hour or two would
pass quietly, without a word on either side, while I watched how
neatly his chisel struck out letter after letter of the names of
the Nortons, the Mayhews, the Luces, the Daggets, and other
immemorial families of the Vineyard. Often, with an artist's
pride, the good old sculptor would speak of favorite productions
of his skill which were scattered throughout the village graveyards of New England. But my chief and most instructive amusement was to witness his interviews with his customers, who held
interminable consultations about the form and fashion of the
desired monuments, the buried excellence to be commemorated,
the anguish to be expressed, and finally, the lowest price in
dollars and cents for which a marble transcript of their feelings
might be obtained. Really, my mind received many fresh ideas
which, perhaps, may remain in it even longer than Mr. Wigglesworth's hardest marble will retain the deepest strokes of his chisel.

An elderly lady came to bespeak a monument for her first
love who had been killed by a whale in the Pacific Ocean no less
than forty years before. It was singular that so strong an impression of early feeling should have survived through the
changes of her subsequent life, in the course of which she had
been a wife and a mother, and, so far as I could judge, a comfortable and happy woman. Reflecting within myself, it appeared
to me that this lifelong sorrow—as, in all good faith, she deemed
it—was one of the most fortunate circumstances of her history.
It had given an ideality to her mind; it had kept her purer and
less earthly than she would otherwise have been, by drawing a
portion of her sympathies apart from earth. Amid the throng
of enjoyments and the pressure of worldly care, and all the warm
materialism of this life, she had communed with a vision, and
had been the better for such intercourse. Faithful to the husband
of her maturity, and loving him with a far more real affection
than she ever could have felt for this dream of her girlhood,
there had still been an imaginative faith to the ocean-buried,
so that an ordinary character had thus been elevated and refined.
Her sighs had been the breath of heaven to her soul. The good

lady earnestly desired that the proposed monument should be ornamented with a carved border of marine plants, intertwined with twisted sea-shells, such as were probably waving over her lover's skeleton, or strewn around it in the far depths of the Pacific. But Mr. Wigglesworth's chisel being inadequate to the task, she was forced to content herself with a rose hanging its head from a broken stem. After her departure, I remarked that the symbol was none of the most apt.

"And yet," said my friend the sculptor, embodying in this image the thoughts that had been passing through my own mind, "that broken rose has shed its sweet smell through forty years of the good woman's life."

It was seldom that I could find such pleasant food for contemplation as in the above instance. None of the applicants, I think, affected me more disagreeably than an old man who came, with his fourth wife hanging on his arm, to bespeak gravestones for the three former occupants of his marriage-bed. I watched with some anxiety to see whether his remembrance of either were more affectionate than of the other two, but could discover no symptom of the kind. The three monuments were all to be of the same material and form, and each decorated, in bass-relief, with two weeping willows, one of these sympathetic trees bending over its fellow, which was to be broken in the midst and rest upon a sepulchral urn. This, indeed, was Mr. Wigglesworth's standing emblem of conjugal bereavement. I shuddered at the gray polygamist who had so utterly lost the holy sense of individuality in wedlock, that methought he was fain to reckon upon his fingers how many women, who had once slept by his side, were now sleeping in their graves. There was even—if I wrong him it is no great matter—a glance sidelong at his living spouse, as if he were inclined to drive a thriftier bargain by bespeaking four gravestones in a lot. I was better pleased with a rough old whaling captain, who gave directions for a broad marble slab, divided into two compartments, one of which was to contain an epitaph on his deceased wife, and the other to be left vacant, till death should engrave his own name there. As is frequently the case among the whalers of Martha's Vineyard, so much of this storm-beaten widower's life had been tossed away on distant seas, that out of twenty years of matrimony he had spent scarce three, and those at scattered intervals, beneath his own roof. Thus the wife of his youth, though she died in his and her declining age, retained the bridal dew-drops fresh around her memory.

My observations gave me the idea, and Mr. Wigglesworth confirmed it, that husbands were more faithful in setting up memorials to their dead wives than widows to their dead husbands. I was not ill-natured enough to fancy that women, less than men, feel so sure of their constancy as to be willing to give a pledge of it in marble. It is more probably the fact that while men are able to reflect upon their lost companions as remembrances apart from themselves, women, on the other hand, are conscious that a portion of their being has gone with the departed whithersoever he has gone. Soul clings to soul; the living dust has a sympathy with the dust of the grave; and, by the very strength of that sympathy, the wife of the dead shrinks the more sensitively from reminding the world of its existence. The link is already strong enough; it needs no visible symbol. And though a shadow walks ever by her side, and the touch of a chill hand is on her bosom, yet life, and perchance its natural yearnings, may still be warm within her, and inspire her with new hopes of happiness. Then would she mark out the grave, the scent of which would be perceptible on the pillow of the second bridal? No—but rather level its green mound with the surrounding earth, as if, when she dug up again her buried heart, the spot had ceased to be a grave. Yet, in spite of these sentimentalities, I was prodigiously amused by an incident, of which I had not the good fortune to be a witness, but which Mr. Wigglesworth related with considerable humor. A gentlewoman of the town, receiving news of her husband's loss at sea, had bespoken a handsome slab of marble, and came daily to watch the progress of my friend's chisel. One afternoon, when the good lady and the sculptor were in the very midst of the epitaph, which the departed spirit might have been greatly comforted to read, who should walk into the workshop but the deceased himself, in substance as well as spirit! He had been picked up at sea, and stood in no present need of tombstone or epitaph.

"And how," inquired I, "did his wife bear the shock of joyful surprise?"

"Why," said the old man, deepening the grin of a death's-head, on which his chisel was just then employed, "I really felt for the poor woman; it was one of my best pieces of marble—and to be thrown away on a living man!"

A comely woman, with a pretty rosebud of a daughter, came to select a gravestone for a twin daughter, who had died a month before. I was impressed with the different nature of their feelings for the dead; the mother was calm and wofully resigned, fully conscious of her loss, as of a treasure which she had not always possessed, and, therefore, had been aware that it might be taken from her; but the daughter evidently had no real knowledge of what death's doings were. Her thoughts knew, but not her heart. It seemed to me, that by the print and pressure which the dead sister had left upon the survivor's spirit, her feelings were almost the same as if she still stood side by side and arm in arm with the departed, looking at the slabs of marble; and once or twice she glanced around with a sunny smile, which, as its sister smile had faded forever, soon grew confusedly overshadowed. Perchance her consciousness was truer than her reflection—perchance her dead sister was a closer companion than in life. The mother and daughter talked a long while with Mr. Wigglesworth about a suitable epitaph, and finally chose an ordinary verse of ill-matched rhymes, which had already been inscribed upon innumerable tombstones. But when we ridicule the triteness of monumental verses, we forget that Sorrow reads far deeper in them than we can, and finds a profound and individual purport in what seems so vague and inexpressive, unless interpreted by her. She makes the epitaph anew, though the selfsame words may have served for a thousand graves.

"And yet," said I afterwards to Mr. Wigglesworth, "they might have made a better choice than this. While you were discussing the subject, I was struck by at least a dozen simple and natural expressions from the lips of both mother and daughter. One of these would have formed an inscription equally original and appropriate."

"No, no," replied the sculptor, shaking his head; "there is a good deal of comfort to be gathered from these little old scraps of poetry; and so I always recommend them in preference to any new-fangled ones. And somehow, they seem to stretch to suit a great grief, and shrink to fit a small one."

It was not seldom that ludicrous images were excited by what took place between Mr. Wigglesworth and his customers. A shrewd gentlewoman, who kept a tavern in the town, was anxious to obtain two or three gravestones for the deceased members of her family, and to pay for these solemn commodities by taking the sculptor to board. Hereupon a fantasy arose in my mind of good Mr. Wigglesworth sitting down to dinner at a broad, flat tombstone, carving one of his own plump little marble cherubs, gnawing a pair of cross-bones, and drinking out of a hollow death's-head, or perhaps a lachrymatory vase, or sepulchral urn, while his hostess's dead children waited on him at the ghastly banquet. On communicating this nonsensical picture to the old man he laughed heartily, and pronounced my humor to be of the right sort.

"I have lived at such a table all my days," said he, "and eaten no small quantity of slate and marble."

"Hard fare!" rejoined I, smiling; "but you seemed to have found it excellent of digestion, too."

A man of fifty, or thereabouts, with a harsh, unpleasant countenance, ordered a stone for the grave of his bitter enemy, with whom he had waged warfare half a lifetime, to their mutual misery and ruin. The secret of this phenomenon was, that hatred had become the sustenance and enjoyment of the poor wretch's soul; it had supplied the place of all kindly affections; it had been really a bond of sympathy between himself and the man who shared the passion; and when its object died the unappeasable foe was the only mourner for the dead. He expressed a purpose of being buried side by side with his enemy.

"I doubt whether their dust will mingle," remarked the old sculptor to me; for often there was an earthliness in his conceptions.

"Oh yes," replied I, who had mused long upon the incident; "and when they rise again, these bitter foes may find themselves dear friends. Methinks what they mistook for hatred was but love under a mask."

A gentleman of antiquarian propensities provided a memorial for an Indian of Chabbiquidick, one of the few of untainted blood remaining in that region, and said to be an hereditary chieftain, descended from the sachem who welcomed Governor Mayhew to the Vineyard. Mr. Wigglesworth exerted his best skill to carve a broken bow and scattered sheaf of arrows, in memory of the hunters and warriors whose race was ended here; but he likewise sculptured a cherub, to denote that the poor Indian had shared the Christian's hope of immortality.

"Why," observed I, taking a perverse view of the winged boy and the bow and arrows, "it looks more like Cupid's tomb than an Indian chief's!"

"You talk nonsense," said the sculptor, with the offended pride of art; he then added with his usual good nature, "How can Cupid die when there are such pretty maidens in the Vineyard?"

"Very true," answered I—and for the rest of the day I thought of other matters than tombstones.

At our next meeting I found him chiselling an open book upon a marble headstone, and concluded that it was meant to express the erudition of some blackletter clergyman of the Cotton Mather school. It turned out, however, to be emblematical of the scriptural knowledge of an old woman who had never read anything but her Bible: and the monument was a tribute to her piety and good works from the Orthodox church, of which she had been a member. In strange contrast with this Christian woman's memorial was that of an infidel, whose gravestone, by his own direction, bore an avowal of his belief that the spirit within him would be extinguished like a flame, and that the nothingness whence he sprang would receive him again. Mr. Wigglesworth consulted me as to the propriety of enabling a dead man's dust to utter this dreadful creed.

"If I thought," said he, "that a single mortal would read the inscription without a shudder, my chisel should never cut a letter of it. But when the grave speaks such falsehoods, the soul of man will know the truth by its own horror."

"So it will," said I, struck by the idea; "the poor infidel may strive to preach blasphemies from his grave; but it will be only another method of impressing the soul with a consciousness of immortality."

There was an old man by the name of Norton, noted throughout the island for his great wealth, which he had accumulated by the exercise of strong and shrewd faculties, combined with a most penurious disposition. This wretched miser, conscious that he had not a friend to be mindful of him in his grave, had himself taken the needful precautions for posthumous remembrance, by bespeaking an immense slab of white marble, with a long epitaph in raised letters, the whole to be as magnificent as Mr. Wigglesworth's skill could make it. There was something very characteristic in this contrivance to have his money's worth even from his own tombstone, which, indeed, afforded him more enjoyment in the few months that he lived thereafter, than it probably will in a whole century, now that it is laid over his bones. This incident reminds me of a young girl,—a pale, slender, feeble creature, most unlike the other rosy and healthful damsels of the Vineyard, amid whose brightness she was fading away. Day after day did the poor maiden come to the sculptor's shop, and pass from one piece of marble to another, till at last she pencilled her name upon a slender slab, which, I think, was of a more spotless white than all the rest. I saw her no more, but soon afterwards found Mr. Wigglesworth cutting her virgin name into the stone which she had chosen.

"She is dead—poor girl," said he, interrupting the tune which he was whistling, "and she chose a good piece of stuff for her headstone. Now which of these slabs would you like best to see your own name upon?"

"Why, to tell you the truth, my good Mr. Wigglesworth," replied I, after a moment's pause,—for the abruptness of the question had somewhat startled me,—"to be quite sincere with you, I care little or nothing about a stone for my own grave, and am somewhat inclined to scepticism as to the propriety of erecting monuments at all over the dust that once was human. The weight of these heavy marbles, though unfelt by the dead corpse of the enfranchised soul, presses drearily upon the spirit of the survivor, and causes him to connect the idea of death with the dungeonlike imprisonment of the tomb, instead of with the freedom of the skies. Every gravestone that you ever made is the visible symbol of a mistaken system. Our thoughts should soar upward with the butterfly—not linger with the exuviæ that confined him. In truth and reason, neither those whom we call the living, and still less the departed, have anything to do with the grave."

"I never heard anything so heathenish!" said Mr. Wigglesworth, perplexed and displeased at sentiments which controverted all his notions and feelings, and implied the utter waste, and worse, of his whole life's labor; "would you forget your dead friends, the moment they are under the sod?"

"They are not under the sod," I rejoined; "then why should I mark the spot where there is no treasure hidden! Forget them? No! But to remember them aright, I would forget what they have cast off. And to gain the truer conception of DEATH, I would forget the GRAVE!"

But still the good old sculptor murmured, and stumbled, as it were, over the gravestones amid which he had walked through life. Whether he were right or wrong, I had grown the wiser from our companionship, and from my observations of nature and character as displayed by those who came, with their old griefs or their new ones, to get them recorded upon his slabs of marble. And yet, with my gain of wisdom, I had likewise gained perplexity; for there was a strange doubt in my mind, whether the dark shadowing of this life, the sorrows and regrets, have not as much real comfort in them—leaving religious influences out of the question—as what we term life's joys.

Epitaphs from Martha's Vineyard

Epitaphs like those described in Hawthorne's "Chippings with a Chisel" are an important genre of New England folk literature. The ones that follow are from graveyards on the Island of Martha's Vineyard off the Massachusetts coast. Very likely Hawthorne saw most of these, but we may be sure he observed the first, on which he comments in an essay titled "Martha's Vineyard" (in *The American Magazine of Useful and Entertaining Knowledge,* April, 1836), and the second, which is the blasphemous one so shocking to the stonecutter Wigglesworth. Original spellings and punctuation have been retained.

1.

Of this epitaph Hawthorne wrote: "It was consecrated to the memory of John and Lydia Claghorne, a young sailor and his wife, the former of whom had perished on the farther side of Cape Horn, about the same time that Lydia died in child-bed. . . . It seems to me that this rude and homely verse may be ranked among the masterpieces of monumental literature."

> John and Lydia, that lovely pair,
> A Whale killed him, her body lies here;
> Their souls, we hope, with Christ shall reign—
> So our great loss is their great gain.
>
> (c. 1771)

2.

Joseph Ripley, Edgartown's only atheist at the time, wrote his own epitaph:

> By the force of vegetation,
> I was brought to life and action;
> And when life and action that shall cease,
> I shall return to the same source.
>
> (1830)

3.

For the victim of a shipwreck at Gay Head, leaving a widow and five children:

> The mighty God that rules the Skys
> Commands tempestuous storms to rise,
> And when his darts are sent abroad
> All must obey and bless the Rod.
> (1782)

4.

On the stone of a man who died at the age of twenty-seven:

> When on this Stone you cast an Eye
> Remember you are Born to Dye
> Like me in Youth or riper Years
> They Reap in Joy who sow in Tears
> It is said indeed He sow'd in Tears
> Although He Dy'd in youthful Years
> Where Godly sorrow is truly Given
> There the Harvest will be Heaven
> (1737)

5.

An epitaph describing how an eleven-year-old boy died:

> The oil of Vitriol he did taste
> Which caused his vitals for to waste
> And forced him to return again
> Unto the earth from whence he came.
> (1787)

6.

The inscriptions that follow need no explanation:

ALL YOU THAT COMS MY GRAVE TO SEE
SUCH AS I AM SO MUST YOU BE
FLEE SIN THEREFORE LIVE GODLY STILL
THEN WELCOME DEATH COME WHEN IT WILL
(1719)

7.

Stay, Reader, yet a moment stay;
mind what this speaking stone doth say.
Remember you was born to die
as well as she who here doth lie.
then as she chose the better Part,
and gave her SAVIOUR all her Heart,
join in her choice, your Heart resign,
And Life Eternal shall be thine.
(1755)

8.

His mind was tranquil and serene,
　　And in his looks no terror seen;
His saviour's smiles dispelled the gloom,
　　And smoothed his passage to the tomb.
(1838)

9.

Remember ye who view this Tomb
Man's days are fix'd nor far his doom,
The tender ties of nature broken,
Tho' in the dust yet not forgotten.

O thou who dost for gracious ends,
Burst the strong ties of dearest friends,
Grant thou thine aid to feeble nature,
To praise thy name, thou great creator.
(1806)

John Greenleaf Whittier

*John Greenleaf Whittier (1807–1892), born into a Quaker
farming family near Haverhill, Massachusetts, had a firsthand
knowledge of rural New England. After a career as a leading
abolitionist, he devoted himself, from the end of the Civil War
onward, to writing about New England life and history. In contrast to his idyllic "Snow-Bound," the "Prelude" to* Among the
Hills and Other Poems *(1869) records several less attractive
aspects of existence in the hill country, which he had come to
know during summer vacations in New Hampshire. The text of
the poem as it appears in this volume is from* The Complete
Poetical Works of John Greenleaf Whittier *(1880).*

"Prelude" to Among the Hills and Other Poems

Along the roadside, like the flowers of gold
That tawny Incas for their gardens wrought,
Heavy with sunshine droops the goldenrod,
And the red pennons of the cardinalflowers
Hang motionless upon their upright staves.
The sky is hot and hazy, and the wind,
Wing-weary with its long flight from the south,
Unfelt; yet, closely scanned, yon maple leaf
With faintest motion, as one stirs in dreams,
Confesses it. The locust by the wall
Stabs the noon-silence with his sharp alarm.

A single hay-cart down the dusty road
Creaks slowly, with its driver fast asleep
On the load's top. Against the neighboring hill,
Huddled along the stone wall's shady side,
The sheep show white, as if a snowdrift still
Defied the dog-star. Through the open door
A drowsy smell of flowers—gray heliotrope,
And white sweet clover, and shy mignonette—
Comes faintly in, and silent chorus lends
To the pervading symphony of peace.

No time is this for hands long overworn
To task their strength: and (unto Him be praise
Who giveth quietness!) the stress and strain
Of years that did the work of centuries
Have ceased, and we can draw our breath once more
Freely and full. So, as yon harvesters
Make glad their nooning underneath the elms
With tale and riddle and old snatch of song,
I lay aside grave themes, and idly turn
The leaves of memory's sketch-book, dreaming o'er
Old summer pictures of the quiet hills,
And human life, as quiet, at their feet.

And yet not idly all. A farmer's son,
Proud of field-lore and harvest craft, and feeling
All their fine possibilities, how rich
And restful even poverty and toil
Become when beauty, harmony, and love
Sit at their humble hearth as angels sat
At evening in the patriarch's tent, when man
Makes labor noble, and his farmer's frock
The symbol of a Christian chivalry
Tender and just and generous to her
Who clothes with grace all duty; still, I know
Too well the picture has another side,—
How wearily the grind of toil goes on
Where love is wanting, how the eye and ear
And heart are starved amidst the plenitude
Of nature, and how hard and colorless
Is life without an atmosphere. I look
Across the lapse of half a century,

And call to mind old homesteads, where no flower
Told that the spring had come, but evil weeds,
Nightshade and rough-leaved burdock in the place
Of the sweet doorway greeting of the rose
And honeysuckle, where the house walls seemed
Blistering in sun, without a tree or vine
To cast the tremulous shadow of its leaves
Across the curtainless windows from whose panes
Fluttered the signal rags of shiftlessness;
Within, the cluttered kitchen-floor, unwashed
(Broom-clean I think they called it); the best room
Stifling with cellar damp, shut from the air
In hot midsummer, bookless, pictureless
Save the inevitable sampler hung
Over the fireplace, or a mourning piece,
A green-haired woman, peony-cheeked, beneath
Impossible willows; the wide-throated hearth
Bristling with faded pine-boughs half concealing
The piled-up rubbish at the chimney's back;
And, in sad keeping with all things about them,
Shrill, querulous women, sour and sullen men,
Untidy, loveless, old before their time,
With scarce a human interest save their own
Monotonous round of small economies,
Or the poor scandal of the neighborhood;
Blind to the beauty everywhere revealed,
Treading the May-flowers with regardless feet;
For them the song-sparrow and the bobolink
Sang not, nor winds made music in the leaves;
For them in vain October's holocaust
Burned, gold and crimson, over all the hills,
The sacramental mystery of the woods.
Church-goers, fearful of the unseen Powers,
But grumbling over pulpit-tax and pew-rent,
Saving, as shrewd economists, their souls
And winter pork with the least possible outlay
Of salt and sanctity; in daily life
Showing as little actual comprehension
Of Christian charity and love and duty,
As if the Sermon on the Mount had been
Outdated like a last year's almanac:
Rich in broad woodlands and in half-tilled fields,

And yet so pinched and bare and comfortless,
The veriest straggler limping on his rounds,
The sun and air his sole inheritance,
Laughed at a poverty that paid its taxes,
And hugged his rags in self-complacency!

Not such should be the homesteads of a land
Where whoso wisely wills and acts may dwell
As king and lawgiver, in broad-acred state,
With beauty, art, taste, culture, books, to make
His hour of leisure richer than a life
Of fourscore to the barons of old time,
Our yeoman should be equal to his home
Set in the fair, green valleys, purple walled,
A man to match his mountains, not to creep
Dwarfed and abased below them. I would fain
In this light way (of which I needs must own
With the knife-grinder of whom Canning sings,
"Story, God bless you! I have none to tell you!")
Invite the eye to see and heart to feel
The beauty and the joy within their reach,—
Home, and home loves, and the beatitudes
Of nature free to all. Haply in years
That wait to take the places of our own,
Heard where some breezy balcony looks down
On happy homes, or where the lake in the moon
Sleeps dreaming of the mountains, fair as Ruth,
In the old Hebrew pastoral, at the feet
Of Boaz, even this simple lay of mine
May seem the burden of a prophecy,
Finding its late fulfilment in a change
Slow as the oak's growth, lifting manhood up
Through broader culture, finer manners, love,
And reverence, to the level of the hills.

O Golden Age, whose light is of the dawn,
And not of sunset, forward, not behind,
Flood the new heavens and earth, and with thee bring
All the old virtues, whatsoever things
Are pure and honest and of good repute,
But add thereto whatever bard has sung
Or seer has told of when in trance and dream

They saw the Happy Isles of prophecy!
Let Justice hold her scale, and Truth divide
Between the right and wrong; but give the heart
The freedom of its fair inheritance;
Let the poor prisoner, cramped and starved so long,
At Nature's table feast his ear and eye
With joy and wonder; let all harmonies
Of sound, form, color, motion, wait upon
The princely guest, whether in soft attire
Of leisure clad, or the coarse frock of toil,
And, lending life to the dead form of faith,
Give human nature reverence for the sake
Of One who bore it, making it divine
With the ineffable tenderness of God;
Let common need, the brotherhood of prayer,
The heirship of an unknown destiny,
The unsolved mystery round about us, make
A man more precious than the gold of Ophir.
Sacred, inviolate, unto whom all things
Should minister, as outward types and signs
Of the eternal beauty which fulfils
The one great purpose of creation, Love,
The sole necessity of Earth and Heaven!

Harriet Beecher Stowe

Harriet Beecher Stowe (1811–1896), the daughter of the famous Calvinist minister Lyman Beecher, was born in Litchfield in the hills of western Connecticut. At the age of twenty-one she accompanied her father to Cincinnati, where he served as president of a theological seminary. Here in 1836 she married one of the professors, Calvin Stowe. In 1850 she and her husband returned to New England, living first at Brunswick, Maine, and later at Andover, Massachusetts. Noted mainly for having writ-
ten *Uncle Tom's Cabin (1851–1852), Mrs. Stowe was also a prolific, enthusiastic, and accurate writer on New England rural life. The Pearl of Orr's Island (1862) is the first and one of the best novels to be written with a Maine coast setting.* Oldtown Folks *(1869) and* Sam Lawson's Oldtown Fireside Stories *(1872), depicting a small Massachusetts village shortly after the Revolution, are compendious and fascinating records of the manners, ideals, and daily living of the people of that time in such a community.* Poganuc People *(1878) provides a similar picture of the inhabitants of a hill town suggestive of Mrs. Stowe's native Litchfield.* The Minister's Wooing *(1859), from which "Views of Divine Government" is taken, has its setting—again, painstakingly presented—in the small but old and somewhat sophisticated coastal town of Newport, Rhode Island, not long after the Revolution. In the chapter given here Mrs. Marvyn, a lady of considerable intellect and education, has learned that her son, who was unconcerned about religion and thus unconverted, has been lost at sea. Mary Scudder and he have been in love but because of his indifference to religion she refuses to marry him. The Dr. Hopkins referred to is a minister who actually served in Newport. Dr. Samuel Hopkins, who was a disciple of the influential theologian and one-time college president, Jonathan Edwards, professed and promulgated a brand of rigid Calvinism that was to dominate most of rural New England*

for fifty years or more, though, as we see, it was meeting oppo-
sition in the older areas. Personally Dr. Hopkins was a kindly
man, but according to his beliefs Mrs. Marvyn's son, having
died in an unregenerate state, must inevitably be consigned to
eternal hellfire. Religious crises like Mrs. Marvyn's must, by the
very nature of Calvinism, have been common in New England.
We should recall that Mrs. Stowe's own son and her sister's
fiancée had died (in drowning accidents!) unconverted. Unable
to accept the unavoidable conclusion of their church, both aban-
doned their father's faith, Mrs. Stowe for Episcopalianism and
her sister for Unitarianism.

The text in this anthology is that of the first edition of The
Minister's Wooing.

Views of Divine Government

We have said before, what we now repeat, that it is impossible
to write a story of New England life and manners for superficial
thought or shallow feeling. They who would fully understand
the springs which moved the characters with whom we now asso-
ciate must go down with us to the very depths.

Never was there a community where the roots of common life
shot down so deeply, and were so intensely grappled around
things sublime and eternal. The founders of it were a body of
confessors and martyrs, who turned their backs on the whole
glory of the visible, to found in the wilderness a republic of which
the God of Heaven and Earth should be the sovereign power.
For the first hundred years grew this community, shut out by a
fathomless ocean from the existing world, and divided by an
antagonism not less deep from all the reigning ideas of nominal
Christendom.

In a community thus unworldly must have arisen a mode of
thought, energetic, original, and sublime. The leaders of thought
and feeling were the ministry, and we boldly assert that the spectacle of the early ministry of New England was one to which

the world gives no parallel. Living an intense, earnest, practical life, mostly tilling the earth with their own hands, they yet carried on the most startling and original religious investigations with a simplicity that might have been deemed audacious, were it not so reverential. All old issues relating to government, religion, ritual, and forms of church organization having for them passed away, they went straight to the heart of things, and boldly confronted the problem of universal being. They had come out from the world as witnesses to the most solemn and sacred of human rights. They had accustomed themselves boldly to challenge and dispute all sham pretensions and idolatries of past ages, —to question the right of kings in the State, and of prelates in the Church; and now they turned the same bold inquiries towards the Eternal Throne, and threw down their glove in the lists as authorized defenders of every mystery in the Eternal Government. The task they proposed to themselves was that of reconciling the most tremendous facts of sin and evil, present and eternal, with those conceptions of Infinite Power and Benevolence which their own strong and generous natures enabled them so vividly to realize. In the intervals of planting and harvesting, they were busy with the toils of adjusting the laws of a universe. Solemnly simple, they made long journeys in their old one-horse chaises, to settle with each other some nice point of celestial jurisprudence, and to compare their maps of the Infinite. Their letters to each other form a literature altogether unique. Hopkins sends to Edwards the younger his scheme of the universe, in which he starts with the proposition, that God is infinitely above all obligations of any kind to his creatures. Edwards replies with the brusque comment,—"This is wrong; God has no more right to injure a creature than a creature has to injure God;" and each probably about that time preached a sermon on his own views, which was discussed by every farmer, in intervals of plough and hoe, by every woman and girl, at loom, spinning-wheel, or wash-tub. New England was one vast sea, surging from depths to heights with thought and discussion on the most insoluble of mysteries. And it is to be added, that no man or woman accepted any theory or speculation simply *as* theory or speculation; all was profoundly real and vital,—a foundation on which actual life was based with intensest earnestness.

The views of human existence which resulted from this course of training were gloomy enough to oppress any heart which did not rise above them by triumphant faith or sink below them by brutish insensibility; for they included every moral problem of natural or revealed religion, divested of all those softening poetries and tender draperies which forms, ceremonies, and rituals had thrown around them in other parts and ages of Christendom. The human race, without exception, coming into existence "under God's wrath and curse," with a nature so fatally disordered, that, although perfect free agents, men were infallibly certain to do nothing to Divine acceptance until regenerated by the supernatural aid of God's Spirit,—this aid being given only to a certain decreed number of the human race, the rest, with enough free agency to make them responsible, but without this indispensable assistance exposed to the malignant assaults of evil spirits versed in every art of temptation, were sure to fall hopelessly into perdition. The standard of what constituted a true regeneration, as presented in such treatises as Edwards on the Affections, and others of the times, made this change to be something so high, disinterested, and superhuman, so removed from all natural and common habits and feelings, that the most earnest and devoted, whose whole life had been a constant travail of endeavor, a tissue of almost unearthly disinterestedness, often lived and died with only a glimmering hope of its attainment.

According to any views then entertained of the evidence of a true regeneration, the number of the whole human race who could be supposed as yet to have received this grace was so small, that, as to any numerical valuation, it must have been expressed as an infinitesimal. Dr. Hopkins in many places distinctly recognizes the fact, that the greater part of the human race, up to his time, had been eternally lost,—and boldly assumes the ground, that this amount of sin and suffering, being the best and most necessary means of the greatest final amount of happiness, was not merely permitted, but distinctly chosen, decreed, and provided for, as essential in the schemes of Infinite Benevolence. He held that this decree not only *permitted* each individual act of sin, but also took measures to make it certain, though, by an exercise of infinite skill, it accomplished this result without violating human free agency.

The preaching of those times was animated by an unflinching consistency which never shrank from carrying an idea to its remotest logical verge. The sufferings of the lost were not kept from view, but proclaimed with a terrible power. Dr. Hopkins boldly asserts, that "all the use which God will have for them is to suffer; this is all the end they can answer; therefore all their faculties, and their whole capacities, will be employed and used for this end. . . . . . The body can by omnipotence be made capable of suffering the greatest imaginable pain, without producing dissolution, or abating the least degree of life or sensibility. . . . . . One way in which God will show his power in punishing the wicked will be in strengthening and upholding their bodies and souls in torments which otherwise would be intolerable."

The sermons preached by President Edwards on this subject are so terrific in their refined poetry of torture, that very few persons of quick sensibility could read them through without agony; and it is related, that, when, in those calm and tender tones which never rose to passionate enunciation, he read these discourses, the house was often filled with shrieks and wailings, and that a brother minister once laid hold of his skirts, exclaiming, in an involuntary agony, "Oh! Mr. Edwards! Mr. Edwards! is God not a God of mercy?"

Not that these men were indifferent or insensible to the dread words they spoke; their whole lives and deportment bore thrilling witness to their sincerity. Edwards set apart special days of fasting, in view of the dreadful doom of the lost, in which he was wont to walk the floor, weeping and wringing his hands. Hopkins fasted every Saturday. David Brainerd gave up every refinement of civilized life to weep and pray at the feet of hardened savages, if by any means he might save *one*. All, by lives of eminent purity and earnestness, gave awful weight and sanction to their words.

If we add to this statement the fact, that it was always proposed to every inquiring soul, as an evidence of regeneration, that it should truly and heartily accept all the ways of God thus declared right and lovely, and from the heart submit to Him as the only just and good, it will be seen what materials of tremendous internal conflict and agitation were all the while working in every bosom. Almost all the histories of religious experience of those times relate paroxysms of opposition to God and fierce rebellion, expressed in language which appalls the very soul,— followed, at length, by mysterious elevations of faith and reactions of confiding love, the result of Divine interposition, which carried the soul far above the region of the intellect, into that of direct spiritual intuition.

President Edwards records that he was once in this state of enmity,—that the facts of the Divine administration seemed horrible to him,—and that this opposition was overcome by no course of reasoning, but by an *"inward and sweet sense,"* which came to him once when walking alone in the fields, and, looking up into the blue sky, he saw the blending of the Divine majesty with a calm, sweet, and almost infinite meekness.

The piety which grew up under such a system was, of necessity, energetic,—it was the uprousing of the whole energy of the human soul, pierced and wrenched and probed from her lowest depths to her topmost heights with every awful life-force possible to existence. He whose faith in God came clear through these terrible tests would be sure never to know greater ones. He might certainly challenge earth or heaven, things present or things to come, to swerve him from this grand allegiance.

But it is to be conceded, that these systems, so admirable in relation to the energy, earnestness, and acuteness of their authors, when received as absolute truth, and as a basis of actual life, had, on minds of a certain class, the effect of a slow poison, producing life-habits of morbid action very different from any which ever followed the simple reading of the Bible. They differ from the New Testament as the living embrace of a friend does from his lifeless body, mapped out under the knife of the anatomical demonstrator;—every nerve and muscle is there, but to a sensitive spirit there is the very chill of death in the analysis.

All systems that deal with the infinite are, besides, exposed to danger from small, unsuspected admixtures of human error, which become deadly when carried to such vast results. The smallest speck of earth's dust, in the focus of an infinite lens, appears magnified among the heavenly orbs as a frightful monster.

Thus it happened, that, while strong spirits walked, palm-crowned, with victorious hymns, along these sublime paths, feebler and more sensitive ones lay along the track, bleeding away in lifelong despair. Fearful to them were the shadows that lay over the cradle and the grave. The mother clasped her babe to her bosom, and looked with shuddering to the awful coming trial of free agency, with its terrible responsibilities and risks; and, as she thought of the infinite chances against her beloved, almost wished it might die in infancy. But when the stroke of death came, and some young, thoughtless head was laid suddenly low, who can say what silent anguish of loving hearts sounded the dread depths of eternity with the awful question, *Where?*

In no other time or place of Christendom have so fearful issues been presented to the mind. Some church interposed its protecting shield; the Christian born and baptized child was supposed in some wise rescued from the curse of the fall, and related to the great redemption,—to be a member of Christ's family, and, if ever so sinful, still infolded in some vague sphere of hope and protection. Augustine solaced the dread anxieties of trembling love by prayers offered for the dead, in times when the Church above and on earth presented itself to the eye of the mourner as a great assembly with one accord lifting interceding hands for the parted soul.

But the clear logic and intense individualism of New England deepened the problems of the Augustinian faith, while they swept away all those softening provisions so earnestly clasped to the throbbing heart of that great poet of theology. No rite, no form, no paternal relation, no faith or prayer of church, earthly or heavenly, interposed the slightest shield between the trembling spirit and Eternal Justice. The individual entered eternity alone, as if he had no interceding relation in the universe.

This, then, was the awful dread which was constantly under-lying life. This it was which caused the tolling bell in green hollows and lonely dells to be a sound which shook the soul and searched the heart with fearful questions. And this it was that was lying with mountain weight on the soul of the mother, too keenly agonized to feel that doubt in such a case was any less a torture than the most dreadful certainty.

Hers was a nature more reasoning than creative and poetic; and whatever she believed bound her mind in strictest chains to its logical results. She delighted in the regions of mathematical knowledge, and walked them as a native home, but the commerce with abstract certainties fitted her mind still more to be stiffened and enchained by glacial reasonings, in regions where spiritual intuitions are as necessary as wings to birds.

Mary was by nature of the class who never reason abstractly, whose intellections all begin in the heart, which sends them colored with its warm life-tint to the brain. Her perceptions of the same subjects were as different from Mrs. Marvyn's as his who revels only in color from his who is busy with the dry details of mere outline. The one mind was arranged like a map, and the other like a picture. In all the system which had been explained to her, her mind selected points on which it seized with intense sympathy, which it dwelt upon and expanded till all else fell away. The sublimity of disinterested benevolence,—the harmony and order of a system tending in its final results to infinite happiness, —the goodness of God,—the love of a self-sacrificing Redeemer,

—were all so many glorious pictures, which she revolved in her mind with small care for their logical relations.

Mrs. Marvyn had never, in all the course of their intimacy, opened her mouth to Mary on the subject of religion. It was not an uncommon incident of those times for persons of great elevation and purity of character to be familiarly known and spoken of as living under a cloud of religious gloom; and it was simply regarded as one more mysterious instance of the workings of that infinite decree which denied to them the special illumination of the Spirit.

When Mrs. Marvyn had drawn Mary with her into her room, she seemed like a person almost in frenzy. She shut and bolted the door, drew her to the foot of the bed, and, throwing her arms round her, rested her hot and throbbing forehead on her shoulder. She pressed her thin hand over her eyes, and then, suddenly drawing back, looked her in the face as one resolved to speak something long suppressed. Her soft brown eyes had a flash of despairing wildness in them, like that of a hunted animal turning in its death-struggle on its pursuer.

"Mary," she said, "I can't help it,—don't mind what I say, but I must speak or die! Mary, I cannot, will not, be resigned!— it is all hard, unjust, cruel!—to all eternity I will say so! To me there is no goodness, no justice, no mercy in anything! Life seems to me the most tremendous doom that can be inflicted on a helpless being! *What had we done,* that it should be sent upon us? Why were we made to love so, to hope so,—our hearts so full of feeling, and all the laws of Nature marching over us,—never stopping for our agony? Why, we can suffer so in this life that we had better never have been born!

"But, Mary, think what a moment life is! think of those awful ages of eternity! and then think of all God's power and knowledge used on the lost to make them suffer! think that all but the merest fragment of mankind have gone into this,—are in it now! The number of the elect is so small we can scarce count them for anything! Think what noble minds, what warm, generous hearts, what splendid natures are wrecked and thrown away by thousands and tens of thousands! How we love each other! how our hearts weave into each other! how more than glad we should be to die for each other! And all this ends—O God, how must it end?—Mary! it isn't *my* sorrow only! What right have I to mourn? Is *my* son any better than any other mother's son? Thousands of thousands, whose mothers loved them as I love mine, are gone there!—Oh, my wedding-day! Why did they rejoice? Brides should wear mourning,—the bells should toll for every wedding; every new family is built over this awful pit of despair, and only one in a thousand escapes!"

Pale, aghast, horror-stricken, Mary stood dumb, as one who in the dark and storm sees by the sudden glare of lightning a chasm yawning under foot. It was amazement and dimness of anguish;—the dreadful words struck on the very centre where her soul rested. She felt as if the point of a wedge were being driven between her life and her life's life,—between her and her God. She clasped her hands instinctively on her bosom, as if to hold there some cherished image, and said, in a piercing voice of supplication, "*My* God! *my* God! oh, where art Thou?"

Mrs. Marvyn walked up and down the room with a vivid spot of red in each cheek, and a baleful fire in her eyes, talking in rapid soliloquy, scarcely regarding her listener, absorbed in her own enkindled thoughts.

"Dr. Hopkins says that this is all best,—better than it would have been in any other possible way,—that God *chose* it because it was for a greater final good,—that He not only chose it, but took means to make it certain,—that He ordains every sin, and does all that is necessary to make it certain,—that He creates the vessels of wrath and fits them for destruction, and that He has an infinite knowledge by which He can do it without violating their free agency.—So much the worse! What a use of infinite knowledge! What if men should do so? What if a father should take means to make it certain that his poor little child should be an abandoned wretch, without violating his free agency? So much the worse, I say!—They say He does this so that He may show to all eternity, by their example, the evil nature of sin and its consequences! This is all that the greater part of the human race have been used for yet; and it is all right, because an overplus of infinite happiness is yet to be wrought out by it!—It is *not* right! No possible amount of good to ever so many can make it right to deprave ever so few;—happiness and misery cannot be measured so! I never can think it right,—never!—Yet they say our salvation depends on our loving God,—loving Him better than ourselves,—loving Him better than our dearest friends.— It is impossible!—it is contrary to the laws of my nature! I can never love God! I can never praise Him!—I am lost! lost! lost! And what is worse, I cannot redeem my friends! Oh, I *could* suffer forever,—how willingly!—if I could save *him!*—But oh, eternity, eternity! Frightful, unspeakable woe! No end!—no bottom!—no shore!—no hope!—O God! O God!"

Mrs. Marvyn's eyes grew wilder,—she walked the floor, wringing her hands,—and her words, mingled with shrieks and moans, became whirling and confused, as when in autumn a storm drives the leaves in dizzy mazes.

Mary was alarmed,—the ecstacy of despair was just verging on insanity. She rushed out and called Mr. Marvyn.

"Oh! come in! do! quick!—I'm afraid her mind is going!" she said.

"It is what I feared," he said, rising from where he sat reading his great Bible, with an air of heartbroken dejection. "Since she heard this news, she has not slept nor shed a tear. The Lord hath covered us with a cloud in the day of his fierce anger."

He came into the room, and tried to take his wife into his arms. She pushed him violently back, her eyes glistening with a fierce light. "Leave me alone!" she said,—"I am a lost spirit!"

These words were uttered in a shriek that went through Mary's heart like an arrow.

At this moment, Candace, who had been anxiously listening at the door for an hour past, suddenly burst into the room.

"Lor' bress ye, Squire Marvyn, we won't hab her goin' on dis yer way," she said. "Do talk *gospel* to her, can't ye?—ef you can't, I will.

"Come, ye poor little lamb," she said, walking straight up to Mrs. Marvyn, "come to ole Candace!"—and with that she gathered the pale form to her bosom, and sat down and began rocking her, as if she had been a babe. "Honey, darlin', ye a'n't right,— dar's a dreful mistake somewhar," she said. "Why, de Lord a'n't like what ye tink,—He *loves* ye, honey! Why, jes' feel how *I* loves ye,—poor ole black Candace,—an' I a'n't better'n Him as made me! Who was it wore de crown o' thorns, lamb?—who was it sweat great drops o' blood?—who was it said, 'Father, forgive dem'? Say, honey!—wasn't it de Lord dat made ye?— Dar, dar, now ye'r' cryin'!—cry away, and ease yer poor little heart! He died for Mass'r Jim,—loved him and *died* for him,— jes' give up his sweet, precious body and soul for him on de cross! Laws, jes' *leave* him in Jesus's hands! Why, honey, dar's de very print o' de nails in his hands now!"

The flood-gates were rent; and healing sobs and tears shook the frail form, as a faded lily shakes under the soft rains of summer. All in the room wept together.

"Now, honey," said Candace, after a pause of some minutes, "I knows our Doctor's a mighty good man, an' larned,—an' in fair weather I ha'n't no 'bjection to yer hearin' all about dese yer great an' mighty tings he's got to say. But, honey, dey won't do for you now; sick folks mus'n't hab strong meat; an' times like dese, dar jest a'n't but one ting to come to, an' dat ar's *Jesus*. Jes' come right down to whar poor ole black Candace has to stay allers,—it's a good place, darlin'! *Look right at Jesus.* Tell ye, honey, ye can't live no other way now. Don't ye 'member how He looked on His mother, when she stood faintin' an' tremblin' under de cross, jes' like you? He knows all about mothers' hearts; He won't break yours. It was jes' 'cause He know'd we'd come into straits like dis yer, dat he went through all dese tings,—Him, de Lord o' Glory! Is dis Him you was a-talkin' about?—Him you can't love? Look at Him, an' see ef you can't. Look an' see what He is!—don't ask no questions, and don't go to no reasonin's,—jes' look at *Him,* hangin' dar, so sweet and patient, on de cross! All dey could do couldn't stop his lovin' 'em; he prayed for 'em wid all de breath he had. Dar's a God you can love, a'n't dar? Candace loves Him,—poor, ole, foolish, black, wicked Candace,—and she knows He loves her,"—and here Candace broke down into torrents of weeping.

They laid the mother, faint and weary, on her bed, and beneath the shadow of that suffering cross came down a healing sleep on those weary eyelids.

"Honey," said Candace, mysteriously, after she had drawn Mary out of the room, "don't ye go for to troublin' yer mind wid dis yer. I'm clar Mass'r James is one o' de 'lect; and I'm clar dar's consid'able more o' de 'lect dan people tink. Why, Jesus didn't die for nothin',—all dat love a'n't gwine to be wasted. De 'lect is more'n you or I knows, honey! Dar's de *Spirit,*—He'll give it to 'em; and ef Mass'r James *is* called an' took, depend upon it de Lord has got him ready,—course He has,—so don't ye go to layin' on your poor heart what no mortal creetur can live under; 'cause, as we's got to live in dis yer world, it's quite clar de Lord must ha' fixed it so we *can;* and ef tings was as some folks suppose, why, we *couldn't* live, and dar wouldn't be no sense in anyting dat goes on."

The sudden shock of these scenes was followed, in Mrs. Marvyn's case, by a low, lingering fever. Her room was darkened, and she lay on her bed, a pale, suffering form, with scarcely the ability to raise her hand. The shimmering twilight of the sick-room fell on white napkins, spread over stands, where constantly appeared new vials, big and little, as the physician made his daily visit, and prescribed now this drug and now that, for a wound that had struck through the soul.

Mary remained many days at the white house, because, to the invalid, no step, no voice, no hand was like hers. We see her there now, as she sits in the glimmering by the bed-curtains,— her head a little drooped, as droops a snowdrop over a grave; —one ray of light from a round hole in the closed shutters falls on her smooth-parted hair, her small hands are clasped on her knees, her mouth has lines of sad compression, and in her eyes are infinite questionings.

Henry David Thoreau

Most readers think of Henry David Thoreau (1817–1862) as a nature writer and a transcendental philosopher. But on occasion he wrote about persons, especially ones who lived close to the soil or sea. Such a person is the Wellfleet Oysterman, whom Thoreau encountered on Cape Cod in the autumn of 1849. The Oysterman is a part and a product of the bleak, windswept locale in which he has passed his eighty-eight years; yet he is very much an individual with his own views on life, religion, and history. His occupation, his home, and his family, which includes an idiot son, are presented in the same detail that Thoreau would observe in describing the habits of a chipmunk or a woodchuck, but we are also made poignantly aware of the old man's human-ity, which has not only survived but in a sense has flourished in an unpromising environment. Thus Thoreau strikes a theme common to most later writers on rural and coastal New England life. The text reproduced here is that of Volume IV of The Writings of Henry David Thoreau, with Bibliographical Introduc-tions and Full Indices *(1894).*

The Wellfleet Oysterman

Having walked about eight miles since we struck the beach, and passed the boundary between Wellfleet and Truro, a stone post in the sand,—for even this sand comes under the jurisdiction of one town or another,—we turned inland over barren hills and valleys, whither the sea, for some reason, did not follow us, and, tracing up a Hollow, discovered two or three sober-looking houses within half a mile, uncommonly near the eastern coast. Their garrets were apparently so full of chambers, that their roofs could hardly lie down straight, and we did not doubt that there was room for us there. Houses near the sea are generally low and broad. These were a story and a half high; but if you merely counted the windows in their gable ends, you would think that there were many stories more, or, at any rate, that the half-story was the only one thought worthy of being illustrated. The great number of windows in the ends of the houses, and their irregularity in size and position, here and elsewhere on the Cape, struck us agreeably,—as if each of the various occupants who had their *cunabula* behind had punched a hole where his necessities required it, and according to his size and stature, without regard to outside effect. There were windows for the grown folks, and windows for the children,—three or four apiece; as a certain man had a large hole cut in his barn-door for the cat, and another smaller one for the kitten. Sometimes they were so low under the eaves that I thought they must have perforated the plate beam for another apartment, and I noticed some which were triangular, to fit that part more exactly. The ends of the houses had thus as many muzzles as a revolver, and, if the inhabitants have the same habit of staring out the windows that some of our neighbors have, a traveler must stand a small chance with them.

Generally, the old-fashioned and unpainted houses on the Cape looked more comfortable, as well as picturesque, than the modern and more pretending ones, which were less in harmony with the scenery, and less firmly planted.

These houses were on the shores of a chain of ponds, seven in number, the source of a small stream called Herring River, which empties into the Bay. There are many Herring Rivers on the Cape; they will, perhaps, be more numerous than herrings soon. We knocked at the door of the first house, but its inhabitants were all gone away. In the meanwhile, we saw the occupants of the next one looking out the window at us, and before we reached it an old woman came out and fastened the door of her bulkhead, and went in again. Nevertheless, we did not hesitate to knock at her door, when a grizzly-looking man appeared, whom we took to be sixty or seventy years old. He asked us, at first, suspiciously, where we were from, and what our business was; to which we returned plain answers.

"How far is Concord from Boston?" he inquired.

"Twenty miles by railroad."

"Twenty miles by railroad," he repeated.

"Didn't you ever hear of Concord of Revolutionary fame?"

"Didn't I ever hear of Concord? Why, I heard guns fire at the battle of Bunker Hill. [They hear the sound of heavy cannon across the Bay.] I am almost ninety; I am eighty-eight year old. I was fourteen year old at the time of Concord Fight,—and where were you then?"

We were obliged to confess that we were not in the fight.

"Well, walk in, we'll leave it to the women," said he.

So we walked in, surprised, and sat down, an old woman taking our hats and bundles, and the old man continued, drawing up to the large, old-fashioned fireplace,—

"I am a poor, good-for-nothing crittur, as Isaiah says; I am all broken down this year. I am under petticoat government here."

The family consisted of the old man, his wife, and his daughter, who appeared nearly as old as her mother, a fool, her son (a brutish-looking, middle-aged man, with a prominent lower face, who was standing by the hearth when we entered, but immediately went out), and a little boy of ten.

While my companion talked with the women, I talked with the old man. They said that he was old and foolish, but he was evidently too knowing for them.

"These women," said he to me, "are both of them poor good-for-nothing critturs. This one is my wife. I married her sixty-four years ago. She is eighty-four years old, and as deaf as an adder, and the other is not much better."

He thought well of the Bible, or at least he *spoke* well, and did not *think* ill, of it, for that would not have been prudent for a man of his age. He said that he had read it attentively for many years, and he had much of it at his tongue's end. He seemed deeply impressed with a sense of his own nothingness, and would repeatedly exclaim,—

"I am a nothing. What I gather from my Bible is just this; that man is a poor good-for-nothing crittur, and everything is just as God sees fit and disposes."

"May I ask your name?" I said.

"Yes," he answered, "I am not ashamed to tell my name. My name is ——. My great-grandfather came over from England and settled here."

He was an old Wellfleet oysterman, who had acquired a competency in that business, and had sons still engaged in it.

Nearly all the oyster shops and stands in Massachusetts, I am told, are supplied and kept by natives of Wellfleet, and a part of this town is still called Billingsgate from the oysters having been formerly planted there; but the native oysters are said to have died in 1770. Various causes are assigned for this, such as a ground frost, the carcasses of blackfish, kept to rot in the harbor, and the like, but the most common account of the matter is,— and I find that a similar superstition with regard to the disappearance of fishes exists almost everywhere,—that when Wellfleet began to quarrel with the neighboring towns about the right to gather them, yellow specks appeared in them, and Providence caused them to disappear. A few years ago sixty thousand bushels were annually brought from the South and planted in the harbor of Wellfleet till they attained "the proper relish of Billingsgate;" but now they are imported commonly full-grown, and laid down near their markets, at Boston and elsewhere, where the water, being a mixture of salt and fresh, suits them better. The business was said to be still good and improving.

The old man said that the oysters were liable to freeze in the winter, if planted too high; but if it were not "so cold as to strain their eyes" they were not injured. The inhabitants of New Brunswick have noticed that "ice will not form over an oyster-bed, unless the cold is very intense indeed, and when the bays are frozen over the oyster-beds are easily discovered by the water above them remaining unfrozen, or as the French residents say, *dégelée*." Our host said that they kept them in cellars all winter.

"Without anything to eat or drink?" I asked.

"Without anything to eat or drink," he answered.

"Can the oysters move?"

"Just as much as my shoe."

But when I caught him saying that they "bedded themselves down in the sand, flat side up, round side down," I told him that my shoe could not do that, without the aid of my foot in it; at which he said that they merely settled down as they grew; if put down in a square they would be found so; but the clam could move quite fast. I have since been told by oystermen of Long Island, where the oyster is still indigenous and abundant, that they are found in large masses attached to the parent in their midst, and are so taken up with their tongs; in which case, they say, the age of the young proves that there could have been no motion for five or six years at least. And Buckland in his "Curiosities of Natural History" (page 50) says: "An oyster, who has once taken up his position and fixed himself when quite young, can never make a change. Oysters, nevertheless, that have not fixed themselves, but remain loose at the bottom of the sea, have the power of locomotion; they open their shells to their fullest extent, and then suddenly contracting them, the expulsion of the water forwards gives a motion backwards. A fisherman at Guernsey told me that he had frequently seen oysters moving in this way."

Some still entertain the question "whether the oyster was indigenous in Massachusetts Bay," and whether Wellfleet Harbor was a "natural habitat" of this fish; but, to say nothing of the testimony of old oystermen, which, I think, is quite conclusive, though the native oyster may now be extinct there, I saw that their shells, opened by the Indians, were strewn all over the Cape. Indeed, the Cape was at first thickly settled by Indians on account of the abundance of these and other fish. We saw many traces of their occupancy after this, in Truro, near Great Hollow, and at High Head, near East Harbor River,—oysters, clams, cockles, and other shells, mingled with ashes and the bones of deer and other quadrupeds. I picked up half a dozen arrowheads, and in an hour or two could have filled my pockets with them. The Indians lived about the edges of the swamps, then probably in some instances ponds, for shelter and water. Moreover, Champlain, in the edition of his "Voyages" printed in 1613, says that in the year 1606 he and Poitrincourt explored a harbor (Barnstable Harbor?) in the southerly part of what is now called Massachusetts Bay, in latitude 42°, about five leagues south, one point west of *Cap Blanc* (Cape Cod), and there they found many good oysters, and they named it *"le Port aux Huistres"* [sic] (Oyster Harbor). In one edition of his map (1632), the *"R. aux Escailles"* is drawn emptying into the same part of the bay, and on the map *"Novi Belgii,"* in Ogilby's America (1670), the words *"Port aux Huistres"* are placed against the same place. Also William Wood, who left New England in 1633, speaks, in his "New England's Prospect," published in 1634, of "a great oyster-bank" in Charles River, and of another in the Mistick, each of which obstructed the navigation of its river. "The oysters," says he, "be great ones in form of a shoe-horn; some be a foot long; these breed on certain banks that are bare every spring tide. This fish without the shell is so big, that it must admit of a division before you can well get it into your mouth." Oysters are still found there.

Our host told us that the sea-clam, or hen, was not easily obtained; it was raked up, but never on the Atlantic side, only cast ashore there in small quantities in storms. The fisherman sometimes wades in water several feet deep, and thrusts a pointed stick into the sand before him. When this enters between the valves of a clam, he closes them on it, and is drawn out. It has been known to catch and hold coot and teal which were preying on it. I chanced to be on the bank of the Acushnet at New Bedford one day since this, watching some ducks, when a man informed me that, having let out his young ducks to seek their food amid the samphire (*Salicornia*) and other weeds along the riverside at low tide that morning, at length he noticed that one remained stationary, amid the weeds, something preventing it from following the others, and going to it he found its foot tightly shut in a quahog's shell. He took up both together, carried them to his home, and his wife opening the shell with a knife released the duck and cooked the quahog. The old man said that the great clams were good to eat, but that they always took out a certain part which was poisonous, before they cooked them. "People said it would kill a cat." I did not tell him that I had eaten a large one entire that afternoon, but began to think that I was tougher than a cat. He stated that pedlers came round there, and sometimes tried to sell the women folks a skimmer, but he told them that their women had got a better skimmer than *they* could make, in the shell of their clams; it was shaped just right for this purpose.—They call them "skim-alls" in some places. He also said that the sun-squall was poisonous to handle, and when the sailors came across it, they did not meddle with it, but heaved it out of their way. I told him that I had handled it that afternoon, and had felt no ill effects as yet. But he said it made the hands itch, especially if they had previously been scratched, or if I put it into my bosom, I should find out what it was.

He informed us that no ice ever formed on the back side of the Cape, or not more than once in a century, and but little snow lay there, it being either absorbed or blown or washed away. Sometimes in winter, when the tide was down, the beach was frozen, and afforded a hard road up the back side for some thirty miles, as smooth as a floor. One winter when he was a boy, he and his father "took right out into the Back Side before daylight, and walked to Provincetown and back to dinner."

When I asked what they did with all that barren-looking land, where I saw so few cultivated fields,—"Nothing," he said.

"Then why fence your fields?"

"To keep the sand from blowing and covering up the whole."

"The yellow sand," said he, "has some life in it, but the white little or none."

When, in answer to his questions, I told him that I was a surveyor, he said that they who surveyed his farm were accustomed, where the ground was uneven, to loop up each chain as high as their elbows; that was the allowance they made, and he wished to know if I could tell him why they did not come out according to his deed, or twice alike. He seemed to have more respect for surveyors of the old school, which I did not wonder at. "King George the Third," said he, "laid out a road four rods wide and straight, the whole length of the Cape," but where it was now he could not tell.

This story of the surveyors reminded me of a Long-Islander, who once, when I had made ready to jump from the bow of his boat to the shore, and he thought that I underrated the distance and would fall short,—though I found afterward that he judged of the elasticity of my joints by his own,—told me that when he came to a brook which he wanted to get over, he held up one leg, and then, if his foot appeared to cover any part of the opposite bank, he knew that he could jump it. "Why," I told him, "to say nothing of the Mississippi, and other small watery streams, I could blot out a star with my foot, but I would not engage to jump that distance," and asked how he knew when he had got his leg at the right elevation. But he regarded his legs as no less accurate than a pair of screw dividers or an ordinary quadrant, and appeared to have a painful recollection of every degree and minute in the arc which they described; and he would have had me believe that there was a kind of hitch in his hip-joint which answered the purpose. I suggested that he should connect his two ankles by a string of the proper length, which should be the chord of an arc, measuring his jumping ability on horizontal surfaces,—assuming one leg to be a perpendicular to the plane of the horizon, which, however, may have been too bold an assumption in this case. Nevertheless, this was a kind of geometry in the legs which it interested me to hear of.

Our host took pleasure in telling us the names of the ponds, most of which we could see from his windows, and making us repeat them after him, to see if we had got them right. They were Gull Pond, the largest and a very handsome one, clear and deep, and more than a mile in circumference, Newcomb's, Swett's, Slough, Horse-Leech, Round, and Herring Ponds, all connected at high water, if I do not mistake. The coast-surveyors had come to him for their names, and he told them of one which they had not detected. He said that they were not so high as formerly. There was an earthquake about four years before he was born, which cracked the pans of the ponds, which were of iron, and caused them to settle. I did not remember to have read of this. Innumerable gulls used to resort to them; but the large gulls were now very scarce, for, as he said, the English robbed their nests far in the north, where they breed. He remembered well when gulls were taken in the gull-house, and when small birds were killed by means of a frying-pan and fire at night. His father once lost a valuable horse from this cause. A party from Wellfleet having lighted their fire for this purpose, one dark night, on Billingsgate Island, twenty horses which were pastured there, and his colt among them, being frightened by it, and endeavoring in the dark to cross the passage which separated them from the neighboring beach, and which was then fordable at low tide, were all swept out to sea and drowned. I observed that many horses were still turned out to pasture all summer on the islands and beaches in Wellfleet, Eastham, and Orleans, as a kind of common. He also described the killing of what he called "wild hens," here, after they had gone to roost in the woods, when he was a boy. Perhaps they were "prairie hens" (pinnated grouse).

He liked the beach pea (*Lathyrus maritimus*), cooked green, as well as the cultivated. He had seen it growing very abundantly in Newfoundland, where also the inhabitants ate them, but he had never been able to obtain any ripe for seed. We read, under the head of Chatham, that "in 1555, during a time of great scarcity, the people about Orford, in Sussex [England] were preserved from perishing by eating the seeds of this plant, which grew there in great abundance upon the sea coast. Cows, horses, sheep, and goats eat it." But the writer who quoted this could not learn that they had ever been used in Barnstable County.

He had been a voyager, then? Oh, he had been about the world in his day. He once considered himself a pilot for all our coast; but now they had changed the names so he might be bothered.

He gave us to taste what he called the Summer Sweeting, a pleasant apple which he raised, and frequently grafted from, but had never seen growing elsewhere, except once,—three trees on Newfoundland, or at the Bay of Chaleur, I forget which, as he was sailing by. He was sure that he could tell the tree at a distance.

At length the fool, whom my companion called the wizard, came in, muttering between his teeth, "Damn book-pedlers,—all the time talking about books. Better do something. Damn 'em. I'll shoot 'em. Got a doctor down here. Damn him, I'll get a gun and shoot him;" never once holding up his head. Whereat the old man stood up and said in a loud voice, as if he was accustomed to command, and this was not the first time he had been obliged to exert his authority there: "John, go sit down, mind your business,—we've heard you talk before,—precious little you'll do,—your bark is worse than your bite." But, without minding, John muttered the same gibberish over again, and then sat down at the table which the old folks had left. He ate all there was on it, and then turned to the apples, which his aged mother was paring, that she might give her guests some apple-sauce for breakfast, but she drew them away and sent him off.

When I approached this house the next summer, over the desolate hills between it and the shore, which are worthy to have been the birthplace of Ossian, I saw the wizard in the midst of a corn-field on the hillside, but, as usual, he loomed so strangely, that I mistook him for a scarecrow.

This was the merriest old man that we had ever seen, and one of the best preserved. His style of conversation was coarse and plain enough to have suited Rabelais. He would have made a good Panurge. Or rather he was a sober Silenus, and we were the boys Chromis and Mnasilus, who listened to his story.

> Not by Haemonian hills the Thracian bard,
> Nor awful Phoebus was on Pindus heard
> With deeper silence or with more regard.

There was a strange mingling of past and present in his conversation, for he had lived under King George, and might have remembered when Napoleon and the moderns generally were born. He said that one day, when the troubles between the Colonies and the mother country first broke out, as he, a boy of fifteen, was pitching hay out of a cart, one Donne, an old Tory, who was talking with his father, a good Whig, said to him, "Why, Uncle Bill, you might as well undertake to pitch that pond into the ocean with a pitchfork, as for the Colonies to undertake to gain their independence." He remembered well General Washington, and how he rode his horse along the streets of Boston, and he stood up to show us how he looked.

"He was a r—a—ther large and portly-looking man, a manly and resolute-looking officer, with a pretty good leg as he sat on his horse."—"There, I'll tell you, this was the way with Washington." Then he jumped up again, and bowed gracefully to right and left, making show as if he were waving his hat. Said he, "*That* was Washington."

He told us many anecdotes of the Revolution, and was much pleased when we told him that we had read the same in history, and that his account agreed with the written.

"Oh," he said, "I know, I know! I was a young fellow of sixteen, with my ears wide open; and a fellow of that age, you know, is pretty wide awake, and likes to know everything that's going on. Oh, I know!"

He told us the story of the wreck of the Franklin, which took place there the previous spring; how a boy came to his house early in the morning to know whose boat that was by the shore, for there was a vessel in distress, and he, being an old man, first ate his breakfast, and then walked over to the top of the hill by the shore, and sat down there, having found a comfortable seat, to see the ship wrecked. She was on the bar, only a quarter of a mile from him, and still nearer to the men on the beach, who had got a boat ready, but could render no assistance on account of the breakers, for there was a pretty high sea running. There were the passengers all crowded together in the forward part of the ship, and some were getting out of the cabin windows and were drawn on deck by the others.

"I saw the captain get out his boat," said he; "he had one little one; and then they jumped into it one after another, down as straight as an arrow. I counted them. There were nine. One was a woman, and she jumped as straight as any of them. Then they shoved off. The sea took them back, one wave went over them, and when they came up there were six still clinging to the boat; I counted them. The next wave turned the boat bottom upward, and emptied them all out. None of them ever came ashore alive. There were the rest of them all crowded together on the forecastle, the other parts of the ship being under water. They had seen all that happened to the boat. At length a heavy sea separated the forecastle from the rest of the wreck, and set it inside of the worst breaker, and the boat was able to reach them, and it saved all that were left, but one woman."

He also told us of the steamer Cambria's getting aground on this shore a few months before we were there, and of her English passengers who roamed over his grounds, and who, he said, thought the prospect from the high hill by the shore, "the most delightsome they had ever seen," and also of the pranks which the ladies played with his scoop-net in the ponds. He spoke of these travelers with their purses full of guineas, just as our provincial fathers used to speak of British bloods in the time of King George the Third.

Quid loquar? Why repeat what he told us?

> Aut Scyllam Nisi, quam fama secuta est,
> Candida succinctam latrantibus inguina monstris,
> Dulichias vexâsse rates, et gurgite in alto
> Ah! timidos nautas canibus lacerâsse marinis?

In the course of the evening I began to feel the potency of the clam which I had eaten, and I was obliged to confess to our host that I was no tougher than the cat he told of; but he answered, that he was a plainspoken man, and he could tell me that it was all imagination. At any rate, it proved an emetic in my case, and I was made quite sick by it for a short time, while he laughed at my expense. I was pleased to read afterward, in Mourt's Relation of the landing of the Pilgrims in Provincetown Harbor, these words: "We found great muscles [the old editor says that they were undoubtedly sea-clams] and very fat and full of sea-pearl; but we could not eat them, for they made us all sick that did eat, as well sailors as passengers, . . . but they were soon well again." It brought me nearer to the Pilgrims to be thus reminded by a similar experience that I was so like them. Moreover, it was a valuable confirmation of their story, and I am prepared now to believe every word of Mourt's Relation. I was also pleased to find that man and the clam lay still at the same angle to one another. But I did not notice sea-pearl. Like Cleopatra, I must have swallowed it. I have since dug these clams on a flat in the Bay and observed them. They could squirt full ten feet before the wind, as appeared by the marks of the drops on the sand.

"Now I am going to ask you a question," said the old man, "and I don't know as you can tell me; but you are a learned man, and I never had any learning, only what I got by natur." —It was in vain that we reminded him that he could quote Josephus to our confusion.—"I've thought, if I ever met a learned man I should like to ask him this question. Can you tell me how *Axy* is spelt, and what it means? *Axy*," says he; "there's a girl over here is named *Axy*. Now what is it? What does it mean? Is it Scripture? I've read my Bible twenty-five years over and over, and I never came across it."

"Did you read it twenty-five years for this object?" I asked.

"Well, *how* is it spelt? Wife, how is it spelt?"

She said, "It is in the Bible; I've seen it."

"Well, how do you spell it?"

"I don't know. A c h, ach, s e h, seh,—Achseh."

"Does that spell Axy? Well, do *you* know what it means?" asked he, turning to me.

"No," I replied, "I never heard the sound before."

"There was a schoolmaster down here once, and they asked him what it meant, and he said it had no more meaning than a bean-pole."

I told him that I held the same opinion with the schoolmaster. I had been a schoolmaster myself, and had had strange names to deal with. I also heard of such names as Zoheth, Beriah, Amaziah, Bethuel, and Shearjashub, hereabouts.

At length the little boy, who had a seat quite in the chimney-corner, took off his stockings and shoes, warmed his feet, and having had his sore leg freshly salved, went off to bed; then the fool made bare his knotty-looking feet and legs, and followed him; and finally the old man exposed his calves also to our gaze. We had never had the good fortune to see an old man's legs before, and were surprised to find them fair and plump as an infant's, and we thought that he took a pride in exhibiting them. He then proceeded to make preparations for retiring, discoursing meanwhile with Panurgic plainness of speech on the ills to which old humanity is subject. We were a rare haul for him. He could commonly get none but ministers to talk to, though sometimes ten of them at once, and he was glad to meet some of the laity at leisure. The evening was not long enough for him. As I had been sick, the old lady asked if I would not go to bed, —it was getting late for old people; but the old man, who had not yet done his stories, said, "You ain't particular, are you?"

"Oh, no," said I, "I am in no hurry. I believe I have weathered the Clam cape."

"They are good," said he; "I wish I had some of them now."

"They never hurt me," said the old lady.

"But then you took out the part that killed a cat," said I.

At last we cut him short in the midst of his stories, which he promised to resume in the morning. Yet, after all, one of the old ladies who came into our room in the night to fasten the fire-board, which rattled, as she went out took the precaution to fasten us in. Old women are by nature more suspicious than old men. However, the winds howled around the house, and made the fire-boards as well as the casements rattle well that night. It was probably a windy night for any locality, but we could not distinguish the roar which was proper to the ocean from that which was due to the wind alone.

The sounds which the ocean makes must be very significant and interesting to those who live near it. When I was leaving the shore at this place the next summer, and had got a quarter of a mile distant, ascending a hill, I was startled by a sudden, loud sound from the sea, as if a large steamer were letting off steam by the shore, so that I caught my breath and felt my blood run cold for an instant, and I turned about, expecting to see one of the Atlantic steamers thus far out of her course, but there was nothing unusual to be seen. There was a low bank at the entrance of the Hollow, between me and the ocean, and suspecting that I might have risen into another stratum of air in ascending the hill,—which had wafted to me only the ordinary roar of the sea,—I immediately descended again, to see if I lost hearing of it; but, without regard to my ascending or descending, it died away in a minute or two, and yet there was scarcely any wind all the while. The old man said that this was what they called the "rut," a peculiar roar of the sea before the wind changes, which, however, he could not account for. He thought that he could tell all about the weather from the sounds which the sea made.

Old Josselyn, who came to New England in 1638, has it among his weather-signs, that "the resounding of the sea from the shore, and murmuring of the winds in the woods, without apparent wind, sheweth wind to follow."

Being on another part of the coast one night since this, I heard the roar of the surf a mile distant, and the inhabitants said it was a sign that the wind would work round east, and we should have rainy weather. The ocean was heaped up somewhere at the eastward, and this roar was occasioned by its effort to preserve its equilibrium, the wave reaching the shore before the wind. Also the captain of a packet between this country and England told me that he sometimes met with a wave on the Atlantic coming against the wind, perhaps in a calm sea, which indicated that at a distance the wind was blowing from an opposite quarter, but the undulation had traveled faster than it. Sailors tell of "tide-rips" and "ground-swells," which they suppose to have been occasioned by hurricanes and earthquakes, and to have traveled many hundred, and sometimes even two to three thousand miles.

Before sunrise the next morning they let us out again, and I ran over to the beach to see the sun come out of the ocean. The old woman of eighty-four winters was already out in the cold morning wind, bareheaded, tripping about like a young girl, and driving up the cow to milk. She got the breakfast with dispatch, and without noise or bustle; and meanwhile the old man resumed his stories, standing before us, who were sitting, with his back to the chimney, and ejecting his tobacco-juice right and left into the fire behind him, without regard to the various dishes which were there preparing. At breakfast we had eels, buttermilk cake, cold bread, green beans, doughnuts, and tea. The old man talked a steady stream; and when his wife told him he had better eat his breakfast, he said, "Don't hurry me; I have lived too long to be hurried." I ate of the apple-sauce and the doughnuts, which I thought had sustained the least detriment from the old man's shots, but my companion refused the apple-sauce, and ate of the hot cake and green beans, which had appeared to him to occupy the safest part of the hearth. But on comparing notes afterward, I told him that the buttermilk cake was particularly exposed, and I saw how it suffered repeatedly, and therefore I avoided it; but he declared that, however that might be, he witnessed that the apple-sauce was seriously injured, and had therefore declined that. After breakfast we looked at his clock, which was out of order, and oiled it with some "hen's grease," for want of sweet oil, for he scarcely could believe that we were not tinkers or pedlers; meanwhile, he told a story about visions, which had reference to a crack in the clock-case made by frost one night. He was curious to know to what religious sect we belonged. He said that he had been to hear thirteen kinds of preaching in one month, when he was young, but he did not join any of them,—he stuck to his Bible. There was nothing like any of them in his Bible. While I was shaving in the next room, I heard him ask my companion to what sect he belonged, to which he answered,—

"Oh, I belong to the Universal Brotherhood."

"What's that?" he asked, "Sons o' Temperance?"

Finally, filling our pockets with doughnuts, which he was pleased to find that we called by the same name that he did, and paying for our entertainment, we took our departure; but he followed us out of doors, and made us tell him the names of the vegetables which he had raised from seeds that came out of the Franklin. They were cabbage, broccoli, and parsley. As I had asked him the names of so many things, he tried me in turn with all the plants which grew in his garden, both wild and cultivated. It was about half an acre, which he cultivated wholly himself. Besides the common garden vegetables, there were yellow dock, lemon balm, hyssop, gill-go-over-the-ground, mouse-ear, chickweed, Roman wormwood, elecampane, and other plants. As we stood there, I saw a fish hawk stoop to pick a fish out of his pond.

"There," said I, "he has got a fish."

"Well," said the old man, who was looking all the while, but could see nothing, "he didn't dive, he just wet his claws."

And, sure enough, he did not this time, though it is said that they often do, but he merely stooped low enough to pick him out with his talons; but as he bore his shining prey over the bushes, it fell to the ground, and we did not see that he recovered it. That is not their practice.

Thus, having had another crack with the old man, he standing bareheaded under the eaves, he directed us "athwart the fields," and we took to the beach again for another day, it being now late in the morning.

It was but a day or two after this that the safe of the Provincetown Bank was broken open and robbed by two men from the interior, and we learned that our hospitable entertainers did at least transiently harbor the suspicion that we were the men.

Rose Terry Cooke

Rose Terry Cooke (1827-1892) was born on a farm not far from Hartford, Connecticut. On both sides she was descended from ancient Puritan stock. Following graduation from Hartford Female Seminary, she taught school for a while, but later gave up teaching in order to take over the upbringing of her dead sister's children. When she was forty-six, she married an iron manufacturer and eventually moved to Pittsfield, Massachusetts, where she remained till her death. In a writing career that covered fifty years she devoted her first efforts to poetry, of which she produced a considerable body in a religious and sentimental vein; but her real talent was for short prose fiction like that contained in her two most notable books, Somebody's Neighbors *(1881) and* Huckleberries Gathered from New England Hills *(1891). As a realist she won the praise of William Dean Howells, and beyond question she deserves a place beside the most skillful and truthful New England regionalists—Sarah Orne Jewett, Mary Wilkins Freeman, and Harriet Beecher Stowe. As a setting for many of her tales she made use of the northwestern Connecticut hill country that she knew so well, placing in this area her fictional town of Bassett, the inhabitants of which keep reappearing from story to story. Mrs. Cooke's narrative tone is a pungent blend of humor and seriousness, which is well illustrated in "Mrs. Flint's Married Experience." She was at once amused and outraged by the tragi-comic excesses and warpings of character commonly found in the isolated and ingrown villages of her region. Quite conventionally religious herself—having undergone conversion in her girlhood—she was nevertheless critical of an atrophied Calvinism that would sanction the hypocritical Deacon Flint's victimizing of his gentle and faithful wife; and she was even more critical of the pious complacency that blinded the village parson to Mrs. Flint's des-*

perate plight. In this long story Mrs. Cooke, mingling irony with indignation, has exhibited a rural Calvinism that was still dominant though far advanced toward senility and ultimate rigor mortis. The text used here is from Somebody's Neighbors *in an edition of 1896.*

Mrs. Flint's Married Experience

"Well, Mindwell, I have counselled a good deal about it. I was happy as the day is long with your father. I don't say but what I cleaved to this world consider'ble more than was good for my growth in grace. He was about the best. But it pleased the Lord to remove him, and it was quite a spell before I could reely submit: the nateral man rebelled, now I tell you! You can't never tell what it is to lose a companion till you exper'ence it."

A faint color, vanishing as rapidly as it came, almost as if ashamed that it bore witness to the emotion within her, rose to Mindwell Pratt's face as her mother spoke. She was a typical New-England woman,—pale, serious, with delicate features, grave dark eyes, a tall, slight, undeveloped figure, graceful from mere unconsciousness, awkward and angular otherwise. You could compare her to nothing but some delicate and slender tree of the forest that waves its fragile but hardy branches fresh and green in spring-time, and abides undaunted the worst blast of winter, rooted in the fissures of the rock, fed by the bitterest showers, the melting snows, the furious hail that bends but never breaks it; perfect in its place, fitted utterly to its surroundings. Her mother, the Widow Gold, was externally like her; but deep in Mindwell's heart lay a strength of character, and acuteness of judgment, the elder woman did not possess, and a reticence that forbade her to express sympathy, even with her mother's sorrow, further than by that reluctant blush; for sympathy implied an expression of her love for her husband,—a hidden treasure she could not profane by speech, which found its only demonstration in deeds, and was the chief spring of her active and devoted life as wife and mother.

Mrs. Gold had been a happy woman, as she said, while her husband lived, and had not yet ceased to reproach herself for mourning him so bitterly. The religion of New England at that time was of a stern type: it demanded a spiritual asceticism of its followers, and virtually forbade them to enjoy the blessings of this life by keeping them in horrid and continual dread of "the pains of hell forever," as their Catechism expresses it. It was their purpose to work out their own salvation with fear and trembling under the curse of the law. The gospel was a profound and awful mystery, to be longed for afar off, no more daily bread than the show-bread of the Temple.

They lived and worked, and suffered and died, with few exceptions, in an awful sense of flying time, brief probation, an angry God, a certain hell, but a very uncertain heaven. No wonder that they were austere and hard: the wonder was that even natural temperament and mental organization should ever resist this outside pressure, and give play to humor, or fancy, or passion of any sort. Yet in this faithless faith lay elements of wonderful strength. The compelling force of duty made men nobly honest, rigidly upright, just, as far as their narrow views allowed, and true to the outward relations of this life, however they violated their inner principle and meaning. Speculation, defalcation, divorce, were crimes they called by other names than these, and abhorred. Can we say as much for ourselves? However we may sneer at Puritanism, it had its strong virtues; and its outgrowth was honesty, decency, and respect for law. A share of such virtues would be worth much to us now.

Mrs. Gold was "a professor," and it behooved her to submit to the will of God when her husband died. He had been a strong, generous, warm-hearted man; and, though undemonstrative as his race, his wife had been loved and cherished as the very blossom of his life. She was a sweet, fair girl when Ethan Gold married her, clinging and dependent by nature, though education had made her a hard worker; but her fragile beauty and soft temper had attracted the strength and fervor of the man, and their short life together had been exceptionally happy. Then fever struck him down in his full prime; and their only child, a girl of six, could but just remember all her life that she once had a father whose very memory was sacred. Fifteen years of

mourning, at first deeply, then steadily, at last habitually, and
rather as a form than a feeling, passed away.

Ethan had left his wife with "means;" so that poverty did
not vex her. And now Mindwell was a grown woman, and married to Samuel Pratt, a well-to-do young farmer of Colebrook,
a hearty, jovial young fellow, whose fun and animal spirits would
bubble over in spite of reproving eyes and tongues, and who
came into Mindwell's restrained and reserved life like a burst
of sunshine. Are the wild blossoms grateful to the sun that draws
them with powerful attraction from the cold sod,

> Where they together,
> All the cold weather,
> Keep house alone?

Perhaps their odor and color are for him who brings them to
light and delight of life. Mindwell's great fear was that she
made an idol of her husband, yet he certainly had not an idea
that she did.

If the good soul had stopped to analyze the relation between
them, his consciousness would have been found, when formulated,
to be, that his wife bore with him as saints do with rather amus-
ing sinners; while he worshipped her as even the most humorous
of sinners do sometimes secretly worship saints. But what the
wife did not acknowledge, or the husband perceive, became in
a few years painfully perceptible to the mother's feminine and
maternal instinct. Mindwell treated her with all possible respect
and kindness, but she was no longer her first object. There is a
strange hunger in the average female heart to be the one and
only love of some other heart, which lies at the root of fearful
tragedies and long agonies of unspoken pain,—a God-given instinct, no doubt, to make the monopoly of marriage dear and
desirable, but, like all other instincts, fatal if it be not fulfilled
or followed. Utterly wanting in men, who grasp the pluralities
of passion as well as of office, this instinct niches itself deepest
in the gentlest of women, and was the ruling yet unrecognized
motive in the Widow Gold's character. If Mindwell had not
had children, perhaps her mother would have been more necessary to her, and more dear; but two babies had followed on
her marriage within three years, and her mother-love was a
true passion. This the grandmother perceived with a tender jeal-

ousy fast growing acute. She loved the little girls, as grand-
mothers do, with unreasoning and lavish fondness. If there had
been a maiden aunt in the family,—that unconsidered maid-of-
all-work, whose love is felt to be intrusive, while yet the demands
on it are insatiable,—the Widow Gold would have had at least
one sympathetic breast to appeal to; but as it was she became
more and more uneasy and unhappy, and began to make herself
wretched with all the commonplaces she could think of,—about
her "room being better than her company," "love runs down,
not up," and the like,—till she was really pining, when just at
this moment an admirer came upon the scene, and made known
the reason of his appearance in a business-like way.

"Deacon Flint's in the keepin'-room, mother, wishful to see
you," said Mindwell one day, about five years after her marriage.
Deacon Flint was an old acquaintance, known to Mrs. Gold
ever since she was a girl in Bassett. When she married, and
moved to Denslow, the acquaintance had been partly dropped,
though only nine miles lay between them; but she had then her
family cares, and Ethan Gold and Amasa Flint were as unlikely
to be friends as a Newfoundland dog and a weasel. Since she had
come to Colebrook to live with her daughter, she was a little farther still from her Bassett friends, and therefore it was a long time
since she had seen the deacon. Meanwhile he had lost his wife,
a silent and sickly woman, who crept about and worried through
her daily duties for years, spent and fainting when the last
supper-dish was washed, and aching at early dawn when she
had to get up to milk. She did not complain: her duty lay there,
in her home, and she did it as long as she could—then she died.
This is a common record among our barren hills, which count by
thousands their unknown and unsung martyrs. It was a year
after her death when Deacon Flint made his first visit to Widow
Gold. He was tired of paying Aunt Polly Morse seventy-five
cents a week to do housework, though she spun and wove, and
made and mended, as faithfully as his wife had done, confiding
only to one trusty ear her opinion of her employer.

"He's a professor, ye know, Isr'el, and I make no doubt but
what he's a good man; but he is dreadful near. Seems as if he
reelly begrutched me my vittles sometimes; and there ain't a grain
o' salt in that house spilt without his findin' of it out. Now, I
don't calc'late *to* spill no salt, nor nothin' else, to waste it; but,
land's sakes! I can't see like a fly, so's to scare up every mite of
sugar that's left onto the edges of the paper he fetches it hum in.

I wish to gracious he'd get somebody else. I'd ruther do chores for Mirandy Huff than for the deacon."

Old Israel's wrinkled face, puckered mouth, and deep-set eyes, twitched with a furtive laugh. He was the village fool, yet shrewder than any man who stopped to jest with him, and a fool only in the satiric sense of jester; for though he had nothing of his own but a tiny brown house and pig-pen, and made his living, such as it was, by doing odd jobs, and peddling yeast from the distilleries at Simsbury, he was the most independent man in Bassett, being regardless of public opinion, and not at all afraid of Parson Roberts.

"Well, Aunt Polly," he answered, "you stay by a spell: the deacon won't want ye too long. He's got a sharp eye, now I tell ye, and he's forehanded as fury. Fust you know, Miss Flint'll *come* home, and you'll *go* home."

"Miss Flint!" screamed Aunt Polly. "Why, Isr'el Tucker, you give me such a turn! Poor cretur, she's safe under the mulleins this year back. I guess I shall go when she comes, but 'twon't be till the day o' judgment."

"Then the day o' judgment's near by, Aunt Polly; and I reckon it is for one poor cretur. But you don't somehow seem to take it in. I tell ye the deacon's gone a-courtin'."

"Courtin'! Isr'el! you be a-foolin' of me now, certain sure."

"Not a mite on't. I see him a-'ilin' up his old harness yesterday, and a-rubbin' down the mare, and I mistrusted he was up to suthin. And Squire Battle he met him a'most to Colebrook this mornin': I heerd him say so. I put this 'n' that together, and drawed my own influences; and I figgered out that he's gone to Colebrook to see if Widder Gold won't hev him. A wife's a lot cheaper than hired help, and this one's got means."

"For mercy's sakes! You don't suppose Sarepty Gold would look at him, do ye?"

"I never see the woman yet that wouldn't look at a man when he axed her to," was the dry answer. But Aunt Polly was too stunned with her new ideas to retort. She went on, as if the sneer at her sex had not reached her ear,—

"Why, she ha'n't no need to marry him: she's got a good home to Sam Pratt's. And there's that farm here that Hi Smith runs on shares, and money in Har'ford bank, they do say. She won't have him: don't ye tell me so."

"Women are mortal queer," replied old Israel.

"If they wa'n't, there wouldn't no men get married," snapped

Aunt Polly, who was a contented old maid, and never suspected she was "queer" herself.

"That's so, Aunt Polly. Mabbe it's what Parson Roberts calls a dispensation, and I guess it is. I say for't, a woman must be extry queer to marry Amasy Flint, ef she's even got a chance at Bassett poor-house."

Yet Israel was right in his prophecy. At that very moment Deacon Flint was sitting bolt-upright in a high-backed chair in Sam Pratt's keeping-room, discoursing with the Widow Gold.

Two people more opposite in aspect could hardly be found. Mrs. Gold was not yet fifty, and retained much of her soft loveliness. Her cheek was still round and fair, her pale brown hair but slightly lined with gray, and the mild light of her eyes shone tenderly yet; though her figure was a little bent, and her hands knotted with work.

She looked fair and young in comparison with the grizzled, stern, hard-favored man before her. A far-off Scotch ancestry had bequeathed to him the high cheek-bones and deep-set eyes that gave him so severe an aspect; and to these an aquiline nose, a cruel, pinched mouth, a low forehead, and a sallow, wrinkled skin, added no charms. But the charm of old association brought him a welcome here. Bassett was the home of Mrs. Gold's childhood, and she had a great many questions to ask. Her face gathered color and light as she recalled old affections and sympathies; and the deacon took a certain satisfaction in looking at her. But this was a mere ripple above his serious intention. He meant business, and could not waste time: so, as soon as there came a little lull in Mrs. Gold's fluent reminiscences, he curtly began,—

"I came over to-day on an arrand, Miss Gold,—I may say quite a ser'ous arrand. I lost my companion, I suppose ye know, a year ago come September the 10th. She was a good woman, Miss Flint was, savin' and reasonable as ever was."

"I always heard her well spoke of," modestly rejoined the widow.

"Yes, her children praise her in the gates,—or they would hev, if she'd had any. I feel her loss. And Scripter says, 'It is not good for man to be alone.' Scripter is right. You are a woman that's seen affliction too, Miss Gold: you've passed under the rod. Well, folks must be resigned: professors like you and me have got to set example. We can't fault the Lord when he takes our companions away, and say, 'Why do ye so?' as though 'twas a man done it. We've got this treasure in earthen vessels. Well, to come to the p'int, I come over to-day to see ef you wa'n't willin' to consider the subject of uniting yourself to me in the bonds of marriage."

"Oh!" said the astonished widow.

"I don't want to hurry ye none," he went on: "take time on't. I should like to get my answer right off: but I can make allowance for bein' onexpected. I'll come agin next week—say this day week. I hope you'll make it a subject of prayer, and I expect you'll get light on your duty by that time. I've got a good house and a good farm, and I'll do well by ye. And, moreover and besides, you know Mr. Pratt's folks are pressed some for room, I expect. I guess they won't stand in the way of your goin' to Bassett. Good-day, good-day."

And the widow received a calm up-and-down handshake, with which decorous caress the deacon—for we cannot call him the lover—departed, leaving Mrs. Gold in a state of pleased amazement, partly because she was a woman and a widow, partly because it was Deacon Flint who had asked her to marry him; for the deacon was a pillar in Bassett church, owned a large farm and a goodly square house, and was a power in the State, having twice been sent to the General Assembly. She could not but be gratified by the preference, and as she pondered on the matter it grew more feasible. Her girl was hers no longer, but a wife and mother herself; and she who had been all in all to Mindwell was now little more than "grandma" in the house,—a sort of suffered and necessary burden on Samuel's hands. But here a home of her own was offered her, a place of dignity among other women,—a place where she could ask her children to come to her, and give rather than receive.

There is nothing so attractive to a woman who is no longer young as the idea of a home. The shadow of age and its infirmities affrights her; loneliness is a terror in the future; and the prospect of drifting about here and there, a dependent, poor, proud, unwelcome, when flesh and heart fail, and the ability to labor is gone, makes any permanent shelter a blessed prospect, and draws many a woman into a far more dreadful fate than the work-house mercies or the colder charity of relatives.

This terror was strong in Mrs. Gold's feeble heart. She was one of the thousands of women who cannot trust what they do not see, and she misjudged her daughter cruelly. Mindwell felt that to-day, as her mother avowed to her Deacon Flint's offer and her own perplexities. When Mrs. Gold asserted that her daughter could never understand what it was to lose a husband, Mindwell felt a sure but unspoken conviction that the terror of such a bereavement, which confronted her whenever her heart leaped up to meet Samuel, was experience enough for her to interpret thereby the longings of a real bereavement; but she only colored faintly, and answered,—

"Well, mother, I don't see my way clear to offer you any advice. You must use your own judgment. You know Samuel and me think every thing of having you here; and the children just begin to know grandma by heart. But I don't want to be self-seeking: if it's for your best good, why, we sha'n't neither of us say a word. I don't skerce know how to speak about it, it's so strange like and sudden. I can't say no more than this: if you're going to be happier and better off with Deacon Flint than with your own folks, we haven't no right to hinder you, and we won't."

Mindwell turned away with trembling lips, silent, because strong emotion choked her. If she had fallen on her mother's neck and wept, and begged her to stay, with repeated kisses and warm embrace, Mrs. Gold never would have become Mrs. Flint; but she could not appreciate Mindwell's feeling. She took her conscientious self-control and candor for indifference, and her elderly lover loomed through this mist in grander proportions than ever. She resolved then and there that it was her duty to accept him.

Mindwell had gone down stairs to find her husband, who sat by the fire, fitting a rake-tail more firmly into a hay-rake. He had been caught in a distant field by a heavy shower, and was steaming now close to the fireplace, where a heap of chips was lighted to boil the kettle for tea. Mindwell stole up to him, and laid one hand on his handsome head. He looked up, astonished at the slight caress, and saw his wife's eyes were full of tears.

"What's the matter, darling?" he said in his cheery voice. It was like a kiss to her to have him say "darling," for sweet words were rare among their class; and this was the only one he ever used, kept sacredly, too, for Mindwell.

"O Sam!" she answered, with a quiver in her delicate voice, "don't you think, Deacon Flint wants to marry mother!"

"Thunder an' guns! You don't mean it, wife? Haw, haw, haw! It's as good as a general trainin'. Of all things! What doos she say to't?"

"Well, I'm 'most afraid she favors him a little. He's given her a week's time to consider of it; but, someway, I can't bear to have it thought of."

"Don't pester your head about it, Miss Pratt; you can't make nor meddle in such things. But I'm free to own that I never was more beat in all my days. Why, Amasy Flint is town-talk for nearness an' meanness. He pretends to be as pious as a basket o' chips, but I hain't no vital faith in that kind o' pious. I b'lieve in my soul he's a darned old hypocrite."

"O Sam, Sam! you hadn't ought to judge folks."

"I suppose I hadn't, reelly; but you know what Scripter says somewhere or 'nother, that some folks's sins are open, an' go to judgment beforehand, and I guess his'n do. I should hate to have mother take up with him."

"What can we do, Sam?"

"Nothin', strenoously. I don't know what 'tis about women-folks in such matters: they won't bear no more meddlin' with than a pa'tridge's nest; you'll spile the brood if you put in a finger. I'd say jest as much as I could about her bein' always welcome here. I'll do my part of that set piece o' music; and that's all we can do. If she's set on havin' him, she will; and you nor me can't stop it, Miss Pratt." With which sound advice, Sam rose from the milking-stool with his reconstructed rake, took down a coarse comb from the clock-case, ran it through his hair by way of toilet, and sat down to supper at the table with the three other hay-makers. Mindwell and her mother were going out to tea, so they did not sup with the men.

After they came home, Sam expressed himself in a succinct but forcible manner to Mrs. Gold on the subject of her marriage, and Mindwell attempted a faint remonstrance again; but her morbid fear of selfishness shut the heart-throbs she longed to express to her mother back into their habitual silence. She and Sam both, trying to do their best, actually helped, rather than hindered, this unpropitious marriage.

Mrs. Gold, in her heart, longed to stay with her children, but feared and disliked so heartily to be a burden on their hands, that she was unjust to herself and them too. A little less self-inspection, and a little more simple honesty of speech, would have settled this matter in favor of Mindwell and Colebrook: as it was, Deacon Flint carried the day. On the Friday following he arrived for his answer; his gray hair tied in a long cue, his Sunday coat of blue, and brass buttons, his tight drab pantaloons, ruffled shirt, and low boots, all indicating a ceremonial occasion.

"Gosh," said old Israel Tucker, jogging along in his yeast-cart, as he met the gray mare in clean harness, whipped up by the deacon in this fine raiment, the old wagon itself being for once washed and greased,—"gosh! it's easy tellin' what he's after. I should think them mulleins an' hardhacks in the buryin'-ground would kinder rustle round. I don't know, though; mabbe Miss Flint's realized by now that she's better off under them beauties of natur' than she ever was in Amasy Flint's house. Good land! what fools women-folks be! They don't never know when they're well off. She's had an easy time along back; but she's seen the last on't, she's seen the last on't.—Get up, Jewpiter."

Nothing daunted by any mystic or magnetic sense of this vaticination by the highway, Deacon Flint whipped up his bony steed still more, and to such good purpose that he arrived in Colebrook before the widow had taken down the last pinned-up curl on her forehead, or decided which of her two worked collars she would put on, and whether it would be incongruous to wear a brooch of blue enamel with a white centre, on which was depicted (in a fine brown tint produced by grinding up in oil a lock of the deceased Ethan Gold's hair) a weeping-willow bending over a tomb, with an urn, and a date on the urn. This did seem a little personal on such an occasion: so she pinned on a blue bow instead, and went down to receive the expecting deacon.

"I hope I see you well, ma'am," said Mr. Flint.

"Comfortably well, I'm obleeged to you," was the prim answer.

But the deacon was not to be daunted at this crisis: he plunged valiantly into the middle of things at once. "I suppose you've took into consideration the matter in hand, Miss Gold?"

The widow creased her handkerchief between her finger and thumb, and seemed to be critical about the hemming of it; but she pretty soon said softly, "Yes, I can't say but what I have thought on't a good deal. I've counselled some with the children too."

"Well, I hope you're fit and prepared to acknowledge the leadin's of Providence to this end, and air about ready to be my companion through the valley of this world up to them fields beyond the swellin' flood stands dressed in livin' green. Amen."

The deacon forgot he was not in a prayer-meeting, and so dropped into the hymn-book, as Mr. Wegg did into secular poetry.

"H'm, well there's a good deal to be thought of for and ag'inst it too," remarked Mrs. Gold, unwilling to give too easy an assent, and so cheapen herself in the eyes of her acute adorer. But, when her thoughts were sternly sifted down, they appeared to be slight matters; and the deacon soon carried his point. He wasted no time in this transaction. Having "shook hands on it," as he expressed himself, he proceeded at once to arrange the programme.

"Well, Sarepty, we're both along in years, and to our time o' life delays is dangerous. I think we'd better get married pretty quick. I'm keepin' that great lazy Polly Morse, and payin' out cash right along; and you no need to fix up any, you've got good clothes enough: besides, what's clothes to worms of the dust sech as we be? The Catechism says 'Man's chief end is to glorify God and enjoy him forever;' and if that's so,—and I expect '*tis* so,—why, 'tain't nothin' to be concerned about what our poor dyin' bodies is clothed in."

Mrs. Gold did not agree with him at all. She liked her clothes, as women ought to; but his preternatural piety awed her, and she said meekly enough, "Well, I don't need no great of gowns. I sha'n't buy but one, I don't believe."

A faint color stole to her cheek as she said it, for she meant a wedding-dress; and Deacon Flint was acute enough to perceive it, and to understand that this was a point he could not carry.

"One gown ain't neither here nor there, Sarepty; but I aim to fix it on your mind that, as I said afore, delays is dangerous. I purpose, with the divine blessin', to be married this day two weeks. I suppose you're agreeable?" The widow was too surprised to deny this soft impeachment; and he went on, "Ye see, there's papers to be drawed up: you've got independent means, and so have I, and it's jest as well to settle things fust as last. Did Ethan Gold leave you a life-int'rest in your thirds, or out an' out?"

The widow's lip trembled; her dead husband had been careful of her, more careful than she knew, till now.

"He didn't will me no thirds at all: he left me use an' privilege, for my nateral life, of every thing that was his'n, and all to go to Mindwell when I'm gone."

"Do tell! He was forehanded, I declare for't!" exclaimed the deacon, both pleased and displeased; for, if his wife's income was to be greater than he supposed, in case of her death before his there would be no increase to his actual possessions.

"Well, I always calc'lated you had your thirds, an' prob'ly, knowin' Ethan was free-handed, you had 'em out an' out. This makes some difference about what papers I'll have to have drawed up. Now, I guess the best way is to have a agreement like this: I agree not to expect to hev an' to hold none of your property, an' you don't none of mine; but I to have the use of your'n, and you to have your livin' out o' mine. You see, you don't have no more'n your livin' out of your'n now: that's all we any of us get in this here world, 'Hevin' food an' raiment, let us therewith be content,' as Scripter says. You agree to this, don't ye?"

Bewildered with the plausible phrases ballasted by a text, unaware that even the Devil can quote Scripture to serve his turn, Mrs. Gold did not see that she was putting herself entirely into the hands of this man, and meekly agreed to his arrangement. If this story were not absolutely true, I should scarce dare to invent such a character as Deacon Flint. But he was once a living man, and hesitating to condemn him utterly, being now defenceless among the dead, we can but hope for him and his like that there are purifying fires beyond this life, where he may be melted and refined into the image of Him who made him a man, and gave him a long life here to develop manhood. Not till after he was gone did Mrs. Gold begin to think that he had left her to explain his arrangements to Mindwell and Sam, and instinctively she shrank from doing so. Like many another weak woman, she hated words, particularly hard words. Her life had flowed on in a gentle routine, so peacefully that she had known but one sorrow, and that was so great, that, with the propensity we all have to balance accounts with Providence, she thought her trouble had been all she could bear. But there was yet reserved for her that sharp attrition of life which is so different from the calm and awful force of sorrow,—so much more exasperating, so much more educating. Some instinct warned her to avoid remonstrance by concealing from her children the contract she was about to make, and she felt, too, the uncertainty of a woman unaccustomed to business, about her own clear understanding of the situation. So she satisfied herself with telling Mindwell of the near approach of her marriage.

"O mother, so soon!" was all Mindwell said, though her eyes and lips spoke far more eloquently.

"Well, now the thing's settled, I don't know but what it may as well be over with. We ain't young folks, Mindwell. 'Tain't as if we had quite a spell to live."

Tears stood in her eyes as she said it. A certain misgiving stole over her: just then it seemed a good thing that she could not live long.

Mindwell forced back the sob that choked her. A woman of single heart, she did not consider a second marriage sacred. For herself, she would rather have taken her children to the town-farm, cold as corporative charity is, than married another man than Samuel, even if he had been dead thirty years; and she bitterly resented this default of respect to her father's memory. But her filial duty came to the rescue.

"Dear mother, I can't bear to think of it. What shall I do? What will the children say? I did hope you would take time to consider."

"It ain't real dutiful in you to take me to do, Mindwell: I'm full old to be lessoned, seems to me. As for you and the children, I don't feel no great distress: love runs down, not up, folks say; and I don't believe you'll any of ye pine a long spell."

This weak and petulant outburst dismayed Mindwell, who had never seen her mother otherwise than gentle and pleasant; but, with the tact of a great heart, she said nothing, only put her arms about the elder woman's neck, and kissed her over and over. At this, Mrs. Gold began to cry; and, in soothing her distress, Mindwell forgot to ask any further questions, but set herself to divert both their minds from this brief and bitter outburst by inquiring what preparation her mother meant to make in the fortnight.

"I don't look to no great preparation," sighed the widow. "I have always had good clothes enough, and there's a piece of linen I wove before we come here that'll do for all I want. I suppose I had ought to have a new gown to be married in. When I was married to Ethan, I had a white dimity gown and a blue levantine petticoat; and if he didn't fetch me a big bunch of sand-violets— they was blossoming then—for to match my eyes and my skirt, he said. But that's past and gone, as the hymn-book says. I do want to have one good gown, Mindwell; and, now I'm a little along in years, I guess I'll have a dark one. T'other night, when we was up to Squire Barnes's to tea, Miss Barnes was telling about a piece of plum-colored paduasoy Mr. Battle bought in Har'ford for 'Lecty's weddin'-gown, and she wouldn't hev it. She said 'twasn't lively enough, and so she's set her mind on a blue levantine. But I should think the plum-color would become me real well."

So the plum-colored silk was bought; and arrayed in its simple folds, with a new worked collar and a white satin bow, the Widow Gold was dressed for her second wedding.

Did she think, as she looked into her oval mirror that morning, what a different vision was this quiet, elderly, sober woman, in decent but not festal garments, from the smiling, blushing, blue-eyed creature in her spotless dimity gown opening over a blue petticoat, and clasped at the throat with a bunch of still bluer violets? What does a woman think who is married the second time? A man is satisfied that now his house will be kept once more, his clothes mended, his whims humored, his table spread to his taste, and his children looked after. If it is needful, he can marry six wives one after the other. They are a domestic necessity: the Lord himself says it is not good for *man* to be alone. But it is quite another thing for the woman. Such a relation is not a movable feast to her: it is once for all; and, if circumstance or pique betray her into this faithlessness, what does she think of herself when it becomes inevitable?

The Widow Gold did not tell. She was paler when she turned from the glass than when she looked into it: and she trembled as she went down stairs to sign the papers before Parson Roberts should arrive.

The best parlor was opened to-day. The high-backed chairs with old brocade cushions, that had belonged to Sam Pratt's grandmother, were ranged along the wall like a row of stiff ghosts; the corner-cupboards were set open to display the old china and glass that filled them; there was a "bow-pot" of great red peonies, abundant and riotous with color and fatness, set under the chimney in the well-whited fireplace; and a few late roses glowed in a blue china jar on the high mantelpiece. On a square table with a leaf lay a legal paper that Sam was reading, with his hands supporting his head as if it was hard to understand the document.

The deacon, in his Sunday garments, was looking at him askance; and Mindwell, with the little girls Ede and Sylvia clinging to her gown, was staring out of the window, down the road, —staring, but not seeing; for the splendid summer day that lavished its bloom and verdure and odor on these gaunt New-England hills, and hid their rude poverty with its royal mantle, was all a dim blur to the heart-wrung woman.

"Mother," said Sam Pratt, raising his head, "do you know what's the sum and substance of these here papers? and do you agree to't?"

The widow glanced aside at Deacon Flint, and caught his "married eye," early as it was to use that ocular weapon.

"Why, yes, Samwell: I don't know but what I do," she said slowly and rather timidly.

"Well," said Sam, rising, and pushing the paper away, "if you

do, why, then you're going right into't, and it's right, I s'pose;
but, by Jinks! I think it's the d—"

Mindwell's touch on his arm arrested the sentence. "There's
Parson Roberts, Samwell. You jest help him out of the gig, will
you? He's quite lame, I see."

Sam Pratt went, with the half-finished sentence on his lips. He
was glad his wife had stopped him, on many accounts; but he
did long to give Deacon Flint his own opinion of that preliminary
contract.

He indulged himself for this deprivation, after the stiff and
somewhat melancholy wedding was over, and the staid couple
had departed for Bassett in the deacon's wagon, by freeing his
mind to his wife.

"Miss Pratt, I was some riled to hev you stop me when I was
a-goin' to tell the deacon what I thought about that there contrack; but I don't never stay riled with you, marm, as you'd ought
to know by this time." And Sam emphasized this statement with
a hearty kiss. "Besides, I will own on second thoughts I was glad
you did stop me; for it's no use pinchin' your fingers in a pair
o' nippers. But I do say now and here, it was the darndest piece
o' swindlin' I ever see,—done under a cover of law an' gospel,
you may say; for the deacon had stuck in a bit of Scripter so's
to salt it like. He's got the best of the bargain, I tell ye, a long
sight. I'm real glad your father went and fixed that prop'ty so
she has the use on't only; for she wouldn't have two cents in two
years' time, if she'd had it to do with what she's a mind to."

"I am glad he did," said Mindwell. "I have felt as though
mother would be better suited if she did have it to do what she
liked to with; but if this was to happen, why, it's as good she is
provided for. She can't want for nothing now."

"I guess she'll want for more'n money, and mabbe for that too.
The paper says she's to have her livin'. Now, that's a wide word.
Folks can live on bread and water, I expect; and he can't be
holden for no more than he's a mind to give."

"O Sam, you don't think Deacon Flint would grudge her a
good living? Why, if he is near, as folks tell he is, he's a professor of religion."

"I'd a durned sight ruther he was a practiser on't, Miss Pratt.
Religion's about the best thing there is, and makin' believe it is
about the wust. I b'lieve in Amasy Flint's religion jest so far
forth as I hear him talk, an' not a inch farther. I know he'll
pinch an' shave an' spare to the outside of a cheese-rind; and I

haven't no great reason to think he'll do better by Mother Gold than he does by himself." Mindwell turned away, full of foreboding; and Sam, following her, put his arm about her, and drew her back to the settle.

"Don't worry, dear. She's made her bed, and she's got to lie on't. But, after all, it's the Lord who lets folks do that way, so's to show 'em, I expect, that beds ain't always meant to sleep on, but sometimes to wake folks up. We're kind of apt to lie long an' get lazy on feathers. I expect that's what's the matter with me. I'll get my husks by and by, I guess."

Mindwell looked up at him, with all her heart in her eyes; but she said nothing, and he gave a shy laugh. Their deep love for each other was "a fountain shut up;" and so far no angel had rolled away the stone, and given it visible life. It was still voiceless and sleeping.

Before her wedding-day was over, Mrs. Flint's new life began; for Polly Morse had been sent off the night before, being the end of an even week, lest she might charge ninepence for an extra day. So her successor without wages had to lay aside her plum-colored silk, put on a calimanco petticoat and short-gown, and proceed to get supper; while Polly, leaning over the half-door of the old red house which she shared with the village tailoress, exchanged pungent remarks with old Israel on the topic of the day in Bassett.

"No, they didn't make no weddin', Isr'el. There wa'n't nobody asked, nor no loaf-cake made for her: he wouldn't hear to't, noway. I'd have staid and fixed up for her to-day; but he was bound I shouldn't. As for me, I'm most amazin' glad to get hum, now I tell ye. I'd a sight ruther be in Simsbury prison for a spell, if it wa'n't for the name on't."

"Say, Polly, do you call to mind what I said three weeks back about Miss Flint comin' home? Oh! ye do, do ye? Well, I ain't nobody's fool, be I? I guess I can see through a millstone, providin' the hole's big enough, as well as the next man. I'm what ye may call mighty obsarvin', now. I can figger consider'ble well on folks, ef I can't on 'rithmetic; and I know'd jest as well, when I see him rigged up in his sabba'-day go-to-meetin's, and his nose p'inted for Colebrook, what he was up to, as though I heerd him a-askin' her to hev him."

"Well, I never did think Sarepty Gold would demean herself to have him. She's got means and a real good home; and Mindwell sets a sight by her, and so does Sam Pratt: but here she's

ben an' gone an' done it. I wouldn't ha' thought it, not if th' angel
Gabriel had have told me on't."

"Guess he's in better business than goin' round with Bassett
gossip, anyhow. But what was you so took back by? Lordy! I
should think you was old enough to git over bein' surprised at
women-folks: them and the weather is two things I don't never
calc'late on. You can't no more tell what a woman'll do, 'specially
about marryin', than you can tell which way in the road a pig'll
go, onless you work it back'ard, same as some folks tell they
drive a pig; and then 'tain't reel reliable: they may go right ahead
when you don't a mite expect it."

"That is one thing about men, I allow, Isr'el: you can always
tell which way they'll go for sartain; and that is after their own
advantage, an' nobody else's, now an' forever."

"Amen! They'd be all fools, like me, if they didn't," assented
the old man, with a dry chuckle, as he drove off his empty cart.
Yet, for all his sneers and sniffs, neither Polly nor the new Mrs.
Flint had a truer friend than Israel. Rough as he was, satiric as
a chestnut burr that shows all its prickles in open defiance, conscious of a sweet white heart within, his words only were bitter:
his nature was generous, kindly, and perceptive. He had become
the peripatetic satirist and philosopher that he was out of this
very nature,

> Dowered with a scorn of scorn, a love of love,

and free with the freedom of independent poverty to express
pungently what he felt poignantly, being in his own kind and
measure the "salt of the earth" to Bassett.

But, in spite of comment and pity, the thing was a fixed fact.
Mrs. Flint's married life had begun under new auspices, and it
was not a path of roses upon which she had entered. Her house-
keeping had always been frugal, with the thrift that is or was
characteristic of her race; but it had been abundant for the wants
of her family. The viands she provided were those of the place
and period, simple and primitive enough; but the great brick
oven was well filled with light bread of wheat and rye both; pies
of whatever material was in season, whose flaky crust and well-
filled interiors testified to her knowledge of the art; deep dishes
of baked beans; jars of winter pears; pans of golden-sweet
apples; and cards of yellow gingerbread, with rows of snowy

and puffy biscuit. Ede and Sylvia knew very well where to find crisp cookies and fat nut-cakes; and pie was reiterated three times a day on Sam Pratt's table.

It was a part of her "pride of life" that she was a good housekeeper; and Mindwell had given her the widest liberty. But now the tide had changed. She soon found that Deacon Flint's parsimony extended into every detail. Her pies were first assailed.

"Sarepty, don't make them pies o' your'n so all-fired rich. They ain't good for the stomach: besides, they use up all the drippin's, and you had ought to make soap next month. Pie is good, and I think it's savin' of meat. But it pompers up the flesh, too good livin' does; and we hev got to give an account, ye know. I don't mean to have no wicked waste laid to my account."

So she left out half the shortening from her crust, and felt ashamed to see the tough substance this economy produced. Next came the sugar question.

"We buy too much sweetenin', Sarepty. There's a kag of tree-molasses down cellar. I expect it's worked some; but you jest take an' bile it up, an' stir consider'ble saleratus into't, an' it'll do. I want to get along jest as reasonable as we can. Wilful waste makes woful want, ye know."

Yet in his own way the deacon was greedy enough. He had the insatiable appetite that belongs to people of his figure far more often than to the stout.

"He's a real racer," said Uncle Israel, reverting to his own experience in pigs,—"slab-sided an' lank. I bet you could count his ribs this minnit; and that's the kind you can feed till the day after never, and they won't do ye no credit. I never see a man could punish vittles the way he can; but there ain't no more fat to him than there is to a hen's forehead."

Mrs. Flint was not "hungry nor hankering," as she expressed it, but a reasonable eater of plain food; but the deacon's mode of procedure was peculiar.

"Say, Sarepty, don't bile but a small piece o' pork with that cabbage to-day. I've got a pain to my head, an' I don't feel no appetite; an' cold pork gets eat up for supper when there ain't no need on't."

Obeying instructions, the small piece of fat pork would be cooked, and, once at the table, transferred bodily to the deacon's plate. "Seems as though my appetite had reelly come back. I guess 'twas a hungry headache." And the tired woman had to make her dinner from cabbage and potatoes seasoned with the salt and greasy water in which they had been cooked.

There were no amusements for her out of the house. The younger people had their berrying frolics, sleighrides, kitchen-dances, nuttings, and the like; and their elders, their huskings, apple-bees, and sewing-societies: but against all these the deacon set his hard face.

"It's jest as good to do your own extry chores yourself as to ask folks to come an' help. That costs more'n it comes to. You've got to feed 'em, and like enough keep a big fire up in the spare room. I'd ruther be diligent in business, as Scripter says, than depend on neighbors."

The sewing-society, too, was denied to poor Mrs. Flint, because they had to have tea got for them. Prayer-meetings he could not deny her; for they cost nothing, and officially he attended them. Meeting on Sunday was another outlet, when she could see friendly faces, receive kind greetings, and read in many eyes a sympathy and pity that at once pleased and exasperated her.

Another woman in her place might have had spirit or guile enough to have resisted the pressure under which she only quailed and submitted. She was one of those feeble souls to whom a hard word is like a blow, and who will bear any thing and every thing rather than be found fault with, and who necessarily become drudges and slaves to those with whom they live, and are de-spised and ill-treated simply because they are incapable of resent-ment. There are some persons who stand in this position not so much from want of strength as from abounding and eager affec-tion for those whom they serve; and their suffering, when they discover how vain has been their labor and self-sacrifice, is known only to Him who was

> At once denied, betrayed, and fled
> By those who shared his daily bread.

But Mrs. Flint had no affection for her husband: she married him because it seemed a good thing to do, and obeyed him be-cause he was her husband, as was the custom in those days. So she toiled on dumbly from day to day, half fed, overworked, desperately lonely, but still uncomplaining; for her constitution was naturally strong, and nerves were unrecognized then.

Her only comfort was the rare visits of her children. Mind-well found it hard to leave home; but, suspicious of her mother's comfort, she made every effort to see her as often as possible, and always to carry her some little present,—a dozen fresh eggs, which the poor woman boiled privately, and ate between her scanty meals, a few peaches, or a little loaf of cake,—small gifts, merely to demonstrate her feeling. She did not know what good purpose they served, for Mrs. Flint did not tell her daughter what she endured. She remembered too well how Mindwell had begged her to delay and consider her marriage; and she would not own to her now that she had made any mistake: for Mrs. Flint had as much human nature in her composition as the rest of us; and who does like to hear even their dearest friend say, "I told you so"?

Matters went on in this way for five years, every day being a little more weary and dreary than the preceding. The plum-colored paduasoy still did duty as the Sunday gown, for none of her own money ever passed into Mrs. Flint's hands. By this time she understood fully what her ante-nuptial contract meant. She had her living, and no more. People could live without finery, even without warmth. A stuff gown of coarse linsey-woolsey for winter wear replaced the soft merinoes she had always bought for that purpose; and homespun linen check was serviceable in summer, though it kept her busy at flax-wheel and loom many an hour. She had outlived the early forbearances of her married life, and learned to ask, to beg, to persist in entreating, for what she absolutely needed; for only in this way could she get her "living." Her only vivid pleasure was in occasional visits from Ede and Sylvia,—lovely little creatures in whom their mother's beauty of character and their father's cheery, genial nature seemed to combine, and with so much of Mindwell's delicate loveliness, her sweet, dark eyes contrasted with the fair hair of their father's family, that to grandmotherly eyes they seemed perfectly beautiful. For them the poor woman schemed and toiled, and grew secretive. She hid a comb of honey sometimes, when the deacon's back was turned, and kept it for Sylvia, who loved honey like a real bee-bird; she stored up red pearmains in the parlor-closet for Ede; and when Sam Pratt went into Hartford with a load of wool, and brought the children as far as Bassett to stay at Deacon Flint's over night, the poor woman would make for them gingerbread such as they remembered, and savory cookies that they loved, though she encountered hard looks, and hard words too, for wasting her husband's substance on another man's children.

Ede, who had a ready memory and a fluent tongue, was the first to report to Mindwell these comments of "Grandsir Flint," as they were taught to call him.

"O mother," she exclaimed, "I do think grandsir is real mean!"

"Edy, Edy, you mustn't talk so about your elders and betters."

"I can't help it," chattered on the irrepressible child. "What did he want to come into the kitchen for when granny was giving us supper, and scold because she made cookies for us? Granny 'most cried; and he kept tellin' how he'd said before she shouldn't do it, and he wouldn't have it."

"Don't talk about it, Edy," said her mother, full of grief and indignation.

"Mother, it's true. I heard him too," interposed Sylvia, who thought Ede's word was doubted; for the voluble and outspoken child was a little apt to embellish her reports.

"Well, Sylvy dear, it isn't best to talk about a good many things that are true."

But, for all that, Mindwell did discuss the matter with Sam before she slept, in that "grand committee of two" which is the strength and comfort of a happy marriage.

"What ever can we do about it, Sam?" she said, with tears in her voice. "I can't bear to keep the children to home,—mother sets by 'em like her life; but, if they're going to make trouble between her and Deacon Flint, don't you think I had ought to prevent their going there?"

"Well, it does seem hard on mother every way; but I guess I can fix it. You know we had a heap of wheat off that east lot last year, and I've sent it to mill to be ground up for us. I guess I'll take and send a barrel on't over to mother for a present. The deacon won't mistrust nothing; nor he can't say nothing about her usin' on't for the children."

"That's the very thing," said Mindwell. And so it was, for that small trouble; yet that was only a drop in the bucket. After a few years of real privation, and a worse hunger of spirit, Mrs. Flint's health began to fail. She grew nervous and irritable, and the deacon browbeat her more than ever. Her temper had long since failed under the hourly exasperation of her husband's companionship, and she had become as cross, as peevish, and as exasperating herself as a feeble nature can become under such a pressure.

"I never see nobody so changed as Miss Flint is," confided

Aunt Polly to old Israel. "I've always heerd tell that 'flictions was sent for folks's good; but her'n don't seem to work that way a mite."

"Well, Polly, I expect there's a reel vital differ'nce in 'flictions, jest as there is in folks. She picked her'n up, as you may say, when she married him. 'Twan't reelly the Lord's sendin'. She no need to ha' married him, if she hadn't ben a min' to."

"I sorta thought the Lord sent every thing't happened to folks."

"Well, in a manner mabbe he doos. But don't ye rek'lect what David said,—how't he'd ruther fall inter the hands of the Lord than inter men's? I expect we're to blame for wilful sins, ain't we? And I guess we fetch 'flictions on ourselves sometimes."

"I don't see how you make them idees jibe with 'lection and fore-ordination," rejoined Aunt Polly, who was a zealous theologian, and believed the Saybrook Platform and the Assembly's Catechism to be merely a skilful abridgment and condensation of Scripture.

"I don't know as I'm called to, Polly. I don't believe the Lord's ways is jest like a primer, for everybody to larn right off. I shouldn't have no great respect for a ruler an' governor, as the Confession sez, that wa'n't no bigger'n I was. Land! ef I was to set sail on them seas o' divinity, I should be snooped up in the fust gale, an' drownded right off. I b'lieve He is good, and doos right, anyhow. Ef I can't see the way on't, why, it's 'cause my spiritooal eyes ain't big enough. I can't see into some littler things than him, and I don't hold to takin' up the sea in a pint cup: 'twon't carry it, nohow." With which aphorism old Israel travelled off with his barrow, leaving Polly amazed and shocked, but perhaps a little wiser after all.

Just about this time a cousin of Deacon Flint's died "over in York State," as he said, and left him guardian of her only daughter, a girl of eighteen. A couple of thousand dollars was all the property that the Widow Eldridge had to give her child; for they had both worked hard for their living after the husband and father left them, and this money was the price of the farm, which had been sold at his death. It was something to get so much cash into his own hands; and the deacon accordingly wrote at once to Mabel, and offered her a home in his house, intimating, that, the interest of her money not being enough to board and clothe her, he would, out of family affection, supply these necessities for that inadequate sum, if she was willing to help a little about the house. Mabel was friendless enough to grasp eagerly this hope of a home; and very soon the stage stopped at Deacon Flint's door, and a new inmate entered his house.

Mabel Eldridge was a capable, spirited, handsome girl, and, before she had been a week in the Flint family, understood her position, and resolved only to endure it till something better could be found. In her heart she pitied Aunt Flint, as she called her, as much as she detested the deacon; and her fresh girlish heart fairly ached with compassion and indignation over the poor woman. But she was a great comfort and help while she staid; though she made that stay as short as possible, and utterly refused to give up her savings-bank book to the deacon, who was unable legally to claim it, since her mother left no will, having only asked him, in a letter written just before her death, to act as Mabel's guardian. Her three months' sojourn in the house made her thoroughly aware of Deacon Flint's character and his wife's sufferings. She could not blame Mrs. Flint that she snapped back at the deacon's snarls, or complained long and bitterly of her wants and distresses.

"You don't know nothing what it is, Mabel," she said one day, sobbing bitterly. "I'm put upon so hard! I want for clothes, and for vittles, and for some time to rest, so's't I don't know but what 'twill clean kill me: and, if 'twa'n't for the childern, I'd wish to die; but I do cleave to them amazingly."

Indignant tears filled Mab's eyes. "I don't know how you bear it, aunty," she said, putting her arms about the old lady's neck. "Can't you get away from him anyhow?"

"I could, but I suppose I hadn't ought to. There's a house on my farm that ain't goin' to be in use come next April. Hiram Smith—him that's rented it along back—wants some repairin' done on't, and Mr. Flint won't hear to't: so Hi he's been and gone and bought a piece of ground acrost the road, an' put up a buildin' for himself. He's got a long lease of the land; but he don't want the house no more, and he won't pay for't. I s'pose I might move over there for a spell, and have some peace. There's enough old furnitoor there that was father's. But then, agin, I do suppose I haven't no right to leave my husband."

"Haven't you got any right to save your life?" indignantly asked Mabel.

"It ha'n't come to that, not quite," said Mrs. Flint sadly.

But before April she began to think it was a matter of life and death to stay any longer with the man. Mabel had left her some months before, and gone into the family of Sam Pratt's mother, in Colebrook, promising her aunt, that, if ever the time came when she needed her in another home, she would come and take care of her.

Toward the middle of February Mrs. Flint was seized with congestion of the lungs, and was very ill indeed. A fear of public opinion made Deacon Flint send for the doctor; but nothing could induce him to let a nurse enter the house, or even to send for Mindwell Pratt. He was able to do for his wife, he said, and nobody could interfere.

It was the depth of winter; and the communication between Bassett and Colebrook was not frequent in the best weather, neither place being dependent on the other for supplies; and now the roads were blocked with heavy drifts, and the inhabitants of both places had hibernated, as New-Englanders must in winter. It was a matter of congratulation with Deacon Flint that he had no out-door work to do just now, and so was spared the expense of a woman to care for his wife. He could do it, too, more economically than a nurse. It did not matter to him that the gruel was lumpy, or burned, or served without flavoring. Sick folks, particularly with serious sickness, ought not to pamper the flesh: their souls were the things to be considered. He did not want to have Sarepta die, for she had an income that helped him much; but he did not want her to be a "bill of expense," as he phrased it. So while he read the Bible to her twice a day, and prayed to, or rather at, her by the hour, he fed her on sloppy gruel and hard bread, sage-tea, and cold toast without butter, and just kept life flickering within her till she could get about and help herself, unknown to him, to draughts of fresh milk, and now and then a raw egg.

But she did not get well: she was feeble, and wasted a long time. The village doctor, knowing what Deacon Flint was, and filled with pity for his wife, called often, carefully stating that his visits were those of a friend, but urging, also, that Mrs. Flint should have a generous diet, and a glass of wine daily, to restore her strength. The deacon heard him through in silence, and when he left began to growl.

"Well, fools a'n't all dead yet. Wine! I guess not. A good drink o' thoroughwort-tea's wuth all the wine in creation. 'Wine's a mocker, an' strong drink is ragin'.' Dr. Grant don't read his Bible as he'd ought to."

"There ain't nothin' in the Bible aginst beef-tea, I guess," feebly piped his wife. "I do feel as though that would fetch me up. Can't you get a piece o' meat down to the slaughter, deacon?"

"I don't see no need on't, Sarepty: you're doin' reasonable well. Meat is reel costly; an' pomperin' the flesh is sinful. I'll git another cod-fish next time I go to the store: that's nourishin'. I don't hold to Grant's idees entire. Besides, 'twa'n't nothin' what he said: he come as a friend."

The poor woman burst into tears. Indignation gave her momentary strength: she did not hear the shed-door open behind her; but she rose in her chair like a spectre, and looked at him with burning eyes.

"Amasy Flint, I b'lieve you'd a sight rather I'd die than live. I hain't had decent vittles since I was took sick, nor no care whatever. You're a loud pray-er an' reader; but, if 'twa'n't for the name of it, I b'lieve you'd kill me with the axe instead of starvation. I've a good mind to send for Squire Battle, and swear the peace against ye."

Deacon Flint at this moment saw a shocked face behind his wife's chair: it was Polly Morse. His acuteness came to the rescue. "She's a leetle out," he said, nodding to the unexpected guest. "Come right along, Polly."

This was too much for the weak woman to bear. She fell back, and fainted. Her indignation had overborne her weakness for a moment, but exhausted it also. And, when she awoke to life, Polly was rubbing her, and crying over her; but her husband had gone. Those tears of sympathy were more than she could endure silently. She put her arms round Polly's neck, and, sobbing like a child, poured out the long list of her sorrows into that faithful ear.

"Bless your dear soul!" said Polly, wiping her eyes, "you can't tell me nothing new about him. Didn't I summer an' winter him, so to speak, afore you come here? Don't I know what killed the fust woman? 'Twa'n't no fever, ef they did call it so. 'Twas livin' with him—want o' food, an' fire, an' lovin'-kindness. Don't tell me. I pitied ye afore ye was married, an' I hain't stopped yit."

But Polly's words were not words only. From that day on, many a cup of broth, vial of currant-wine, or bit of hot stewed chicken, found its way surreptitiously to Mrs. Flint; and her strength of mind and body returned fast, with this sympathy for one, and food for the other. She made up her mind at last that she would leave her husband, at least for a time, and in her own house endeavor to find the peace and rest necessary to her entire recovery. If she could have seen Mindwell and Sam, and taken counsel with them, her course might have been different; but the roads were now well-nigh impassable from deep mud, and she could not get to Colebrook, and in sheer desperation she resolved to leave her present home as soon as Hiram Smith moved from the farmhouse. Fortunately for her, the deacon had to attend town-meeting, three miles off, on the first Monday in April; and, with Polly and Israel to help her, Mrs. Flint was established in the other house before he returned, and found her flown. His wrath was great but still. He said and did nothing, never went near her, and, for very shame's sake, did not speak of her—for what could he say?

Perhaps in that solitary house, whose silence was like balm to her weary and fevered soul, she might have starved but for the mercy of her neighbors. Polly Morse had a tongue of swiftness, and it never wagged faster than in Mrs. Flint's behalf. Dr. Grant sent half a barrel of flour to that destitute dwelling, and Israel, a bushel of apples. Polly, out of her poverty, shared her kit of pork with the poor woman; and Hiram Smith brought in a barrel of potatoes and a bag of meal, which he duly charged against her account with the farm. But there were many who dared not help her; for the deacon held notes and mortgages on many a house and of many a man in Bassett who could not afford to offend him. And old Parson Roberts was just then shut up with an attack of low fever: so he knew nothing about the matter. However, the deacon was not long to be left nursing his wrath. Food and fire are not enough for life sometimes. The old house was leaky, damp, comfortless; and in a few weeks Mrs. Flint was taken again with disease of the lungs, and Polly Morse found her in her bed, unable to speak loud, her fire gone out, and the rain dripping down in the corner of her bedroom. Polly had come to tell her that Israel was going to Colebrook to buy a pig, and would take any message. She did not tell her, but, stepping to the door, called to him across the yard to tell Sam Pratt he must come over to Bassett directly. This done, she hunted about for something to make a fire, and then looked for the tea; but there was none. Nothing like food remained but a half-loaf of bread and some cold potatoes: so she had to break the bread up in some hot water, and feed the exhausted woman slowly, while she chafed her icy feet, and covered her closely with her own shawl. The next day Sam and Mindwell came over, shocked and indignant, their wagon loaded with provisions; and the old house was soon filled with odors of beef-broth, milk-porridge, fragrant tea and toast, and the sharp crackle of a great fire in two rooms; while, best of all, tender hands fed and soothed the poor woman, and soft filial kisses comforted her starved soul.

Mindwell could not stay,—there was a little baby at home,— but Sam would be left behind while old Israel drove her back to Colebrook, and fetched Mabel Eldridge to take her place.

Mab burst into a passion of tears when she entered the kitchen.

"I knew it!" she sobbed: "I knew that old wretch would kill her!" And it was long before Sam could calm her anger and grief, and bring her in to the invalid.

In the course of two or three weeks, however, Mab's faithful nursing, and Sam's care and providing, brought back life and some strength to the perishing woman. And meanwhile Polly's tongue had wagged well: it flew all over Bassett that Deacon Flint's wife had left him, and almost died of cold and hunger.

To-day such a rumor would have had some direct effect on its object; but then to find fault with authorities was little less than a sin, and for a wife to leave her husband, a fearful scandal. In spite of the facts and all their witnesses, the sentiment of Bassett went with the deacon. Conjugal subjection was the fashion, or rather the principle and custom, of the day, and was to be upheld in spite of facts. However, Parson Roberts by this time had heard of the matter, and called Deacon Flint to account, thinking it to be his duty.

"This is the hull sum and substance on't, parson," explained the deacon: "Miss Flint is a miser'ble hystericky female, a dreadful weak vessel, and noways inclined to foller Scripter in the marriage-relation. I've gin her the same livin' I had myself. I hain't denied her food an' raiment wherewith she had ought to be content, as the 'Postle Poll says. But she is real pernickity, and given to the lusts of the flesh about her eatin'; and I feel it to be my dooty to be a faithful stooard of my substance, and not pomper up our poor perishin' bodies, while there is forty million more or less o' heathen creturs lyin' in wickedness in foreign parts. Ye know, parson, I hain't never stented my contributions to them things: I've ben constant to means of grace allus, and I may say a pillar—mabbe a small and creaky one, but still a pillar —in the temple sech as 'tis. I don't know as I had ought to be disturbed by this strife of tongues."

Parson Roberts was a little confounded. He himself loved a

bit of good eating,—a cantle of chicken-pie, a tender roast pig, a young chicken broiled on hickory coals, or a succulent shad from the Connecticut, washed down with sparkling cider or foaming flip,—and the consciousness of this mild weakness gave undue exaltation to Deacon Flint's boasted asceticism. The parson was too honestly humble to see that Deacon Flint loved money with a greed far surpassing that of any epicure; that his own fault was but a failing, while the other was a passion. Besides, he considered that Mrs. Flint had made light of the sacred ordinance of marriage, and set an awful example to the wives of the parish: so he went away from this interview convinced that the deacon was a stern saint, and his wife a weak sinner.

Next day, however, the deacon himself was surprised by another visit. Pale and worn, clinging tight to Sam Pratt's arm, and followed by Mabel carrying a cushion, his wife entered the kitchen, where he sat devouring salt pork and potatoes with the zest of a dog who gnaws his bone unmolested.

"I come back, Amasy, to see if we couldn't agree to get along together agin," she said weakly and meekly. "I hear there's ben consider'ble talk about my leavin' on ye, and I don't want to cast no reflections. I was tired all out, an' I wanted to rest a spell. Sam an' Mab has nursed me up, so't I could get along now, I guess."

The man turned his cold green-gray eyes on her slowly. "I don't know what you want to come back for now," he said.

"Why, I want for to do my duty so far as I can."

"You had oughter have considered that afore you went off," was the dogged answer.

Tears ran down the poor woman's face: she could not speak. Mabel's beautiful eyes blazed with wrath: she made a step forward; but Sam Pratt gently put her back, and said,—

"Look here, Deacon Flint. Mother left you because she hadn't food, nor care, nor nothing she needed, nyther when she was sick, nor when she was gettin' better. She thought a spell o' rest would do her good. She knowed by that smart contrack you got out of her that you owed her a livin' anyhow; and you hain't done a thing to'rds it sence she went to her own house. Now, I don't call that conduct honest, by no means, much less Christian."

"Jedge not, Samwell Pratt. Scripter, no less'n statoot law, commands a wife to be subjeck to her husband. Sarepty had what I had. I done what I jedged best for her; and, instead of submittin' to her head, she up and went off to live by herself, and lef' me to git along as I could. I wa'n't noway bound by no law nor no contrack to supply her with means, so long as she went away from her dooties, and made me an astonishment an' a hissin' in Israel, so to speak."

"Stop right there!" broke in Mabel, furious. "I've heard say the Devil could fetch Scripter to further his own purposes, and I b'lieve it. Didn't you have no duties to your wife? Don't the Bible say you've got to love and cherish her? Don't tell me! I lived here long enough to see you starve and browbeat and torment her. I know your mean, hateful, crabbed ways; and I don't know how she lived with you so long. She ought to have run away years ago; and, if folks do hiss at you, it's more'n time they did. Christian!—*you* a Christian! You're a dyed-in-the-wool hypocrite. If you're pious, I hope I shall be a reprobate."

"I ha'n't no doubt but what you will be, young woman," answered the deacon with cold fury. "You'd ought to be put under the pump this minnit, for a common scold. Get out of my house, right off!"

And with this he advanced upon her. But Sam Pratt, lifting the old lady in his arms, carried her away, and gently shoved Mabel, glowing with rage, before them till they reached the wagon. Then he himself went back, and tried to make terms with the deacon. At last, moved by the worldly wisdom of Sam's argument, that it would put him in a bad light before people if he refused to do any thing for his wife, he did agree to let her have half of his share of the produce from her farm, if Sam and Mindwell would provide for her other wants. And, making the best of a bad bargain, the poor woman retired to the old house, which Sam had repaired, so that most of it was habitable; and Mabel, who had agreed to teach the district school the next year, took up her abode with her.

Now the deacon had a clear field, and appeared in the arena of Bassett in the character of an injured and forsaken husband. His prayers at meeting were longer and more eloquent than ever; and the church, sympathizing with his sorrows,—the male members especially deprecating Mrs. Flint's example, lest it should some time be followed by their own wives,—unanimously agreed to withdraw their fellowship from Mrs. Flint,—a proceeding in kind, if not in degree, like the anathema of the papacy. The poor old woman quivered under the blow, imparted to her by Parson Roberts, awful in the dignity of his office and a new wig. But the parson was human; and the meek grief of the woman, set off by Mab's blazing indignation, worked upon his honest soul, and caused him to doubt a little the church's wisdom. Mab had followed him across the door-yard to the gate in order to "free her mind."

"I want to know what you wanted that poor woman to do, Parson Roberts. She was dyin' by inches for want of vittles fit to eat, and the care most folks would give a sick ox. Do you think, now, honest, she'd ought to have staid with that old wretch?"

"Speak not evil of dignities, young woman. Amasy Flint is a deacon of Bassett church. It does not become you so to revile him."

This glittering generality did not daunt Mab a moment.

"I don't care if he was deacon in the New Jerusalem, or minister either. If he was the angel Gabriel, and acted the way he did act, I shouldn't have no faith in his piety, nor no patience with his prayers."

Parson Roberts glared at her over his spectacles with pious horror. "What, what, what!" he sternly cried. "Who be you that set in judgment on your elders and betters?"

"I'm one that's seen him where you haven't, anyway, nor your church-members. I've lived to his house, and I know him like a book."

Was it possible, the parson thought, that brother Flint might have been in fault,—just a little? But he was faithful to his dogmas and his education.

"Do not excuse the woman's sin. She has left her lawful husband, threatened to swear the peace against a Christian man whom she was bound by human and divine law to obey, and caused a scandal and a disturbance in the fold of Christ. Is this a light matter, you daughter of Belial?"

Mab laughed,—laughed in the parson's face, in full front of his majestic wig, his awful spectacles, his gold-headed cane uplifted in the heat of argument. He could not see that she was a little hysterical. He grew red with ungodly rage, but Mab did not care a pin.

"You ain't a fool, Parson Roberts," she said undauntedly. "You've got eyes in your head; and you'd know, if you'd use 'em, that Aunt Flint is a weak sister anyway. She wouldn't turn no sooner'n the least worm that ever was; but *they* will turn, if you tread right on 'em. And, whatever you say, you know, jest as well as I do, that Amasy Flint drove her into leavin' him, and drove her with a whip of scorpions, as the Bible tells about."

"Woman, do you mean to say I lie?" thundered the parson.

"Well, yes—if you don't tell the truth," returned Mab, completely at bay now. An audible chuckle betrayed some listener; and the parson, turning round, beheld old Israel silently unloading a wheelbarrow-load of potatoes at the corner of the fence, and wondered in his soul how long the man had been there, but considered it the better part of valor to leave the scene, now that it had ceased to be a *tête-à-tête:* so he waved his hand at Mab with a gloomy scowl, and went his way.

"Land o' liberty!" ejaculated the old man, drawing the back of his hand across his mouth to smother a laugh. "Didn't you give him jesse! I swan you're the gal for a free fight, now. He's heerd the fac's in the case, if he never did afore. Of all things! What be you a-cryin' for now, eh?" For Mab, a real woman, had flung her apron over her face, and was sobbing violently. Uncle Israel gently tried to pull the check screen away; but she held on to it.

"Let me cry," she said. "I ain't sorry: I'm mad, and I've got to cry it out."

"Well," said Israel, returning to his potatoes, and slowly shaking his head, "women-folks air the beateree. I don't know nothing about 'em, and I'm five an' sixty year old come Friday. Lordy! there ain't no riddles nor Chinee puzzle-rings to compare with 'em. I've hed a wife, an' lost a wife, praise the Lord! but I never was sure o' her even. I wouldn't no more try it agin than I'd slip down into a bee-tree; for there's full as much stings as honey to 'em, and, take an everidge, I guess there's more."

Whether or not the parson's silent ideas coincided with those Israel expressed is not for the ignorant chronicler to say; but it is certain that his candid and generous soul was so far moved by Mab's tirade, however he denied and defied it during its delivery, that the next day he resolved to call in a council of his neighboring brethren to discuss the matter, and indorse or reprobate the action of his own church.

So he wrote to the Rev. Ami Dobbins of Dorset, and the Rev. Samuel Jehoram Hill of Bassington, better known as Father Hill; and, in compliance with his request, they repaired to Bassett, and investigated the matter. Being advised of the pastor, who had had his experiences, they went to Mrs. Flint's during school-hours; and Mabel had no chance to pour out her soul before them. They encountered only a pale, depressed, weak woman, who was frightened out of what little heart was left her by past trials, when these two august personages came into her presence, and with severe countenances began their catechism of her life with Deacon Flint. As in the case of many another woman, her terror, her humiliation, and a lingering desire to shield her husband from his own misdeeds, all conspired against her. Her testimony was tearful, confused, and contradictory; though through it all she did feebly insist on her own sufferings, and depicted them in honest colors. From her they went to the deacon, whom they found resigned, pious, and loftily superior to common things; then he was a man, and a deacon! Is it to be wondered at that their letter to the church at Bassett was in the deacon's favor? They did indeed own that Mrs. Flint had "peculiar trials," but went on to say,—

"Nevertheless, she cannot be fully justified, but has departed from meekness and a Christian spirit . . . particularly in indulging angry and passionate expressions, tending to provoke and irritate her husband; and, however unjustifiable his conduct may be, that doth not exculpate her. We think that it would be proper and suitable for her to make suitable reflections, acknowledge she hath given her brethren and sisters of the church occasion of stumbling and to be dissatisfied; and, upon her manifesting a becoming spirit of meekness and love, we think they ought to restore her; but if she should refuse to make such reflections, they cannot consistently receive her."

And with a few added remarks on the perplexity of the case, and advising the church to call the ecclesiastical council, the Rev. Ami Dobbins and Father Hill retired for the present.

But Bassett was not content. Weeks passed, and no act of confession or contrition came from this poor old offender. To tell the truth, Mabel stood behind her now, afire with honest rage at the way she had been put upon.

"You sha'n't do it, aunty!" she said, with all her native vehemence.

"You confess! I like that! It is that old hypocrite's place to confess. He drove you out, now when you get down to it; and he hain't asked you to come back, that I've heard tell. I'd let him and the church, and Bassett too, go to thunder, if they're a mind to. If you make 'suitable reflections,' they'll reflect on old Flint and Bassett church-members. Dear me! I know one thing: I'd rather be an old maid ten times over than married to that man."

A faint smile crept over the old woman's pale face. From her high pillows she had a good outlook, and more than once she had seen an interview by the little gate that did not augur long maidenhood for Mab.

"Well, Mabel, if that's your say, why, it behooves you to be real cautious, though I don't know as Sam Pratt's brother could be anyways other than good."

Mab blushed like a Provence rose, but said nothing, yet day after day kept hardening her aunt's heart as well as she knew how; and Parson Roberts, receiving no "reflections" from the offender, and having great faith in Father Hill's power of persuasion, invited him to come again by himself, and hold a conversation with sister Flint on the subject of her trials and her contumacy.

Father Hill was a quaint, gentle, sweet-natured old man, steeped, however, in the prejudices of his time and his faith. He, too, went to the house mailed with his fixed assurance of ecclesiastical dignity and marital supremacy. Sympathy, pity, comprehension of her side of the case, would have disarmed Mrs. Flint completely; she would have sobbed, confessed, laid her hand on her mouth, and her mouth in the dust, and been ready to own herself the chief of sinners: but to be placed in the wrong from the first, reproved, admonished, and treated as an impenitent and hardened culprit, made it easier for her weak nature to accept the situation than to defy or to deny it. Nothing Father Hill could say moved her, but her dull and feeble obstinacy stirred his tender heart to its depths: he felt a despair of human means and a yearning tenderness that could find no outlet but in prayer. He fell on his knees before the chair in which he had been sitting, and lifted his earnest face to heaven.

"O dear Lord and Master," he said, speaking even as a man unto his friend, "thou hast borne our griefs, and carried our sorrows. Thou knowest by heart every pain and woe that we feel. A stranger cannot intermeddle, but, O thou Hope of Israel, why shouldst thou be as a stranger that passeth by, and a wayfaring man that tarrieth but a night, in this dwelling of thy handmaid? Dear Lord, it is not in man that walketh to direct his own steps, how much less the steps of others! Come thou in the might of thy great gentleness and thine all-knowing sympathy and love, and show this child of thine the right way, saying, 'Walk ye in it.' Thou knowest every sorrow she has passed through, every bitter draught she has drunk, every sin she has been led into: yea, when she said there was no comforter, thine eye pitied and thine arm waited to save her, though the eye of flesh saw it not. Come now, and place beneath her weary heart and failing flesh the everlasting arms of thy overflowing love and care; give her peace and rest; give her an understanding heart; above all, with thy love and pity redeem her, as thou didst the elder Israel, and bring her with tender leading and divine affection, not only into thy fold on earth, but to the general assembly and church of the first-born in heaven. And to thee shall be praise and love and glory forever. Amen."

When he arose, his old face fair with the shining of the mount from whence he came down, the poor woman, who had dropped her head on her hand, lifted it, and tried to thank him; but streaming tears choked her, and behind the door into the shed a stifled sob betrayed some hidden auditor.

"Farewell!" said Father Hill, and with a look of heavenly benignity went out from the house. His deep and earnest piety had got the better of his dogmas; and, so strange is human nature, he was a little ashamed of it. But on his departing steps the shed-door opened, and Mab came in, her face all washed with tears.

"*That* man's got religion," she said decisively. "I never heerd a mortal creature pray like that: seemed as though he see right into glory, and talked face to face with the Lord. If that's bein' pious, I wish I was as pious as fury myself."

"He's a good man," sobbed Mrs. Flint; "one of the Lord's an'inted, I make no doubt. And, Mabel, I don't know but what I have did wrong. I ain't noways heavenly-minded like him: mabbe I had ought to have put up with every thing."

"No, you hadn't: that ain't so. But if it's goin' to make you easier, aunty, to 'make reflections,' as old Parson Roberts says, why, make 'em: only don't tell no lies to the church because you've got into a heavenly mood all to once. Folks that ain't just to themselves don't never get justice elsewheres, now I tell you."

Father Hill, despairing of having impressed Mrs. Flint, had cast the matter into his Master's hands, and from his study in Bassington sent a letter to Parson Roberts, running thus:—

"Rev'd and dear Brother,—I have had Opportunity with Mrs. Flint, and find that she conceived her leaving the Deacon was a real duty at that time; that her Recovery under Providence turned upon it; that she did not then foresee the Consequences that such a step would issue in her final Separation. . . . She stands ready to reflect upon herself as far as she can be convinced she ought to do so, but thinks the fault is not on her Side as things now are.

"I feel unable to direct or advise further. The cause of Religion, the cause of the Christian Church, you are very sensible, is of more Consequence than the Honor or Pease of any individual. If such a settlement can be made as may secure Religion from suffering, it must be an object to be desired. . . . Sensible of the Embarrassments you and the church labor under, and desirous to contribute my mite, I use this Freedom.

"This from your affectionate Brother,
"Samuel J. Hill.

To Rev'd Mr. Roberts.
"To be communicated if you think expedient."

But, while the ministers were in this strait about their obstinate parishioner, the Lord had answered Father Hill, unknown to himself, while he was yet speaking. Moved, and indeed melted, by the love and sympathy that prayer showed, Mrs. Flint, no longer hindered by Mabel, prepared herself to write "proper reflections" to the church; but in doing so was also perpetually prompted by Mabel not to traitorously deny her own cause, or slip aside from the truth in a voluntary humility; and in due time the following confession was laid before that august body:—

"I, the subscriber, Sarepta Flint, a member of the church of Christ in Bassett, sensible that the Church are dissatisfied with me on account of the Separation that has taken place between Deacon Flint and myself, and that they are Apprehensive that I have not been innocent as to measures which have led to this unhappy Event, whereby Religion is wounded and the Pease of the Church disturbed, take this opportunity to publickly acknowledge myself a poor, imperfect Creture, and to own that under my Weak state of Body and weakness of mind, with which I was attended at one Time or another, I no doubt manifested on certain Occasions an unsuitable Temper of mind, said and Did things which under other Circumstances I should not have said or done. I am far from justifying myself in all my conduct. Particular I would reflect on myself for that Expression in regard to swearing the Pease against Deacon Flint. . . . I ask the Forgivness of God and this church, and of all others who are aggrieved, and request the prayers of my Christian Brethren and

Sisters that I henceforth conduct as a true and faithful Disciple of Christ, and adorn the Solem Vocation by which I am called.

"Sarepta Flint.

"P.S.—I stand ready also to return to my Husband as soon as a suitable Door opens for that Purpose."

Perhaps something in the self-respecting yet honest humility of this document touched the heart of Bassett church; or perhaps only their self-love and pride of place was soothed by it. Be that as it may, the confession was accepted; and Parson Roberts, with a valor and persistence that did him honor, insisted that Deacon Flint should go with him to inform his wife of her release from interdict, and also to open that "Door" of reconciliation to which she had so pathetically alluded. The parson's wig was fresh buckled, the deacon's cue new wound and tied, and their sabbath-day garments prim and speckless, as the next morning they opened the door of the old house where Sarepta Flint had taken refuge from her oppressor. A scene they little expected met their eyes. On the low bed, covered with its rough blue homespun spread, lay an evidently dying figure. A more "Solem Vocation" than life had called Deacon Flint's wife, and she was about to obey. Mindwell and Sam Pratt upheld her as she gasped for breath, and the two children clung together sobbing at her feet; while Mabel, with Joe Pratt's arm about her, and her face streaming with tears she did not feel, stood by the bedside gazing at her friend. Her face blazed as the deacon and Parson Roberts entered; but, roused by the click of the latch, Mrs. Flint opened her eyes, and looked at the youthful pair with a gentle smile. They had been the one bright outlook of her latter life, and to them she gave her last smile; for, as her eyes turned toward her husband, a cold terror filled them, the lids fell, her head drooped on Mindwell's shoulder, and with one long, shuddering sigh she escaped forever. The forgiveness of the church and the condescension of her husband came too late: she was already safe where the wicked cease from troubling, and the Consoler dries all mortal tears.

Deacon Flint stood like a stone. Did remorse trouble him? Was regret busy at his heart? Or did he feel a bitter and deep chagrin at the loss of so much income?

Mabel's tears ceased: she withdrew from Joe's arm, and went round to where Deacon Flint stood. "Are you proper pleased now?" she said in a low voice of concentred contempt and rage.

"You've got her turned out of church, and into heaven. You won't never see her again,—no, never! not to all eternity. But you've killed her as good as if you took an axe to her. You can take that hum to sleep on."

"Hush!" said Parson Roberts, with all the dignity a little man could give to his voice and manner. "When the Lord giveth quietness, who, then, can make trouble?"

But even as he spoke, Joe Pratt—his face full of black wrath —set his hand to the deacon's collar, and walked him summarily into the road. Mabel had spoken truth: never again did he see his wife's face, not even in the fair peace of death. Whether ever, in that far world of souls, they met again, is perhaps doubtful: let us pray not. Mrs. Flint's married experience was over in this world a hundred years ago, and in the next "they neither marry nor are given in marriage."

Emily Dickinson

Emily Dickinson (1830–1886), daughter of an Amherst, Massachusetts, lawyer, is a poet of international reputation. Though her depths of feeling and perception and her technical virtuosity can in no sense be described as merely regional, she nevertheless wrote in meters derived from her Congregational hymnbook and employed images, symbols, and situations common to New England village life. Recognizing the narrowness of her experience, she made do with what was physically, intellectually, and spiritually available in Amherst, at that time a farming community that happened also to be the location of a newly established, religiously orthodox college. As she herself asserts, she sees "New Englandly." She envisages heaven as a country town and God as the proprietor of a village store. Christ is imagined as a teacher in a rural school. Though probably not a strict believer, she shared the Calvinists' sense of individual destiny—the soul engulfed in a "polar privacy" as it faces its maker, who alone can save it. Death is an unforgettable reality, making its presence felt in village funerals and disused country graveyards. As a backdrop to the townspeople's activities is the cycle of the seasons, each suggesting its own mystery in "a certain slant of light" or in an "altered air." Justice can scarcely be done to Emily Dickinson in the space available here. The few selections from her work have been chosen in an attempt to illustrate the manner in which she draws on her Amherst surroundings. World poet though she may be, she is also a village poet—the greatest that New England has produced.

The poems reprinted here are from Thomas H. Johnson's three-volume The Poems of Emily Dickinson *(1958), or from the same editor's one-volume* The Complete Poems of Emily Dickinson *(1960), in both of which the capitalization and punctuation of the original manuscripts have been retained.*

125

Thirteen Poems

1.

On the Bleakness of my Lot
Bloom I strove to raise—
Late—My Garden of a Rock—
Yielded Grape—and Maise—

Soil of Flint, if steady tilled
Will refund the Hand—
Seed of Palm, by Lybian Sun
Fructified in Sand—

2.

The Robin's my Criterion for Tune—
Because I grow—where Robins do—
But, were I Cuckoo born—
I'd swear by him—
The ode familiar—rules the Noon—
The Buttercup's, my Whim for Bloom—
Because, we're Orchard sprung—
But, were I Cuckoo born—
I'd Daisies spurn—
None but the Nut—October fit—
Because, through dropping it,
The Seasons flit—I'm taught—
Without the Snow's Tableau
Winter, were lie—to me—
Because I see—New Englandly—
The Queen, discerns like me—
Provincially—

3.

The Butterfly's Assumption Gown
In Chrysoprase Apartments hung
This afternoon put on—

How condescending to descend
And be of Buttercups the friend
In a New England Town—

4.

I went to Heaven—
'Twas a small Town—
Lit—with a Ruby—
Lathed—with Down—

Stiller—than the fields
At the full Dew—
Beautiful—as Pictures—
No Man drew.
People—like the Moth—
Of Mechlin—frames—
Duties—of Gossamer—
And Eider—names—
Almost—contented—
I—could be—
'Mong such unique
Society—

5.

I'm sorry for the Dead—Today—
It's such congenial times
Old Neighbors have at fences—
It's time o' year for Hay.

And Broad—Sunburned Acquaintance
Discourse between the Toil—
And laugh, a homely species
That makes the Fences smile—

It seems so straight to lie away
From all the noise of Fields—
The Busy Carts—the fragrant Cocks—
The Mower's Metre—Steals

A Trouble lest they're homesick—
Those Farmers—and their Wives —
Set separate from the Farming—
And all the Neighbor's lives—

A wonder if the Sepulchre
Dont feel a lonesome way—
When Men—and Boys—and Carts—and June,
Go down the fields to "Hay"—

6.

I asked no other thing—
No other—was denied—
I offered Being—for it—
The Mighty Merchant sneered—

Brazil? He twirled a Button—
Without a glance my way—
"But—Madam—is there nothing else—
That We can show—Today?"

7.

I cautious, scanned my little life—
I winnowed what would fade
From what w'd last till Heads like mine
Should be a-dreaming laid.

I put the latter in a Barn—
The former, blew away.
I went one winter morning
And lo—my priceless Hay

Was not upon the "Scaffold"—
Was not upon the "Beam"—
And from a thriving Farmer—
A Cynic, I became.

Whether a thief did it—
Whether it was the wind—
Whether Deity's guiltless—
My business is, to find!

So I begin to ransack!
How is it Hearts, with thee?
Art thou within the little Barn
Love provided Thee?

8.

There is a solitude of space
A solitude of sea
A solitude of death, but these
Society shall be
Compared with that profounder site
That polar privacy
A soul admitted to itself—
Finite Infinity.

9.

I shall know why—when Time is over—
And I have ceased to wonder why—
Christ will explain each separate anguish
In the fair schoolroom of the sky—

He will tell me what "Peter" promised—
And I—for wonder at his woe—
I shall forget the drop of Anguish
That scalds me now—that scalds me now!

10.

These are the days when Birds come back—
A very few—a Bird or two—
To take a backward look.

These are the days when skies resume
The old—old sophistries of June—
A blue and gold mistake.

Oh fraud that cannot cheat the Bee—
Almost thy plausibility
Induces my belief.

Till ranks of seeds their witness bear—
And softly thro' the altered air
Hurries a timid leaf.

Oh Sacrament of summer days,
Oh Last Communion in the Haze—
Permit a child to join.

Thy sacred emblems to partake—
Thy consecrated bread to take
And thine immortal wine!

11.

There's a certain Slant of Light,
Winter Afternoons—
That oppresses, like the Heft
Of Cathedral Tunes—

Heavenly Hurt, it gives us—
We can find no scar,
But internal difference,
Where the Meanings, are—

None may teach it—Any—
'Tis the Seal Despair—
An imperial affliction
Sent us of the Air—

When it comes, the Landscape listens—
Shadows—hold their breath—
When it goes, 'tis like the Distance
On the look of Death—

12.

There's been a Death, in the Opposite House,
As lately as Today—
I know it, by the numb look
Such Houses have—alway—

The Neighbors rustle in and out—
The Doctor—drives away—
A window opens like a Pod—
Abrupt—mechanically—

Somebody flings a Mattrass out—
The Children hurry by—
They wonder if it died—on that—
I used to—when a Boy—

The Minister—goes stiffly in—

As if the House were His—
And He owned all the Mourners—now—
And little Boys—Besides—

And then the Milliner—and the Man
Of the Appalling Trade—
To take the measure of the House—

There'll be that Dark Parade—

Of Tassels—and of Coaches—soon—
It's easy as a Sign—
The Intuition of the News—
In just a Country Town—

13.

After a hundred years
Nobody knows the Place
Agony that enacted there
Motionless as Peace

Weeds triumphant ranged
Strangers strolled and spelled
At the lone Orthography
Of the Elder Dead

Winds of Summer Fields
Recollect the way—
Instinct picking up the Key
Dropped by memory—

Rowland Evans Robinson

Rowland Evans Robinson (1833–1900) was born into a Quaker farming family at Ferrisburg in the Champlain Valley of Vermont. Except for a short period that he spent in New York City attempting to live by his modest talent as an artist, he passed his life in Vermont working the family farm and writing. The territory about which he wrote is a small slice of the state extending from Lake Champlain to the Green Mountains. The villages of Lincoln and Starksboro, included in this area, served as models for the fictional hill town of Danvis which, like Rose Terry Cooke's Bassett, was the setting for many of his stories and sketches. Farmer, sportsman, student of nature, Rowland Robinson knew his little corner of New England as well as Thoreau knew Concord, and he wrote about it as lovingly. His Uncle Lisha's Shop: Life in a Corner of Yankee-Land *(1887)* and Danvis Folks *(1894) are real treasuries of local color. Afflicted with blindness in his later years, he continued his literary output with the aid of a grooved writing board.*

Rowland Robinson was proud of his Quaker ancestry, which had its origins in Newport, Rhode Island. In the farmhouse at Ferrisburg—the house was named Rokeby in honor of Sir Walter Scott—was a room used by fugitive slaves escaping into Canada by the Underground Railway. Stemming from his memories of these times, the story "The Mole's Path" illustrates an important chapter in the history of Robinson's family and of the State of Vermont. "The Purification of Cornbury" reveals the meanness and poverty that were aspects of rural New England life, presents the selectmen in action, and betrays the still potent Puritanism of the region. "An Old-Time March Meeting" doubtless reflects scores of such meetings that Robinson attended in his own town. In its humor, its phonetic transcription of dialect, and its amiable depiction of rural characters it is typical of Robinson's art. Here we have the town meeting in its most primitive but perhaps most effective form. Though concerned mainly with such matters as the impounding of stray hogs, this meeting is pure participatory democracy. The sketch was first published, posthumously, in the Atlantic Monthly *in 1902 (Vol. 89), from which it is reprinted here. The texts of "The Mole's Path" and of "The Purification of Cornbury" are those in Robinson's* Out of Bondage and Other Stories *as published in the Centennial Edition (Rutland, Vermont, 1936).*

The Mole's Path

When Hannah Wray was left alone, more than seventy years ago, by the death of her father, an active worker in the anti-slavery cause, it was not the least of her sorrows that she could not continue his work. The Wray house, so easily distinguishable by strangers and wayfarers because of its gambrel roof and the two tall Lombardy poplars that were its landmarks afar off, was no longer a frequented station of that dark thoroughfare that, unseen and often unsuspected, like the mole's path beneath the meadow turf, formed a network through our Northern States. Along its secret lines many dusky travelers passed in safety on their long journey through the Land of the Free to the liberty denied them in it.

Hannah was of too timid a nature to take a place in the aggressive ranks of the Abolitionists. She could not, even though the Spirit moved vehemently, bring herself to bear testimony in Friends' meeting among her own people. It was out of the question for a lone woman to harbor unknown men coming at all hours of the night. So she tried to content herself with subscribing to the state anti-slavery paper, with making her small contributions to the cause, and with gathering donations of clothing for the fugitives in Canada West. Thither had gone, in accordance with his wishes, her father's entire wardrobe, shad-bellied brown coats, long drab waistcoats, and barn-door breeches, with underclothes made of free-labor goods, the broad-brimmed drab felt hat and honest home made foot-gear.

If Hannah had been one of the world's people instead of a self-controlled Quakeress, she would have confessed to being worried one fall morning, as she nervously folded, sealed carefully with a red wafer, and addressed a letter at her kitchen table, and going to the door, looked intently up the road. She was aware of being "considerably concerned" when the stretch of black thoroughfare, now frozen hard, revealed no sign of life nor of motion, between its borders of naked trees and dun grass, save a scurry of withered leaves, here and there, caught by a swoop of the November wind and tossed by it like a flock of frightened birds.

At the bend of the road stood the old Friends' meeting-house, gray and lonely beside its treeless yard of unmarked graves. The shade of anxiety clouding her placid face changed to an expression of quiet sadness as her eyes dwelt on the deserted building, and she wished that her father could be with her, if but for a moment, to advise her in her present strait.

"I say for it, it's strange what keeps Joseph to-day of all days," she soliloquized, as was her habit like that of many who are much alone and crave the sound of a human voice. "Well, watching won't bring him any sooner."

She reentered the kitchen and made pretense of busying herself with the impossibility of making it more neat and orderly. She set a waiting coffee pot a little farther back on the stove, mended the fire, and swept vigorously where the litter of the wood was supposed to have fallen. While she was going through the form of emptying this into the stove, the clear, melodious winding of a horn caught her ear above the clatter of dustpan and griddle.

Hastening to the door, she saw a man on horseback turning the bend by the meeting-house at a gallop. The sound of the postman's horn was pleasant to her ears, though it came perilously near being a tune. She watched the rider until he was within thirty rods of her, his eyes being curiously intent on some object above her. Then, going to the stove, she poured a steaming cup of coffee and was at the threshold with it when he drew rein before the broad stepping-stone.

"Here is thy coffee," she said, stepping out; "I'm afraid it ain't so good as common, thee is so late. What made thee?"

Joe Bagley drew the latest number of "The Voice of Freedom" from the right-hand saddle-bag and reached it toward her to exchange for his accustomed stirrup cup, answering, explaining, and asking, continuously, as he did so:—

"Oh, to'able, haow be you? Had tu stop an' git a shoe sot. Say, Miss Wray, who you got stayin' wi' ye? See someb'dy peekin' aout the gerrit winder. Looked kinder dark-complected."

Hannah started back, the hand that held the proffered cup drew it toward her and she took her other hand from the pocket where her letter was. Joe's pale gray eyes opened wider as he leaned over to his utmost balance for the fragrant cup, tantalizing his nostrils and palate. Her face at once regained its wonted calmness, and her voice was steady as she asked:—

"Is n't thee mistaken, Joseph?"

"I seen 'em jest as plain as I see you, Miss Wray, someb'dy peekin' aout the gerrit winder. Did n't you know there was someb'dy?"

"Hitch thy horse a minute an' come in to drink thy coffee. I must speak to thee in private." For she saw her nearest neighbor, quick-eared Betsey Lane, coming out of her house, and Betsey "hated niggers, and 'ould lick ev'ry one on 'em an' send 'em straight back tu where they come f'om."

"He don't need no hitchin', but I 'm kinder late a'ready. Ol' hoss is gittin' bunged an' slower 'n a snail"; but the coffee and his curiosity were stronger than his sense of duty, and throwing his crippled right leg over the saddle pommel, he slid to the ground and limped inside the door, which was closed carefully behind him. Just inside, he stopped, apparently appalled by the neatness of the room.

"Sit down and drink thy coffee," she said, setting a chair for him.

Without removing his close-fitting sealskin cap,—the coarse, black, shiny hair worn to the skin in spots,—or even untying the half oval lappets tied under the chin with two strings of black tape, he obeyed her and began sipping the coffee, while his eyes slowly ranged the spotless purity of the room, and returned to its no less immaculate mistress.

"I 've got tu hev me a new hoss, the' hain't no tew ways 'baout it," he explained, perched on the edge of his chair with his feet crooked far under him, "but haow I 'm goin' tu 's more 'n I know. Airnin's is desp't slow."

"Joseph Bagley," she said in her quiet voice, giving no heed to his words, but seating herself before him and looking straight into his wavering, colorless eyes so different from the clear blue of her own, "I think thee has a kind heart and that I can trust thee with a weighty secret."

"Yis, marm."

"What thee saw at the window is a poor hunted runaway woman. She and her child have been here since last First Day night. I heard yesterday that the slave hunters are close behind on her track. They have handbills out describing her and her child, and they offer a hundred dollars for them."

"A hundred dollars?" he burst out. "Gol, I 'll bet that 's one o' them papers on the meetin'-'ouse door, as I come along."

"On the meeting-house? Oh,"—Hannah's cheek flushed, "but never mind that, now. What I want of thee is to say nothing of what thee has seen to any one,—any one, mind."

"Yis, marm," Joe answered, and she went on:—

"James is a good tenant and does well by my farm, but I can't trust this to him, and I don't keep any horse that I can drive. Now, I want thee to take this letter to Aaron Varney just as quick as thee can and do thy business as thee goes along. Of course, thee must do that, but don't dally on the way nor stop anywhere to talk to any one,—as thee has with me," she added, smiling at the incongruity of her precept and example. "Now thee understands. Remember I depend on thee to help me. It would be dreadful to have these poor creatures taken back to slavery. I can't bear to think of it."

"No, marm, an' you 'd better tell the fool of a nigger to keep away f'm the winder."

"Please don't call these unfortunate colored people by that name, Joseph; it hurts me."

"Seems 's 'ough that was the name on 'em,—same 's we 're Yankees."

"Never mind, now. Thee 's not to mention having seen any, and thee 'll get my letter to Aaron as soon as thee can. Now thee 's finished thy coffee, put some doughnuts in thy pocket and go on."

Joe pocketed a generous supply of Hannah's delicately browned and puffy cakes, and with the letter in the breast pocket of his coat, he limped out to his horse.

"Farewell, Joseph, thee understands I am trusting thee greatly in this matter."

Hannah watched through a crack of the rush curtain until assured of the carrier's speedy passage by her inquisitive and dangerous neighbor. Then she climbed the stairs to the chambers and thence to the low-roofed attic where her charge was bestowed in a closet-like room behind the great chimney. Sliding aside the secret panel, she stooped low and entered the chamber of refuge where during her girlhood many a fugitive had found rest from his weary journeying. It was a place made almost holy to her in its defiance of unrighteous laws.

A dark negress with the scared, alert look of a hunted wild animal, sat on the low bed where a mulatto child lay quietly sleeping.

"Milly, thee poor foolish thing," Hannah began in a tone of mild reproach, "why will thee go to the window? The post-rider saw thee and it may bring us great trouble. Thee must be more careful. Thy Heavenly Father will help thee if thee trusts Him. But remember thee must help thyself and thee must not be seen at the window. I'll bring thy dinner presently and then thee try to sleep, for it 's likely thee 'll have to ride a long way tonight, and thee must be ready to start at a moment's notice." She laid a gentle hand on the turbaned head as she spoke. The woman caught it in her hard palms, crying out:—

"De Lawd 'll sholy bless yo', missus, whateber happens to we uns."

Closing the panel behind her, Hannah went down to the kitchen, and putting on her hood and drab shawl, she locked the door behind her and set forth for the performance of another duty. She walked briskly up the road, stirring the leaves to further flights before the north wind. In stately fashion a procession of crows was faring before the wind on their southward journey, and a grand progress of white clouds drifting against the sunlit sky.

That atrocious advertisement, displayed on the old meeting-house, sanctified by long-continued testimony against the sin of slavery, was an affront not to be endured. She mounted the broad, rough stone and stood a moment to read:—

"One Hundred Dollars' Reward for the Apprehension of my slave woman Milly and her girl. Said woman is 28, tall, very dark, with scar on left cheek. Girl light, 5 years old."

If they had put it on the door of a steeple-house whose hireling priest excused the crime, it would have been fittingly placed, she thought, and her cheeks flushed with an anger for which her conscience condemned her. She snatched the paper from its fastening, tore it in small fragments and threw them to the winds. Then turning away she retraced her steps homeward.

The postman did not need to blow his horn for the notification of Betsey Lane, for she was already at her gate, her head hooded with her apron, her inquisitive eyes boring him at long

range, her lips tremulous with questions as he slackened his pace
and drew her paper from his pouch as he approached.

"Here 's your 'Rutlan' Herald,' Mis' Lane."

"What was you a-stoppin' so long for at Hanner's? I 've
stood here a-waitin' for ye till I 'm 'mos' froze."

"Gittin' a maouse aouten a trap," he answered. "Beats all
haow feared women folks be of a leetle maouse."

"Has Hanner got comp'ny? See any black critters hengin'
raoun' there? Thought I heerd a young un yellin' bloody murder,
once yist'd'y."

"Why, yis, I did see a black cat lyin' 'n under the stove."

As Joe handed her the paper he dug his heels into his horse's
flanks and made an unspellable sound with his tongue against
his teeth.

"It took ye an awful spell an' me aout here a-freezin'. What
be you in sech a pucker for? Hain't you got any news?"

"You 'll find it in the paper. That 's what they print it for,"
Joe said, speaking over his shoulder with increasing volume as
he started away, leaving Mrs. Lane slowly searching for the
marriages and deaths as she groped her way to her door. It
required some self-denial for Joe to shorten an interview with
one of his most loquacious patrons, for he was of a sociable
turn and enjoyed the brief opportunities for gossip that were
snatched here and there along his weekly route. As he jogged
along from house to house he held conversation with his horse
wherein he took both parts.

"A hundred dollars for ketchin' tew niggers! What ye think
o' that, Bob? You would n't, hey? Land! you could n't. You
could n't ketch a rollin' berril o' potash. I tell ye what, I 'm a
dum good min' ter tell an' git the hundred dollars an' buy me a
hoss 'at c'ld git som'eres, sometime, an' you could hev a good
time aout to parster. What if I have gin my word? Ev'ybody 's
mean, meaner 'n pusley, an' we 've got tu be mean tu keep up
aour row an' live. If you run'd away, I 'd want ye back an' a
feller 'at kep' ye 'ould be a dum thief. What if I would n't hom-
mer an' hell peck ye when I got ye, it would n't be that feller's
business. You think folks hain't no right tu own folks? That
ain't fer me tu settle, an' hosses are a dum sight more humern
tu me 'an what niggers be. Oh, Bob, go 'long! When you s'pose
we 'll git tu Uncle Aaron's?"

The two passed a cross road that led far back into the hill
country beyond whose mantle of living green the helmet of
Camel's Hump towered, shining like frosted silver with the first

snow. The road ran beside a stretch of gray woodland with a zigzag rail fence dividing them. Joe's eye caught a glimpse of white flashing in and out, from corner to corner. It was a weasel unduly conspicuous in his too early donned winter guise, in sharp pursuit of a field mouse. The hard-pressed quarry dodged into a knot-hole in a hollow rail. The weasel ran over it, then finding itself at fault, beat back, and recovering the lost scent, began worming itself into the loophole. Joe slid off his horse, and picking up a stout stick as he ran to the fence in his peculiar galloping gait, struck and broke the back of the savage little hunter when the lithe body had wriggled itself half its length into the hole. He drew it forth and dashed the grinning, snarling head against a rail.

"'T wa'n't nothin' but a dum maouse," he said as he undulated toward his horse, complacently regarding his prize, "but I 'd ruther be for the maouse 'an agin him with this bloody lettle cuss, would n't you, Bob? I guess we won't help 'em ketch their niggers, seein' Hanner 's dependin' on us."

As he mounted, he saw rapidly approaching from the direction in which he was going, a vehicle called by courtesy a "light wagon" drawn by a span of swift-footed Morgans. There were three occupants of the wagon,—one, who was driving, an alert, keen-eyed man, the well-known deputy sheriff. The other two were strangers, and there was a suggestive empty seat.

"Hello, Joe," the sheriff called, pulling up as they met. "Seen or heard anything of a nigger woman an' a young un as you come along? Think hard, now, there 's a hundred dollars' reward. That 'ould come in handy toward a-gettin' on ye a new hoss. This ol' feller 's on his last laigs. I hear 'em talkin' o' gettin' a new paper-carrier wi' a new hoss."

"A nigger woman an' a baby? Le' me see;" and he seemed to be searching his memory, but in fact he was wrestling with temptation. "Ben a-stealin', hes she?"

"Wal, yes, her laigs is a-kerryin' off this gentleman's prop'ty. Did ye stop at the Quaker ol' maid's? Like 'nough, she 's a-hidin' of 'em."

"Lord, no, the' hain't nob'dy there," Joe answered promptly. "I stopped and went in as I come along. She 's all alone. The haouse stiller 'n last year's bird's-nest. Is yer nigger womern black as Tony, an' the young un yaller?"

"Yes, yes. Where did you see 'em?" The sheriff asked eagerly, already tightening his reins for a start.

"I hain't seen 'em nowheres, but come tu think on 't, I met a feller back at the cross road, come f'm the east, he did, an' he ast me who I s'posed they was an' where I s'posed they was a-goin'. Said he met 'em 'baout four mild back, a-pikin' their pootiest."

Joe became so interested in his fiction that he slid to the ground and stood by the near fore wheel, picking the mud from the hub as he talked. "If ye git 'em on this track will you give me suthin' for puttin' of you ontu it?"

"Suttinly, suh, suttinly, I 'll give you twenty-five dollars," said one of the strangers, a cool-looking man who somehow reminded Joe of his weasel.

"Wal," Joe continued, looking straight at the three, one by one, after noting that the notch of the hub was on the upper side and the head of the linchpin directly under it, "if I was a-lookin' arter 'em, I should put right for Lindley M. Meader's. The Quakers is mostly in the same kittle."

"That 's so," the sheriff assented heartily. "We 've just come f'm ol' Aaron Varney's. We s'arched from suller to gerrit but did n't find no niggers, only a good place for 'em."

"You don't say! Wal, I 'd go tu Lindley M.'s; it 's 'baout ten mild, I cal'late." Joe slipped something into the pocket with Hannah's doughnuts and slowly wiped the wheel grease from his fingers on the seat of his trousers, with the foot of his game leg still on the hub.

The sheriff, impatient to be on the new trail, tightened the reins, and the horses started, bringing Joe's foot to the ground with a sudden jerk that almost upset him. He drew Bob from the withered roadside grasses he was cropping, remounted and went his way. Presently he drew forth something from his pocket which he tossed far afield without even looking at it. Then taking one of the doughnuts he began eating it, passing alternate mouthfuls to Bob, who turned his head aside to receive them. Joe listened to the retreating clatter of the sheriff's wagon, munching slowly for better listening, until he heard a sudden crash, followed by silence.

"I hope the' hain't none of 'em broke the' blasted necks," he ejaculated, and blowing a loud resounding blast on his horn, he dug his heels into Bob's sides.

Two hours later he rode into the back yard of Aaron Varney's great square house, setting the mixed multitude of poultry into a commotion and clamor with his melodious horn. Thereat the owner came forth, a stately man of firm countenance who looked sharply at the post rider from under the wide brim of his hat.

Joe handed him the letter, which he ead at once. "Does thee know what this is about, Joseph?"

"Pooty nigh, I guess, an' my idee is you 'd better be a-hustlin' as soon as it gits dark. Hed visitors, hain't ye, Mr. Varney?"

"What makes thee think so?"

Joe went on to tell of his meeting the sheriff's party and how he had sent them off on a false scent, ending with, "I shouldn't wonder if they lost a linchpin er suthin'. I heard a kind of a smash as they went down the hill."

"Why, Joseph," said Friend Varney, his keen eyes twinkling although the corners of his mouth were drawn down to a serious expression, "I had n't any idee thee was so zealous in the cause. I hope if there was an accident, them poor, misguided men were not injured."

"I did n't go back tu see. Hed n't no time an' git my papers delivered. Here 's yourn, "V'ice o' Freedom" an' "The Frien' " an' "Rutlan' Herald." Like tu forgot 'em. You tell Hanner I done her arrent."

"Farewell, Joseph, thee will be remembered in the latter day;" but the post rider was gone beyond the hearing of the kindly words.

While Joe was yet pursuing his unfinished route in the slanted light of the low sun and beguiling the time with bites of doughnut uncertainly caught as he rode along, Aaron Varney, in his empty lumber wagon drawn by a pair of well fed horses, was traveling at a smart pace on his way to Hannah Wray's. The shadows of night had long since fallen upon the earth, blotting its dun and gray to universal blackness, and house lights were going out, one by one like setting stars, when he reached her home. As he passed a curtained window, he tapped lightly on it with the hickory handle of his rarely used whip. The curtain was drawn a little, and he whispered, "It 's Aaron come for the goods. Be spry as thee can, Hannah. Is all well so far?"

He drove cautiously into the barn, and for a time there were hushed mysterious movements, until the wagon emerged with a hogshead standing on end, behind the seat.

"Farewell, Aaron, may the Heavenly Father protect thy precious lading," Hannah said reverently. He heaved a suppressed, assenting groan as he climbed into his seat and the wagon moved with caution down the road.

A mile on his way, Aaron met three men driving a pair of

jaded horses. They eyed him sharply in the faint light that shone from a sky beginning to brighten with the rising moon, but there was nothing to excite suspicion in the solitary figure and the innocent-looking hogshead. He drove on through the growing moonlight and its sudden changes of cloud shadow and unveiled radiance, alert, silent, and lonely, though with companions near. When the moon was growing pale against the sky and the shadows it cast were fading in the gray of morning he entered the yard of a tidy farmhouse. A horse neighed a welcome to the stable as the wagon entered the gloom of the neighboring shed. A pebble cast against an upper window caused its cautious opening and the appearance of a shirted figure.

"Is that thee, David? This is Aaron an' I 've brought thee a hogshead of free labor goods."

In a few moments a small man of silent, quick movements, emerged from the house. The two exchanged whispered greetings and Aaron led the way to the wagon, where they laid hold of the inverted hogshead and raising it bodily, disclosed the slave woman and child. David conducted the cramped tired fugitives inside the house, followed by Aaron's portly form, where they were welcomed with as gentle cordiality as if the hostess had expected their early call.

"Wal, Sary, here 's Aaron agin, with some more stolen prop'ty. Pooty Quaker you are, Aaron, stealin' them poor Southerners' goods." His twinkling eyes and firm set mouth expressed a love of fun and adventure perhaps more than humanitarian sentiment. "I 'm a good min' to report you to the Monthly Meetin', Aaron. Some o' the ol' blue bellies 'd turn ye out o' meetin' if they got wind o' your goin's on. Wal, I s'pose I'll hafter help ye smuggle the goods into Canerdy. Feed 'em an' stow 'em away, Sary," and the dusky passengers again passed out of sight in another station of the dark, wide-reaching, many-branched road that stretched from the sunlit Southern fields to Canadian snows.

The post rider jogged leisurely southward on his return trip with no object but to get home and be ready for the next journey over the old route. Bob might take his time now without detriment to the newspaper service, so Joe tied him to Hannah Wray's hitching-post and went in to learn how her affairs had prospered.

After their interchange of information she said, "And now I think thee said thee wanted a new horse."

"Yis, marm."

"Well, I 've been thinking about that. I 'm told thee 's a careful hand with horses and I 've a notion to let thee take my three-year-old bay mare and break her to the saddle. Thee can turn thy horse out in my rowan to be used a little perhaps if James needs him. How will that suit thee?"

"That 's tew good, marm," Joe said, his pale eyes actually shining with surprise and delight. "But I guess I c'n manage the mare if you want me tu try it."

The colt, being intelligent and good tempered, took kindly to the saddle and saddle-bags and to Joe on top of them. He, riding away the happiest man in the country, was soon engaged in friendly converse with her as he had lately been with her predecessor. He explained to her all strange objects on the road and gradually accustomed her to the sound of the horn blown just above her sensitive ears. Thus traveling they met the Sheriff engaged in better business than when last met.

"Hello, Joe," he hailed, after recognizing the postman on the new horse.

"Hello, Mr. Barnes. You got that twenty-five dollars for me?" Joe asked, playing with a wisp of the mare's mane.

"Twenty-five your grandmother!" said the sheriff scornfully. "Drove fifteen mild, lickaty split arter nothin' an' back agin, besides a wheel comin' off an' pooty nigh breakin' all our necks."

"You don't say. That 's all killin' bad. I was a-lottin' on that twenty-five dollars."

"Say, where did you get your hoss, Joe?" critically studying the new mount.

"This 'ere mare?" Joe asked, apparently then first aware he was not astride old Bob. "Oh, she hain't nothin' but a green cult Mis' Wray wanted me for tu take an' ride a spell tu saddle-break an' git waywise."

"O-oh!" The sheriff's long drawn exclamation comprehended many expressions. Running his eyes over the insignificant figure before him, his newly awakened admiration took form in words. "You can't allers tell by the looks of a toad how fur he 'll jump. I swear you be an innercent lookin' cuss."

Quite different were Hannah Wray's thoughts of the post rider, as she sat at her kitchen window and musingly looked out on the peaceful autumnal landscape: "What poor, feeble instruments our Heavenly Father will sometimes strengthen for His use!"

The Purification of Cornbury

One September morning, sixty years ago, the three selectmen of Cornbury were holding an informal council in front of the kitchen door of Squire Dana. He, a tall, athletic man, with a strongly moulded and not unkindly face, stood on the ground, resting one foot on the hub of a vehicle called by courtesy a light wagon, in which sat, elevated high above him, the second and third members of the triumvirate. One of them, a short, important-looking man, held the reins of a fat Morgan mare that stood quite undisturbed by his meditative flicking of the grass with the woodchuck-skin lash of the hickory-handled whip. The other, a lean, mild-faced person, picked nervously at the hair of the buffalo skin that temporarily upholstered the wagon seat, while he listened to the conversation of his associates.

"The long an' short on 't is," said he who held the reins, giving a sharp cut at a late-blooming dandelion, "folks is a-gittin' so stirred up abaout them a-livin' tugether the way they du 'at we 've got tu raout 'em aout."

"Wal, I s'pose so," Squire Dana admitted reluctantly, taking his foot from the hub as he drew his knife from his pocket, picked up a chip that had strayed from the woodshed into the neatness of the yard, and began to whittle; "but I swan it goes agin my grain tu tackle a woman."

"That 's jest it," said Captain Fay, the rotund second selectman. "All aour women folks is tur'bly riled up abaout it, an' for my part, I 'd a good deal druther hev a bresh wi' that 'ere one woman an' done with it 'an tu hev all the women in taown a-buzzin' araound aour ears the hul endurin' time."

"Why not set the constable arter 'em?" Deacon Palmer suggested. "Seems 's 'ough 't was more his business 'n what it is aourn."

Squire Dana shook his head in slow dissent. "No, 't would make the taown expense. I guess we 'll hafter 'tend tu it."

Mrs. Dana, hovering near the open door, conducted her house-work in such unusual silence that her alert ears caught the drift of the conversation, to which she felt it her duty, as a member of the Moral Reform Society and the wife of the first selectman, to add her voice for the quick removal of a blot on the town's good name.

"Good-mornin', Captain. Good-mornin', Deacon," she said, stepping out on to the stoop, the welcome smile on her genial face hardening to fitting severity as she asked, "Was you a-talkin' abaout that Lem Tyler an' that woman? It's a disgrace tu the hul town an' every respectable woman in it tu have them mis'able creeturs a-livin' the way they du. It's a burnin' shame, an' I say if the selec'men hain't got enough spunk tu take a holt an' turn 'em aou' door, the women 'll haftu."

"Sartainly, we're a-cal'latin' tu, Mis' Dany," Captain Fay answered, with prompt decision; "but you see we want tu ketch 'em aou' door if we possibly can, an' then we can set their stuff aou' door an' not hev no rumpus."

"That's it ezackly," her husband assented emphatically; and Deacon Palmer added acquiescence without taking his eyes from an unfamiliar prairie burr he was plucking at in the buffalo hair.

"Wal, if that's what you want, he's gone away," declared Mrs. Dana. "He went off up the road whilst aour folks was a-milkin', an' I hain't seen him go back. If you three men can't git one woman an' one young one aout of a haouse, the taown hed better elect a new board."

"I guess they won't heftu, Mis' Dany," Captain Fay said confidently. "Say, Square, if we're a-goin' tu-day tu lay that new road, why can't we take in this 'ere job as we go along? 'T won't be no gret of a chore. Come, put on your kut, an' git right in here."

"You come in an' let me put a clean dicky on, Mr. Dany," said his wife, and she bustled indoors, presently reappearing with the supplementary collar and bosom, with which she proceeded to invest her husband, while he elevated his chin, pursed his lips, shut his eyes, and held his breath, in dread of pins. Then she brought his second-best blue coat and his black fur hat, in which he permitted himself to be arrayed without audible protest.

"There! naow you look more like payin' your respec's to a lady," she said, after a brief, comprehensive inspection that lingered with least approval on trousers and boots.

He climbed to the seat, and the three drove away, watched by Mrs. Dana till they were hidden by the copse of crimson sumac at the road.

"Wal, I only hope their spunk 'll hold aout," she soliloquized as the apex of the pyramid of three bell-crowned hats disappeared, and she reentered to a brisk and noisy resumption of her interrupted labors. "I wish 't I was a man a spell: I'd drive 'em aout o' the taown. But then, I s'pose if I was a man I should be jest like the rest on 'em."

Captain Fay drove the Morgan mare at a pace that soon brought him and his associates to a house of such forlorn exterior and surroundings that one would have thought it untenanted, if the smoke crawling from the crumbling chimney and the heap of freshly gathered wood at the door had not betokened occupancy. Naked scars where the wind had torn shingles from the sagging mossy roof; broken windows; lichen-scaled clapboards dropping away from their places, disclosing raw strips of unweathered boarding like unhealed wounds; the dying lilac-tree, hedged around by its own sprouts, beside the unused front door; the lilies and peonies running wild with a vagabond company of weeds; the untrodden, weed-grown path to the ruinous barn; the curbless well, and its broken sweep lying beside it, with the leaky bucket still attached to the pole and chain,—all told of a house abandoned by its owners and given over to careless tenants.

"They run a pretty good fire," said the Squire, observing the smoke.

"Yes, wood a-plenty for the picking up," said Captain Fay; and then, casting a critical eye along a rail fence which had sunken somewhat below lawful height, "Guess Davis's fences hes begun to winter-kill a'ready."

"I don't see what in tunket Davis ever let the critturs in here fur!" Squire Dana said impatiently. "Folks ortu be more pa-'tic'lar. My tenant haousen has ben empty more 'n three months 'cause I can't find the right sort of a family tu let int' it."

"Wal, mebby Davis 'll git a day's work naow an' agin, an' that 's better 'n nothin'," said Palmer. "Shh! there 's the woman naow. Say, she hain't bad-lookin'."

A dark-haired, dark-eyed woman, comely in spite of a look too worn for her years, which were not more than twenty-five, and neatly though poorly clad, came out at the side door with a pail in her hand. She halted a moment to cast a startled glance upon the visitors alighting at the broken gate, and then hurried to the well and hastily lowered the bucket by its clumsy attachment.

Squire Dana's first impulse was to help her; but while he hesitated she drew up the dribbling bucket with swift, strong hands, and emptying what remained of its wasted contents into the pail, sped back to the house without bestowing another look on the strangers at the gate, though their chief called out:—

"Hol' on a minute, won't ye, marm? There, Fay, if you had n't 'a' ben forever a-hitchin' your hoss, we might 'a' run in ahead on her."

"Wal, what hendered you an' Palmer?" the Captain asked, chuckling as he joined his companions. "I could tend the mare."

"Say," said Palmer, edging toward the wagon, "le' 's go an' lay that road, an' leave this 'ere job for the constable. It hain't aourn."

"What! flunk aout naow an' hev aour women folks givin' us Hail Columby?" asked the Squire. "No, siree, I 've ben hetcheled all I want tu be. Come on."

With that he led the way up the path, but with as little stomach as the others for the unpleasant duty. He knocked at the door where the woman had gone in; but there was no response, though he could hear her stepping lightly across the floor. He tried the latch and found it fastened; then knocked more loudly. A window over the door was opened, and the woman's voice descended:—

"What d' you want?"

There was a little penthouse roof jutting out over the door, and the Squire backed from beneath it that he might see the speaker. Her face was flushed and defiant, and beside her, peering over the window ledge, was the curious, scared face of a fair-haired little girl.

"We want tu come in," he said, answering her question as he looked up at her.

"Wal, you can't, 'cause Mr. Tyler 's gone away, an' he tol' me not tu let nob'dy in till he come back."

"Oh, come naow, what 's the use? We 're the selec'men, ye know. You'd better let us in."

"I can't help it if you 're the hul taown. I can't let you in, I can't!"

"Wal, then we 'll hafter bust in the door, for we 're a-comin' in, one way or 'nother," said the Squire, taking a more decided tone. "Fay, you an' Palmer fetch a rail off'en the fence." He turned away, and stood with his arms akimbo watching the somewhat slow execution of the order by his companions.

The two figures disappeared from the window; there was a clatter of stove furniture, a sound of pouring water, and the woman reappeared at her coign of vantage as the storming party advanced, carrying a stout rail as a battering ram.

"I give you good warnin'," she said, with her voice higher pitched than before. "If you come anigh, you 'll git scalt."

There was a reek of steam about her, and as she spoke she lifted a large dipper of hot water from a pail and rested it on the window sill.

"Sho, she won't dast tu!" said the Squire contemptuously as his comrades hesitated. "Come on. Let drive nighest tu the latch an' bust it."

They advanced more briskly, and she, drawing back the dipper, called out, "Ta' care, or you 'll ketch it!" and then flung out the contents at them.

The shot fell short of the bearers of the battering ram, and the Squire dodged under shelter of the narrow pent roof and flattened himself against the door, while the charge overshot him and dribbled from the eaves.

"Gosh, hain't she a spunky one!" he exclaimed, in a burst of admiration that exceeded his vexation. "Come on, naow. Quick afore she gits loaded up agin."

But before the order could be executed another volley descended upon the assaulting party, who dropped the rail and retired precipitately; Captain Fay nursing a scalded finger, and Deacon Palmer, whose hat had fallen off within range of the battery, striving to express his feelings within the limits of such mild profanity as a church member might be allowed.

"Wal, you be smart fellers," the Squire commented. "Naow, if I 'd hed a holt o' that 'ere rail"—

"You can hev a holt o' my sheer on 't an' welcome," the Captain generously offered, as he alternately inspected and blew his injured finger.

"Mine tew, gol darn it!" the Deacon declared, venturing near the danger line with a pole, and attempting to insert the end of it in the crown of his hat. Before he could effect a rescue down came a scalding shower, deluging the upturned beaver and barely missing its owner.

The Squire made a determined attack upon the door, kicking

lustily at the panels and throwing his shoulder with all his might against it; but it would not yield, and he desisted when a dash of hot water caught his foot thrust beyond the shelter of the door's hood. Direct attack did not seem to promise success, so he sallied out to his comrades beyond the fire of the garrison, and began plotting strategy.

"We wanter kinder squirmish 'raound till she gits her ammernition used up," said he; "when that 's gone, I 'll resk her claws."

"I do' know 'baout that, the darn' she-cat!" Deacon Palmer remarked dubiously; but he had no thought of raising the siege now, for his fighting blood was up. "I 'm a-goin' tu make a-nother try for that 'ere hat."

"Yes, du, an' me an' Captain 'll make b'lieve go at the door agin."

The Deacon clawed at the hat with the pole at arm's length, the others made a show of attack with the rail, and all drew frequent fire from the enemy, ineffectual but for a further drenching of the hat, which the owner at last secured and hung on a stake to dry.

"My sakes!" he groaned, as he contemplated its limp and bedraggled condition. "I do' know what in time Mis' Palmer 'll say when she sees that 'ere hat. I 've kep' it as good as new for fifteen year, an' naow jest look at it! Looks as if I 'd took a head dive int' the river an' forgot tu take it off."

"If I was you, I 'd ruther hev her see it 'an tu hev her hear what you said. Pretty nigh cussin' for a deacon."

"That I can keep tu myself. The hat I can't."

"Wal, you want tu keep that 'ere tu show your gran'childern when you tell 'em abaout the capture o' Fort Davis," said the Captain.

"It hain't captured yet."

"Wal, it 's a-goin' tu be," said the Squire confidently. "I can hear her scrapin' the dipper in the bottom of the kittle, an' her ammernition 's 'baout spent. Le' 's draw her fire agin."

The feint excited a feeble volley; another brought no response, and it became evident that the amazon's ammunition was exhausted. The besiegers now advanced boldly to the assault. The door yielded to the first vigorous stroke of the battering ram, and victory at last perched on the banner of the selectmen.

"Wal, marm," said the Squire, in his severest official voice, addressing the woman who stood sullenly defiant at the farther side of the scantily furnished kitchen, with one hand on the head of the frightened child, "you ortu be 'shamed o' yourself a-scaldin' taown officers."

"Shamed!" she flared up indignantly. "I sh'd think you was the ones tu be 'shamed! Three men a-tacklin' a woman an' a little girl an' bustin' in doors! Scald you! I wish I c'd bile you!"

"No daoubt on 't, marm, but we won't waste no time a-passin' compliments," and the Squire turned away. "Come, men, le' 's git these 'ere things aout."

The victors hurried as if in fear of relenting before the dis-agreeable duty was accomplished, and soon set the poor and meagre furniture out of doors, yet with a degree of care they felt was due to its valiant defender, who now, without further attempt at useless resistance, went out, leading the child by the hand. Then they fastened the door, and clambered out through a window and went their way, leaving the woman and child standing in silent, dazed despair among their unshrined house-hold gods.

"Gosh! I do' know but I sh'd feel as mean 'f I'd ben stealin' sheep an' got ketched at it." The Squire broke the silence in which the selectmen held self-communion as they drove along the highway. His associates grunted a sympathetic response, and the Deacon ran his hand tenderly over the blistered hat crown.

"I do' know what the critturs live on," the Captain remarked. "All the vituals I see was a bag o' 'taters I fetched aout, an' the' wa'n't more 'n a ha' bushel o' them."

As the Squire's wife set her kitchen in order and put the finishing touches to its neatness (for she was just then, as she expressed it, "aout of a girl, an' duin' my own work"), she often went to the door and looked down the road, wondering what progress the town fathers were making, and with what thorough-ness they would perform their duty. No hopeful sign was given her out of the haze of smoke with which a shift of wind to the northward was thickening the atmosphere, from some distant forest fire, and chilling it with what seemed an unnatural breath, since it choked one with the odor of burnt leaves, and even bore their charred and ashy shapes, wavering as silently as ghosts of dead leaves, in long slants to the ground. The sumac copse shone like a red flame in the blue mist that blurred near objects, and blotted out all beyond the middle distance.

" I p'sume tu say they won't du nothin'," she said to herself.

"Square Dany 's tew soft-hearted, an' the others is afeard o' maddin' someb'dy nuther tu vote agin 'em. My! I wish 't women voted; we 'd show 'em which side their bread was buttered on. Wal, I 'll see if I can spin part of a knot 'fore it 's time tu git dinner a-goin'."

She drew the big wheel, with its white saddle of rolls, from the corner, and set it to humming its musical song while she stepped back and forth beside it; now twirling the wheel swiftly in one way, now slowly the other. After a time the merrier sound of the kettle and the clatter of dinner-getting succeeded the noise of the wheel; then the dinner horn sounded a note pleasant to the ear of the hired man wrestling with the plumed ranks of ripe corn, when, sticking his sickle into the last vanquished shock, he declared an hour's truce. When he had resumed hostilities, and Mrs. Dana, leaving the table uncleared, was assisting digestion by a perusal of the Advocate of Moral Reform, she was disturbed by a timid knock at the door.

Opening it, she was confronted by the unfamiliar faces of a young woman and a little girl. Both bore traces of recent tears, and the child's breath was still broken by an irrepressible sob.

"I would n't 'a' bothered you, ma'am, but 'Mandy was cryin' for somethin' tu eat, an' there wa'n't nothin' tu give her." The young woman spoke in a soft voice, and her dark eyes had a pleading expression that a harder heart than Mrs. Dana's could not have resisted.

"Hungry, is she? Why, good land, come right in. I guess you be, tew, if you hed n't nothin' for her. Set up to the stove. It 's turned raound real cold, an' the fire feels good." She put chairs for her guests, and gave the fire a hospitable punch, and set herself to rearranging the table; piling dirty plates, cups, and saucers, clawing the rumpled cloth into place, brushing the crumbs with one hand into the other, and bustling to the pantry for a fresh supply of bread and the indispensable pie.

"I don't want you tu take no trouble," the woman protested, looking apprehensively at the preparations. "I—I hain't no money tu pay you, but I can spin a spell for you," her eyes dwelling on the wheel.

"Good land, I don't want no pay, an' I hain't goin' tu take no trouble," Mrs. Dana declared. "Trav'lin' fur? Goin' tu see some o' your folks, I p'sume tu say? The little girl hain't yourn? Some related, mebby, but she don't favor you a mite. Mebby you hain't married?"

It was not Mrs. Dana's habit to wait for answers to her questions, but she did now, while the visitor, with downcast eyes, shook her head.

"I you 'd ha' come an hour sooner, you might ha' eat a hot dinner with us," the hostess went on. "But there 's enough left, such as it is, thank goodness. There wa'n't nob'dy but me an' the hired man tu dinner. My husband, he 's gone off on taown business tu-day. He 's fust selec'man, an' they 've gone off 'mongst 'em a-transactin' business. Naow, then, you an' she take right off your bunnets an' shawls, an' set up tu the table."

The visitor arose hastily, and gasped in a scared voice: "No, no! Give 'Mandy a piece o' bread an' butter in her hand, an' we 'll go. We can't stop! Oh no, we can't stop!"

"Be you crazy? I sh'd like to know what 's the reason you can't stop an' eat?"

"Oh, I can't," the woman protested. "We must go right off."

"Wal, then, you hain't a-goin', an' that child hain't a-goin' afore she 's eat a meal o' victuals! Naow tell me your trouble," Mrs. Dana said, in a tone so masterful that, aided by the entreating, hungry eyes of the little girl, it compelled compliance.

"If you 've got tu know," the stranger answered half defiantly, "your man an' the other selec'men come over there," indicating the direction with a sidewise motion of the head; "an' Mr. Tyler, he was gone, an' they was comin' in, an' I hove hot water ontu 'em! Yes, I did. But they broke in the door, an' they sot all the things aout door an' fastened us aout; an', oh dear, I do' know what 's goin' tu be become of us! I wish 't I was dead!" With that she broke down utterly, covered her face with her hands, and sobbed as if her heart would break.

"Wal, I never!" Mrs. Dana gasped, her breath so completely taken away by the revelation that she was obliged to sit down to await its return, burying beneath her ample form the crumpled pages of the "Advocate" where it lay on the cushion into which she sank. The blankness of her face gradually hardened into an expression of proper severity; her gaping mouth closed tightly, then opened again as speech came with renewed breath. "So you 're that woman, be you? You don't look like her. I would n't ha' thought it of you. Haow ever come you tu du so?"

No answer came but sobs from the hidden face. Impelled by an impulse of motherly pity, Mrs. Dana laid her hand gently on the bowed head, and said as gently, "Don't you believe you 'd better tell me all abaout your trouble?"

Then the woman began in a broken voice that grew steadier

as she went on: "I was took sick at the place where I was a-workin', an' they was a-goin' to throw me on t' the taown, but Mr. an' Mis' Tyler took me in an' kep' me till I got well; an' then Mis' Tyler, she took sick, an' there wa'n't nob'dy tu ta' care of her only me, an' so I did till she died; an' then there wa'n't nob'dy tu keep haouse for him, an' so I stayed an' kep' a-stayin', like a fool, but I could n't seem tu help it, they 'd ben so good tu me. An' everybody turned agin us, an' he could n't git no work, an' so we come away from there an' got in here, but it 's jes' as bad; an' this mornin' he started off for Brinkford lookin' for work, an' them men come an' turned us aout, an' now I do' know what we be goin' tu du! Oh dear, I wish 't I was dead!"

Her sobs broke out afresh, and Mrs. Dana waited a little before she asked, "Why wa'n't you married?"

"He wanted tu, but I would n't so soon after she died, an' so we kep' livin' along; an' he said 't wa'n't nob'dy's business 's long 's we sot so by one 'nother as we did."

The moral reformer of Cornbury, suddenly recollecting neglected hospitality, said in a gentler voice: "It don't signify, a-lettin' folks starve afore my face an' eyes! Now set up tu the table. Yes, you 've got tu, an' the little girl 'll set right by, an' help her an' yourself;" and having seated her guests at the table, she busied herself in ministering to them while she silently pondered and cast frequent searching glances up the road.

"When was you expectin' 'Mandy's pa 'd be comin' back?"

"Any time 'most."

"Well, I want tu ketch him when he comes along. An' naow, if you won't eat nothin' more, you may spin a little while if you are a mind tu. You was sayin' you could, wa'n't you? What did you say your name was?"

"Roxy," the woman answered, taking her place at the wheel with the alacrity of accustomed use.

Mrs. Dana watched her, at first doubtfully, then with growing admiration of her agile and skillful movements; and when she had examined the yarn with critical eye and touches, she declared: "I never see nob'dy that could spin sprier an' better. I could n't myself. There, naow, you sit daown an' rest. You need n't spin no more. Sis, is n't that your pa?"

She hastened out to intercept a man whose form seemed to acquire substance as he drew near, as if materializing out of the blue haze. He yielded to her entreaty, which was as much a command. His heavy, good-humored face was blank. While he was wiping his dusty boots on the dooryard knot-grass, she was further gratified by the arrival of the selectmen.

"Hitch your hoss, and come right in, Captain, you an' the Deacon. Oh yes, you got tu. I want you tu," she urged against all excuses, and getting in the rear of her guests left no way open to them but the one she desired them to take. Her husband walked behind her, dumbly wondering at her and went to the depths of speechless astonishment with his colleagues when he found their late antagonist installed in his own kitchen.

"Square Dany," his wife began, without any detail of explanation, "these folks wants tu git married right off, an' I want you tu merry 'em. Stan' right up here, naow, Lem'wil, an' you, Roxy, take a holt o' his han'. There, naow, Square, perform the ceremony."

The matrimonial candidates obediently did as told, but the Squire protested:

"Why, Mis' Dany, I never married a couple in my life."

"Wal, if you 've ben Justice o' the Peace tew hul year, goin' on three, an' do' know haow tu merry folks, the taown 'd better 'lect someb'dy else in your place," she said, in a tone that put him upon his mettle; and since the eyes of his fellow fathers were upon him, he manfully essayed the performance of the unaccustomed duty.

"Du you, j'intly an' severally, solemnly promise, in the presence o' these witnesses, tu take one 'nother for husban' an' wife, for better or wus, be the same more or less, an' promise well an' truly tu perform the same without fear or favor of any man— or woman?" he added, with a happy afterthought.

Lemuel Tyler responded with a hearty affirmative, and Roxy bashfully nodded, as the mistress of ceremonies, with a ready hand, would perforce have obliged her to, had she hesitated. Then the Squire declared, in his best official voice: "By the authority in me vested by the State of Vermont, I du pronounce you man an' wife, tu hev an' tu hol' till death du you part. Asy Dany, Justice of the Peace.—There, I guess that 'll hold, won't it?" he asked, turning to his associates as he wiped his perspiring face.

"I don't see no flaw in the indictment," Captain Fay admitted; "but hain't you goin' tu make no remarks? It 's usuil on sech occasions."

"Wal, yes, I s'pose it is." The Squire pondered as he cleared his throat for further speech. "I will say tu you, Mr. Tyler, that ef you want tu keep peace in the fam'ly you 'd better du putty nigh as Mis Tyler wants you tu; an' tu you, Mis' Tyler, not tu want onreasonable; an' tu both on ye, if one gits sassy, for t' other not to sass back,—in the words of the poet,—

> Ef one throws fire an' the other water,
> Peace will reign in every quarter.

"S'posin' it 's hot water?" the Captain asked, as he tended his forefinger.

"I do' know 's I 've got anything more tu remark," said the Squire.

"Naow set daown, all on ye," his wife commanded, as she bustled into the pantry, where her voice, pitched in a high key, could still be heard: "The' wa'n't no time for preparation, so the' hain't no weddin' cake; but the' 's nut cakes an' cheese a-plenty, an' punkin pie, which is good if I did make it." These she presently brought and pressed upon the company.

Captain Fay picked up the crumpled "Advocate" from the chair in which he was about to seat himself, and studying the title a moment remarked, "Mis' Dany, your Moral Reform paper looks as if it hed ben sot daown on."

Without heeding him she went on: "Naow, ef you hain't no objections, Square Dany, I 'll blow the horn for Hiram, an' he an' Lem'wil can hitch ontu the hay riggin', an' go an' git the things an' put 'em in your tenant haouse. You ben wantin' a good stubbed man in 't, which Lem'wil looks tu be, an' Roxy is the beater tu spin, as I know."

As Squire Dana parted with his associates at the hitching-post he spoke only one word,—"Gosh!"

An Old-Time March Meeting

One day in the latter part of February, Asahel Peck was observed to be abroad on horseback; for, owing to a recent thaw, sleighing was bad, and wheeling worse. Those in the neighborhood of the town house saw him alight in front of that ancient and variously used structure and nail a paper to the battered and punctured door. It read as follows:—

MARCH MEETING

These are to notify and to warn all the Inhabitants of this Town who are legal Voters in Town Meeting to meet at the Town House on the first Tuesday in March the 3rd (proximo) at ten o'clock in the forenoon to transact the following business, viz.

1st to choose a moderator to Govern said meeting, 2nd a town clerk, 3rd, three or more persons to be Select men, Also Over Seeors of the poor, a Town Treasurer, Three or more Listers, a constable and Collector of Town rates or taxes, Grand and petit jurors, One or more Grand Jurymen for the town, Surveyors of the Highways, Fence viewers, pound keepers, Sealers of weights and measures, Sealers of Leather, also one or more tything men and hay wards. Also a committee to Settle with the Overseeors of the Poor also a Committee to settle with the Treasurer and report the state of the Treasury, a Superintending committee for schools, also to consider of the Propriety of adjoining Uriah Cruttenden's Farm to the School District known by the name of the New District and lastly to vote to defray the expenses of the Town the Current year.

ASAHEL PECK ⎫
JONATHAN YOUNG ⎬ Select men.
SEYMOUR HAYS ⎭

Feby 18, 184—.[1]

But few persons troubled themselves to read what could more easily be heard for only twelve days' waiting; and, moreover, every proposed measure of importance had been a subject for discussion at Hamner's tavern, the store, the blacksmith's shop, the shoemaker's, and the mill, as also at the town house itself, on several Sundays, before and after the services, held there alternately by the Methodists and Congregationalists: so that saints and sinners were already informed.

The days went by in sunshine and south wind. On the appointed day many voters came of choice on foot, across fields bare

---

1. Copied from a Ferrisburgh Warning for Town Meeting.

of snow but for drifts still enduring along the fences, while others jolted in wagons over the rutted main highways, superficially dried rough-cast memorials of former difficult travel, one wind-swept mile of it now yielding dust enough for the ransom of a whole tribe of Israel. Others came floundering and splashing along the crossroads, which were narrow lanes of mud between banks of snow sullied with the blown dust of ploughed land and muddy tracks of men and dogs. Overhead, straggling flocks of returning crows drove northward through their broad, clean, aerial thoroughfare. All terrestrial travelers tended, by different routes, toward the town house. Rows of horses lengthened along the neighboring fences. Freemen of all ages, from those newly assuming the responsibilities of voting and the burden of taxation to those beyond the demand of a poll tax, swarmed in at the door. There was a considerable attendance of boys, to whom the bustle inside was more novel and attractive than the feeble beginning of a game of ball outside.

The town house was an unpainted, weather-beaten, clapboarded building of one story, with one rough, plastered room, furnished with rows of pine seats, originally severely plain, but now profusely ornamented with carved initials, dates, and strange devices. A desk and seat on a platform at the farther end, for the accommodation of the town officers, and a huge box stove, so old and rusty that it seemed more like the direct product of a mine than of a furnace, completed the furniture of the room, wherein were now gathered a majority of the male inhabitants of the town. Its fathers, maintaining the dignity of office in stiff, high shirt collars and bell-crowned hats, were grouped behind the desk, planning in semi-privacy the business of the day, while some self-appointed guardians of the public weal stood near, craning their necks and cocking their ears to catch scattered crumbs of the wise discourse. Old acquaintances from the farthest opposite corners of the township, who rarely met but on such occasions, exchanged greetings and neighborhood gossip. Hunters and trappers recounted their exploits to one another and an interested audience of boys. Invalids enjoyed their poor health to the utmost in the relation of its minutest details. Pairs of rough jokers were the centers of applauding groups, while other pairs exchanged experiences in the wintering of stock or discussed weather probabilities. From all arose a babble of voices, the silentest persons present being two or three of the town's poor, who had come to get the earliest intelligence of their disposal.

"Wal, I cal'late we 're goin' tu git an airly spring," said one of a knot of elderly men and middle-aged wiseacres. "When the ol' bear come aout he did n't see no shadder."

"What, the twenty-sixt' o' Febwary?" one of the latter chuckled. "Why, good land o' massy, the sun was er-shinin' jest as bright as 't is today!"

"The twenty-sixt' haint the day! It's the secont, an' it snowed all day!"

"Sho! It 's the twenty-sixt'," the other asserted. "Ev'ybody knows that 'at knows anythin' about signs."

"Wal, I know it 's the secont."

"No, 't ain't nuther!"

"'T is tuther!"

"Wal," drawled big John Dart, "s'posin' the' wan't no bear ary day? What then?"

"What ye think o' this fur a sign?" a tall newcomer asked, pushing his way into the group, carefully holding in his hand a red and yellow cotton handkerchief, gathered at its corners, which he now unfolded, displaying three full-grown grasshoppers, not very active, but unmistakably alive. "There! I picked them up as I come across lots. What ye think o' that?"

There was a general expression of wonder, and Dart exclaimed, after a critical examination of the insects, "Good Lord, deliver us! Ef the grasshoppers is all ready tu transack business as soon 's the snow 's off'n the graound, it won't make no odds tu us if we du hev an airly spring. They 'll eat ev'ry identical thing as soon as it starts."

"Wal, I swanny, Billy Williams 's dressed up consid'able scrumptious fur taown meetin'," the discoverer of the grasshoppers remarked irrelevantly, after a careful survey of the dignitaries grouped behind the desk. "S'pose he cal'lates he 's goin' tu rep'sent the taown next fall?"

"Oh yes. It would n't be usin' on him well tu let him die a ye'rlin'," another responded.

"I do' know 's we 're 'bleeged tu send him on that accaount," the first speaker said. "We don't send folks tu Montpelier fur their health, but fur aour benefit. I never hear'd o' his duin' anythin' gret whilst he was up there."

"I wonder 'f he ever delivered the speech up there 't he prepared," a farmer asked, with a merry twinkle in his eyes, and inquiring faces were turned toward him.

"You never hear'd on 't? Wal, I tell ye 't was a buster. Tom Hamlin hear'd him a-practicin' of it one day when he went there on some errant tu Billy, an' the women folks sent him aout tu the barn tu find him; an' he hear'd him-a-talkin' turrible airnest on the barn floor, an' so he peeked through a crack o' the door tu see who he was a-talkin' tu, an' there stood Billy wi' a paper in his hand, a-motionin' of it aout, an' nob'dy nor nothin' afore him but an ol' poll ram a-stan'in' back in the furder eend. 'Mister Speaker,' says Billy, 'I rise tu make a motion'—Then, as he turned araound tu git the light on his paper, the ol' ram let drive at him an' knocked him a-sprawlin' clean acrost the barn floor. Tom cal'lated Billy hed made his motion."

"Ruther more of a turnaout 'n the' was tu the fust taown meetin' 'at I went tu in this taown," Gran'ther Hill remarked to an old man who sat beside him, looking nearly his own age, but whose simple, almost childlike features were in marked contrast to the strong, grim visage of the veteran ranger.

"I s'pose likely," responded the other, glancing vaguely around. "I wa'n't there."

"Ef you was, you hed n't no business there, fur you wa'n't much more 'n borned," said Gran'ther Hill. "No, sir, the' hain't a livin' man here but me 'at was tu it."

"I s'pose there wa'n't a turrible sight on ye?" his companion suggested.

"Not over twenty on us, all told; an' we hel' it in a log barn 'at stood t' other side o' the river, on Moses Benham's pitch, an' we sot raound on the log mangers, an' the clark writ on the head of a potash berril. We hed n't no sech fix-uppances as these 'ere," pounding the seat with his fist; "an' as fur that 'ere," punching the stove with his cane, "we jest stomped raound tu keep warm, an' did n't fool away much time no longer 'n we was 'bleeged tu."

"I s'pose you git your pension right along, reg'lar?" the younger old man asked.

"Sartainly; it comes as sure as death an' taxes," said Gran'ther Hill. "An' what in blazes is the reason you don't git yourn?"

"Wal, ye see," said the other, "they claim 'at they can't find the roll o' my comp'ny, daown there tu Wash'n'ton,—Comp'ny B, 'Leventh Regiment,—but they say they can't find hide ner hair on't; an' my discharge, that got burnt up 'long wi' all I hed, time o' the fire: so here I be, on the taown." The old man smiled in feeble resignation.

"It 's a damned shame, an' you'd ortu hev your pension," Gran'ther Hill declared.

"Sarved him right fur bein' sech a plaguy fool," said a hard-featured man standing near, speaking not to the two old men, but for their hearing, as he explained to those about him: "He went 'n under his bed, when the haouse was afire, an' got a peck o' wa'nuts 't he 'd fetched up f'm the Lake, an' left his chist wi' all his papers in 't tu burn up. Yis, an' a bran'-new pair o' calf-skin boots."

"I s'pose I kinder lost my head," the old soldier said apologetically, and still striving to smile in spite of a quivering of his chin; "an' the wa'nuts, I fetched 'em a-purpose fur my tew leetle gran'childern; an' I do' know 's I'm sorry 'at I saved 'em, fur they died wi' canker rash, both on 'em, next spring, an' the loss on 'em, jest killed their mother, an' he married agin an' went off West, an' here I be. The' was one leetle chap 'at lived, but he was tew leetle tu remember me, an' they would n't never tell him nothin' 'bout his ol' gran'ther, I s'pose," said the old man, with a sigh and a more pathetic smile.

"Lost his head!" the hard-faced man sneered. "An almighty loss that must ha' ben!"

Certain inarticulate sounds issued from Gran'ther Hill's tooth-less jaws, accompanied by a nervous handling of his staff, which indicated a rising storm that his companion at once strove to prevent, whispering anxiously into the veteran's ear, from which a tuft of grizzled hair bristled like an abatis:—

"Don't fur massy's sake say nothin' tu mad him, Cap'n Hill. He 's a-goin' tu run fur poormarster, an' if he don't git it he 's a-goin' tu bid for aour keepin'. If he gits a spite agin me, he 'll gi' me gowdy. Don't say nothin'."

Thus admonished, Gran'ther Hill corked the vials of his wrath, and contented himself with glowering savagely on its intended object and offering consolation to his friend.

"You need n't be 'shamed on 't, Ros'il. Misfortin hain't no disgrace tu a man 'at 's fit in the 'Leventh agin the British tu Chippewa an' that what-you-call-him's Lane. The disgrace is fur them 'at hain't no respect fur sech duin's. What ye s'pose I'd care 'f I was on the taown? By the Lord Harry, I'd tell 'em 't was an honor tu any taown tu hev a man on it 'at took Ticonderogue, an' was tu Hubbar't'n an' Bennin'ton! The country's goin' tu the divil, it 's a-gittin' so corrup', an' we 'll all be on the taown in a heap in less 'n twenty year, wi' the people's money bein' flung right an' left. I hear 'em a-talkin' o' hevin' ruffs over some o' the bridges. Lord Harry, what next?"

"Good airth an' seas!" exclaimed the good-natured-looking

shoemaker, who had just taken a seat near the veterans. "'T ain't more 'n what we 're all lierble tu. 'T ain't many year sen' the constable useter warn ev'ry man jack of a newcomer tu clear aout lest he come on t' the taown. There was ol' Mister Van Brunt, 'at lived tu New York when he was tu hum, 'at owned more 'n tew thaousan' acres here, come up an' stayed quite a spell; an' so the constable, he up an' warned him aout o' the taown. Van Brunt, says he tu him, 'You go an' ask the selec'men what they 'll take fur this mis'able leetle insi'nificant taown, an' I'll buy the hul on 't.' "

"I tell ye, it don't signify, Ros'il Adams," Gran'ther Hill began, when reminiscences and prophecies were cut short by the clerk's calling the meeting to order.

Comparative quiet fell upon the assembly, that was for a few moments thridded by the thin, whining voice of one of the invalids, who had not completed the details of his last bad spell. The clerk then read the warning that had been taken from the door, and announced the first business to be the choice of a moderator. Thereupon Squire Waite was nominated, and being unanimously elected, took his place beside the clerk behind the desk. He was a tall, portly old man, whose venerable presence was somewhat impaired by a curly chestnut wig. With a voice deep and strong enough to have outborne the clamor of many ordinary ones, he addressed his assembled townsmen:—

"Gentlemen, the next business afore the meetin' is to choose a town clark. Please nomernate some one so to sarve you."

"I nomernate the exper'enced an' deficient present incumberent, Joel Bartlett!" cried Solon Briggs, and the nomination was quickly seconded.

"Joel Bartlett is nomernated and seconted," thundered the moderator. "You 'at 's in favor of him a-sarvin' of you as town clark, say 'Aye.' "

There was a loud affirmative response, and when the squire called, "Contrary-minded, say 'No,' " only Beri Burton answered, though he endeavored to make the noise of a majority.

"Gentlemen, the Ayes appear to hev it, and you hev made ch'ice of Joel Bartlett to sarve you as clark fur the ensuin' year."

The reëlected officer pursed his lips to their roundest and set himself to record the proceedings of the meeting; his choice of implements being divided between a sputtering quill pen and a lead pencil so hard that its only mark upon the paper, unless frequently moistened, was a deep corrugation. The arrangement of his lips seemed especially adapted to the moistening process.

"The next business in order," the moderator declared, after studying the warning, "is tu choose three, four, or five selec'men. Haow many is it your pleasure tu hev?"

It was decided that there should be three, and two separate nominations and elections followed. According to the usual and wise custom, the first member of the old board was retired, the second elected to his place, the third to the second place, and a new man to the third place, for which there were three candidates, each with so considerable a following that a ballot was called for by three or more voters, and a spirited contest ensued. The readiest writers scribbled the names of their candidates on whatever scraps of paper came to hand, which were then cut into slips with jack-knives. These ballots were distributed to the eager voters who crowded around each writer, or were urged upon the wavering and indifferent. Each, when so provided, pushed into the swarming aisle and struggled forward, as if the fate of the nation depended on the immediate deposit of his ballot in the constable's bell-crowned hat, which was now devoted to this sacred service under the vigilant guardianship of its owner. Here, a tall, strong man forced a passage through the crowd, with some smaller, weaker men following easily in his wake. There, a small man, nearly overwhelmed, almost within reach of the voting place, held his ballot at arm's length above his head, like a craft, foundering within sight of port, flying a signal of distress. Having cast their votes, some got out of the press as quickly as possible, while others clung about the voting place, curious to see the last ballot dropped into the hat and to watch the counting.

"Gentlemen, are your votes all in?" called the moderator.

No one responded during the five minutes of grace, and at their expiration the improvised ballot box was emptied on the desk. The counting began, by the clerk and the constable, while the hum of conversation again arose, continuing until the result of the ballot was announced. The rival candidates strove to hide their different emotions under the mask of unconcern, and their adherents soon forgot the brief contest in the strife for a board of listers and other important officers.

The old treasurer, who had through many years' service proved faithful to his charge, was continued as custodian of the town money, kept for the most part in a canvas shot bag conspicuously marked "B. B. Twenty four lbs;" and no one underbidding the old collector's offer to collect the tax for two per cent thereof, he was unanimously reëlected to the dual office of constable and collector.

When it was voted that the selectmen should be overseers of the poor, Roswell Adams was greatly relieved of his anxiety, for he felt sure that at least two of the board were men who would have consideration for an unfortunate old soldier, and he entered quite heartily into the humor of some of the minor elections.

Reuben Black, a blind man, was nominated for fence viewer, and came near being elected.

"You might ha' done wus 'n tu elec' me," said Reuben, "for I c'n smell aout a new fence an' feel aout a lawful one, an' du it in the darkest night jes' 's well as in daylight, an' thet 's more 'n most on 'em c'n du."

John Dart, whose gigantic frame was supported by a more than ample foundation, nominated the shoemaker for inspector of leather, an office without duties or emoluments, and he was unanimously elected.

"Ef I make an' mend your boots, John Dart, I cal'late I'll handle the heft o' the luther in Danvis!" he roared, in a voice that excited the envy of the moderator.

It was a common custom in Vermont, in the first half of this century, to permit all kinds of stock to run at large in the highways, which made it necessary to appoint several poundkeepers, and as many haywards, or hog-howards,* as they were commonly called, whose duty was to keep road-ranging swine within the limits of the highways. Six pound-keepers were now elected, and their barnyards constituted pounds. There was a merry custom, of ancient usage, of electing the most recently married widower to the office of hayward, and it then chanced that Parson Nehemiah Doty, the worthy pastor of the Congregationalists, had been but a fortnight married to his second wife. So an irreverent member of his own flock nominated him for hayward. The nomination was warmly seconded, and he was almost unanimously elected, even the deacons responding very faintly when the negative vote was called; for the parson was a man of caustic humor, and each of its many victims realized that this was a rare opportunity for retaliation. Laughter and applause subsided to decorous silence when the venerable man arose to acknowledge the doubtful honor which had been conferred upon him; and he spoke in the solemn and measured tones that marked the delivery

---

* Impounders of stray hogs (Ed.).

of his sermons, but the clerical austerity of his face was lightened a little by a twinkle of his cold gray eyes:—

"Mr. Moderator and fellow townsmen, in the more than a score of years that I have labored among you, I have endeavored faithfully to perform, so far as in me lay, the duties of a shepherd: to keep within the fold the sheep which were committed to my care, to watch vigilantly that none strayed from it, and to be the humble means of leading some into its shelter. Thus while you were my sheep I have acted as your shepherd, but since you are no longer sheep I will endeavor to perform as faithfully the office of your hayward."

"Wal, haow is 't?" John Dart inquired of the nominator. "Hev ye got much the start o' the parson? Or hev ye?"

When every office of the town had been filled, a tax of eight per cent on the grand list was voted, after violent opposition by a considerable minority of economists. Then a sharp-featured man, who had for some time awaited the opportunity, perched on the edge of his seat like some ungainly bird about to take flight, arose and spoke:—

"Mr. Moderator, it 's my 'pinion, an' I guess 't is most ev'rybody's else's, 'at we ben a-payin' aout more money fur taown 'xpenses 'an we ortu, in p'rtic'lar fur keepin' aour porpers. You look a' one item,—fifty dollars fur keepin' the Bassett boy! Fifty dollars fur keepin' of a idjit,—as much as 't would ha' cost tu ha' wintered tew yoke o' oxen, pooty nigh! Why, it 's ridic'lous!" He paused to give his audience time to consider the extravagant cost of supporting the Bassett boy, who had been a town charge for many years, yet by title, at least, seemed possessed of perennial youth, having been designated in the town reports for forty years as "the Bassett boy." "Course we wanter du what 's right an' proper by aour porpers, but we don't wanter parmper 'em, an' we got tu be equinomercal. Naow what I was a-goin' tu say is 'at we hev sometimes heretobefore let aout the keepin' of aour poor to the lowest bidder, an' it hes ben quite a savin' tu the taown; an' considerin' haow hefty aour expenses hes ben durin' the past year, we might du wus 'an tu try it agin."

As Esquire Hard parted his coat tails and resumed his perch on the edge of the seat, another thrifty townsman arose to say, "I think the idee 's a good one, an' if the gentleman 'll put it in the shape of a motion, I'll secont it."

Thereupon the esquire got up such a little way and for such a little while that he began at once to part his coat tails while he said, "I move 'at the s'lec'men let aout the keepin' of the taown poor tu the lowest bidder," which was immediately seconded.

Yet before it could be put to vote a few made earnest protest against this barbarous but then not uncommon custom. The veteran of Ticonderoga got upon his feet with alacrity, and commanded attention with vigorous thumps of his staff as much as by his imperative voice, shaken and cracked by the heat of his indignation.

"Mr. Moderator, is the voters o' this 'ere taown white folks, or be they a pack o' damned heatherns?"

"Order! Order!" the moderator thundered.

"I did n't say they was damned, but they will be if they don't quit sech cussedness. A-biddin' off the poor tu vandew is a cussed shame! I don't keer whether they be God's poor or the divil's poor, or poor divils. 'T 'ould be humaner tu fat 'em up an' boocher 'em fur the' taller 'an what it 'ould be to starve 'em the way they will be. Yes, by a damned sight!"

Again Squire Waite thundered, "Order! Order! We must hev order!" while Gran'ther Hill continued, "You need n't take no pride in what I say, Square Waite, but I swear I will hev vent, an' I do' know but I've hed all I kin 'thaout hittin' someb'dy," and he sat down, still snorting and growling.

His phlegmatic son declared, "It did n't somehow sca'cely seem Christian duin's fur tu bid off humern white folks."

"The heft of aour poor aire in no ways tu blame fur bein' where they be, an' we'd better skimp some'eres else!" shouted the shoemaker.

"Gol dum th' poor tax!" mumbled Beri Burton. "Give 'em puddin' an' milk the year raoun', I say. Gol dum the poor tax!"

Before this many of the voters had dispersed, thinking all important business had been done, and others were impatient to get home by chore time, which was close at hand, as the waning afternoon admonished them: so that when the motion was put to vote, it was passed by a large majority. Then the first selectman announced that "bids for the support of our town's poor would now be received," while the old soldier of 1812 and his fellow paupers awaited the degree of misery to which they should be consigned.

One of the minority, whose plump, good-humored face gave proof that no living thing would suffer under his care, bid a little below the last year's cost. The anxious faces of the paupers brightened during the pause that succeeded this offer; but it only lasted while Peter Flint, the late reviler of the old soldier, after a brief mental computation, made a lower bid; and then another competitor entered the lists, and after a sharp contest of alternately decreasing bids, from which the rosy-faced farmer retired, the contract was awarded to Peter Flint.

"That means short rations fur us poor folks," said Roswell. "Why did n't a cannern ball knock my mis'able head off? I wish 't it hed!"

"No, ye don't nuther, I tell ye," Gran'ther Hill declared, with emphatic thumps of his staff on the floor. "An' you hain't a-goin' tu starve nuther, if aour 'tater bin an' pork berril hol's aout. I'm a-goin' tu take ye hum along wi' me tu visit a year, an' the taown may go tu the divil fur all o' me. A-sellin' off men 'at fit fur the' country! By the Lord Harry, I would n't never fit fur it if I 'd ha' knowed what a passel o' maggits it was a-goin' tu breed. I swear I won't agin, come what may!"

"You 're turrible good, Cap'n Hill," faltered Roswell, overcome by this hospitable offer of a comfortable home, "but I don't b'lieve I 'd ortu trouble ye, an' mebby they—they won't let me."

"Shet yer head, an' go 'long an' git int' the waggin. I sh'ld like tu see 'em stop ye!" Gran'ther Hill growled hoarsely, glowering fiercely on every one within range of his vision. "Jozeff, onhitch the team, an' le's be a-goin' hum."

"I p'sume like 'nough it 'll be all right wi' M'ri, his a-comin' in so sort o' onexpected," Joseph confided to Sam Lovel as he untied the halters; "but, Sam Hill, I guess by the time father 's put him through Ticonderogue ev'ry day for three four weeks a-runnin', he 'll think he 'd ortu hev tew pensions. Gosh! it 'most seems sometimes 's 'ough I 'd ortu hev one, arter all I 've endured in them 'ere battles."

"Wal, if ary one on 'em gits sick on 't, you can send Ros'ell over tu aour haouse a spell," said Sam Lovel.

"An' when he gits Hill's folks an' you all eat aout, Lovel, we 'll give him a try down tu aour haouse," said John Dart, in a loud, confidential whisper that was like a gust of welcome south wind to the two old men already in the lumber wagon. "Skin Flint 'll haf ter wait awhile fur a chance tu starve Uncle Ros'ell an' git paid for it."

There was a stir of curiosity among the groups before the town house, and sentences were left unfinished, or finished unheard by the audience, as a stranger appeared there, a traveler, evidently, for he carried a carpet-bag, and the newness of his well-fitting clothes was worn off with far-journeying. He searched the faces that were turned toward him, not as if in quest of a familiar one, but as if for one that promised the readiest answer to a question.

"Can you tell me, sir, if old Mr. Adams is here?" he asked a genial-looking farmer.

"That 's him 'at 's jest got inter Joe Hill's waggin," was the answer, and a half dozen ready forefingers indicated the vehicle.

Giving hasty thanks for the information, the stranger, a bright, alert-looking young fellow, hurried over, and asked with some embarrassment, dividing his inquiring glances between Gran'ther Hill and the shabby old man, "Is this Mr. Adams?"

"That 's my name," the latter answered, staring blankly at the questioner; and Gran'ther Hill, looking very grim, nodded in confirmation.

"Why, gran'pa, how d' ye do?" cried the young man, in a hearty voice. "You don't know me, do you?" he said, as the old man, still staring, responded in a maze of wonder, "Haow d' ye du, sir?"

"I 'm your gran'son, John White."

"Good Lord! you hain't!" the old man exclaimed, half incredulous; and then, studying the smiling face: "Oh, you be! I can see your ma's looks in your eyes jest as plain! Oh, my good Lord!" and he quite broke down.

The young man's eyes were moist, and he was making futile efforts to swallow a lump in his throat. Gran'ther Hill cleared his own with a sound between a growl and a howl, and cursing under his breath his "damned ol' dried-up gullet," and Joseph and Sam looked intently at nothing away off in the fields, while they groped blindly in their pockets for handkerchiefs.

"I do' know, but it kinder seems 's 'ough I ketched cold in that 'ere dumbed taown haouse," said Joseph, snuffling. "I du reg'lar 'most every March meetin'."

"I guess we all did," Sam urged, with a weak little laugh.

"Well, gran'pa," the stranger said, steadying his voice, "where be you stayin'? Or shall we go over to the hotel?"

"I—I don't stay nowheres,—not yit," his grandfather replied.

"The' hain't no hotel!" growled Gran'ther Hill,—"nothin' only Harmner's cussed tarvern. You 're a-goin' hum 'long wi' me, both on ye, jes' 's yer gran'sir sot aout tu! Come, pile in here, young man. Hurry up yer cakes, Jozeff, an' le's be a-pikin'."

The newcomer demurred in vain, and presently the party went lumbering on its homeward way.

The band chariot of a circus could not have attracted more attention, for the news had run like wildfire through the dispersing assembly that "ol' Uncle Ros'ell's gran'son had come fr'm aout West arter the ol' man, an' was a-goin' tu take him right off'n the taown."

It was as wonderful as a story out of a book.

The freeholders dispersed from the town house more rapidly than they had gathered. The company of ball players on the common was reduced to the few boys whose homes were nearest. The chimney of the deserted town house was scattering on the wind the last wisp of smoke from the expiring fire as Gran'ther Hill, with his captured guests beside him, driving over the crest of Stony Brook Hill, cast a last triumphant glance back upon the scene.

Charles W. Eliot

Charles W. Eliot (1834–1926), scion of a Boston Brahmin family, was president of Harvard from 1869-1909. Though he is out of place in the generally rural company of writers in this volume, his "John Gilley," first published in The Century Magazine *(November, 1899) as one of a series titled "The Forgotten Millions," can not justifiably be excluded. Eliot's lifelike and sympathetic portraiture of John Gilley, whom he had known during many summers on Mt. Desert Island, is a minor classic that long enjoyed high esteem but for a generation or two has gone into undeserved eclipse. Perhaps the most significant aspect of this little biography is Eliot's feeling for his subject. Antipodally separated by occupation, class, and education, the university president and the Maine islander share a certain cultural and spiritual heritage traceable back to their New England and ultimately English origins. The text reprinted here is that of* The Century Magazine, *Volume 59.*

John Gilley

To be absolutely forgotten in a few years is the common fate of mankind. Isaac Watts did not exaggerate when he wrote:

> Time, like an ever-rolling stream,
>   Bears *all* its sons away;
> They fly forgotten, as a dream
>   Dies at the opening day.

With the rarest exceptions, the death of each human individual is followed in a short time by complete oblivion, so far as living human memories are concerned. Even family recollection or tradition quickly becomes dim, and soon fades utterly away. Few of us have any clear transmitted impression of our great-grandparents; some of us could not describe our grandparents. Even men accounted famous at their deaths slip from living memories and become mere shadows or word-pictures—shadows or pictures which too often distort or misrepresent the originals. Not one human being in ten million is really long remembered. For the mass of mankind absolute oblivion, like death, is sure. But what if it is? Should this indubitable fact affect injuriously the mortal life in this world of the ordinary human being? Not at all. For most men and women the enjoyments, interests, and duties of this world are just as real and absorbing at the moment, as they would be if the enjoying, interested, and dutiful individuals could imagine that they were long to be remembered on this earthly stage. A few unusually imaginative and ambitious persons are doubtless stimulated and supported by the hope of undying fame—a hope which in the immense majority of such cases proves to be a pure delusion. The fact is that forelooking is not a common occupation of the human mind. We all live, as a rule, in the present and the past, and take very little thought for the future. Now, in estimating the aggregate well-being and happiness of a community or a nation, it is obviously the condition of the obscure millions, who are sure to be absolutely forgotten, that it is most important to see and weigh aright; yet history and biography alike neglect these humble, speechless multitudes, and modern fiction finds it profitable to portray the most squalid and vicious sides of the life of these millions rather than the best and the commonest. Thus the facts about the life of the common multitude go unobserved, or at least unrecorded, while fiction paints that life in false colors.

This paper describes with accuracy the actual life of one of the to-be-forgotten millions. Is this life a true American type? If it is, there is good hope for our country.

John Gilley was born February 22, 1822, at the Fish Point on Great Cranberry Island, Maine, whither his mother, who lived on Baker's Island, had gone to be confined at the house of Mrs. Stanley, a midwife. Baker's Island lies nearly four miles from the island of Mount Desert. It is a roundish island, a little more than half a mile long from north to south, and a little less than half a mile wide from east to west. At low tide it is connected with another much larger island, called Little Cranberry, by a reef and bar about a mile long; but by half-tide this bar is entirely covered. Almost all the coasting-vessels which come from the westward, bound to the Bay of Fundy or to the coast of Maine east of Frenchman's Bay, pass just outside of Baker's Island; and, as this island has some dangerous ledges near it, the United States built a lighthouse on its highest part in the year 1828. The island has no good harbor; but in the summer small vessels find a safe anchorage on the north side of it, except in easterly storms. The whole shore of the island is bare rock, and the vegetation does not approach the ordinary level of high water, the storm-waves keeping the rocks bare far above and behind the smooth-water level of high tide. There are many days in every year when it is impossible to land on the island or to launch a boat from it. In the milder half of the year the island is of course a convenient stopping-place for offshore fishermen, for it is several miles nearer the fishing-grounds than the harbors of Mount Desert proper. In the first years of this century the island was uninhabited, and was covered by a growth of good-sized trees, both evergreen and deciduous.

About the year 1812, William Gilley of Norwood's Cove, at the foot of Somes Sound on its west side, and Hannah Lurvey, his wife, decided to move on to Baker's Island with their three little children and all their goods. Up to that time he had got his living chiefly on fishing- or coasting-vessels; but, like most young men of the region, he was also something of a wood-cutter and farmer. He and his wife had already accumulated a little store of household goods and implements, and tools for fishing and farming. They needed no money wherewith to buy Baker's Island. There it lay in the sea, unoccupied and unclaimed; and they simply took possession of it.

William Gilley was a large, strong man, six feet tall, and weighing over two hundred pounds. His father is said to have come from Great Britain at fourteen years of age. Hannah Gilley was a robust woman, who had lived in Newburyport and Byfield, Massachusetts, until she was thirteen years old, and had there had much better schooling than was to be had on the island of Mount Desert. She was able to teach all her children to read, write, and cipher; and all her life she valued good reading, and encouraged it in her family. Her father, Jacob Lurvey, was born in Gloucester, Massachusetts, and married Hannah Boynton of Byfield. The name Lurvey is a good transliteration of the German Loewe, which is a common name among German Jews; and there is a tradition in the Lurvey family that the first Lurvey, who emigrated to Massachusetts in the seventeenth century, was of Jewish descent and came from Archangel in Russia. It is noticeable that many of the Lurveys have Old Testament names, such as Reuben, Levi, Samuel, Isaac, and Jacob, and that their noses tend to be aquiline. This was the case with most of the children of William and Hannah Gilley. The father of Hannah served in the Revolutionary army as a boy. He lived to the age of ninety-two, and had ten children and seventy-seven grandchildren. The Lurveys are therefore still numerous at South-West Harbor and the vicinity.

For William Gilley the enterprise of taking possession of Baker's Island involved much heavy labor, but few unaccustomed risks. For Hannah, his wife, it was different. She already had three little children, and she was going to face for herself and her family a formidable isolation which was absolute for considerable periods in the year. Moreover, she was going to take her share in the severe labors of a pioneering family. Even to get a footing on this wooded island—to land lumber, live stock, provisions, and the implements of labor, and to build the first shelter—was no easy task. A small, rough beach of large stones was the only landing-place, and just above the bare rocks of the shore was the forest. However, health, strength, and fortitude were theirs; and in a few years they had established themselves on the island in considerable comfort. Nine more children were born to them there; so that they ultimately had a family of twelve children, of whom six were sons and six daughters. All these children grew to maturity. Fortunately, the eldest child was a girl, for it was the mother that most needed help. Three of the children are still (1899) living, two of them over eighty years of age and one over ninety. Nine of the twelve children married, and to them were born fifty-eight children, of whom forty-five are still living.

John Gilley was the tenth child and also the youngest son, and when he was born the family had already been ten years on the island, and had transformed it into a tolerable farm. When he began to look about him, his father was keeping about six cows, a yoke of oxen, two or three young cattle, about fifty sheep, and three or four hogs. Several of the children were already contributing by their labor to the support of the family. The girls, by the time they were twelve years old, were real helpers for the mother. They tended the poultry, made butter, and spun wool. [A] photograph [seen by Eliot] of one of the daughters is declared by a surviving brother to be the perfect image of their mother. The boys naturally helped in the work of the father. He, unaided except by his boys, had cleared a considerable portion of the island, burning up in so doing a fine growth of trees— spruce, fir, birth, and beech. With his oxen he had broken up the cleared land, hauled off part of the stones and piled them on the protruding ledges, and gradually made fields for grass and other crops. In the earlier years, before flour began to be cheap at the Mount Desert "stores," he had even raised a little wheat on the island; but the main crops besides hay were potatoes and other vegetables for the use of the family and cattle. The son is still living who carried a boat-load of wheat to Somesville, had it ground and sifted into three grades, and carried all three back to the island for winter use. The potato-bug and potato-rot were then unknown, and the island yielded any wished-for amount of potatoes. The family often dug from two to three hundred bushels of potatoes in a season, and fed what they did not want to their cattle and hogs.

Food at the island was habitually abundant. It was no trouble to get lobsters. No traps were needed; they could be picked up in the shallow water along the rocky shore. Fresh fish were always to be easily procured, except in stormy weather and in cold and windy February and March. A lamb could be killed at any time in the summer. In the fall, in sorting the flock of sheep, the family killed from ten to fifteen sheep; and what they could not use as fresh mutton they salted. Later in the season, when the weather turned cold, they killed a "beef-critter," and sometimes two when the family grew large. Part of this beef was salted, but part was kept frozen throughout the winter to be used fresh. Sea-birds added to their store of food. Shooting them made sport for the boys. Ducks and other sea-fowl were so abundant in the fall that the gunners had to throw away the bodies of the birds, after picking off all the feathers. The family never bought any salt pork, but every winter made a year's supply. Although codfish were easily accessible, the family made no use of salt cod. They preferred mackerel, which were to be taken in the near waters in some month of every year. They had a few nets, but they also caught mackerel on the hook. During the summer and early autumn the family had plenty of fresh vegetables.

For clothing the family depended mostly on wool from their own sheep. They used very little cotton. There were spinning-wheels and looms in the house, and the mother both spun and wove. Flax they raised on the island, and from it made a coarse kind of linen, chiefly for towels. They did, however, buy a cotton warp, and filled it with wool, thus making a comfortable sort of sheet for winter use or light blanket for summer. The wool of at least fifty sheep was used every year in the household, when the family had grown large. The children all went barefoot the greater part of the year; but in the winter they wore shoes or boots, the eldest brother having learned enough of the shoe-maker's art to keep the family supplied with footwear in winter. At that time there were no such things as rubber boots, and the family did not expect to have dry feet.

Their uses for money were few; but some essentials to comfort they must procure at the store, seven miles away, at South-West Harbor, in return for money or its equivalent. Their available resources for procuring money were very much like those of similar families to-day in the same neighborhood. They could sell or exchange butter and eggs at the store, and they could sell in Boston dried fish and feathers. One of John's elder brothers shot birds enough in a single year to yield over a hundredweight of feathers, worth fifty cents a pound in Boston. The family shipped their feathers to Boston every year by a coasting-vessel; and this product represented men's labor, whereas the butter and eggs represented chiefly the women's labor. The butter was far the best of the cash resources; and so it remains to this day in these islands. It sold in the vicinity at twelve and a half cents a pound. There was one other source of money, namely, smoked herring. The herring which abound in these waters had at that time no value for bait; but smoked herring could be sold in New York, which was the best market for them, at from seventy-five cents to one dollar and ten cents a box, each box holding half a bushel. The herring were caught, for the most part, in gill-nets; for there were then no weirs and no seines. The family had their own smoke-house, and made the boxes themselves from lumber which was sawed for them at the Somesville or the Duck Brook saw-mill. Each of these saw-mills was at least nine miles distant from Baker's Island; so that it was a serious undertaking, requiring favorable weather, to boat the lumber from the mill and land it safely at the rough home beach. The family nailed the boxes together out of the sawed lumber in the early fall, and packed them with the fragrant fish; and then some coasting-vessel, usually a schooner owned in a neighboring island, carried the finished product to distant New York, and brough back, after a month or two, clear cash to pay for the winter's stores.

In this large and united family the boys stayed at home and worked for their parents until they were twenty-one years of age, and the girls stayed at home until they were married and had homes of their own or had come of age. All the boys and three of the girls were ultimately married. The three girls who did not marry went away from home to earn money by household labor, factory work, nursing, or sewing. It was not all work for the children on the island, or, indeed, for the father and mother. In the long winter evenings they played checkers and fox and geese; and the mother read to the family until the children grew old enough to take their share in reading aloud. Out of doors they played ball, and in winter coasted on the snow. The boys, as soon as they were ten or twelve years of age, were in and out of boats much of the time, and so attained that quick, instinctive use of oar, sail, and tiller in which lies safety. When they grew older they had the sport of gunning, with the added interest of profit from the feathers. Their domestic animals were a great interest as well as a great care. Then, they always had before them some of the most splendid aspects of nature. From their sea-girt dwelling they could see the entire hemisphere of the sky; and to the north lay the grand hills of Mount Desert, with outline clear and sharp when the northwest wind blew, but dim and soft when southerly winds prevailed. In every storm a magnificent surf dashed up on the rock-bound isle. In winter the low sun made the sea toward the south a sheet of shimmering silver; and all the year an endless variety of colors, shades, and textures played over the surfaces of hills and sea. The delight in such visions is often but half conscious in persons who have not the habit of reflection; but it is nevertheless a real source of happiness, which is soon missed when one brought up amid such pure and noble scenes is set down among the straitened, squalid, ugly sights of a city. On the whole, the survivors of that isolated family look back on their childhood as a happy one; and they feel a strong sense of obligation to the father and mother—particularly to the mother, because she was a person of excellent faculties and an intellectual outlook. Like most of her people for two generations, she was a member of the Congregational Church; and in the summer-time she took the eldest children nearly every Sunday in

mild weather to the church at South-West Harbor, going seven
miles each way in an open boat. To be sure, the minister taught
that hell was paved with infants' skulls, and descriptions of hellfire and the undying worm formed an important part of every
discourse. Some of the children supposed themselves to accept
what they heard at church; but the mother did not. She bought
books and read for herself; and by the time she had borne half
a dozen children she could no longer accept the old beliefs, and
became a Universalist, to which more cheerful faith she adhered
till her death.

It is obvious that this family on its island domain was much
more self-contained and independent than any ordinary family is
today, even under similar circumstances. They got their fuel,
food, and clothing as products of their own skill and labor, their
supplies and resources being almost all derived from the sea and
from their own fields and woods. In these days of one crop on a
farm, one trade for a man, and factory labor for whole families,
it is not probable that there exists a single American family which
is so little dependent on exchange of products, or on supplies resulting from the labor of others, as was the family of William
and Hannah Gilley from 1812 to 1842. It should also be observed that sea-shore people have a considerable advantage in
bringing up boys, because boys who become good boatmen must
have an admirable training in alertness, prompt decision, resource
in emergencies, and courageous steadiness in difficulties and dan-
gers. The shore fisherman or lobsterman on the coast of Maine,
often going miles to sea alone in a half-decked boat, is liable to
all sorts of vexatious or formidable weather changes—in summer
to fog, calms, and squalls, in winter to low-lying icy vapor, blinding snow, and the sudden northwester at zero, against which he
must beat homeward with the flying spray freezing fast to hull,
sails, and rigging. The youth who learns to wring safety and
success out of such adverse conditions has been taught by these
struggles with nature to be vigilant, patient, self-reliant, and
brave. In these temperate regions the adverse forces of nature
are not, as they sometimes are in the tropics, irresistible and over-
whelming. They can be resisted and overcome by man; and so
they develop in successive generations some of the best human
qualities.

It resulted from the principles in which the children had been
brought up that no one of the boys began to save much of anything for himself until he was twenty-one years of age. It was

therefore 1843 before John Gilley began to earn money on his own account. Good health, a strong body, skill as a sailor, and some knowledge of farming, stock-raising, and fishing, he had acquired. In what way should he now begin to use these acquisitions for his own advantage? A fortunate change in his father's occupation fifteen years before probably facilitated John's entrance on a career of his own. William Gilley had been appointed light-keeper in 1828, with a compensation of three hundred and fifty dollars a year in money, the free occupation of a house, and all the sperm-oil he could use in his household. He held this place until the year 1849, when, on the coming into power of the Whig party, he was turned out and a Whig was appointed in his place. Perhaps in recognition of his long service, it was considerately suggested to him that he might retain his position if he should see fit to join the dominant party; but to this overture he replied, with some expletives, that he would not change his political connection for all the lighthouses in the United States. Now, three hundred and fifty dollars a year in cash, besides house and light, was a fortune to any coast-of-Maine family seventy years ago,— indeed, it still is,—and William Gilley undoubtedly was able to lay up some portion of it, besides improving his buildings, live stock, boats, tools, and household furniture. From these savings the father was able to furnish a little money to start his sons each in his own career. This father was himself an irrepressible pioneer, always ready for a new enterprise. In 1837, long before he was turned out of the lighthouse, he bought for three hundred dollars Great Duck Island, an uninhabited island about five miles southwest of Baker's Island, and even more difficult of access, his project being to raise live stock there. Shortly after he ceased to be lightkeeper, when he was about sixty-three years old and his youngest children were grown up, he went to live on Great Duck, and there remained almost alone until he was nearly eighty years of age. His wife Hannah had become somewhat infirm, and was unable to do more than make him occasional visits on Duck Island. She died at sixty-nine, but he lived to be ninety-two. Each lived in their declining years with one of their married sons, Hannah on Little Cranberry and William on Baker's. Such is the natural mode of taking care of old parents in a community where savings are necessarily small and only the able-bodied can really earn their livelihood.

John Gilley's first venture was the purchase of a part of a small coasting-schooner called the *Preference,* which could carry about one hundred tons, and cost between eight and nine hundred dollars. He became responsible for one third of her value, paying down one or two hundred dollars, which his father probably lent him. For the rest of the third he obtained credit for a short time from the seller of the vessel. The other two owners were men who belonged on Great Cranberry Island. The owners proceeded to use their purchase during all the mild weather—perhaps six months of each year—in carrying paving-stones to Boston. These stones, unlike the present rectangular granite blocks, were smooth cobblestones picked up on the outside beaches of the neighboring islands. They of course were not found on any inland or smooth-water beaches, but only where heavy waves rolled the beach-stones up and down. The crew of the *Preference* must therefore anchor her off an exposed beach, and then, with a large dory, boat off to her the stones which they picked up by hand. This work was possible only during moderate weather. The stones must be of tolerably uniform size, neither too large nor too small; and each one had to be selected by the eye and picked up by the hand. When the dory was loaded, it had to be lifted off the beach by the men standing in the water, and rowed out to the vessel; and there every single stone had to be picked up by hand and thrown on to the vessel. A hundred tons having been thus got aboard by sheer hard work of human muscle, the old craft, which was not too seaworthy, was sailed to Boston, to be discharged at what was then called the "Stone Wharf" in Charlestown. There the crew threw the stones out of her hold on to the wharf by hand. They therefore lifted and threw these hundred tons of stone three times at least before they were deposited on the city's wharf. The cobblestones were the main freight of the vessel; but she also carried dried fish to Boston, and fetched back goods to the island stores of the vicinity. Some of the island people bought their flour, sugar, dry-goods, and other family stores in Boston through the captain of the schooner. John Gilley soon began to go as captain, being sometimes accompanied by the other owners and sometimes by men on wages. He was noted among his neighbors for the care and good judgment with which he executed their various commissions, and he knew himself to be trusted by them. This business he followed for several years, paid off his debt to the seller of the schooner, and began to lay up money. It was an immense satisfaction to him to feel himself thus established in an honest business which he understood, and in which he was making his way. There are few solider satisfactions to be won in this world by anybody, in any condition of life. The scale of the business—large or small—makes little difference in the measure of content.

At that time—about 1843 to 1850—there were very few guides to navigation between Mount Desert and Boston compared with the numerous marks that the government now maintains. Charts were lacking, and the government had issued no coast-pilot. Blount's "Coast-Pilot" was the only book in use among the coastwise navigators, and its description of the coast of Maine, New Hampshire, and Massachusetts was very incomplete, though tolerably accurate in the few most important regions. It was often anxious business for the young owners of an old, uninsured vessel to encounter the various weather of the New England coast between the 1st of April and the 1st of December. Their all and sometimes their lives were at stake on their own prudence, knowledge, and skill. None of them had knowledge of navigation in the technical sense; they were coasting sailors only, who found their way from point to point along the shore by practice, keen observation, and good memory for objects once seen and courses once safely steered. The young man who can do this work successfully has some good grounds for self-respect. At this business John Gilley laid up several hundred dollars. In a few years he was able to sell the *Preference* and buy half of a much better vessel called the *Express*. She was larger, younger, and a better sailer, and cost her purchasers between fifteen and sixteen hundred dollars. He followed the same business in the *Express* for several years more, laying her up in the late autumn and fitting her out again every spring. The winters he generally spent with his father and mother, or with one of his married brothers; but even in such periods of comparative repose he kept busy, and was always trying to make a little money. He was fond of gunning, and liked it all the better because it yielded feathers for sale. In December, 1853, he was staying with his brother Samuel Gilley on Little Cranberry Island, and gunning as usual; but his brother observed that he did not sell the feathers which he assiduously collected. That winter there was a school-teacher from Sullivan on Little Cranberry, who seemed to be an intelligent and pleasing girl. He made no remarks on the subject to his brother; but that brother decided that John was looking for a wife—or, as this brother expressed it at the age of eighty-two, "John was thinking of looking out for the woman; he saved his feathers—and actions speak louder than words." Moreover, he sold his vessel at Rockland, and found himself in possession of nine or ten hundred dollars in money, the product of patient industry, and not the result of drawing a prize or two in the fishing lottery. In the following spring he went with six or seven other men, in a low-priced fishing-vessel of about thirty-five tons which his brother Samuel and he had bought, up the Bay of Fundy and to the banks between Mount Desert and Cape Sable, fishing for cod and haddock. Every fortnight or three weeks the brothers came home to land their fish and get supplies; but the schoolmistress had gone home to Sullivan. During that spring John Gilley crossed more than once to Sutton's Island, an island about a mile long, which lies between the Cranberry Islands and the island of Mount Desert, with its long axis lying nearly east and west. On this island he bought that season a rough, neglected farm of about fifty acres, on which stood a house and barn. It was a great undertaking to put the buildings into habitable condition and clear up and improve the few arable fields. But John Gilley looked forward to the task with keen interest and a good hope, and he had the definite purpose of providing here a permanent home for himself and a wife.

When cold weather put an end to the fishing season, John Gilley, having provided all necessary articles for his house, sailed over to Sullivan, distant about eighteen miles, in his fishing-vessel, and brought back to the home on Sutton's Island Harriet Bickford Wilkinson, the schoolmistress from Sullivan. The grandfather of Harriet Wilkinson came to Sullivan from Portsmouth, New Hampshire, in 1769, and her mother's family came from York, Maine. The marriage took place on December 25, 1854, when John was thirty-two and Harriet was twenty-five; and both entered with joy upon married life at their own island farm. She was a pretty woman, but delicate, belonging to a family which was thought to have a tendency to consumption. . . . In the summer of 1855 he spent about half his time on this same vessel which had brought home his wife, and made a fair profit on the fishing; and the next year he sometimes went on short trips of shore fishing, but that was the last of his going away from the farm. Whatever fishing he did afterward he did in an open boat not far from home, and he went coasting no more. A son was born to them, but lived only seven months; and soon the wife's health began to fail. A wife's sickness, in the vast majority of families, means, first, the loss of her labor in the care and support of the household, and, secondly, the necessity of hiring some woman to do the work which the wife cannot do. This necessity of hiring is a heavy burden in a family where little money is earned, although there may be great comfort so far as food, fire, and clothing are concerned. His young wife continuing to grow worse, John Gilley tried all means that were possible to him to restore her health. He consulted the neighboring physicians, bought quantities of medicine in great variety, and tried in every way that love or duty could suggest to avert the threatening blow. It was all in vain. Harriet Gilley lived only two years and a half after her marriage, dying in June, 1857. At this period, his expenses being large and his earning power reduced, John Gilley was forced to borrow a little money. The farm and the household equipment had absorbed his whole capital.

On April 27, 1857, there came from Sullivan, to take care of Harriet, Mary Jane Wilkinson, her cousin. This cousin was only twenty-one years of age; but her father was dead, and her mother had married again. She had helped her mother till she was almost twenty-one years of age, but now felt free. Until this cousin came, nieces and a sister of John Gilley had helped him to take care of his dying wife. The woman relatives must always come to the aid of a family thus distressed. To help in taking care of the farm and in fishing, John Gilley habitually hired a man all through the season, and this season of 1857 the hired man was his wife's brother. When Harriet Gilley died, there was still the utmost need of a woman on the farm; so Mary Jane Wilkinson stayed during the summer and through the next winter, and before the end of that winter she had promised to marry John Gilley. There were at that time eight houses on Sutton's Island, and more permanent residents than there are now. Mary Jane Wilkinson was fond of the care of animals and of farm duties in general. She found at the farm only twelve hens, a cow, and a calf, and she set to work at once to increase the quantity of live stock; but in April, 1858, she returned to her mother's house at West Gouldsboro', that she might prepare her wardrobe and some articles of household linen. When, later in the season, John Gilley came after Mary Jane Wilkinson at Jones's Cove, he had to transport to Sutton's Island, besides Mary Jane's personal possessions, a pair of young steers, a pig, and a cat. They were married at North-East Harbor by Squire Kimball, in the old tavern on the west side of the harbor, in July, 1858; and then these two set about improving their condition by unremitting industry and frugality, and an intelligent use of every resource the place afforded. The new wife gave her attention to the poultry and made butter whenever the milk could not be sold as such. The price of butter had greatly improved since John Gilley was a boy on Baker's Island. It could not be sold at from twenty to twenty-five cents a pound. In summer Squire Kimball, at the tavern, bought their milk. All summer eggs could be sold at the stores on the neighboring islands; but in the fall it was necessary to send them to Boston. During the fishing season the husband frequently went for fish in an open boat with one sail; but he no longer absented himself from home for weeks at a time. His labor on the farm was incessant. On the crest of the island a small field had been cleared by the former occupant of the house. With the help of a yoke of oxen John Gilley proceeded to add to this field on the east and on the west. The piles of stones which he heaped up on the bare ledges remain to this day to testify to his industry. One of them is twenty-four feet long, fifteen feet wide, and five feet high. In after years he was proud of these piles, regarding them as monuments to his patient industry and perseverance in the redemption, or rather creation, of this precious mowing-field.

In these labors three or four years passed away, when the Civil War broke out, and soon, linseed-oil becoming scarce, porgy-oil attained an unheard-of value. Fortunately for the New England shore people, the porgies arrived in shoals on the coast in every season for rather more than ten years. At various places along the shore from Long Island Sound to the Bay of Fundy, large factories were built for expressing the oil from these fish; but this was an industry which could also be well conducted on a small scale with a few nets, a big kettle, and a screw-press worked by hand. For an enterprising and energetic man here was a new chance of getting profit from the sea. Accordingly, John Gilley, like thousands of other fishermen along the New England coast, set up a small porgy-oil factory, and during the porgy season this was his most profitable form of industry. During the last part of the war porgy-oil sold at a dollar or even a dollar and ten cents a gallon. The chum, or refuse from the press, was a valuable element in manure. All of John Gilley's porgy-chum went to enrich his precious fields. We may be sure that this well-used opportunity gave him great satisfaction.

The farm, like most farms on the Maine shore, not sufficing for the comfortable support of his family, John Gilley was always looking for another industry by which he could add to his annual income. He found such an industry in the manufacture of smoked herring. This was at that time practised in two ways among the island people. Fresh herring were caught near home, and were immediately corned and smoked; and salted herring brought from the Magdalen Islands were bought by the vessel-load, soaked in fresh water to remove a part of the salt, and then smoked. John Gilley built a large smoke-house on his shore close to a safe and convenient anchorage, and there pursued the herring business in both forms, whenever supplies of herring could be obtained. This is an industry in which women can bear a part. They can pull out the gills and string the wet fish on the sticks by which they are hung up in the smoke-house; and they can pack the dried fish into the boxes in which they are marketed. So the wife and the eldest daughter, as time went on, took a hand in this herring work. The sawed lumber for the boxes was all brought from the saw-mill at the head of Somes Sound, eight miles away. The men did that transportation, and nailed the boxes together. It was characteristic of John Gilley that he always took pains to have his things better than anybody else's. He was careful and particular about all his work, and thoroughly believed in the good results of this painstaking care. He was always confident that his milk, butter, eggs, fowls, porgy-oil, and herring were better than the common, and were worth a higher price; and he could often induce purchasers to think so, too.

Of the second marriage there came three girls, who all grew to maturity, and two of whom were married in due season; but when John Gilley was seventy-four years old he had but two grandchildren, of whom the elder was only eight years old, his fate in this respect being far less fortunate than that of his father. Late marriage caused him to miss some of the most exquisite of natural human delights. He could not witness the coming of grandchildren to maturity. He had the natural, animal fondness —so to speak—for children, the economic liking for them as helpers, and the real love for them as affectionate comrades and friends.

The daughters were disposed to help in the support of the family and the care of the farm. The eldest went through the whole course of the Normal School at Castine, and became a teacher. The youngest was best at household and farm work, having her father's head for business. The other daughter was married early, but had already gone from her father's house to Little Cranberry Island as a helper in the family of the principal storekeeper on that island. Since the household needed the assistance of another male, it was their custom to hire a well-grown boy or a man during the better part of the year, the wages for such services being not more than from fifteen to twenty dollars a month in addition to board and lodging.

Although the island lay much nearer to the shores of Mount Desert than Baker's Island did, the family had hardly more intercourse with the main island than William Gilley's family on Baker's Island had had a generation before. They found their pleasures chiefly at home. In the winter evenings they read aloud to one another, thus carrying down to another generation the habit which Hannah Lurvey Gilley had established in her family. The same good habit has been transmitted to the family of one of John Gilley's married daughters, where it is now in force.

In the early autumn of 1874 a serious disaster befell this industrious and thriving family. One evening Mr. and Mrs. Gilley were walking along the southern shore of the island toward a neighbor's house, when John suggested that it was time for Mary Jane to get the supper, and for him to attend to the fire in the smoke-house, which was full of herring hung up to smoke, and also contained on the floor a large quantity of packed herring, the fruit of the entire summer's work on herring. The smoke-house was large, and at one end there stood a carpenter's bench with a good many tools. It was also used as a place of storage for rigging, anchors, blocks, and other seaman's gear. Mrs. Gilley went home and made ready the supper. John Gilley arranged the fire as usual in the smoke-house, and went up to the house from the shore. As the family were sitting at supper, a neighbor, who had been calling there and had gone out, rushed back, exclaiming, "Your smoke-house is all afire!" So indeed it was; and in a few minutes John Gilley's chief investment and all his summer's work went up in flames. The whole family ran to the scene, but it was too late to do more than save the fish-house, which stood near. John opened the door of the smoke-house and succeeded in rescuing a pair of oiled trousers and his precious compass, which stood on a shelf by the door. Everything else was burned up clean. John said but little at the moment, and looked calmly on at the quick destruction; but when he went to bed that night, he broke down and bewailed his loss with tears and sobs. He had lost not only a sum of money which was large for him,—perhaps five hundred dollars,—but, what was more, he had lost an object of interest and affection, and a means of livelihood which represented years of patient labor. It was as if a mill-owner had lost his mill without insurance, or the owner of a noble vessel had seen her go down within sight of home. This was the only time in all their married life that his wife ever saw him overcome by such emotion. In consequence of this disaster, it was necessary for John Gilley, in order to buy stores enough for the ensuing winter, to sell part of the live stock off his farm. This fact shows how close may be the margin of livelihood for a family on the New England coast which really owns a good deal of property and is justly held by its neighbors to be well off. If the cash proceeds of a season's work are lost or destroyed, extraordinary and undesirable means have to be taken to carry over the family to another season. This may happen to a healthy, industrious, frugal household. Much worse, of course, may happen in consequence of sudden disaster in an unthrifty or sickly family. The investments of poor men are apt to be very hazardous. They put their all into farming-tools or live stock; they risk everything they have on an old vessel or on a single crop, and therefore on the weather of a single season; with their small savings they build a barn or a smoke-house, which may be reduced to ashes with all its contents in fifteen minutes. Insurance they can seldom afford. If the investments of the rich were as hazardous as are those of the poor, theirs would be a lot even more worrisome than it is now.

The smoke-house was never rebuilt. At first the money to rebuild was lacking, and later a new prospect opened before the family. After the fire John Gilley went more into cows and less into fat oxen. Hitherto he had always kept a good yoke of oxen and some steers, and he had been accustomed to do their hauling and plowing for all the families on the island. Thereafter he generally had as many as five cows, but often only a single young ox to do the hauling for the island. He always trained his oxen himself, and had pleasure in the company of these patient and serviceable creatures.

In 1880 the Gilleys on Sutton's Island heard that three "Westerners," or "rusticators," had bought land at North-East Harbor. One was said to be a bishop, another the president of a college, and the third and earliest buyer a landscape-gardener— whatever that might be. It was even reported that one of these pioneers had landed on the western end of Sutton's Island and walked the length of the island. The news was intensely interesting to all the inhabitants. They had heard of the fabulous prices of land at Bar Harbor, and their imaginations began to play over their own pastures and wood-lots. John Gilley went steadily on his laborious and thrifty way. He served the town in various capacities, such as selectman and collector of taxes. He was one of the school committee for several years, and later one of the board of health. He was also road-surveyor on the island —there being but one road, and that grass-grown. As a town officer John Gilley exhibited the same uprightness and frugality which he showed in all his private dealings. To be chosen to responsible office by his fellow-townsmen, every one of whom knew him personally, was to him a source of rational gratification; and in each of his offices he had occasion to enlarge his knowledge and to undertake new responsibilities.

In 1884 the extreme western point of Sutton's Island was sold to a "Westerner," a professor in Harvard College, and shortly after a second sale in the same neighborhood was effected; but it was not until 1886 that John Gilley made his first sale of land for summering purposes. In the next year he made another sale, and in 1894 a third. The prices he obtained, though moderate compared with the prices charged at Bar Harbor or North-East Harbor, were forty or fifty times any price which had ever been put on his farm by the acre. Being thus provided with what was for him a considerable amount of ready money, he did what all his like do when they come into possession of ready money—he first gave himself and his family the pleasure of enlarging and improving his house and other buildings, and then lent the balance on small mortgages on village real estate. Suddenly he became a prosperous man, at ease, and a leader in his world. Up to this time he had merely earned a comfortable livelihood by means of diversified industry; since his second marriage now he had a secured capital in addition to his farm and its buildings. Now, at last, he was highly content, but nevertheless ready as ever for new undertakings. His mind was active, and his eye and hand were steady.

When three cottages had stood for several years on the eastern foreside of North-East Harbor,—the nearest point of the shore of Mount Desert to Sutton's Island,—John Gilley, at the age of seventy-one, undertook to deliver at these houses milk, eggs, and fresh vegetables every day, and chickens and fowls when they were wanted. This undertaking involved his rowing in all weathers nearly two miles from his cove to the landings of these houses, and back again, across bay waters which are protected indeed from the heavy ocean swells, but are still able to produce what the natives call "a big chop." Every morning he arrived with the utmost punctuality, in rain or shine, calm or blow, and alone, unless it blew heavily from the northwest (a head wind from Sutton's), or his little grandson—his mate, as he called the boy—wanted to accompany him on a fine, still morning. Soon he extended his trips to the western side of North-East Harbor, where he found a much larger market for his goods than he had found thirty-five years before, when he first delivered milk at Squire Kimball's tavern. This business involved what was new work for John Gilley, namely, the raising of fresh vegetables in much larger variety and quantity than he was accustomed to. He entered on this new work with interest and intelligence, but was of course sometimes defeated in his plans by wet weather in spring, a drought in summer, or by the worms and insects which unexpectedly attacked his crops. On the whole he was decidedly successful in this enterprise undertaken at seventy-one. Those who bought of him liked to deal with him, and he found in the business fresh interest and pleasure. Not many men take up a new out-of-door business at seventy, and carry it on successfully by their own brains and muscles. It was one of the sources of his satisfaction that he thus supplied the two daughters who still lived at his house with a profitable outlet for their energies. One of these—the school-teacher—was an excellent laundress, and the other was devoted to the work of the house and the farm, and was helpful in her father's new business. John Gilley transported the washes from North-East Harbor and back again in his rowboat, and under the new conditions of the place washing and ironing proved to be more profitable than school-keeping.

In the fall of 1896 the family which had occupied that summer one of the houses John Gilley was in the habit of supplying with milk, eggs, and vegetables, and which had a young child dependent on the milk, lingered after the other summer households had departed. He consented to continue his daily trips a few days into October that the child's milk might not be changed, although it was perfectly clear that his labor could not be adequately recompensed. On the last morning but one that he was to come across from the island to the harbor a strong northeast wind was blowing, and some sea was running through the deep passage between Sutton's Island and Bear Island, which he had to cross on his way to and fro. He took with him in his boat the young man who had been working for him on the farm the few weeks past. They delivered the milk, crossed to the western side of North-East Harbor, did some errands there, and started cheerfully for home, as John Gilley had done from that shore hundreds of times before. The boy rowed from a seat near the bow, and the old man sat on the thwart near the stern, facing the bow, and pushing his oars from him. They had no thought of danger; but to ease the rowing they kept to windward under Bear Island, and then pushed across the deep channel, south by west, for the western point of Sutton's Island. They were more than half-way across when, through some inattention or lack of skill on the part of the young man in the bow, a sea higher or swifter than the rest threw a good deal of water into the boat. John Gilley immediately began to bail, and told the rower to keep her head to the waves. The overweighted boat was less manageable than before, and in a moment another roller turned her completely over. Both men clung to the boat and climbed on to her bottom. She drifted away before the wind and sea toward South-West Harbor. The oversetting of the boat had been seen from both Bear Island and Sutton's Island; but it was nearly three quarters of an hour before the rescuers could reach the floating boat, and then the young man, though unconscious, was still clinging to the boat's keel, but the old man, chilled by the cold water and stunned by the waves which beat about his head, had lost his hold and sunk into the sea. In half an hour John Gilley had passed from a hearty and successful old age in this world, full of its legitimate interests and satisfactions, into the voiceless mystery of death. No trace of his body was ever found. It disappeared into the waters on which he had played and worked as boy and man all his long and fortunate life. He left his family well provided for, and full of gratitude and praise for his honorable career and his sterling character.

This is the life of one of the forgotten millions. It contains no material for distinction, fame, or long remembrance; but it does contain the material and present the scene for a normal human development through mingled joy and sorrow, labor and rest, adversity and success, and through the tender loves of childhood, maturity, and age. We cannot but believe that it is just for countless quiet, simple lives like this that God made and upholds this earth.

Celia Thaxter

Celia Thaxter (1835–1894) was born in Portsmouth, New Hampshire. When she was four years old her father took the position of lighthouse keeper on White Island, one of the Isles of Shoals some eight miles off the New Hampshire coast. After marrying at sixteen, she lived for a time on the mainland, but the greater part of her life was spent on these little islands, where her father had established a summer hotel. Here, in the summers at least, she met vacationing men and women of culture and of artistic attainment and became one of their circle. Though she wrote much verse that was popular in its day, her claim to literary fame must rest on a series of sketches that she wrote for the Atlantic Monthly *and soon thereafter published in book form under the title* Among the Isles of Shoals *(1873), from which the following excerpt is taken. The greatest merit of these sketches is their success in evoking the atmosphere of their author's beloved islands, as is admirably exemplified in the accompanying excerpt describing Mrs. Thaxter's childhood pastimes and impressions. Attachment to place, even though the place may have serious drawbacks as a home, is the keynote of all her writing, as it is of so much writing in this collection. A rocky offshore island or a windswept hill farm may be dreary places for living, but on those who have made their lives on them they exert a pull which is all but impossible to break.*

From *Among the Isles of Shoals*

I well remember my first sight of White Island, where we took up our abode on leaving the mainland. I was scarcely five years old; but from the upper windows of our dwelling in Portsmouth, I had been shown the clustered masts of ships lying at the wharves along the Piscataqua River, faintly outlined against the sky, and, baby as I was, even then I was drawn, with a vague longing, seaward. How delightful was that long, first sail to the Isles of Shoals! How pleasant the unaccustomed sound of the incessant ripple against the boat-side, the sight of the wide water and limitless sky, the warmth of the broad sunshine that made us blink like young sandpipers as we sat in triumph, perched among the household goods with which the little craft was laden! It was at sunset in autumn that we were set ashore on that loneliest, lovely rock, where the lighthouse looked down on us like some tall, black-capped giant, and filled me with awe and wonder. At its base a few goats were grouped on the rock, standing out dark against the red sky as I looked up at them. The stars were beginning to twinkle; the wind blew cold, charged with the sea's sweetness; the sound of many waters half bewildered me. Some one began to light the lamps in the tower. Rich red and golden, they swung round in mid-air; everything was strange and fascinating and new. We entered the quaint little old stone cottage that was for six years our home. How curious it seemed, with its low, whitewashed ceiling and deep window-seats, showing the great thickness of the walls made to withstand the breakers, with whose force we soon grew acquainted! A blissful home the little house became to the children who entered it that quiet evening and slept for the first time lulled by the murmur of the encircling sea. I do not think a happier triad ever existed than we were, living in that profound isolation. It takes so little to make a healthy child happy; and we never wearied of our few resources. True, the winters seemed as long as a whole year to our little minds, but they were pleasant, nevertheless. Into the deep win-

dow-seats we climbed, and with pennies (for which we had no
other use) made round holes in the thick frost, breathing on
them till they were warm, and peeped out at the bright, fierce,
windy weather, watching the vessels scudding over the intensely
dark blue sea, all "feather-white" where the short waves broke
hissing in the cold, and the sea-fowl soaring aloft or tossing on
the water; or, in calmer days, we saw how the stealthy Star-
Islander paddled among the ledges, or lay for hours stretched on
the wet sea-weed, with his gun, watching for wild-fowl. Sometimes the round head of a seal moved about among the kelp-
covered rocks. A few are seen every winter, and are occasionally
shot; but they are shyer and more alert even than the birds.

We were forced to lay in stores of all sorts in the autumn, as
if we were fitting out a ship for an Arctic expedition. The lower
story of the lighthouse was hung with mutton and beef, and the
store-room packed with provisions.

In the long, covered walk that bridged the gorge between the
lighthouse and the house, we played in stormy days; and every
evening it was a fresh excitement to watch the lighting of the
lamps, and think how far the lighthouse sent its rays, and how
many hearts it gladdened with assurance of safety. As I grew
older I was allowed to kindle the lamps sometimes myself. That
was indeed a pleasure. So little a creature as I might do that
much for the great world! But by the fireside our best pleasure
lay,—with plants and singing birds and books and playthings
and loving care and kindness the cold and stormy season wore
itself at last away, and died into the summer calm. We hardly
saw a human face beside our own all winter; but with the spring
came manifold life to our lonely dwelling,—human life among
other forms. Our neighbors from Star rowed across; the pilot-
boat from Portsmouth steered over, and brought us letters, newspapers, magazines, and told us the news of months. The faint
echoes from the far-off world hardly touched us little ones. We
listened to the talk of our elders. "Winfield Scott and Santa
Anna!" "The war in Mexico!" "The famine in Ireland!" It
all meant nothing to us. We heard the reading aloud of details
of the famine, and saw tears in the eyes of the reader, and were
vaguely sorry; but the fate of Red Riding-Hood was much more
near and dreadful to us. We waited for the spring with an eager
longing; the advent of the growing grass, the birds and flowers
and insect life, the soft skies and softer winds, the everlasting
beauty of the thousand tender tints that clothed the world,—

these things brought us unspeakable bliss. To the heart of Nature one must needs be drawn in such a life; and very soon I learned how richly she repays in deep refreshment the reverent love of her worshipper. With the first warm days we built our little mountains of wet gravel on the beach, and danced after the sandpipers at the edge of the foam, shouted to the gossiping kittiwakes that fluttered above, or watched the pranks of the burgomaster gull, or cried to the crying loons. The gannet's long, white wings stretched overhead, perhaps, or the dusky shag made a sudden shadow in mid-air, or we startled on some lonely ledge the great blue heron that flew off, trailing legs and wings, storklike, against the clouds. Or, in the sunshine on the bare rocks, we cut from the broad, brown leaves of the slippery, varnished kelps, grotesque shapes of man and bird and beast that withered in the wind and blew away; or we fashioned rude boats from bits of driftwood, manned them with a weird crew of kelpies, and set them adrift on the great deep, to float we cared not whither.

We played with the empty limpet-shells; they were mottled gray and brown, like the song-sparrow's breast. We launched fleets of purple mussel-shells on the still pools in the rocks, left by the tide,—pools that were like bits of fallen rainbow with the wealth of the sea, with tints of delicate sea-weeds, crimson and green and ruddy brown and violet; where wandered the pearly eolis with rosy spines and fairy horns; and the large, round sea-urchins, like a boss upon a shield, were fastened here and there on the rock at the bottom, putting out from their green, prickly spikes transparent tentacles to seek their invisible food. Rosy and lilac star-fish clung to the sides; in some dark nook, perhaps, a holothure unfolded its perfect ferns, a lovely, warm buff color, delicate as frost-work; little forests of coralline moss grew up in stillness, gold-colored shells crept about, and now and then flashed the silver-darting fins of slender minnows. The dimmest recesses were haunts of sea-anemones that opened wide their starry flowers to the flowing tide, or drew themselves together, and hung in large, half-transparent drops, like clusters of some strange, amber-colored fruit, along the crevices as the water ebbed away. Sometimes we were cruel enough to capture a female lobster hiding in a deep cleft, with her millions of mottled eggs; or we laughed to see the hermit-crabs challenge each other, and come out and fight a deadly battle till the stronger overcame, and, turning the weaker topsy-turvy, possessed himself of his ampler cockle-shell, and scuttled off with it triumphant.

Or, pulling all together, we dragged up the long kelps, or devil's-aprons; their roots were almost always fastened about large, living mussels; these we unclasped, carrying the mussels home to be cooked; fried in crumbs or batter, they were as good as oysters. We picked out from the kelp-roots a kind of star-fish which we called sea-spider; the moment we touched it an extraordinary process began. One by one it disjointed all its sections,—whether from fear or anger we knew not; but it threw itself away, bit by bit, until nothing was left of it save the little, round body whence the legs had sprung!

With crab and limpet, with grasshopper and cricket, we were friends and neighbors, and we were never tired of watching the land-spiders that possessed the place. Their webs covered every window-pane to the lighthouse top, and they rebuilt them as fast as they were swept down. One variety lived among the round gray stones on the beach, just above high-water mark, and spun no webs at all. Large and black, they speckled the light stones, swarming in the hot sun; at the first footfall they vanished beneath the pebbles.

All the cracks in the rocks were draped with swinging veils like the window-panes. How often have we marvelled at them, after a fog or a heavy fall of dew, in the early morning, when every slender thread was strung with glittering drops,—the whole symmetrical web a wonder of shining jewels trembling in the breeze! Tennyson's lines,

> The cobweb woven across the cannon's throat
> Shall shake its threaded tears in the wind no more,

always bring back to my mind the memory of those delicate, spangled draperies, more beautiful than any mortal loom could weave, that curtained the rocks at White Island and "shook their threaded tears" in every wind.

Sometimes we saw the bats wheel through the summer dusk, and in profoundly silent evenings heard, from the lighthouse top, their shrill, small cries, their voices sharper and finer than needle-points. One day I found one clinging to the under side of a shutter,—a soft, dun-colored, downy lump. I took it in my hand, and in an instant it changed to a hideous little demon, and its fierce white teeth met in the palm of my hand. So much fury in so small a beast I never encountered, and I was glad enough to give him his liberty without more ado.

A kind of sandhopper about an inch long, that infested the beach, was a great source of amusement. Lifting the stranded sea-weed that marked the high-water line, we always startled a gray and brown cloud of them from beneath it, leaping away, like tiny kangaroos, out of sight. In storms these were driven into the house, forcing their way through every crack and cranny till they strewed the floors,—the sea so encircled us! Dying immediately upon leaving the water from which they fled, they turned from a clear brown, or what Mr. Kingsley would call a "pellucid gray," to bright brick-color, like a boiled lobster, and many a time I have swept them up in ruddy heaps; they looked like bits of coral.

I remember in the spring kneeling on the ground to seek the first blades of grass that pricked through the soil, and bringing them into the house to study and wonder over. Better than a shop full of toys they were to me! Whence came their color? How did they draw their sweet, refreshing tint from the brown earth, or the limpid air, or the white light? Chemistry was not at hand to answer me, and all her wisdom would not have dispelled the wonder. Later the little scarlet pimpernel charmed me. It seemed more than a flower; it was like a human thing. I knew it by its homely name of poor-man's weather-glass. It was so much wiser than I, for, when the sky was yet without a cloud, softly it clasped its small red petals together, folding its golden heart in safety from the shower that was sure to come! How could it know so much? Here is a question science cannot answer. The pimpernel grows everywhere about the islands, in every cleft and cranny where a suspicion of sustenance for its slender root can lodge; and it is one of the most exquisite of flowers, so rich in color, so quaint and dainty in its method of growth. I never knew its silent warning fail. I wondered much how every flower knew what to do and to be; why the morning-glory didn't forget sometimes, and bear a cluster of elder-bloom, or the elder hang out pennons of gold and purple like the iris, or the golden-rod suddenly blaze out a scarlet plume, the color of the pimpernel, was a mystery to my childish thought. And why did the sweet wild primrose wait till after sunset, to unclose its pale yellow buds; why did it unlock its treasure of rich perfume to the night alone? Few flowers bloomed for me upon the lonesome rock; but I made the most of all I had, and neither knew of nor desired more. Ah, how beautiful they were! Tiny stars of crimson sorrel threaded on their long brown stems; the blackberry blossoms in bridal white; the surprise of the blue-eyed grass; the crowfoot flowers, like drops of yellow gold spilt about among the short grass and over the moss; the rich, blue-purple beach-pea, the sweet, spiked germander, and the homely, delightful yarrow that grows thickly on all the islands. Sometimes its broad clusters of dull white bloom are stained a lovely reddish-purple, as if with the light of sunset. I never saw it colored so elsewhere. Quantities of slender, wide-spreading mustard-bushes grew about the house; their delicate flowers were like fragrant golden clouds. Dandelions, buttercups, and clover were not denied to us; though we had no daisies nor violets nor wild roses, no asters, but gorgeous spikes of golden-rod, and wonderful wild morning-glories, whose long, pale, ivory buds I used to find in the twilight, glimmering among the dark leaves, waiting for the touch of dawn to unfold and become each an exquisite incarnate blush,—the perfect color of a South Sea shell. They ran wild, knotting and twisting about the rocks, and smothering the loose boulders in the gorges with lush green leaves and pink blossoms.

Many a summer morning have I crept out of the still house before any one was awake, and, wrapping myself closely from the chill wind of dawn, climbed to the top of the high cliff called the Head to watch the sunrise. Pale grew the lighthouse flame before the broadening day as, nestled in a crevice at the cliff's edge, I watched the shadows draw away and morning break. Facing the east and south, with all the Atlantic before me, what happiness was mine as the deepening rose-color flushed the delicate cloudflocks that dappled the sky, where the gulls soared, rosy too, while the calm sea blushed beneath. Or perhaps it was a cloudless sunrise with a sky of orange-red, and the sea-line silver-blue against it, peaceful as heaven. Infinite variety of beauty always awaited me, and filled me with an absorbing, unreasoning joy such as makes the song-sparrow sing,—a sense of perfect bliss. Coming back in the sunshine, the morning-glories would lift up their faces, all awake, to my adoring gaze. Like countless rosy trumpets sometimes I thought they were, tossed everywhere about the rocks, turned up to the sky, or drooping toward the ground, or looking east, west, north, south, in silent loveliness. It seemed as if they had gathered the peace of the golden morning in their still depths even as my heart had gathered it.

In some of those matchless summer mornings when I went out to milk the little dun cow, it was hardly possible to go farther than the doorstep, for pure wonder, as I looked abroad at the

sea lying still, like a vast, round mirror, the tide drawn away
from the rich brown rocks, a sail or two asleep in the calm, not
a sound abroad except a few bird voices; dew lying like jewel-
dust sifted over everything,—diamond and ruby, sapphire, topaz,
and amethyst, flashing out of the emerald deeps of the tufted
grass or from the bending tops. Looking over to the mainland, I
could dimly discern in the level sunshine the depths of glowing
green woods faintly revealed in the distance, fold beyond fold
of hill and valley thickly clothed with the summer's splendor. But
my handful of grass was more precious to me than miles of
green fields, and I was led to consider every blade where there
were so few. Not long ago I had watched them piercing the
ground toward the light; now, how strong in their slender grace
were these stems, how perfect the poise of the heavy heads that
waved with such harmony of movement in the faintest breeze!
And I noticed at mid-day when the dew was dry, where the tall,
blossoming spears stood in graceful companies that, before they
grew purple, brown, and ripe, when they began to blossom, they
put out first a downy ring of pollen in tiny, yellow rays, held by
an almost invisible thread, which stood out like an aureole from
each slow-waving head,—a fairy-like effect. On Seavey's Island
(united to ours by a narrow beach covered at high tide with
contending waves) grew one single root of fern, the only one
within the circle of my little world. It was safe in a deep cleft,
but I was in perpetual anxiety lest my little cow, going there daily
to pasture, should leave her cropping of the grass and eat it up
some day. Poor little cow! One night she did not come home
to be milked as usual, and on going to seek her we found she
had caught one foot in a crevice and twisted her hoof entirely
off! That was a calamity; for we were forced to summon our
neighbors and have her killed on the spot.

I had a scrap of garden, literally not more than a yard square,
wherein grew only African marigolds, rich in color as barbaric
gold. I knew nothing of John Keats at that time,—poor Keats,
"who told Severn that he thought his intensest pleasure in life
had been to watch the growth of flowers,"—but I am sure he
never felt their beauty more devoutly than the little, half-savage
being who knelt, like a fire-worshipper, to watch the unfolding
of those golden disks. When, later, the "brave new world" of
poets was opened to me, with what power those glowing lines of
his went straight to my heart,

Open afresh your rounds of starry folds,
Ye ardent marigolds!

All flowers had for me such human interest, they were so dear and precious, I hardly liked to gather them, and when they were withered, I carried them all to one place and laid them tenderly together, and never liked to pass the spot where they were hidden.

Once or twice every year came the black, lumbering old "oil-schooner" that brought supplies for the lighthouse, and the inspector, who gravely examined everything, to see if all was in order. He left stacks of clear red and white glass chimneys for the lamps, and several doe-skins for polishing the great, silver-lined copper reflectors, large bundles of wicks, and various pairs of scissors for trimming them, heavy black casks of ill-perfumed whale-oil, and other things, which were all stowed in the round, dimly-lighted rooms of the tower. Very awe-struck, we children always crept into corners, and whispered and watched the intruders till they embarked in their ancient, clumsy vessel, and, hoisting their dark, weather-stained sails, bore slowly away again. About ten years ago that old white lighthouse was taken away, and a new, perpendicular brick tower built in its place. The lantern, with its fifteen lamps, ten golden and five red, gave place to Fresnel's powerful single burner, or, rather, three burners in one, enclosed in its case of prisms. The old lighthouse was by far the most picturesque; but perhaps the new one is more effective, the light being, undoubtedly, more powerful.

Often, in pleasant days, the head of the family sailed away to visit the other islands, sometimes taking the children with him, oftener going alone, frequently not returning till after dark. The landing at White Island is so dangerous that the greatest care is requisite, if there is any sea running, to get ashore in safety. Two long and very solid timbers about three feet apart are laid from the boathouse to low-water mark, and between those timbers the boat's bow must be accurately steered; if she goes to the right or the left, woe to her crew unless the sea is calm! Safely lodged in the slip, as it is called, she is drawn up into the boat-house by a capstan, and fastened securely. The lighthouse gave no ray to the dark rock below it; sending its beams far out to sea, it left us at its foot in greater darkness for its lofty light. So when the boat was out late, in soft, moonless summer nights, I used to light a lantern, and, going down to the water's edge, take my station between the timbers of the slip, and, with the lantern at my feet, sit waiting in the darkness, quite content, knowing my little star was watched for, and that the safety of the boat depended in a great measure upon it. How sweet the summer wind blew, how softly plashed the water round me, how refreshing was the odor of the sparkling brine! High above, the lighthouse rays streamed out into the humid dark, and the cottage windows were ruddy from the glow within. I felt so much a part of the Lord's universe, I was no more afraid of the dark than the waves or winds; but I was glad to hear at last the creaking of the mast and the rattling of the rowlocks as the boat approached; and, while yet she was far off, the lighthouse touched her one large sail into sight, so that I knew she was nearing me, and shouted, listening for the reply that came so blithely back to me over the water.

Unafraid, too, we watched the summer tempests, and listened to the deep, melodious thunder rolling away over the rain-calmed ocean. The lightning played over the iron rods that ran from the lighthouse-top down into the sea. Where it lay on the sharp ridgepole of the long, covered walk that spanned the gorge, the strange fire ran up the spikes that were set at equal distances, and burnt like pale flame from their tips. It was fine indeed from the lighthouse itself to watch the storm come rushing over the sea and ingulf us in our helplessness. How the rain weltered down over the great panes of plate glass,—floods of sweet, fresh water that poured off the rocks and mingled with the bitter brine. I wondered why the fresh floods never made the salt sea any sweeter. Those pale flames that we beheld burning from the spikes of the lightning-rod, I suppose were identical with the St. Elmo's fire that I have since seen described as haunting the spars of ships in thunder-storms. And here I am reminded of a story told by some gentleman visiting Appledore sixteen or eighteen years ago. They started from Portsmouth for the Shoals in a whaleboat, one evening in summer, with a native Star-Islander, Richard Randall by name, to manage the boat. They had sailed about half the distance, when they were surprised at seeing a large ball of fire, like a rising moon, rolling toward them over the sea from the south. They watched it eagerly as it bore down upon them, and, veering off, went east of them at some little distance, and then passed astern, and there, of course, they expected to lose sight of it; but while they were marvelling and speculating, it altered its course, and suddenly began to near them, coming back upon its track against the wind and steadily following in their wake. This was too much for the native Shoaler. He took off his jacket and turned it inside out to exorcise the fiend, and lo, the apparition most certainly disappeared! We heard the excited account of the strange gentlemen and witnessed the holy horror of the boatmen on the occasion; but no one could imagine what had set the globe of fire rolling across the sea. Some one suggested that it might be an exhalation, a phosphorescent light, from the decaying body of some dead fish; but in that case it must have been taken in tow by some living finny creature, else how could it have sailed straight "into the teeth of the wind"? It was never satisfactorily accounted for, and must remain a mystery.

One autumn at White Island our little boat had been to Portsmouth for provisions, etc. With the spy-glass we watched her returning, beating against the head wind. The day was bright, but there had been a storm at sea, and the breakers rolled and roared about us. The process of "beating" is so tedious that, though the boat had started in the morning, the sun was sending long yellow light from the west before it reached the island. There was no cessation in those resistless billows that rolled from the Devil's Rock upon the slip; but still the little craft sailed on, striving to reach the landing. The hand at the tiller was firm, but a huge wave swept suddenly in, swerving the boat to the left of the slip, and in a moment she was overturned and flung upon the rocks, and her only occupant tossed high upon the beach, safe except for a few bruises; but what a moment of terror it was for us all, who saw and could not save! All the freight was lost except a roll of iron wire and a barrel of walnuts. These were spread on the floor of an unoccupied eastern chamber in the cottage to dry. And they did dry; but before they were gathered up came a terrible storm from the southeast. It raved and tore at lighthouse and cottage; the sea broke into the windows of that eastern chamber where the walnuts lay, and washed them out till they came dancing down the stairs in briny foam! The sea broke the windows of the house several times during our stay at the lighthouse. Everything shook so violently from the concussion of the breakers, that dishes on the closet shelves fell to the floor, and one member of the family was at first always made sea-sick in storms, by the tremor and deafening confusion. One night when, from the southeast, the very soul of chaos

seemed to have been let loose upon the world, the whole pon-
derous "walk" (the covered bridge that connected the house and
lighthouse) was carried thundering down the gorge and dragged
out into the raging sea.

It was a distressing situation for us,—cut off from the precious
light that must be kept alive; for the breakers were tearing
through the gorge so that no living thing could climb across. But
the tide could not resist the mighty impulse that drew it down;
it was forced to obey the still voice that bade it ebb; all swollen
and raging and towering as it was, slowly and surely, at the
appointed time, it sank away from our rock, so that, between
the billows that still strove to clutch at the white, silent, golden-
crowned tower, one could creep across, and scale the height, and
wind up the machinery that kept the great clustered light revolving till the gray daylight broke to extinguish it.

I often wondered how it was possible for the sea-birds to live
through such storms as these. But, when one could see at all, the
gulls were always soaring, in the wildest tumult, and the stormy
petrels half flying, half swimming in the hollows of the waves.

Would it were possible to describe the beauty of the calm
that followed such tempests! The long lines of silver foam that
streaked the tranquil blue, the "tender-curving lines of creamy
spray" along the shore, the clear-washed sky, the peaceful yellow
light, the mellow breakers murmuring slumberously!

Of all the storms our childish eyes watched with delighted
awe, one thunder-storm remains fixed in my memory. Late in
an August afternoon it rolled its awful clouds to the zenith, and,
after the tumult had subsided, spread its lightened vapors in an
under-roof of gray over all the sky. Presently this solemn gray
lid was lifted at its western edge, and an insufferable splendor
streamed across the world from the sinking sun. The whole
heaven was in a blaze of scarlet, across which sprang a rainbow
unbroken to the topmost clouds, "with its seven perfect colors
chorded in a triumph" against the flaming background; the sea
answered the sky's rich blush, and the gray rocks lay drowned
in melancholy purple. I hid my face from the glory,—it was too
much to bear. Ever I longed to *speak* these things that made
life so sweet; to speak the wind, the cloud, the bird's flight, the
sea's murmur. A vain longing! I might as well have sighed for
the mighty pencil of Michael Angelo to wield in my impotent
child's hand. Better to "hush and bless one's self with silence";
but ever the wish grew. Facing the July sunsets, deep red and

golden through and through, or watching the summer northern lights,—battalions of brilliant streamers advancing and retreating, shooting upward to the zenith, and glowing like fiery veils before the stars; or when the fog-bow spanned the silver mist of morning, or the earth and sea lay shimmering in a golden haze of noon; in a storm or calm, by day or night, the manifold aspects of Nature held me and swayed all my thoughts until it was impossible to be silent any longer, and I was fain to mingle my voice with her myriad voices, only aspiring to be in accord with the Infinite harmony, however feeble and broken the notes might be.

It has been my good fortune to witness but few wrecks at the Shoals. The disasters of which we hear faintly from the past were many and dreadful; but since the building of the lighthouse on White Island, and also on Boone Island (which seems like a neighbor, though fifteen miles distant), the danger of the place is much lessened. A resident of Star Island told me of a wreck which took place forty-seven years ago, during a heavy storm from the eastward. It blew so that all the doors in the house opened as fast as they shut them, and in the night a vessel drove against "Hog Island Head," which fronts the village on Star. She went to pieces utterly. In the morning the islanders perceived the beach at Londoners heaped with some kind of drift; they could not make out what it was, but, as soon as the sea subsided, went to examine and found a mass of oranges and picture-frames, with which the vessel had been freighted. Not a soul was saved. "She struck with such force that she drove a large spike out of her forefoot" into a crevice in the rock, which was plainly to be seen till a few years ago. My informant also told me that she remembered the wreck of the Sagunto, in 1813; that the beaches were strewn with "almond-nuts" long after; and that she picked up curiously embroidered vests and "work-bags" in all directions along the shores.

During a storm in 1839, while living at White Island, we were startled by the heavy booming of guns through the roar of the tempest,—a sound that drew nearer and nearer, till at last, through a sudden break in the mist and spray, we saw the heavy rolling hull of a large vessel driving by, to her sure destruction, toward the coast. It was as if the wind had torn the vapor apart on purpose to show us this piteous sight; and I well remember the hand on my shoulder which held me firmly, shuddering child that I was, and forced me to look in spite of myself. What a day of pain it was! how dreadful the sound of those signal-guns, and how much more dreadful the certainty, when they ceased, that all was over! We learned afterward that it was the brig Pocahontas, homeward bound from Spain, and that the vessel and all her crew were lost. In later years a few coasters and fishermen have gone ashore at the islands, generally upon the hidden ledges at Duck. Many of these have been loaded with lime,—a most perilous freight; for as soon as the water touches it there is a double danger; and between fire and water there is little chance of escape.

I wish I could recall the graphic language of a Star Islander who described to me a wreck of this kind. The islanders saw at sunrise, one bitter winter day, a schooner ashore among the dreadful ledges at Duck Island, and, though the wind blew half a gale, they took their boats and ran down toward her before the northwester. Smoke and steam and spray and flame were rising from her and about her when they reached the spot. Only one man was found alive. From the davits, hanging head downward, was the lifeless body of a fair-haired boy of sixteen or thereabouts. The breakers swept him to and fro, and, drawing away, left his long yellow hair dripping with the freezing brine. The mate's story was that he had gone to unfasten the boat which hung at the stern, that a sea had struck him, and he had fallen headforemost with his feet entangled in the ropes of the davits. He was the only son of his mother, who was a widow. They carried his body home to that most unhappy mother. The vessel was a total loss, with all on board, except the mate.

One winter night at Appledore when it was blowing very hard northwest, with a clear sky, we were wakened by a violent knocking at the door. So unaccustomed a sound, at that time of night too, was enough to startle us all, and very much amazed we were. The door was opened to admit four or five shipwrecked men, whose hands, feet, and ears were all frozen stiff,—pitiable objects they were indeed. Their vessel had struck full on York Ledge, a rock lying off the coast of Maine far east of us, and they had taken to the boat and strove to make a landing on the coast; but the wind blew off shore so fiercely they failed in their attempt, their hands became useless from the cold, they dropped their oars, and, half steering with one of the seats of the boat, managed to reach Appledore, more dead than alive. They were obliged to remain there several days before finding an opportunity of going on shore, the gale was so furious. Next morning, in the glare of the winter sunshine, we saw their vessel, still with all sail set, standing upright upon the ledge,—a white column looming far away. One of the most hideous experiences I have heard befell a young Norwegian now living at the Shoals. He and a young companion came out from Portsmouth to set their trawl, in the winter fishing, two years ago. Before they reached the island, came a sudden squall of wind and snow, chilling and blinding. In a few moments they knew not where they were, and the wind continued to sweep them away. Presently they found themselves under the lee of White Island Head; they threw out the road-lines of their trawl, in desperate hope that they might hold the boat till the squall abated. The keepers at the lighthouse saw the poor fellows, but were powerless to help them. Alas! the road-lines soon broke, and the little boat was swept off again, they knew not whither. Night came down upon them, tossed on that terrible black sea; the snow ceased, the clouds flew before the deadly cold northwest wind, the thermometer sank below zero. One of the men died before morning; the other, alone with the dead man, was still driven on and on before the pitiless gale. He had no cap nor mittens; had lost both. He bailed the boat incessantly, for the sea broke over him the live-long time. He told me the story himself. He looked down at the awful face of his dead friend and thought "how soon he should be like him"; but still he never ceased bailing,—it was all he could do. Before night he passed Cape Cod and knew it as he rushed by. Another unspeakably awful night, and the gale abated no whit. Next morning he was almost gone from cold, fatigue, and hunger. His eyes were so swollen he could hardly see; but afar off, shining whiter than silver in the sun, the sails of a large schooner appeared at the edge of the fearful wilderness. He managed to hoist a bit of old canvas on an oar. He was then not far from Holmes' Hole, nearly two hundred miles from the Shoals! The schooner saw it and bore down for him, but the sea was running so high that he expected to be swamped every instant. As she swept past, they threw from the deck a rope with a loop at the end, tied with a bow-line knot that would not slip. It caught him over the head, and clutching it at his throat with both hands, in an instant he found himself in the sea among the ice-cold, furious waves, drawn toward the vessel with all the strength of her crew. Just before he emerged, he heard the captain shout, "We've lost him!" Ah the bitter moment! For a horrible fear struck through him that they might lose their hold an instant on the rope, and then he knew it would be all over. But they saved him. The boat with the dead man in it, all alone, went tossing, heaven knows where.

Sarah Orne Jewett

Sarah Orne Jewett (1849-1909) was born of patrician stock and brought up in South Berwick, Maine, a few miles inland from York. As a girl she accompanied her father, a physician, on his rounds in the adjacent countryside, and the knowledge of rural character that she acquired on these visits to the households of the ill provided material and insight not only for her semiautobiographical novel, A Country Doctor *(1884), but for many of her stories and sketches. On the whole her best work deals with coastal people and settings of her own section of Maine as well as of the eastern sections of the state where she went on summer vacations. It is the rocky eastern coast and its isolated communities that she writes about in* The Country of the Pointed Firs *(1896) and in "The King of Folly Island" (1886). Like so many of the authors in this anthology, she made a name for herself by contributing to the* Atlantic Monthly, *but unlike them she was at home among the literary and intellectual élite of Boston, where she made long visits with her friend Annie Fields, the wife of the great publisher and editor, James T. Fields. Her reputation has worn better than that of any other of her rural contemporaries, for she is now generally recognized as one of America's foremost writers.*

The selections from Miss Jewett's writings printed here are typical but have escaped widespread inclusion in anthologies. "The King of Folly Island" has the same eastern Maine setting as The Country of the Pointed Firs *and like that book introduces us to the area through the deepening perceptions of a visiting outsider whose general outlook on life is modified by his Down-East experiences. But in "The King of Folly Island" the warpings of character and the abnormal development of the post-Puritan will, in isolated communities, are more destructive. The scenery in each is presented with fidelity to detail and atmosphere, the emphasis being on the blending of human habitations*

205

*and works with the natural environment. In both there is a
funeral, a walking one in* The Country of the Pointed Firs *and
a floating one in "The King of Folly Island," and in each case
the funeral reminds us of the eternal presence of death. But in
"The King of Folly Island" the funeral, seen by a dying girl
through a spyglass over miles of water, whelms the reader with
emotion of almost unbearable poignancy. This description of the
funerary dories slowly gliding over the waters of death is one
of the triumphs of Miss Jewett's art. Her awareness of death,
indeed, adds a dimension of profundity that characterizes much
of her work. It is this that makes "The Gray Man" (1892) so
overpowering an evocation of the pathos of desertion that
clouded, and still clouds, the New England scene as by a pall.*

*In a different vein, one of life-affirmation, is "The Gray Mills
of Farley" (1898), which treats that cancerous growth, the mill-
town, on New England's green and pleasant land. Miss Jewett's
sympathy for, and admiration of, the Irish and the French-
Canadian operatives, especially the former, is an indication of
the breadth of her feelings, though it was, unfortunately, uncommon among native New Englanders of her class.*

*The text of "The Gray Mills of Farley," which never ap-
peared in any of the volumes of her collected stories, is from*
Cosmopolitan, *vol. 15 (1898). "The Gray Man" is from* The
White Heron and Other Stories *(1886), and "The King of Folly
Island" is from* The King of Folly Island, and Other People
(1888).

The King of Folly Island

I.

The September afternoon was nearly spent, and the sun was
already veiled in a thin cloud of haze that hinted at coming
drought and dustiness rather than rain. Nobody could help feeling sure of just such another golden day on the morrow; this was
as good weather as heart could wish. There on the Maine coast,

where it was hard to distinguish the islands from the irregular outline of the main-land, where the summer greenness was just beginning to change into all manner of yellow and russet and scarlet tints, the year seemed to have done its work and begun its holidays.

Along one of the broad highways of the bay, in the John's Island postmaster's boat, came a stranger—a man of forty-two or forty-three years, not unprosperous but hardly satisfied, and ever on the quest for entertainment, though he called his pleasure by the hard name of work, and liked himself the better for such a wrong translation. Fate had made him a business man of good success and reputation; inclination, at least so he thought, would have led him another way, but his business ventures pleased him more than the best of his holidays. Somehow life was more interesting if one took it by contraries; he persuaded himself that he had been looking forward to this solitary ramble for many months, but the truth remained that he had found it provokingly hard to break away from his city office, his clerks, and his accounts. He had grown much richer in this last twelve-month, and as he leaned back in the stern of the boat with his arm over the rudder, he was pondering with great perplexity the troublesome question what he ought to do with so much money, and why he should have had it put into his careless hands at all. The bulk of it must be only a sort of reservoir for the sake of a later need and ownership. He thought with scorn of some liberal gifts for which he had been aggravatingly thanked and praised, and made such an impatient gesture with his shoulder that the boat gave a surprised flounce out of its straight course, and the old skipper, who was carefully inspecting the meagre contents of the mailbag, nearly lost his big silver spectacles overboard. It would have been a strange and awesome calamity. There were no new ones to be bought within seven miles.

"Did a flaw strike her?" asked Jabez Pennell, who looked curiously at the sky and sea and then at his passenger. "I've known of a porpus h'isting a boat, or mought be you kind o' shifted the rudder?"

Whereupon they both laughed; the passenger with a brilliant smile and indescribably merry sound, and the old postmaster with a mechanical grimace of the face and a rusty chuckle; then he turned to his letters again, and adjusted the rescued spectacles to his weather-beaten nose. He thought the stranger, though a silent young man, was a friendly sort of chap, boiling over with fun, as it were; whereas he was really a little morose—so much for Jabez's knowledge of human nature. "Feels kind o' strange, 't is likely; that 's better than one o' your forrard kind," mused Jabez, who took the visitor for one of the rare specimens of commercial travelers who sometimes visited John's Island—to little purpose it must be confessed. The postmaster cunningly concealed the fact that he kept the only store on John's Island; he might as well get his pay for setting the stranger across the bay, and it was nobody's business to pry into what he wanted when he got there. So Jabez gave another chuckle, and could not help looking again at the canvas-covered gun case with its neat straps, and the well-packed portmanteau that lay alongside it in the bows.

"I suppose I can find some place to stay in overnight?" asked the stranger, presently.

"Do' know 's you can, I'm sure," replied Mr. Pennell. "There ain't no reg'lar boarding places onto John's Island. Folks keep to theirselves pretty much."

"I suppose money is of some object?" gently inquired the passenger.

"Waal, yes," answered Jabez, without much apparent certainty. "Yes, John's Island folks ain't above nippin' an' squeezin' to get the best of a bargain. They 're pretty much like the rest o' the human race, an' want money, whether they 've got any use for it or not. Take it in cold weather, when you 've got pork enough and potatoes and them things in your sullar, an' it blows an' freezes so 't ain't wuth while to go out, 'most all that money 's good for is to set an' look at. Now I need to have more means than most on 'em," continued the speaker, plaintively, as if to excuse himself for any rumor of his grasping ways which might have reached his companion. "Keeping store as I do, I have to handle"—But here he stopped short, conscious of having taken a wrong step. However, they were more than half across now, and the mail was overdue; he would not be forced into going back when it was ascertained that he refused to even look at any samples.

But the passenger took no notice of the news that he was sailing with the chief and only merchant of John's Island, and even turned slowly to look back at the shore they had left, far away now, and fast growing dim on the horizon. John's Island was, on the contrary, growing more distinct, and there were some

smaller fragments of land near it; on one he could already distinguish a flock of sheep that moved slowly down a barren slope.
It was amazing that they found food enough all summer in that
narrow pasture. The suggestion of winter in this remote corner
of the world gave Frankfort a feeling of deep pity for the sheep,
as well as for all the other inhabitants. Yet it was worth a cheer-
less year to come occasionally to such weather as this; and he
filled his lungs again and again with the delicious air blown to
him from the inland country of bayberry and fir balsams across
the sparkling salt-water. The fresh northwest wind carried them
straight on their course, and the postmaster's passenger could
not have told himself why he was going to John's Island, except
that when he had apparently come to the end of everything on
an outreaching point of the main-land, he had found that there
was still a settlement beyond—John's Island, twelve miles distant, and communication would be that day afforded. "Sheep
farmers and fishermen—a real old-fashioned crowd," he had
been told. It was odd to go with the postmaster: perhaps he was
addressed by fate to some human being who expected him. Yes,
he would find out what could be done for the John's-Islanders;
then a wave of defeat seemed to chill his desire. It was better to
let them work toward what they needed and wanted; besides,
"the gift without the giver were dumb." Though after all it
would be a kind of satisfaction to take a poor little neighborhood under one's wing, and make it presents of books and various
enlightenments. It would n't be a bad thing to send it a Punch
and Judy show, or a panorama.

"May I ask your business?" interrupted Jabez Pennell, to
whom the long silence was a little oppressive.

"I am a sportsman," responded John Frankfort, the partner
in a flourishing private bank, and the merchant-postmaster's face
drooped with disappointment. No bargains, then, but perhaps a
lucrative boarder for a week or two; and Jabez instantly resolved that for not a cent less than a dollar a day should this
man share the privileges and advantages of his own food and
lodging. Two dollars a week being the current rate among John's-
Islanders, it will be easily seen that Mr. Pennell was a man of
far-seeing business enterprise.

II.

On shore, public attention was beginning to centre upon the
small white sail that was crossing the bay. At the landing there

was at first no human being to be seen, unless one had sharp eyes enough to detect the sallow, unhappy countenance of the post-master's wife. She sat at the front kitchen window of the low-storied farm-house that was perched nearly at the top of a long green slope. The store, of which the post-office department was a small fraction, stood nearer the water, at the head of the little harbor. It was a high, narrow, smartly painted little building, and looked as if it had strayed from some pretentious inland village, but the tumble-down shed near by had evidently been standing for many years, and was well acquainted with the fish business. The landing-place looked still more weather-beaten; its few timbers were barnacled and overgrown with sea-weeds below high-water mark, and the stone-work was rudely put together. There was a litter of drift-wood, of dilapidated boats and empty barrels and broken lobster pots, and a little higher on the shore stood a tar kettle, and, more prominent still, a melancholy pair of high chaise wheels, with their thorough-braces drawn uncomfortably tight by exposure to many seasonings of relentless weather.

The tide was high, and on this sheltered side of the island the low waves broke with a quick, fresh sound, and moved the pebbles gently on the narrow beach. The sun looked more and more golden red, and all the shore was glowing with color. The faint reddening tinge of some small oaks among the hemlocks farther up the island shore, the pale green and primrose of a group of birches, were all glorified with the brilliant contrast of the sea and the shining of the autumn sky. Even the green pastures and browner fields looked as if their covering had been changed to some richer material, like velvet, so soft and splendid they looked. High on a barren pasture ridge that sheltered the landing on its seaward side the huckleberry bushes had been brightened with a touch of carmine. Coming toward John's Island one might be reminded of some dull old picture that had been cleansed and wet, all its colors were suddenly grown so clear and gay.

Almost at the same moment two men appeared from different quarters of the shore, and without apparently taking any notice of each other, even by way of greeting, they seated themselves side by side on a worm-eaten piece of ship timber near the tar pot. In a few minutes a third resident of the island joined them, coming over the high pasture slope, and looking for one moment giant-like against the sky.

"Jabez need n't grumble to-day on account o' no head-wind," said one of the first comers. "I was mendin' a piece o' wall that was overset, an' I see him all of a sudden, most inshore. My woman has been expecting a letter from her brother's folks in Castine. I s'pose ye 've heard? They was all down with the throat distemper last we knew about 'em, an' she was dreadful put about because she got no word by the last mail. Lor', now wa'n't it just like Jabe's contrairiness to go over in that fussin' old dory o' his with no sail to speak of?"

"Would n't have took him half the time in his cat-boat," grumbled the elder man of the three. "Thinks he can do as he 's a mind to, an' we 've got to make the best on 't. Ef I was post-master I should look out, fust thing, for an abler boat nor any he 's got. He 's gittin nearer every year, Jabe is."

" 'T ain't fa'r to the citizens," said the first speaker. "Don't git no mail but twice a week anyhow, an' then he l'iters round long 's he 's a mind to, dickerin' an' spoutin' politics over to the Foreside. Folks may be layin' dyin', an' there 's all kinds o' urgent letters that ought to be in owners' hands direct. Jabe need n't think we mean to put up with him f'rever"; and the irate islander, who never had any letters at all from one year's end to another's looked at both his companions for their assent.

"Don't ye git riled so, Dan'el," softly responded the last-comer, a grizzled little fisherman-farmer, who looked like a pirate, and was really the most amiable man on John's Island— "don't ye git riled. I don' know as, come to the scratch, ary one of us would want to make two trips back an' forrard every week the year round for a hunderd an' twenty dollars. Take it in them high December seas, now, an' 'long in Jenoary an' March. Course he accommodates himself, an' it comes in the way o' his business, an' he gits a passenger now an' then. Well, it all counts up, I s'pose."

"There 's somebody or 'nother aboard now," said the opponent. "They may have sent over for our folks from Castine. They was headin' on to be dangerous, three o' the child'n and Wash-'n'ton himself. I may have to go up to-night. Dare say they 've sent a letter we ain't got. Darn that Jabe! I've heard before now of his looking over everything in the bag comin' over— sortin' he calls it, to save time—but 't would n't be no wonder ef a letter blowed out o' his fingers now an' again."

"There 's King George a-layin' off, ain't he?" asked the peace-maker, who was whittling a piece of dry kelp stalk that he had picked up from the pebbles, and all three men took a long look at the gray sail beyond the moorings.

"What a curi's critter that is!" exclaimed one of the group.

"I suppose, now, nothin 's goin' to tempt him to set foot on John's Island long 's he lives—do you?" but nobody answered.

"Don' know who he 's spitin' but himself," said the peacemaker. "I was underrunning my trawl last week, an' he come by with his fare o' fish, an' hove to to see what I was gittin'. Me and King George 's al'a's kind o' fellowshiped a little by spells. I was off to the Banks, you know, that time he had the gran' flare up an' took himself off, an' so he ain't counted me one o' his enemies."

"I always give my vote that he wa'n't in his right mind; 't wa'n't all ugliness, now. I went to school with him, an' he was a clever boy as there was," said the elder man, who had hardly spoken before. "I never more 'n half blamed him, however 't was, an' it kind o' rankled me that he should ha' been drove off an' outlawed hisself this way. 'T was Jabe Pennell; he thought George was stan'in' in his light 'bout the postmastership, an' he worked folks up, an' set 'em agin him. George's mother's folks did have a kind of a punky spot somewhere in their heads, but he never give no sign o' anything till Jabe Pennell begun to hunt him an' dare him."

"Well, he 's done a good thing sence he bought Folly Island. I hear say King George is gittin' rich," said the peaceful pirate. "'T was a hard thing for his folks, his wife an' the girl. I think he 's been more scattery sence his wife died, anyway. Darn! how lonesome they must be in winter! I should think they 'd be afeared a sea would break right over 'em. Pol'tics be hanged, I say, that 'll drive a man to do such things as them—never step foot on any land but his own agin! I tell ye we 've each on us got rights."

This was unusual eloquence and excitement on the speaker's part, and his neighbors stole a furtive look at him and then at each other. He was an own cousin to King George Quint, the recluse owner of Folly Island—an isolated bit of land several miles farther seaward—and one of the listeners reflected that this relationship must be the cause of his bravery.

The post-boat was nearly in now, and the three men rose and went down to the water's edge. The sail was furled, and the old dory slipped about uneasily on the low waves. The postmaster was greeted by friendly shouts from his late maligners, but he was unnecessarily busy with his sail and with his packages amidships, and took his time, as at least one spectator grumbled, about coming in. King George had also lowered his sail and taken to his oars, but just as he would have been alongside, the postmaster caught up his own oars, and pulled smartly toward the landing. This proceeding stimulated his pursuer to a stern-chase, and presently the boats were together, but Pennell pushed straight on through the low waves to the strand, and his pursuer lingered just outside, took in his oars, and dropped his killock over the bow. He knew perfectly well that the representative of the government would go ashore and take all the time he could to sort the contents of the mail-bag in his place of business. It would even be good luck if he did not go home to supper first, and keep everybody waiting all the while. Sometimes his constituents had hailed him from their fishing-boats on the high seas, and taken their weekly newspaper over the boat's side, but it was only in moments of great amiability or forgetfulness that the King of Folly Island was so kindly served. This was tyranny pure and simple. But what could be done? So was winter cold, and so did the dog-fish spoil the trawls. Even the John's-Islanders needed a fearless patriot to lead them to liberty.

The three men on the strand and King George from the harbor were all watching with curious eyes the stranger who had crossed in Jabez Pennell's boat. He was deeply interested in them also; but at that moment such a dazzling glow of sunlight broke from the cloud in the west that Frankfort turned away to look at the strange, remote landscape that surrounded him. He felt as if he had taken a step backward into an earlier age—these men had the look of pioneers or of colonists—yet the little country-side showed marks of long occupancy. He had really got to the outer boundary of civilization.

"Now it 's too bad o' you, Jabez, to keep George Quint a-waitin'," deprecated the peace-maker. "He 's got a good ways to go 'way over to Folly Island, an' like 's not he means to underrun his trawl too. We all expected ye sooner with this fair wind." At which the postmaster gave an unintelligible growl.

"This 'ere passenger was comin' over, calc'latin' to stop a spell, an' wants to be accommodated," he announced presently.

But one of the group on the strand interrupted him. He was considered the wag of that neighborhood. "Ever b'en to Folly Island, stranger?" he asked, with great civility. "There's the King of it, layin' off in his boat. George!" he called lustily, "I want to know ef you can't put up a trav'ler that wants to view these parts o' the airth?"

Frankfort somehow caught the spirit of the occasion, and

understood that there was a joke underlying this request. Folly Island had an enticing sound, and he listened eagerly for the answer. It was well known by everybody except himself that Jabez Pennell monopolized the entertainment of the traveling public, and King George roared back, delightedly, that he would do the best he could on short notice, and pulled his boat farther in. Frankfort made ready to transfer his luggage, and laughed again with the men on the shore. He was not sorry to have a longer voyage in that lovely sunset light, and the hospitality of John's Island, already represented by these specimens of house-holders, was not especially alluring. Jabez Pennell was grumbling to himself, and turned to go to the store. King George reminded him innocently of some groceries which he had promised to have ready, and always fearful of losing one of his few customers, he nodded and went his way. It seemed to be a strange combination of dependence and animosity between the men. The King followed his purveyor with a blasting glance of hatred, and turned his boat, and held it so that Frankfort could step in and reach back afterward for his possessions.

In a few minutes Mr. Pennell returned with some packages and a handful of newspapers.

"Have ye put in the cough drops?" asked the fisherman, gruffly, and was answered by a nod of the merchant's head.

"Bring them haddick before Thu'sday," he commanded the island potentate, who was already setting his small sail.

The wind had freshened. They slid out of the bay, and presently the figures on the shore grew indistinct, and Frankfort found himself outward bound on a new tack toward a low island several miles away. It seemed to be at considerable distance from any other land; the light of the sun was full upon it. Now he certainly was as far away as he could get from city life and the busy haunts of men. He wondered at the curious chain of circumstances that he had followed that day. This man looked like a hermit, and really lived in the outermost island of all.

Frankfort grew more and more amused with the novel experiences of the day. He had wished for a long time to see these Maine islands for himself. A week at Mount Desert had served to make him very impatient of the imported society of that renowned watering-place, so incongruous with the native simplicity and quiet. There was a serious look to the dark forests and bleak rocks that seemed to have been broken into fragments by some convulsion of nature, and scattered in islands and reefs along the coast. A strange population clung to these isolated bits of the world, and it was rewarding to Frankfort's sincere interest in such individualized existence that he should now be brought face to face with it.

The boat sailed steadily. A colder air, like the very breath of the great sea, met the voyagers presently. Two or three light-house lamps flashed out their first pale rays like stars, and evening had begun. Yet there was still a soft glow of color over the low seaboard. The western sky was slow to fade, and the islands looked soft and mirage-like in the growing gloom. Frankfort found himself drifting away into dreams as if he were listening to music; there was something lulling in the motion of the boat. As for the King, he took no notice of his passenger, but steered with an oar and tended the sheet and hummed a few notes occasionally of some quaint minor tune, which must have been singing itself more plainly to his own consciousness. The stranger waked from his reverie before very long, and observed with delight that the man before him had a most interesting face, a nobly moulded forehead, and brave, commanding eyes. There was truly an air of distinction and dignity about this King of Folly Island, an uncommon directness and independence. He was the son and heir of the old Vikings who had sailed that stormy coast and discovered its harborage and its vines five hundred years before Columbus was born in Italy, or was beggar to the surly lords and gentlemen of Spain.

The silence was growing strange, and provoking curiosity between the new-made host and guest, and Frankfort asked civilly some question about the distance. The King turned to look at him with surprise, as if he had forgotten his companionship. The discovery seemed to give him pleasure, and he answered, in a good clear voice, with a true fisherman's twang and brogue: "We 're more 'n half there. Be you cold?" And Frankfort confessed to a stray shiver now and then, which seemed to inspire a more friendly relationship in the boat's crew. Quick as thought, the King pulled off his own rough coat and wrapped it about the shoulders of the paler city man. Then he stepped forward along the boat, after handing the oar to his companion, and busied himself ostentatiously with a rope, with the packages that he had bought from Pennell. One would have thought he had freed himself from his coat merely as a matter of convenience; and Frankfort, who was not a little touched by the kindness, paid his new sovereign complete deference. George Quint was evidently a man whom one must be very careful about thanking, however, and there was another time of silence.

"I hope my coming will not make any trouble in your family," ventured the stranger, after a little while.

"Bless ye, no!" replied the host. "There 's only Phebe, my daughter, and nothing would please her better than somebody extra to do for. She 's dreadful folksy for a girl that 's hed to live alone on a far island, Phebe is. 'T ain't every one I 'd pick to carry home, though," said the King, magnificently. "'T has been my plan to keep clear o' humans much as could be. I had my fill o' the John's-Islanders a good while ago."

"Hard to get on with?" asked the listener, humoring the new tone which his ears had caught.

"I could get on with 'em ef 't was anyways wuth while," responded the island chieftain. "I did n't see why there was any need o' being badgered and nagged all my days by a pack o' curs like them John's-Islanders. They 'd hunt ye to death if ye was anyways their master; and I got me a piece o' land as far off from 'em as I could buy, and here I be. I ain't stepped foot on any man's land but my own these twenty-six years. Ef anybody wants to deal with me, he must come to the water's edge."

The speaker's voice trembled with excitement, and Frankfort was conscious of a strange sympathy and exhilaration.

"But why did n't you go ashore and live on the main-land, out of the way of such neighbors altogether?" he asked, and was met by a wondering look.

"I did n't belong there," replied the King, as if the idea had never occurred to him before. "I had my living to get. It took me more than twelve years to finish paying for my island, besides what hard money I laid down. Some years the fish is mighty shy. I always had an eye to the island sence I was a boy; and we 've been better off here, as I view it. I was some sorry my woman should be so fur from her folks when she was down with her last sickness."

The sail was lowered suddenly, and the boat rose and fell on the long waves near the floats of a trawl, which Quint pulled over the bows, slipping the long line by with its empty hooks until he came to a small haddock, which he threw behind him to flop and beat itself about at Frankfort's feet as if imploring him not to eat it for his supper. Then the sprit-sail was hoisted again, and they voyaged toward Folly Island slowly with a failing breeze. The King stamped his feet, and even struck his arms together as if they were chilled, but took no notice of the coat which his guest had taken off again a few minutes before. To Frankfort the evening was growing mild, and his blood rushed through his veins with a delicious thrill. The island loomed high and black, as if it were covered with thick woods; but there was a light ashore in the window of a small house, and presently the pilgrim found himself safe on land, quite stiff in his legs, but very serene in temper. A brisk little dog leaped about him with clamorous barks, a large gray cat also appeared belligerent and curious; then a voice came from the doorway: "Late, ain't you, father?"

Without a word of reply, the King of that isle led the way to his castle, haddock in hand. Frankfort and the dog and cat followed after. Before they reached the open door, the light shone out upon a little wilderness of bright flowers, yellow and red and white. The King stepped carefully up the narrow pathway, and waited on the step for his already loyal subject to enter.

"Phebe," he said, jokingly, "I 've brought ye some company— a gentleman from Lord knows where, who could n't seem to content himself without seeing Folly Island."

Phebe stepped forward with great shyness, but perfect appreciation of the right thing to be done. "I give you welcome," she said, quietly, and offered a thin affectionate hand. She was very plain in her looks, with a hard-worked, New England plainness, but as Frankfort stood in the little kitchen he was immediately conscious of a peculiar delicacy and refinement in his surroundings. There was an atmosphere in this out-of-the-way corner of civilization that he missed in all but a few of the best houses he had ever known.

The ways of the Folly Island housekeeping were too well established to be thrown out of their course by even so uncommon an event as the coming of a stranger. The simple supper was eaten, and Frankfort was ready for his share of it. He was touched at the eagerness of his hostess to serve him, at her wistful questioning of her father to learn whom he had seen and what he had heard that day. There was no actual exile in the fisherman's lot after all; he met his old acquaintances almost daily on the fishing grounds, and it was upon the women of the household that an unmistakable burden of isolation had fallen. Sometimes a man lived with them for a time to help cultivate the small farm, but Phebe was skilled in out-door handicrafts. She could use tools better than her father, the guest was told proudly, and that day she had been digging potatoes—a great pleasure evidently, as anything would have been that kept one out-of-doors in the sunshiny field.

When the supper was over, the father helped his daughter to clear away the table as simply and fondly as could be, and as if it were as much his duty as hers. It was very evident that the cough drops were for actual need; the poor girl coughed now and then with a sad insistence and hollowness. She looked ill already, so narrow-chested and bent-shouldered, while a bright spot of color flickered in her thin cheeks. She had seemed even elderly to Frankfort when he first saw her, but he discovered from something that was said that her age was much less than his own. What a dreary lifetime! he thought, and then re-proached himself, for he had never seen a happier smile than poor Phebe gave her father at that moment. The father was evidently very anxious about the cough; he started uneasily at every repetition of it, with a glance at his guest's face to see if he also were alarmed by the foreboding. The wind had risen again, and whined in the chimney. The pine-trees near the house and the wind and sea united in a solemn, deep sound which af-fected the new-comer strangely. Above this undertone was the lesser, sharper noise of waves striking the pebbly beach and retreating. There was a loneliness, a remoteness, a feeling of being an infinitesimal point in such a great expanse of sea and stormy sky, that was almost too heavy to be borne. Phebe knitted steadily, with an occasional smile at her own thoughts. The tea-kettle sang and whistled away; its cover clicked now and then as if with hardly suppressed cheerfulness, and the King of Folly Island read his newspaper diligently, and doled out bits of infor-mation to his companions. Frankfort was surprised at the tenor of these. The reader was evidently a man of uncommon depth of thought and unusual common-sense. It was both less and more surprising that he should have chosen to live alone; one would imagine that his instinct would have led him among people of his own sort. It was no wonder that he had grown impatient of such society as the postmaster's; but at this point of his medita-tion the traveler's eyes began to feel strangely heavy, and he fell asleep in his high-backed rocking-chair. What peacefulness had circled him in! the rush and clamor of his business life had fallen away as if he had begun another existence, without the fretful troubles of this present world.

"He 's a pretty man," whispered Phebe to her father, and the old fisherman nodded a grave assent, and folded his hands upon the county newspaper while he took a long honest look at the stranger within his gates.

The next morning Frankfort made his appearance in the kitchen at a nobly early hour, to find that the master of the house had been out in his boat since four o'clock, and would not be in for some time yet. Phebe was waiting to give him his breakfast, and soon after he saw her going to the potato field, and joined her. The sun was bright, and the island was gay with color; the asters were in their best pale lavender and royal purple tints; the bay was flecked with sails of fishing-boats, because the mackerel had again struck in; and outside the island, at no great distance, was the highway of the coasting vessels to and from the eastern part of the state and the more distant provinces. There were near two hundred craft in sight, great and small, and John Frankfort dug his potatoes with intermittent industry as he looked off east and west at such a lovely scene. They might have been an *abbé galant* and a dignified *marquise,* he and Phebe—it did not matter what work they toyed with. They were each filled with a charming devotion to the other, a grave reverence and humoring of the mutual desire for quiet and meditation. Toward noon the fishing-boat which Phebe had known constantly and watched with affectionate interest was seen returning deep laden, and she hastened to the little landing. Frankfort had already expressed his disdain of a noonday meal, and throwing down his hoe, betook himself to the highest point of the island. Here was a small company of hemlocks, twisted and bent by the northeast winds, and on the soft brown carpet of their short pins, our pilgrim to the outer boundaries spent the middle of the day. A strange drowsiness, such as he had often felt before in such bracing air, seemed to take possession of him, and to a man who had been perplexing himself with hard business problems and erratic ventures in financiering, potato-digging on a warm September day was not exciting.

The hemlocks stood alone on the summit of the island, and must have been a landmark for the King to steer home by. Before Frankfort stretched a half-cleared pasture, where now and then, as he lazily opened his eyes, he could see a moving sheep's back among the small birches and fern and juniper. Behind him were the cleared fields and the house, and a fringe of forest trees stood all round the rocky shore of the domain. From the water one could not see that there was such a well-arranged farm on

Folly Island behind this barrier of cedars, but the inhabitants of that region thriftily counted upon the natural stockade to keep the winter winds away.

The sun had changed its direction altogether when he finally waked, and shone broadly down upon him from a point much nearer the western horizon. At that moment the owner of the island made his appearance, looking somewhat solicitous.

"We did n't know what had become of ye, young man," he said, in a fatherly way. " 'T ain't nateral for ye to go without your dinner, as I view it. We 'll soon hearten ye up, Phebe an' me; though she don't eat no more than a chippin'-sparrer, Phebe don't," and his face returned to its sadder lines.

"No," said Frankfort; "she looks very delicate. Don't you think it might be better to take her inland, or to some more sheltered place, this winter?"

The question was asked with hesitation, but the speaker's kind-heartedness was in all his words. The father turned away and snapped a dry hemlock twig with impatient fingers.

"She would n't go withouten me," he answered, in a choked voice, "an' my vow is my vow. I shall never set foot on another man's land while I 'm alive."

The day had been so uneventful, and Folly Island had appeared to be such a calm, not to say prosaic place, that its visitor was already forgetting the thrill of interest with which he had first heard its name. Here again, however, was the unmistakable tragic element in the life of the inhabitants; this man, who should be armed and defended by his common-sense, was yet made weak by some prejudice or superstition. What could have warped him in this strange way? for, indeed, the people of most unenlightened communities were prone to herd together, to follow each other's lead, to need a dictator, no matter how much they might rebel at his example or demands. This city gentleman was moved by a deep curiosity to know for himself the laws and charts of his new-found acquaintance's existence; he had never felt a keener interest in a first day's acquaintance with any human being.

"Society would be at a stand-still," he said, with apparent lightness, "if each of us who found his neighbors unsatisfactory should strike out for himself as you have done."

The King of Folly Island gave a long shrewd look at his companion, who was still watching the mackerel fleet; then he blushed like a girl through all the sea-changed color of his cheeks.

"Look out for number one, or else number two 's got to look

out for you," he said, with some uncertainty in the tone of his voice.

"Yes," answered Frankfort, smiling. "I have repeated that to myself a great many times. The truth is, I don't belong to my neighbors any more than you do."

"I expect that you have got a better chance nor me; ef I had only been started amon'st Christians, now!" exclaimed Quint, with gathering fury at the thought of his John's-Islanders.

"Human nature is the same the world over," said the guest, quietly, as if more to himself than his listener. "I dare say that the fault is apt to be our own"; but there was no response to this audacious opinion.

Frankfort had risen from the couch of hemlock pins, and the two men walked toward the house together. The cares of modern life could not weigh too heavily on such a day. The shining sea, the white sails, gleaming or gray-shadowed, and the dark green of the nearer islands made a brilliant picture, and the younger man was impatient with himself for thinking the armada of small craft a parallel to the financial ventures which were made day after day in city life. What a question of chance it was, after all, for either herring or dollars—some of these boats were sure to go home disappointed, or worse, at night; but at this point he shrugged his shoulders angrily because he could not forget some still undecided ventures of his own. How degraded a man became who chose to be only a money-maker! The zest of the chase for wealth and the power of it suddenly seemed a very trivial and foolish thing to Frankfort, who confessed anew that he had no purpose in making his gains.

"You ain't a married man; live a bachelor life, don't ye?" asked the King, as if in recognition of these thoughts, and Frankfort, a little startled, nodded assent.

"Makes it a sight easier," was the unexpected response. "You don't feel as if you might be wronging other folks when you do what suits you best. Now my woman was wuth her weight in gold, an' she lays there in the little yard over in the corner of the field —she never fought me, nor argued the p'int again after she found I was sot, but it aged her, fetchin' of her away from all her folks, an' out of where she was wonted. I did n't foresee it at the time."

There was something martyr-like and heroic in the exile's appearance as he spoke, and his listener had almost an admiration for such heroism, until he reminded himself that this withdrawal from society had been willful, and, so far as he knew, quite self-ish. It could not be said that Quint had stood in his lot and place as a brave man should, unless he had left John's Island as the Pilgrim Fathers left England, for conscientious scruples and a necessary freedom. How many pilgrims since those have falsely made the same plea for undeserved liberty!

"What was your object in coming here?" the stranger asked, quietly, as if he had heard no reason yet that satisfied him.

"I wanted to be by myself"; and the King rallied his powers of eloquence to make excuses. "I wa'n't one that could stand them folks that overlooked an' harried me, an' was too mean to live. They could go their way, an' I mine; I would n't harm 'em, but I wanted none of 'em. Here, you see, I get my own livin'. I raise my own hog, an' the women-folks have more hens than they want, an' I keep a few sheep a-runnin' over the other side o' the place. The fish o' the sea is had for the catchin', an' I owe no man anything. I should ha' b'en beholden if I 'd stopped where we come from"; and he turned with an air of triumph to look at Frankfort, who glanced at him in return with an air of interest.

"I see that you depend upon the larger islands for some sup-plies—cough drops, for instance?" said the stranger, with need-less clearness. "I cannot help feeling that you would have done better to choose a less exposed island—one nearer the main-land, you know, in a place better sheltered from the winds."

"They do cut us 'most in two," said the King, meekly, and his face fell. Frankfort felt quite ashamed of himself, but he was conscious already of an antagonistic feeling. Indeed, this was an island of folly; this man, who felt himself to be better than his neighbors, was the sacrificer of his family's comfort; he was heaping up riches, and who would gather them? Not the poor pale daughter, that was certain. In this moment they passed the corner of the house, and discovered Phebe herself standing on the doorstep, watching some distant point of the sea or sky with a heavy, much battered spy-glass.

She looked pleased as she lowered the glass for a moment, and greeted Frankfort with a silent welcome.

"Oh, so 't is; now I forgot 't was this afternoon," said Quint. "She 's a-watchin' the funeral; ain't you, daughter? Old Mis' Danforth, over onto Wall Island, that has been layin' sick all summer—a cousin o' my mother's," he confessed, in a lower tone, and turned away with feigned unconcern as Frankfort took the spy-glass which Phebe offered. He was sure that his hostess had been wishing that she could share in the family gathering. Was it possible that Quint was a tyrant, and had never let this grown woman leave his chosen isle? Freedom, indeed!

He forgot the affairs of Folly Island the next moment, as he caught sight of the strange procession. He could see the coffin with its black pall in a boat rowed by four men, who had pushed out a little way from shore, and other boats near it. From the low gray house near the water came a little group of women stepping down across the rough beach and getting into their boats; then all fell into a rude sort of orderliness, the hearse-boat going first, and the procession went away across the wide bay toward the main-land. He lowered the glass for an instant, and Phebe reached for it eagerly.

"They were just bringing out the coffin before you came," she said, with a little sigh; and Frankfort, who had seen many pageants and ceremonials, rebuked himself for having stolen so much of this rare pleasure from his hostess. He could still see the floating funeral. Though it was only a far-away line of boats, there was a strange awe and fascination in watching them follow their single, steady course.

"Danforth's folks bury over to the Foreside," explained the King of Folly Island; but his guest had taken a little book from his pocket, and seated himself on a rock that made one boundary of the gay, disorderly garden. It was very shady and pleasant at this side of the house, and he was too warm after his walk across the unshaded pastures. It was very hot sunshine for that time of the year, and his holiday began to grow dull. Was he, after all, good for nothing but money-making? The thought fairly haunted him; he had lost his power of enjoyment, and there might be no remedy.

The fisherman had disappeared; the funeral was a dim speck off there where the sun glittered on the water, yet he saw it still, and his book closed over his listless fingers. Phebe sat on the door-step knitting now, with the old glass laid by her side ready for use. Frankfort looked at her presently with a smile.

"Will you let me see your book?" she asked, with a child's eagerness; and he gave it to her.

"It is an old copy of Wordsworth's shorter poems," he said. "It belonged to my mother. Her name was the same as yours."

"She spelled it with the *o*," said Phebe, radiant with interest in this discovery, and closely examining the flyleaf. "What a pretty hand she wrote! Is it a book you like?"

"I like it best because it was hers, I am afraid," replied Frankfort, honestly. "Yes, it does one good to read such poems; but I find it hard to read anything in these days; my business fills my mind. You know so little, here on your island, of the way the great world beyond pushes and fights and wrangles."

"I suppose there are some pleasant folks," said Phebe, simply. "I used to like to read, but I found it made me lonesome. I used to wish I could go ashore and do all the things that folks in books did. But I don't care now; I would n't go away from the island for anything."

"No," said Frankfort, kindly; "I would n't if I were you. Go on dreaming about the world; that is better. And it does people good to come here and see you so comfortable and contented," he added, with a tenderness in his voice that was quite foreign to it of late years. But Phebe gave one quick look at the far horizon, her thin cheeks grew very rosy, and she looked down again at her knitting.

Presently she went into the house. At tea-time that evening the guest was surprised to find the little table decked out for a festival, with some flowered china, and a straight-backed old mahogany chair from the best room in his own place of honor. Phebe looked gay and excited, and Frankfort wondered at the feast, as well as the master of the house, when they came to take their places.

"You see, you found me unawares last night, coming so unexpected," said the poor pale mistress. "I did n't want you to think that we had forgotten how to treat folks."

And somehow the man whose face was usually so cold and unchanging could hardly keep back his tears while, after the supper was cleared away, he was shown a little model of a meeting-house, steeple and all, which Phebe had made from cardboard and covered with small shells a winter or two before. She brought it to him with a splendid sense of its art, and Frankfort said everything that could be said except that it was beautiful. He even begged to be told exactly how it was done, and they sat by the light together and discussed the poor toy, while the King of Folly Island dozed and waked again with renewed pleasure as he contemplated his daughter's enjoyment. But she coughed very often, poor Phebe, and the guest wondered if the postmaster's supply of drugs were equal to this pitiful illness. Poor Phebe! and winter would be here soon!

Day after day, in the bright weather, Frankfort lingered with his new friends, spending a morning now and then in fishing with his host, and coming into closer contact with the inhabitants of that part of the world.

Before the short visit was over, the guest was aware that he had been very tired and out of sorts when he had yielded to the desire to hide away from civilization, and had drifted, under some pilotage that was beyond himself, into this quiet haven. He felt stronger and in much better spirits, and remembered afterward that he had been as merry as a boy on Folly Island in the long evenings when Phebe was busy with her knitting-work, and her father told long and spirited stories of his early experiences along the coast and among the fishermen. But business cares began to fret this holiday-maker, and as suddenly as he had come he went away again on a misty morning that promised rain. He was very sorry when he said good-by to Phebe; she was crying as he left the house, and a great wave of compassion poured itself over Frankfort's heart. He never should see her again, that was certain; he wished that he could spirit her away to some gentler climate, and half spoke his thought as he stood hesitating that last minute on the little beach. The next moment he was fairly in the boat and pushing out from shore. George Quint looked as hardy and ruddy and weather-beaten as his daughter was pale and faded, like some frost-bitten flower that tries to lift itself when morning comes and it feels the warmth of the sun. The tough fisherman, with his pet doctrines and angry aversions, could have no idea of the loneliness of his wife and daughter all these unvarying years on his Folly Island. And yet how much they had been saved of useless rivalries and jealousies, of petty tyranny from narrow souls! Frankfort had a bitter sense of all that, as he leaned back against the side of the boat, and sailed slowly out into the bay, while Folly Island seemed to retreat into the gathering fog and slowly disappear. His thoughts flew before him to his office, to his clerks and accounts; he thought of his wealth which was buying him nothing, of his friends who were no friends at all, for he had pushed away some who might have been near, strangely impatient of familiarity, and on the defense against either mockery or rivalry. He was the true King of Folly Island, not this work-worn fisherman; he had been a lonelier and a more selfish man these many years.

George Quint was watching Frankfort eagerly, as if he had been waiting for this chance to speak to him alone.

"You seem to be a kind of solitary creatur'," he suggested,

with his customary frankness. "I expect it never crossed your thought that 't would be nateral to git married?"

"Yes, I thought about it once, some years ago," answered Frankfort, seriously.

"Disapp'inted, was you? Well, 't was better soon nor late, if it had to be," said the sage. "My mind has been dwellin' on Phebe's case. She was a master pooty gal 'arlier on, an' I was dreadful set against lettin' of her go, though I call to mind there was a likely chap as found her out, an' made bold to land an' try to court her. I drove him, I tell you, an' ducked him under when I caught him afterward out a-fishin', an' he took the hint. Phebe did n't know what was to pay, though I dare say she liked to have him follerin' about."

Frankfort made no answer,—he was very apt to be silent when you expected him to speak,—and presently the King resumed his suggestions.

"I 've been thinking that Phebe ought to have some sort o' brightenin' up. She pines for her mother: they was a sight o' company for each other. Now I s'pose you could n't take no sort o' fancy for her in course o' time? I 've got more hard cash stowed away than folks expects, an' you should have everything your own way. I could git a cousin o' mine, a widow woman, to keep the house winters, an' you an' the gal need n't only summer here. I take it you 've got some means?"

Frankfort found himself smiling at this pathetic appeal, and was ashamed of himself directly, and turned to look seaward. "I 'm afraid I could n't think of it," he answered. "You don't suppose"—

"Lor' no," said George Quint, sadly, shifting his sail. "*She* ain't give no sign, except that I never see her take to no stranger as she has to you. I thought you might kind of have a feelin' for her, an' I knowed you thought the island was a sightly place; 't would do no harm to speak, leastways."

They were on their way to John's Island, where Frankfort was to take the postmaster's boat to the main-land. Quint found his fog-bound way by some mysterious instinct, and at their journey's ends the friends parted with little show of sentiment or emotion. Yet there was much expression in Quint's grasp of his hand, Frankfort thought, and both men turned more than once as the boats separated, to give a kindly glance backward. People are not brought together in this world for nothing, and poor Quint had no idea of the confusion that his theories and his manner of life had brought into the well-regulated affairs of John Frankfort. Jabez Pennell was brimful of curiosity about the visit, but he received little satisfaction. "Phebe Quint was the pootiest gal on these islands some ten years ago," he proclaimed, "an' a born lady. Her mother's folks was ministers over to Castine."

The winter was nearly gone when Frankfort received a letter in a yellow envelope, unbusiness-like in its appearance. The King of Folly Island wrote to say that Phebe had been hoping to get strength enough to thank him for the generous Christmas-box which Frankfort had sent. He had taxed both his imagination and memory to supply the minor wants and fancies of the islanders.

But Phebe was steadily failing in health, and the elderly cousin had already been summoned to take care of her and to manage the house-keeping. The King wrote a crabbed hand, as if he had used a fish-hook instead of a pen, and he told the truth about his sad affairs with simple, unlamenting bravery. Phebe only sent a message of thanks, and an assurance that she liked to think of Frankfort's being there in the fall. She would soon send him a small keepsake.

One morning Frankfort opened a much-crushed bundle which lay upon his desk, and found this keepsake, the shell meeting-house, which looked sadly trivial and astray. He was entirely confused by its unexpected appearance; he did not dare to meet the eyes of an office-boy who stood near; there was an uncomfortable feeling in his throat, but he bravely unfastened a letter from the battered steeple, and read it slowly, without a very clear understanding of the words: —

"DEAR FRIEND" (said poor Phebe),—"I was very thankful for all that you sent in the box—I take such pleasure in the things. I find it hard to write, but I think about you every day. Father sends his best respects. We have had rough weather, and he stays right here with me. You must keep your promise, and come back to the island; he will be lonesome, and you are one that takes father just right. It seems as if I had n't been any use in the world, but it rests me, laying here, to think what a sight of use you must be. And so good-by."

A sudden vision of the poor girl came before his eyes as he

saw her stand on the door-step the day they watched the boat funeral. She had worn a dress with a quaint pattern, like gray and yellowish willow leaves as one sees them fallen by the country roadsides. A vision of her thin, stooping shoulders and her simple, pleasant look touched him with real sorrow. "Much use in the world!" Alas! alas! how had her affection made her fancy such a thing!

The day was stormy, and Frankfort turned anxiously to look out of the window beside him, as he thought how the wind must blow across the distant bay. He felt a strange desire to sweep away everything that might vex poor Phebe or make her less comfortable. Yet she must die, at any rate, before the summer came. The King of Folly Island would reign only over his sheep pastures and the hemlock-trees and pines. Much use in the world! The words stung him more and more.

The office-boy still stood waiting, and now Frankfort became unhappily conscious of his presence. "I used to see one o' them shell-works where I come from, up in the country," the boy said, with unexpected forbearance and sympathy; but Frankfort dismissed him with a needless question about the price of certain railroad bonds, and dropped the embarrassing gift, the poor little meeting-house, into a deep lower drawer of his desk. He had hardly thought of the lad before except as a willing, half mechanical errand-runner; now he was suddenly conscious of the hopeful, bright young face. At that moment a whole new future of human interests spread out before his eyes, from which a veil had suddenly been withdrawn, and Frankfort felt like another man, or as if there had been a revivifying of his old, uninterested, self-occupied nature. Was there really such a thing as taking part in the heavenly warfare against ignorance and selfishness? Had Phebe given him in some mysterious way a legacy of all her unsatisfied hopes and dreams?

The Gray Man

High on the southern slope of Agamenticus there may still be seen the remnant of an old farm. Frost-shaken stone walls surround a fast-narrowing expanse of smooth turf which the forest is overgrowing on every side. The cellar is nearly filled up, never having been either wide or deep, and the fruit of a few mossy apple-trees drops ungathered to the ground. Along one side of the forsaken garden is a thicket of seedling cherry-trees to which the shouting robins come year after year in busy flights; the caterpillars' nests are unassailed and populous in this untended hedge. At night, perhaps, when summer twilights are late in drawing their brown curtain of dusk over the great rural scene,— at night an owl may sit in the hemlocks near by and hoot and shriek until the far echoes answer back again. As for the few men and women who pass this deserted spot, most will be repulsed by such loneliness, will even grow impatient with those mistaken fellow-beings who choose to live in solitude, away from neighbors and from schools,—yes, even from gossip and petty care of self or knowledge of the trivial fashions of a narrow life.

Now and then one looks out from this eyrie, across the wide-spread country, who turns to look at the sea or toward the shining foreheads of the mountains that guard the inland horizon, who will remember the place long afterward. A peaceful vision will come, full of rest and benediction into busy and troubled hours, to those who understand why some one came to live in this place so near the sky, so silent, so full of sweet air and woodland fragrance; so beaten and buffeted by winter storms and garlanded with summer greenery; where the birds are nearest neighbors and a clear spring the only wine-cellar, and trees of the forest a choir of singers who rejoice and sing aloud by day and night as the winds sweep over. Under the cherry thicket or at the edge of the woods you may find a stray-away blossom, some half-savage, slender grandchild of the old flower-plots, that you gather gladly to take away, and every year in June a red rose blooms toward which the wild pink roses and the pale sweet briars turn wondering faces as if a queen had shown her noble face suddenly at a peasant's festival.

There is everywhere a token of remembrance, of silence and secrecy. Some stronger nature once ruled these neglected trees and this fallow ground. They will wait the return of their master as long as roots can creep through mould, and the mould make way for them. The stories of strange lives have been whispered to the earth, their thoughts have burned themselves into the cold rocks. As one looks from the lower country toward the long slope of the great hillside, this old abiding-place marks the dark covering of trees like a scar. There is nothing to hide either the sunrise or the sunset. The low lands reach out of sight into the west and the sea fills all the east.

The first owner of the farm was a seafaring man who had through freak or fancy come ashore and cast himself upon the bounty of nature for support in his later years, though tradition keeps a suspicion of buried treasure and of a dark history. He cleared his land and built his house, but save the fact that he was a Scotsman no one knew to whom he belonged, and when he died the state inherited the unclaimed property. The only piece of woodland that was worth anything was sold and added to another farm, and the dwelling-place was left to the sunshine and the rain, to the birds that built their nests in the chimney or under the eaves. Sometimes a strolling company of country boys would find themselves near the house on a holiday afternoon, but the more dilapidated the small structure became, the more they believed that some uncanny existence possessed the lonely place, and the path that led toward the clearing at last became almost impassable.

Once a number of officers and men in the employ of the Coast Survey were encamped at the top of the mountain, and they smoothed the rough track that led down to the spring that bubbled from under a sheltering edge. One day a laughing fellow, not content with peering in at the small windows of the house, put his shoulder against the rain-blackened door and broke the simple fastening. He hardly knew that he was afraid as he first stood within the single spacious room, so complete a curiosity took possession of him. The place was clean and bare, the empty cupboard doors stood open, and yet the sound of his companions' voices outside seemed far away, and an awful sense that some unseen inhabitant followed his footsteps made him hurry out again pale and breathless to the fresh air and sunshine. Was this really a dwelling-place of spirits, as had been already hinted? The story grew more fearful, and spread quickly like a mist of terror among the lowland farms. For years the tale of the coast-surveyor's adventure in the haunted house was slowly magnified and told to strangers or to wide-eyed children by the dim firelight. The former owner was supposed to linger still about his old home, and was held accountable for deep offense in choosing for the scene of his unsuccessful husbandry a place that escaped the proprieties and restraints of life upon lower levels. His grave was concealed by the new growth of oaks and beeches, and many a lad and full-grown man beside has taken to his heels at the flicker of light from across a swamp or under a decaying tree in that neighborhood. As the world in some respects grew wiser, the good people near the mountain understood less and less the causes of these simple effects, and as they became familiar with the visible world, grew more shy of the unseen and more sensitive to unexplained foreboding.

One day a stranger was noticed in the town, as a stranger is sure to be who goes his way with quick, furtive steps straight through a small village or along a country road. This man was tall and had just passed middle age. He was well made and vigorous, but there was an unusual pallor in his face, a grayish look, as if he had been startled by bad news. His clothes were somewhat peculiar, as if they had been made in another country, yet they suited the chilly weather, being homespun of undyed wools, just the color of his hair, and only a little darker than his face or hands. Some one observed in one brief glance as he and this gray man met and passed each other, that his eyes had a strange faded look; they might, however, flash and be coal-black in a moment of rage. Two or three persons stepped forward to watch the wayfarer as he went along the road with long, even strides, like one taking a journey on foot, but he quickly reached a turn of the way and was out of sight. They wondered who he was; one recalled some recent advertisement of an escaped criminal, and another the appearance of a native of the town who was supposed to be long ago lost at sea, but one surmiser knew as little as the next. If they had followed fast enough they might have tracked the mysterious man straight across the country, threading the by-ways, the shorter paths that led across the fields where the road was roundabout and hindering. At last he disappeared in the leafless, trackless woods that skirted the mountain.

That night there was for the first time in many years a twinkling light in the window of the haunted house, high on the hill's great shoulder; one farmer's wife and another looked up curiously, while they wondered what daring human being had chosen that awesome spot of all others for his home or for even a transient shelter. The sky was already heavy with snow; he might be a fugitive from justice, and the startled people looked to the fastening of their doors unwontedly that night, and waked often from a troubled sleep.

An instinctive curiosity and alarm possessed the country men and women for a while, but soon faded out and disappeared. The newcomer was by no means a hermit; he tried to be friendly, and inclined toward a certain kindliness and familiarity. He bought a comfortable store of winter provisions from his new acquaintances, giving every one his price, and spoke more at length, as time went on, of current events, of politics and the weather, and the town's own news and concerns. There was a sober cheerfulness about the man, as if he had known trouble and perplexity, and was fulfilling some mission that gave him pain; yet he saw some gain and reward beyond; therefore he could be contented with his life and such strange surroundings. He was more and more eager to form brotherly relations with the farmers near his home. There was almost a pleading look in his kind face at times, as if he feared the later prejudice of his associates. Surely this was no common or uneducated person, for in every way he left the stamp of his character and influence upon men and things. His reasonable words of advice and warning are current as sterling coins in that region yet; to one man he taught a new rotation of crops, to another he gave some priceless cures for devastating diseases of cattle. The lonely women of those remote country homes learned of him how to achieve their household toil with less labor and drudgery, and here and there he singled out promising children and kept watch of their growth, giving freely a most affectionate companionship, and a fair start in the journey of life. He taught those who were guardians of such children to recognize and further the true directions and purposes of existence; and the easily warped natures grew strong and well-established under his thoughtful care. No wonder that some people were filled with amazement, and thought his wisdom supernatural, from so many proofs that his horizon was wider than their own.

Perhaps some envious soul, or one aggrieved by being caught in treachery or deception, was the first to find fault with the stranger. The prejudice against his dwelling-place, and the superstition which had become linked to him in consequence, may have led back to the first suspicious attitude of the community. The whisper of distrust soon started on an evil way. If he were not a criminal, his past was surely a hidden one, and shocking to his remembrance, but the true foundation of all dislike was the fact that the gray man who went to and fro, living his simple, harmless life among them, *never was seen to smile.* Persons who remember him speak of this with a shudder, for nothing is more evident than that his peculiarity became at length intolerable to those whose minds lent themselves readily to suspicion. At first, blinded by the gentle good fellowship of the stranger, the changeless expression of his face was scarcely observed, but as the winter wore away he was watched with renewed disbelief and dismay.

After the first few attempts at gayety nobody tried to tell a merry story in his presence. The most conspicuous of a joker's audience does a deep-rankling injustice if he sits with unconscious, unamused face at the receipt of raillery. What a chilling moment when the gray man softly opened the door of a farmhouse kitchen and seated himself like a skeleton at the feast of walnuts and roasted apples beside the glowing fire! The children whom he treated so lovingly, to whom he ever gave his best, though they were won at first by his gentleness, when they began to prattle and play with him would raise their innocent eyes to his face and hush their voices and creep away out of his sight. Once only he was bidden to a wedding, but never afterward, for a gloom was quickly spread through the boisterous company; the man who never smiled had no place at such a festival. The wedding guests looked over their shoulders again and again in strange foreboding, while he was in the house, and were burdened with a sense of coming woe for the newly-married pair. As one caught sight of his, among the faces of the rural folk, the gray man was like a sombre mask, and at last the bridegroom flung open the door with a meaning gesture, and the stranger went out like a hunted creature, into the bitter coldness and silence of the winter night.

Through the long days of the next summer the outcast of the wedding, forbidden, at length, all the once-proffered hospitality, was hardly seen from one week's end to another's. He cultivated his poor estate with patient care, and the successive crops of his small garden, the fruits and berries of the wilderness, were food enough. He seemed unchangeable, and was always ready when he even guessed at a chance to be of use. If he were repulsed, he only turned away and went back to his solitary home. Those persons who by chance visited him there tell wonderful tales of the wild birds which had been tamed to come at his call and cluster about him, of the orderliness and delicacy of his simple life. The once-neglected house was covered with vines that he had brought from the woods, and planted about the splintering, decaying walls. There were three or four books in worn bindings on a shelf above the fire-place; one longs to know what volumes this mysterious exile had chosen to keep him company!

There may have been a deeper reason for the withdrawal of friendliness; there are vague rumors of the gray man's possession of strange powers. Some say that he was gifted with amazing strength, and once when some belated hunters found shelter at his fireside, they told eager listeners afterward that he did not sleep but sat by the fire reading gravely while they slumbered uneasily on his own bed of boughs. And in the dead of night an empty chair glided silently toward him across the floor as he softly turned his pages in the flickering light.

But such stories are too vague, and in that neighborhood too common to weigh against the true dignity and bravery of the man. At the beginning of the war of the rebellion he seemed strangely troubled and disturbed, and presently disappeared, leaving his house key with a neighbor as if for a few days' absence. He was last seen striding rapidly through the village a few miles away, going back along the road by which he had come a year or two before. No, not last seen either; for in one of the first battles of the war, as the smoke suddenly lifted, a farmer's boy, reared in the shadow of the mountain, opened his languid pain-dulled eyes as he lay among the wounded, and saw the gray man riding by on a tall horse. At that moment the poor lad thought in his faintness and fear that Death himself rode by in the gray man's likeness; unsmiling Death who tries to teach and serve mankind so that he may at the last win welcome as a faithful friend!

The Gray Mills of Farley

I.

The mills of Farley were close together by the river, and the gray houses that belonged to them stood, tall and bare, alongside. They had no room for gardens or even for little green side-yards where one might spend a summer evening. The Corporation, as this compact village was called by those who lived in it, was small but solid; you fancied yourself in the heart of a large town when you stood midway of one of its short streets, but from the street's end you faced a wide green farming country. On spring and summer Sundays, groups of the young folks of the Corporation would stray out along the country roads, but it was very seldom that any of the older people went. On the whole, it seemed as if the closer you lived to the mill-yard gate, the better. You had more time to loiter on a summer morning, and there was less distance to plod through the winter snows and rains. The last stroke of the bell saw almost everybody within the mill doors.

There were always fluffs of cotton in the air like great white bees drifting down out of the picker chimney. They lodged in the cramped and dingy elms and horse-chestnuts which a former agent had planted along the streets, and the English sparrows squabbled over them in eaves-corners and made warm, untidy great nests that would have contented an Arctic explorer. Somehow the Corporation homes looked like make-believe houses or huge stage-properties, they had so little individuality or likeness to the old-fashioned buildings that made homes for people out on the farms. There was more homelikeness in the sparrows' nests, or even the toylike railroad station at the end of the main street, for that was warmed by steam, and the station-master's wife, thriftily taking advantage of the steady heat, brought her house-plants there and kept them all winter on the broad window-sills.

The Corporation had followed the usual fortunes of New England manufacturing villages. Its operatives were at first eager young men and women from the farms near by, these being joined quickly by pale English weavers and spinners, with their hearty-looking wives and rosy children; then came the flock of Irish families, poorer and simpler than the others but learning the work sooner, and gayer-hearted; now the Canadian-French contingent furnished all the new help, and stood in long rows before the noisy looms and chattered in their odd, excited fashion. They were quicker-fingered, and were willing to work cheaper than any other workpeople yet.

There were remnants of each of these human tides to be found as one looked about the mills. Old Henry Dow, the overseer of the cloth-hall, was a Lancashire man and some of his grandchildren had risen to wealth and prominence in another part of the country, while he kept steadily on with his familiar work and authority. A good many elderly Irishmen and women still kept their places; everybody knew the two old sweepers, Mary Cassidy and Mrs. Kilpatrick, who were looked upon as pillars of the Corporation. They and their compatriots always held loyally together and openly resented the incoming of so many French.

You would never have thought that the French were for a moment conscious of being in the least unwelcome. They came gayly into church and crowded the old parishioners of St. Michael's out of their pews, as on week-days they took their places at the looms. Hardly one of the old parishioners had not taken occasion to speak of such aggressions to Father Daley, the priest, but Father Daley continued to look upon them all as souls to be saved and took continual pains to rub up the rusty French which he had nearly forgotten, in order to preach a special sermon every other Sunday. This caused old Mary Cassidy to shake her head gravely.

"Mis' Kilpatrick, ma'am," she said one morning. "Faix, they ain't folks at all, 'tis but a pack of images they do be, with all their chatter like birds in a hedge."

"Sure then, the holy Saint Frances himself was after saying that the little birrds was his sisters," answered Mrs. Kilpatrick, a godly old woman who made the stations every morning, and was often seen reading a much-handled book of devotion. She was moreover always ready with a friendly joke.

"They ain't the same at all was in them innocent times, when there was plinty saints living in the world," insisted Mary Cassidy. "Look at them thrash, now!"

The old sweeping-women were going downstairs with their brooms. It was almost twelve o'clock, and like the old dray-horses in the mill yard they slackened work in good season for the noonday bell. Three gay young French girls ran downstairs past them; they were let out for the afternoon and were hurrying home to dress and catch the 12:40 train to the next large town.

"That little one is Meshell's daughter; she's a nice child too, very quiet, and has got more Christian tark than most," said Mrs. Kilpatrick. "They live overhead o' me. There's nine o' themselves in the two rooms; two does be boarders."

"Those upper rooms bees very large entirely at Fitzgibbon's," said Mary Cassidy with unusual indulgence.

" 'Tis all the company cares about is to get a good rent out of the pay. They're asked every little while by honest folks 'on't they build a trifle o' small houses beyond the church up there, but no, they'd rather the money and kape us like bees in them old hives. Sure in winter we're better for having the more fires, but summer is the pinance!"

"They all says 'why don't folks build their own houses'; they does always be talking about Mike Callahan and how well he saved up and owns a pritty place for himself convanient to his work. You might tell them he'd money left him by a brother in California till you'd be black in the face, they'd stick to it 'twas in the picker he earnt it from themselves," grumbled Mary Cassidy.

"Them French spinds all their money on their backs, don't they?" suggested Mrs. Kilpatrick, as if to divert the conversation from dangerous channels. "Look at them three girls now, off to Spincer with their fortnight's pay in their pocket!"

"A couple o' onions and a bag o' crackers is all they want and a pinch o' lard to their butter," pronounced Mary Cassidy with scorn. "The whole town of 'em 'on't be the worse of a dollar for steak the week round. They all go back and buy land in Canada, they spend no money here. See how well they forget their pocketbooks every Sunday for the collection. They do be very light too, they've more laugh than ourselves. 'Tis myself's getting old anyway, I don't laugh much now."

"I like to see a pritty girl look fine," said Mrs. Kilpatrick. "No, they don't be young but once——"

The mill bell rang, and there was a moment's hush of the jarring, racketing machinery and a sudden noise of many feet trampling across the dry, hard pine floors. First came an early flight of boys bursting out of the different doors, and chasing one another down the winding stairs two steps at a time. The old sweepers, who had not quite reached the bottom, stood back against the wall for safety's sake until all these had passed, then they kept on their careful way, the crowd passing them by as if they were caught in an eddy of the stream. Last of all they kept sober company with two or three lame persons and a cheerful delayed little group of new doffers, the children who minded bobbins in the weave-room and who were young enough to be tired and even timid. One of these doffers, a pale, pleasant-looking child, was all fluffy with cotton that had clung to her little dark plaid dress. When Mrs. Kilpatrick spoke to her she answered in a hoarse voice that appealed to one's sympathy. You felt that the hot room and dry cotton were to blame for such hoarseness; it had nothing to do with the weather.

"Where are you living now, Maggie, dear?" the old woman asked.

"I'm in Callahan's yet, but they won't keep me after to-day," said the child. "There's a man wants to get board there, they're changing round in the rooms and they've no place for me. Mis' Callahan couldn't keep me 'less I'd get my pay raised."

Mrs. Kilpatrick gave a quick glance at Mary Cassidy. "Come home with me then, till yez get a bite o' dinner, and we'll talk about it," she said kindly to the child. "I'd a wish for company the day."

The two old companions had locked their brooms into a three-cornered closet at the stair-foot and were crossing the mill yard together. They were so much slower than the rest that they could only see the very last of the crowd of mill people disappearing along the streets and into the boardinghouse doors. It was late autumn, the elms were bare, one could see the whole village of Farley, all its poverty and lack of beauty, at one glance. The large houses looked as if they belonged to a toy village, and had been carefully put in rows by a childish hand; it was easy to lose all sense of size in looking at them. A cold wind was blowing bits of waste and paper high into the air; now and then a snowflake went swiftly by like a courier of winter. Mary Cassidy and Mrs. Kilpatrick hugged their old woolen shawls closer about their round shoulders, and the little girl followed with short steps alongside.

II.

The agent of the mills was a single man, keen and business-like, but quietly kind to the people under his charge. Sometimes, in times of peace, when one looks among one's neighbors wondering who would make the great soldiers and leaders if there came a sudden call to war, one knows with a flash of recognition the presence of military genius in such a man as he. The agent spent his days in following what seemed to many observers to be only a dull routine, but all his steadiness of purpose, all his simple intentness, all his gifts of strategy and powers of foresight, and of turning an interruption into an opportunity, were brought to bear upon this dull routine with a keen pleasure. A man in his place must know not only how to lead men, but how to make the combination of their force with the machinery take its place as a factor in the business of manufacturing. To master workmen and keep the mills in running order and to sell the goods success-fully in open market is as easy to do badly as it is difficult to do well.

The agent's father and mother, young people who lived for a short time in the village, had both died when he was only three years old, and between that time and his ninth year he had learned almost everything that poverty could teach, being left like little Maggie to the mercy of his neighbors. He remembered with a grateful heart those who were good to him, and told him of his mother, who had married for love but unwisely. Mrs. Kilpatrick was one of these old friends, who said that his mother was a lady, but even Mrs. Kilpatrick, who was a walking history of the Corporation, had never known his mother's maiden name, much less the place of her birth. The first great revelation of life had come when the nine-years-old boy had money in his hand to pay his board. He was conscious of being looked at with a dif-ference; the very woman who had been hardest to him and let him mind her babies all the morning when he, careful little soul, was hardly more than a baby himself, and then pushed him out into the hungry street at dinner time, was the first one who beck-oned him now, willing to make the most of his dollar and a quarter a week. It seemed easy enough to rise from uttermost poverty and dependence to where one could set his mind upon the highest honor in sight, that of being agent of the mills, or to work one's way steadily to where such an honor was grasped at thirty-two. Every year the horizon had set its bounds wider and wider, until the mills of Farley held but a small place in the manufacturing world. There were offers enough of more salary and higher position from those who came to know the agent, but he was part of Farley itself, and had come to care deeply about his neighbors, while a larger mill and salary were not exactly the things that could tempt his ambition. It was but a lonely life for a man in the old agent's quarters where one of the widows of the Corporation, a woman who had been brought up in a gentleman's house in the old country, kept house for him with a certain show of propriety. Ever since he was a boy his room was never without its late evening light, and books and hard study made his chief companionship.

As Mrs. Kilpatrick went home holding little Maggie by the hand that windy noon, the agent was sitting in the company's counting-room with one of the directors and largest stockholders, and they were just ending a long talk about the mill affairs. The agent was about forty years old now and looked fifty. He had a pleasant smile, but one saw it rarely enough, and just now he looked more serious than usual.

"I am very glad to have had this long talk with you," said the old director. "You do not think of any other recommendations to be made at the meeting next week?"

The agent grew a trifle paler and glanced behind him to be sure that the clerks had gone to dinner.

"Not in regard to details," he answered gravely. "There is one thing which I see to be very important. You have seen the books, and are clear that nine per cent. dividend can easily be declared?"

"Very creditable, very creditable," agreed the director; he had recognized the agent's ability from the first and always upheld him generously. "I mean to propose a special vote of thanks for your management. There isn't a minor corporation in New England that stands so well to-day."

The agent listened. "We had some advantages, partly by accident and partly by lucky foresight," he acknowledged. "I am going to ask your backing in something that seems to me not only just but important. I hope that you will not declare above a six per cent. dividend at that directors' meeting; at the most, seven per cent.," he said.

"What, what!" exclaimed the listener. "No, sir!"

The agent left his desk-chair and stood before the old director as if he were pleading for himself. A look of protest and disappointment changed the elder man's face and hardened it a little, and the agent saw it.

"You know the general condition of the people here," he explained humbly. "I have taken great pains to keep hold of the best that have come here; we can depend upon them now and upon the quality of their work. They made no resistance when we had to cut down wages two years ago; on the contrary, they were surprisingly reasonable, and you know that we shut down for several weeks at the time of the alterations. We have never put their wages back as we might easily have done, and I happen to know that a good many families have been able to save little or nothing. Some of them have been working here for three generations. They know as well as you and I and the books do when the mills are making money. Now I wish that we could give them the ten per cent. back again, but in view of the general depression perhaps we can't do that except in the way I mean. I think that next year we're going to have a very hard pull to get along, but if we can keep back three per cent., or even two, of this dividend we can not only manage to get on without a shut-down or touching our surplus, which is quite small enough, but I can have some painting and repairing done in the tenements. They've needed it for a long time——"

The old director sprang to his feet. "Aren't the stockholders going to have any rights then?" he demanded. "Within fifteen years we have had three years when we have passed our dividends, but the operatives never can lose a single day's pay!"

"That was before my time," said the agent, quietly. "We have averaged nearly six and a half per cent. a year taking the last twenty years together, and if you go back farther the average is even larger. This has always been a paying property; we've got our new machinery now, and everything in the mills themselves is just where we want it. I look for far better times after this next year, but the market is glutted with goods of our kind, and nothing is going to be gained by cut-downs and forcing lower-cost goods into it. Still, I can keep things going one way and another, making yarn and so on," he said pleadingly. "I should like to feel that we had this extra surplus. I believe that we owe it to our operatives."

The director had walked heavily to the window and put his hands deep into his side-pockets. He had an angry sense that the agent's hands were in his pockets too.

"I've got some pride about that nine per cent., sir," he said loftily to the agent.

"So have I," said the agent, and the two men looked each other in the face.

"I acknowledge my duty to the stockholders," said the younger man presently. "I have tried to remember that duty ever since I took the mills eight years ago, but we've got an excellent body of operatives, and we ought to keep them. I want to show them this next year that we value their help. If times aren't as bad as we fear we shall still have the money——"

"Nonsense. They think they own the mills now," said the director, but he was uncomfortable, in spite of believing he was right. "Where's my hat? I must have my luncheon now, and afterward there'll hardly be time to go down and look at the new power-house with you—I must be off on the quarter-to-two train."

The agent sighed and led the way. There was no use in saying anything more and he knew it. As they walked along they met old Mrs. Kilpatrick returning from her brief noonday meal with little Maggie, whose childish face was radiant. The old woman recognized one of the directors and dropped him a decent curtsey as she had been taught to salute the gentry sixty years before.

The director returned the salutation with much politeness. This was really a pleasant incident, and he took a silver half dollar from his pocket and gave it to the little girl before he went on.

"Kape it safe, darlin'," said the old woman; "you'll need it yet. Don't be spending all your money in sweeties; 'tis a very cold world to them that haves no pince in their pocket."

The child looked up at Mrs. Kilpatrick apprehensively; then the sunshine of hope broke out again through the cloud.

"I am going to save fine till I buy a house, and you and me'll live there together, Mrs. Kilpatrick, and have a lovely coal fire all the time."

"Faix, Maggie, I have always thought some day I'd kape a pig and live pritty in me own house," said Mrs. Kilpatrick. "But I'm the old sweeper yet in Number Two. 'Tis a world where some has and more wants," she added with a sigh. "I got the manes for a good buryin', the Lord be praised, and a bitteen more beside. I wouldn't have that if Father Daley was as croping as some."

"Mis' Mullin does always be scolding 'bout Father Daley having all the collections," ventured Maggie, somewhat adrift in so great a subject.

"She's no right then!" exclaimed the old woman angrily;

"she'll get no luck to be grudging her pince that way. 'Tis hard work anny priest would have to kape the likes of hersilf from being haythens altogether."

There was a nine per cent. annual dividend declared at the directors' meeting the next week, with considerable applause from the board and sincere congratulations to the agent. He looked thinner and more sober than usual, and several persons present, whose aid he had asked in private, knew very well the reason. After the meeting was over the senior director, and largest stockholder, shook hands with him warmly.

"About that matter you suggested to me the other day," he said, and the agent looked up eagerly. "I consulted several of our board in regard to the propriety of it before we came down, but they all agreed with me that it was no use to cross a bridge until you come to it. Times look a little better, and the operatives will share in the accession of credit to a mill that declares nine per cent. this year. I hope that we shall be able to run the mills with at worst only a moderate cut-down, and they may think themselves very fortunate when so many hands are being turned off everywhere."

The agent's face grew dark. "I hope that times will take a better turn," he managed to say.

"Yes, yes," answered the director. "Good-bye to you. Mr. Agent! I am not sure of seeing you again for some time," he added with unusual kindliness. "I am an old man now to be hurrying round to board meetings and having anything to do with responsibilities like these. My sons must take their turn."

There was an eager protest from the listeners, and presently the busy group of men disappeared on their way to the train. A nine per cent. dividend naturally made the Farley Manufacturing Company's stock go up a good many points, and word came presently that the largest stockholder and one or two other men had sold out. Then the stock ceased to rise, and winter came on apace, and the hard times which the agent had foreseen came also.

III.

One noon in early March there were groups of men and women gathering in the Farley streets. For a wonder, nobody was hurrying toward home and dinner was growing cold on some of the long boarding-house tables.

"They might have carried us through the cold weather; there's but a month more of it," said one middle-aged man sorrowfully.

"They'll be talking to us about economy now, some o' them big thinkers; they'll say we ought to learn how to save; they always begin about that quick as the work stops," said a youngish woman angrily. She was better dressed than most of the group about her and had the keen, impatient look of a leader. "They'll say that manufacturing is going to the dogs, and capital's in worse distress than labor——"

"How is it those big railroads get along? They can't shut down, there's none o' them stops; they cut down sometimes when they have to, but they don't turn off their help this way," complained somebody else.

"Faith then! they don't know what justice is. They talk about their justice all so fine," said a pale-faced young Irishman—"justice is nine per cent. last year for the men that had the money and no rise at all for the men that did the work."

"They say the shut-down's going to last all summer anyway. I'm going to pack my kit to-night," said a young fellow who had just married and undertaken with unusual pride and ambition to keep house. "The likes of me can't be idle. But where to look for any work for a mule spinner, the Lord only knows!"

Even the French were sobered for once and talked eagerly among themselves. Halfway down the street, in front of the French grocery, a man was haranguing his compatriots from the top of a packing-box. Everybody was anxious and excited by the sudden news. No work after a week from to-morrow until times were better. There had already been a cut-down, the mills had not been earning anything all winter. The agent had hoped to keep on for at least two months longer, and then to make some scheme about running at half time in the summer, setting aside the present work for simple yarn-making. He knew well enough that the large families were scattered through the mill rooms and that any pay would be a help. Some of the young men could be put to other work for the company; there was a huge tract of woodland farther back among the hills where some timber could be got ready for shipping. His mind was full of plans and anxieties and the telegram that morning struck him like a blow. He had asked that he might keep the card-room prices up to where the best men could make at least six dollars and a half a week and was hoping for a straight answer, but the words on the yellow paper seemed to dance about and make him dizzy. "Shut down Saturday 9th until times are better!" he repeated to himself. "Shut down until times are worse here in Farley!"

The agent stood at the counting-room window looking out at the piteous, defenseless groups that passed by. He wished bitterly that his own pay stopped with the rest; it did not seem fair that he was not thrown out upon the world too.

"I don't know what they're going to do. They shall have the last cent I've saved before anybody suffers," he said in his heart. But there were tears in his eyes when he saw Mrs. Kilpatrick go limping out of the gate. She waited a moment for her constant companion, poor little Maggie the doffer, and they went away up the street toward their poor lodging holding each other fast by the hand. Maggie's father and grandfather and great-grandfather had all worked in the Farley mills; they had left no heritage but work behind them for this orphan child; they had never been able to save so much that a long illness, a prolonged old age, could not waste their slender hoards away.

IV.

It would have been difficult for an outsider to understand the sudden plunge from decent comfort to actual poverty in this small mill town. Strange to say, it was upon the smaller families that the strain fell the worst in Farley, and upon men and women who had nobody to look to but themselves. Where a man had a large household of children and several of these were old enough to be at work, and to put aside their wages or pay for their board; where such a man was of a thrifty and saving turn and a ruler of his household like old James Dow in the cloth-hall he might feel sure of a comfortable hoard and be fearless of a rainy day. But with a young man who worked single-handed for his wife and a little flock, or one who had an invalid to work for, that heaviest of burdens to the poor, the door seemed to be shut and barred against prosperity, and life became a test of one's power of endurance.

The agent went home late that noon from the counting-room. The street was nearly empty, but he had no friendly look or word for anyone whom he passed. Those who knew him well only pitied him, but it seemed to the tired man as if every eye must look at him with reproach. The long mill buildings of gray stone with their rows of deep-set windows wore a repellent look of strength and solidity. More than one man felt bitterly his

own personal weakness as he turned to look at them. The ocean
of fate seemed to be dashing him against their gray walls—
what use was it to fight against the Corporation? Two great
forces were in opposition now, and happiness could come only
from their serving each other in harmony.

The stronger force of capital had withdrawn from the league;
the weaker one, labor, was turned into an utter helplessness of
idleness. There was nothing to be done; you cannot rebel against
a shut-down, you can only submit.

A week later the great wheel stopped early on the last day of
work. Almost everyone left his special charge of machinery in
good order, oiled and cleaned and slackened with a kind of affectionate lingering care, for one person loves his machine as
another loves his horse. Even little Maggie pushed her bobbin-
box into a safe place near the overseer's desk and tipped it up
and dusted it out with a handful of waste. At the foot of the
long winding stairs Mrs. Kilpatrick was putting away her broom,
and she sighed as she locked the closet door; she had known
hard times before. "They'll be wanting me with odd jobs; we'll
be after getting along some way," she said with satisfaction.

"March is a long month, so it is—there'll be plinty time for
change before the ind of it," said Mary Cassidy hopefully. "The
agent will be thinking whatever can he do; sure he's very in-
genious. Look at him how well he persuaded the directors to
l'ave off wit' making cotton cloth like everybody else, and catch
a chance wit' all these new linings and things! He's done very
well, too. There bees no sinse in a shut-down anny way, the
looms and cards all suffers and the bands all slacks if they don't
get stiff. I'd sooner pay folks to tind their work whatever it cost."

" 'Tis true for you," agreed Mrs. Kilpatrick.

"What'll ye do wit' the shild, now she's no chance of pay,
any more?" asked Mary relentlessly, and poor Maggie's eyes
grew dark with fright as the conversation abruptly pointed her
way. She sometimes waked up in misery in Mrs. Kilpatrick's
warm bed, crying for fear that she was going to be sent back
to the poorhouse.

"Maggie an' me's going to kape together awhile yet," said the
good old woman fondly. "She's very handy for me, so she is.
We 'on't part with 'ach other whativer befalls, so we 'on't," and
Maggie looked up with a wistful smile, only half reassured. To
her the shut-down seemed like the end of the world.

Some of the French people took time by the forelock and

boarded the midnight train that very Saturday with all their possessions. A little later two or three families departed by the same train, under cover of the darkness between two days, without stopping to pay even their house rent. These mysterious flittings, like that of the famous Tartar tribe, roused a suspicion against their fellow countrymen, but after a succession of such departures almost everybody else thought it far cheaper to stay among friends. It seemed as if at any moment the great mill wheels might begin to turn, and the bell begin to ring, but day after day the little town was still and the bell tolled the hours one after another as if it were Sunday. The mild spring weather came on and the women sat mending or knitting on the doorsteps. More people moved away; there were but few men and girls left now in the quiet boarding-houses, and the spare tables were stacked one upon another at the end of the rooms. When planting-time came, word was passed about the Corporation that the agent was going to portion out a field that belonged to him a little way out of town on the South road, and let every man who had a family take a good-sized piece to plant. He also offered seed potatoes and garden seeds free to anyone who would come and ask for them at his house. The poor are very generous to each other, as a rule, and there was much borrowing and lending from house to house, and it was wonderful how long the people seemed to continue their usual fashions of life without distress. Almost everybody had saved a little bit of money and some had saved more; if one could no longer buy beefsteak he could still buy flour and potatoes, and a bit of pork lent a pleasing flavor, to content an idle man who had nothing to do but to stroll about town.

V.

One night the agent was sitting alone in his large, half-furnished house. Mary Moynahan, his housekeeper, had gone up to the church. There was a timid knock at the door.

There were two persons waiting, a short, thick-set man and a pale woman with dark, bright eyes who was nearly a head taller than her companion.

"Come in, Ellen; I'm glad to see you," said the agent. "Have you got your wheelbarrow, Mike?" Almost all the would-be planters of the field had come under cover of darkness and contrived if possible to avoid each other.

" 'Tisn't the potatoes we're after asking, sir," said Ellen. She was always spokeswoman, for Mike had an impediment in his speech. "The childher come up yisterday and got them while you'd be down at the counting-room. 'Twas Mary Moynahan saw to them. We do be very thankful to you, sir, for your kindness."

"Come in," said the agent, seeing there was something of consequence to be said. Ellen Carroll and he had worked side by side many a long day when they were young. She had been a noble wife to Mike, whose poor fortunes she had gladly shared for sake of his good heart, though Mike now and then paid too much respect to his often infirmities. There was a slight flavor of whisky now on the evening air, but it was a serious thing to put on your Sunday coat and go up with your wife to see the agent.

"We've come wanting to talk about any chances there might be with the mill," ventured Ellen timidly, as she stood in the lighted room; then she looked at Mike for reassurance. "We're very bad off, you see," she went on. "Yes, sir, I got them potaties, but I had to bake a little of them for supper and more again the day, for our breakfast. I don't know whatever we'll do whin they're gone. The poor children does be entreating me for them, Dan!"

The mother's eyes were full of tears. It was very seldom now that anybody called the agent by his christian name; there was a natural reserve and dignity about him, and there had come a definite separation between him and most of his old friends in the two years while he had managed to go to the School of Technology in Boston.

"Why didn't you let me know it was bad as that?" he asked. "I don't mean that anybody here should suffer while I've got a cent."

"The folks don't like to be begging, sir," said Ellen sorrowfully, "but there's lots of them does be in trouble. They'd ought to go away when the mills shut down, but for nobody knows where to go. Farley ain't like them big towns where a man'd pick up something else to do. I says to Mike: 'Come, Mike, let's go up after dark and tark to Dan; he'll help us out if he can,' says I—"

"Sit down, Ellen," said the agent kindly, as the poor woman began to cry. He made her take the armchair which the weave-room girls had given him at Christmas two years before. She sat there covering her face with her hands, and trying to keep back her sobs and go quietly on with what she had to say. Mike was sitting across the room with his back to the wall anxiously twirling his hat round and round. "Yis, we're very bad off," he contrived to say after much futile stammering. "All the folks in the Corporation, but Mr. Dow, has got great bills run up now at the stores, and thim that had money saved has lint to thim that hadn't—'twill be long enough before anybody's free. Whin the mills starts up we'll have to spind for everything at once. The children is very hard on their clothes and they're all dropping to pieces. I thought I'd have everything new for them this spring, they do be growing so I minds them and patches them the best I can." And again Ellen was overcome by tears. "Mike an' me's always been conthrivin' how would we get something laid up, so if anny one would die or be long sick we'd be equal to it, but we've had great pride to see the little gerrls go looking as well as anny, and we've worked very steady, but there's so manny of us we've had to pay rint for a large tenement and we'd only seventeen dollars and a little more when the shut-down was. Sure the likes of us has a right to earn more than our living, ourselves being so willing-hearted. 'Tis a long time now that Mike's been steady. We always had the pride to hope we'd own a house ourselves, and a pieceen o' land, but I'm thankful now—'tis as well for us; we've no chances to pay taxes now."

Mike made a desperate effort to speak as his wife faltered and began to cry again, and seeing his distress forgot her own, and supplied the halting words. "He wants to know if there's anny work he could get, some place else than Farley. Himself's been sixteen years now in the picker, first he was one of six and now he is one of the four since you got the new machines, yourself knows it well."

The agent knew about Mike; he looked compassionate as he shook his head. "Stay where you are, for a while at any rate. Things may look a little better, it seems to me. We will start up as soon as anyone does. I'll allow you twenty dollars a month after this; here are ten to start with. No, no, I've got no one depending on me and my pay is going on. I'm glad to share it with my friends. Tell the folks to come up and see me, Ahern and Sullivan and Michel and your brother Con; tell anybody you know who is really in distress. You've all stood by me!"

" 'Tis all the lazy ones 'ould be coming if we told on the poor boy," said Ellen gratefully, as they hurried home. "Ain't he got the good heart? We'd ought to be very discrate, Mike!" and

Mike agreed by a most impatient gesture, but by the time summer had begun to wane the agent was a far poorer man than when it had begun. Mike and Ellen Carroll were only the leaders of a sorrowful procession that sought his door evening after evening. Some asked for help who might have done without it, but others were saved from actual want. There were a few men who got work among the farms, but there was little steady work. The agent made the most of odd jobs about the mill yards and contrived somehow or other to give almost every household a lift. The village looked more and more dull and forlorn, but in August, when a traveling show ventured to give a performance in Farley, the Corporation hall was filled as it seldom was filled in prosperous times. This made the agent wonder, until he followed the crowd of workless, sadly idle men and women into the place of entertainment and looked at them with a sudden comprehension that they were spending their last cent for a little cheerfulness.

VI.

The agent was going into the counting room one day when he met old Father Daley and they stopped for a bit of friendly talk. "Could you come in for a few minutes, sir?" asked the younger man. "There's nobody in the counting-room."

The busy priest looked up at the weather-beaten clock in the mill tower.

"I can," he said. " 'Tis not so late as I thought. We'll soon be having the mail."

The agent led the way and brought one of the directors' comfortable chairs from their committee-room. Then he spun his own chair face-about from before his desk and they sat down. It was a warm day in the middle of September. The windows were wide open on the side toward the river and there was a flicker of light on the ceiling from the sunny water. The noise of the fall was loud and incessant in the room. Somehow one never noticed it very much when the mills were running.

"How are the Duffys?" asked the agent.

"Very bad," answered the old priest gravely. "The doctor sent for me—he couldn't get them to take any medicine. He says that it isn't typhoid; only a low fever among them from bad food and want of care. That tenement is very old and bad, the drains from the upper tenement have leaked and spoiled the whole west side of the building. I suppose they never told you of it?"

"I did the best I could about it last spring," said the agent. "They were afraid of being turned out and they hid it for that reason. The company allowed me something for repairs as usual and I tried to get more; you see I spent it all before I knew what a summer was before us. Whatever I have done since I have paid for, except what they call legitimate work and care of property. Last year I put all Maple Street into first-rate order—and meant to go right through the Corporation. I've done the best I could," he protested with a bright spot of color in his cheeks. "Some of the men have tinkered up their tenements and I have counted it toward the rent, but they don't all know how to drive a nail."

" 'Tis true for you; you have done the best you could," said the priest heartily, and both the men were silent, while the river, which was older than they and had seen a whole race of men disappear before they came—the river took this opportunity to speak louder than ever.

"I think that manufacturing prospects look a little brighter," said the agent, wishing to be cheerful. "There are some good orders out, but of course the buyers can take advantage of our condition. The treasurer writes me that we must be firm about not starting up until we are sure of business on a good paying margin."

"Like last year's?" asked the priest, who was resting himself in the armchair. There was a friendly twinkle in his eyes.

"Like last year's," answered the agent. "I worked like two men, and I pushed the mills hard to make that large profit. I saw there was trouble coming, and I told the directors and asked for a special surplus, but I had no idea of anything like this."

"Nine per cent. in these times was too good a prize," said Father Daley, but the twinkle in his eyes had suddenly disappeared.

"You won't get your new church for a long time yet," said the agent.

"No, no," said the old man impatiently. "I have kept the foundations going as well as I could, and the talk, for their own sakes. It gives them something to think about. I took the money they gave me in collections and let them have it back again for work. 'Tis well to lead their minds," and he gave a quick glance at the agent. " 'Tis no pride of mine for church-building and no good credit with the bishop I'm after. Young men can be satisfied with those things, not an old priest like me that prays to be a father to his people."

Father Daley spoke as man speaks to man, straight out of an honest heart.

"I see many things now that I used to be blind about long ago," he said. "You may take a man who comes over, him and his wife. They fall upon good wages and their heads are turned with joy. They've been hungry for generations back and they've always seen those above them who dressed fine and lived soft, and they want a taste of luxury too; they're bound to satisfy themselves. So they'll spend and spend and have beefsteak for dinner every day just because they never had enough before, but they'd turn into wild beasts of selfishness, most of 'em, if they had no check. 'Tis there the church steps in. 'Remember your Maker and do Him honor in His house of prayer,' says she. 'Be self-denying, be thinking of eternity and of what's sure to come." And you will join with me in believing that it's never those who have given most to the church who come first to the ground in a hard time like this. Show me a good church and I'll show you a thrifty people." Father Daley looked eagerly at the agent for sympathy.

"You speak the truth, sir," said the agent. "Those that give most are always the last to hold out with honest independence and the first to do for others."

"Some priests may have plundered their parishes for pride's sake; there's no saying what is in poor human nature," repeated Father Daley earnestly. "God forgive us all for unprofitable servants of Him and His church. I believe in saying more about prayer and right living, and less about collections, in God's house, but it's the giving hand that's the rich hand all the world over."

"I don't think Ireland has ever sent us over many misers; Saint Patrick must have banished them all with the snakes," suggested the agent with a grim smile. The priest shook his head and laughed a little and then both men were silent again in the counting-room.

The mail train whistled noisily up the road and came into the station at the end of the empty street, then it rang its loud bell and puffed and whistled away again.

"I'll bring your mail over, sir," said the agent, presently. "Sit here and rest yourself until I come back and we'll walk home together."

The leather mail-bag looked thin and flat and the leisurely postmaster had nearly distributed its contents by the time the agent had crossed the street and reached the office. His clerks were both off on a long holiday; they were brothers and were glad of the chance to take their vacations together. They had been on lower pay; there was little to do in the counting-room— hardly anybody's time to keep or even a letter to write.

Two or three loiterers stopped the agent to ask him the usual question if there were any signs of starting up; an old farmer who sat in his long wagon before the post-office asked for news too, and touched his hat with an awkward sort of military salute.

"Come out to our place and stop a few days," he said kindly. "You look kind of pinched up and bleached out, Mr. Agent; you can't be needed much here."

"I wish I could come," said the agent, stopping again and looking up at the old man with a boyish, expectant face. Nobody had happened to think about him in just that way, and he was far from thinking about himself. "I've got to keep an eye on the people that are left here; you see they've had a pretty hard summer."

"Not so hard as you have!" said the old man, as the agent went along the street. "You've never had a day of rest more than once or twice since you were born!"

There were two letters and a pamphlet for Father Daley and a thin handful of circulars for the company. In busy times there was often all the mail matter that a clerk could bring. The agent sat down at his desk in the counting-room and the priest opened a thick foreign letter with evident pleasure. "'Tis from an old friend of mine; he's in a monastery in France," he said. "I only hear from him once a year," and Father Daley settled himself in his armchair to read the close-written pages. As for the agent of the mills, he had quickly opened a letter from the treasurer and was not listening to anything that was said.

Suddenly he whirled round in his desk chair and held out the letter to the priest. His hand shook and his face was as pale as ashes.

"What is it? What's the matter?" cried the startled old man, who had hardly followed the first pious salutations of his own letter to their end. "Read it to me yourself, Dan; is there any trouble?"

"Orders—I've got orders to start up; we're going to start— I wrote them last week—"

But the agent had to spring up from his chair and go to the window next the river before he could steady his voice to speak. He thought it was the look of the moving water that made him dizzy. "We're going to start up the mills as soon as I can get things ready." He turned to look up at the thermometer as if it were the most important thing in the world; then the color rushed to his face and he leaned a moment against the wall.

"Thank God!" said the old priest devoutly. "Here, come and sit down, my boy. Faith, but it's good news, and I'm the first to get it from you."

They shook hands and were cheerful together; the foreign letter was crammed into Father Daley's pocket, and he reached for his big cane.

"Tell everybody as you go up the street, sir," said Dan. "I've got a hurricane of things to see to; I must go the other way down to the storehouses. Tell them to pass the good news about town as fast as they can; 'twill hearten up the women." All the anxious look had gone as if by magic from the agent's face.

Two weeks from that time the old mill bell stopped tolling for the slow hours of idleness and rang out loud and clear for the housekeepers to get up, and rang for breakfast, and later still for all the people to go in to work. Some of the old hands were gone for good and new ones must be broken in in their places, but there were many familiar faces to pass the counting-room windows into the mill yard. There were French families which had reappeared with surprising promptness. Michel and his pretty daughter were there, and a household of cousins who had come to the next tenement. The agent stood with his hands in his pockets and nodded soberly to one group after another. It seemed to him that he had never felt so happy in his life.

"Jolly-looking set this morning," said one of the clerks whose desk was close beside the window; he was a son of one of the directors, who had sent him to the agent to learn something about manufacturing.

"They've had a bitter hard summer that you know nothing about," said the agent slowly.

Just then Mrs. Kilpatrick and old Mary Cassidy came along, and little Maggie was with them. She had got back her old chance at doffing and the hard times were over. They all smiled with such blissful satisfaction that the agent smiled too, and even waved his hand.

Mary E. Wilkins Freeman

Mary E. Wilkins Freeman (1852–1930) was the daughter of a carpenter in Randolph, in her day a typical eastern Massachusetts village of farmers and artisans. In her fifteenth year her family removed to Brattleboro, Vermont, where Mary lived for the next seventeen years. In 1884, her mother and father both dead, she returned to Randolph to live. In 1902 she married Dr. Charles Freeman of Metuchen, New Jersey, remaining there for the rest of her life. She had done considerable writing in Brattleboro, and the economically depressed hill towns of the surrounding region supplied her with settings and materials for her fiction—as did her native Randolph, especially in her later years. Her first volume of adult fiction was A Humble Romance and Other Stories *(1887); other collections were* A New England Nun and Other Stories *(1891),* The People of Our Neighborhood *(1898), and* The Winning Lady and Others *(1909). Her two most impressive novels are* Pembroke *(1894), a probing study of village character, and* The Portion of Labor *(1901), which treats the problems of the poor in a mill town reminiscent of Miss Jewett's Farley.*

In her short fiction Mrs. Freeman's technique is an elaboration of that of the village gossips she had listened to in so many New England kitchens and livingrooms. "Old Woman Magoun" (from The Winning Lady and Others*) and "A Conflict Ended" (from* A Humble Romance and Other Stories*), both in this volume, are good examples of her methods. The former begins with some gossipy details about Barry's Ford—its location, the origin of its name, the means of crossing the river there. Our first introduction to the main character is in connection with her instrumentality in getting the bridge built, and we are given snatches of her comments about the need for the bridge. Finally we emerge into the main part of the bleak story of a strong-willed but compassionate woman's dealing with a terrible di-*

lemma. Similarly, "A Conflict Ended" begins with some mean-derings about the two churches in Acton and the attendance at each. With Mrs. Freeman, however, we find that the gossip's obsession with irrelevant detail is transformed to an instinct for details that bring to life a place or a situation, or symbolically bring a theme into focus.

Mrs. Freeman was preoccupied with the meanness and poverty and with the abnormalities of character in backcountry areas that one critic has described as "the terminal moraine of New England Puritanism." The poverty is present to some degree in many of the stories in this volume, but it figures most grimly in the stark, Chekhov-like "Sister Liddy" (from A New England Nun and Other Stories), the best of the many tales of poor-houses—which were ubiquitous on the New England countryside —written by Mrs. Freeman's contemporaries. "A Conflict End-ed" exemplifies her interest in the workings of a pathologically warped will. "An Honest Soul" (from A Humble Romance and Other Stories) presents us with the New England conscience de-veloped to a degree that transcends the pathetic and becomes ridiculous, and "A Poetess" (from A New England Nun and Other Stories) exhibits an equally excessive overdevelopment of sensitivity and personal pride. In both these stories, as in many others by Mrs. Freeman, there is an ironical humor that derives from the pettiness of the situations in contrast with the grotesque overreactions of the protagonists.

Though at the height of her career she was extremely popular and later won the acclaim of such critics as Paul Elmer More and F. O. Matthiessen, Mrs. Freeman's reputation has proved less durable than Miss Jewett's. Yet of the two she is unques-tionably the more perceptive in her psychological insights, and she is in no way inferior in narrative skill. Miss Jewett takes undisputed first place only in the polish and refinement of her prose style. The texts in this anthology are from the first edi-tions of the volumes in which they appear.

An Honest Soul

"Thar's Mis' Bliss's pieces in the brown kaliker bag, an' thar's Mis' Bennet's pieces in the bed-tickin' bag," said she, surveying complacently the two bags leaning against her kitchen-wall. "I'll get a dollar for both of them quilts, an' thar'll be two dollars. I've got a dollar an' sixty-three cents on hand now, an' thar's plenty of meal an' merlasses, an' some salt fish an' pertaters in the house. I'll get along middlin' well, I reckon. Thar ain't no call fer me to worry. I'll red up the house a leetle now, an' then I'll begin on Mis' Bliss's pieces."

The *house* was an infinitesimal affair, containing only two rooms besides the tiny lean-to which served as wood-shed. It stood far enough back from the road for a pretentious mansion, and there was one curious feature about it—not a door nor window was there in front, only a blank, unbroken wall. Strangers passing by used to stare wonderingly at it sometimes, but it was explained easily enough. Old Simeon Patch, years ago, when the longing for a home of his own had grown strong in his heart, and he had only a few hundred dollars saved from his hard earnings to invest in one, had wisely done the best he could with what he had.

Not much remained to spend on the house after the spacious lot was paid for, so he resolved to build as much house as he could with his money, and complete it when better days should come.

This tiny edifice was in reality simply the L of a goodly two-story house which had existed only in the fond and faithful fancies of Simeon Patch and his wife. That blank front wall was designed to be joined to the projected main building; so, of course, there was no need of doors or windows. Simeon Patch came of a hard-working, honest race, whose pride it had been to keep out of debt, and he was a true child of his ancestors. Not a dollar would he spend that was not in his hand; a mortgaged house was his horror. So he paid cash for every blade of grass on his lot of land, and every nail in his bit of a house, and settled down patiently in it until he should grub together enough more to buy a few additional boards and shingles, and pay the money down.

That time never came: he died in the course of a few years, after a lingering illness, and only had enough saved to pay his doctor's bill and funeral expenses, and leave his wife and daughter entirely without debt, in their little fragment of a house on the big, sorry lot of land.

There they had lived, mother and daughter, earning and saving in various little, petty ways, keeping their heads sturdily above water, and holding the dreaded mortgage off the house for many years. Then the mother died, and the daughter, Martha Patch, took up the little homely struggle alone. She was over seventy now—a small, slender old woman, as straight as a rail, with sharp black eyes, and a quick toss of her head when she spoke. She did odd housewifely jobs for the neighbors, wove rag-carpets, pieced bed-quilts, braided rugs, etc., and contrived to supply all her simple wants.

This evening, after she had finished putting her house to rights, she fell to investigating the contents of the bags which two of the neighbors had brought in the night before, with orders for quilts, much to her delight.

"Mis' Bliss has got proper handsome pieces," said she— "proper handsome; they'll make a good-lookin' quilt. Mis' Bennet's is good too, but they ain't quite ekal to Mis' Bliss's. I reckon some of 'em's old."

She began spreading some of the largest, prettiest pieces on her white-scoured table. "Thar," said she, gazing at one admiringly, "that jest takes my eye; them leetle pink roses is pretty, an' no mistake. I reckon that's French caliker. Thar's some big pieces too. Lor', what bag did I take 'em out on! It must hev been Mis' Bliss's. I mustn't git 'em mixed."

She cut out some squares, and sat down by the window in a low wooden rocking-chair to sew. This window did not have a very pleasant outlook. The house was situated so far back from the road that it commanded only a rear view of the adjoining one. It was a great cross to Martha Patch. She was one of those women who like to see everything that is going on outside, and who often have excuse enough in the fact that so little is going on with them.

"It's a great diversion," she used to say, in her snapping way, which was more nervous than ill-natured, bobbing her head violently at the same time—"a very great diversion to see Mr. Peters's cows goin' in an' out of the barn day arter day; an' that's about all I do see—never git a sight of the folks goin' to meetin' nor nothin'."

The lack of a front window was a continual source of grief to her.

"When the minister's prayin' for the widders an' orphans he'd better make mention of one more," said she, once, "an' that's women without front winders."

She and her mother had planned to save money enough to have one some day, but they had never been able to bring it about. A window commanding a view of the street and the passers-by would have been a great source of comfort to the poor old woman, sitting and sewing as she did day in and day out. As it was, she seized eagerly upon the few objects of interest which did come within her vision, and made much of them. There were some children who, on their way from school, could make a short cut through her yard and reach home quicker. She watched for them every day, and if they did not appear quite as soon as usual she would grow uneasy, and eye the clock, and mutter to herself, "I wonder where them Mosely children can be?" When they came she watched their progress with sharp attention, and thought them over for an hour afterwards. Not a bird which passed her window escaped her notice. This innocent old gossip fed her mind upon their small domestic affairs in lieu of larger ones. To-day she often paused between her stitches to gaze absorbedly at a yellow-bird vibrating nervously round the branches of a young tree opposite. It was early spring, and the branches were all of a light-green foam.

"That's the same yaller-bird I saw yesterday, I do b'lieve," said she. "I recken he's goin' to build a nest in that ellum."

Lately she had been watching the progress of the grass gradually springing up all over the yard. One spot where it grew much greener than elsewhere her mind dwelt upon curiously.

"I can't make out," she said to a neighbor, "whether that 'ere spot is greener than the rest because the sun shines brightly thar, or because somethin's buried thar."

She toiled steadily on the patchwork quilts. At the end of a fortnight they were nearly completed. She hurried on the last one morning, thinking she would carry them both to their owners that afternoon and get her pay. She did not stop for any dinner.

Spreading them out for one last look before rolling them up in bundles, she caught her breath hastily.

"What hev I done?" said she. "Massy sakes! I hevn't gone an' put Mis' Bliss's caliker with the leetle pink roses on't in Mis' Bennet's quilt? I hev, jest as sure as preachin'! What shell I do?"

The poor old soul stood staring at the quilts in pitiful dismay. "A hull fortni't's work," she muttered. "What shell I do? Them pink roses is the prettiest caliker in the hull lot. Mis' Bliss will be mad if they air in Mis' Bennet's quilt. She won't say nothin', an' she'll pay me, but she'll feel it inside, an' it won't be doin' the squar' thing by her. No; if I'm goin' to airn money I'll airn it."

Martha Patch gave her head a jerk. The spirit which animated her father when he went to housekeeping in a piece of a house without any front window blazed up within her. She made herself a cup of tea, then sat deliberately down by the window to rip the quilts to pieces. It had to be done pretty thoroughly on account of her admiration for the pink calico, and the quantity of it—it figured in nearly every square. "I wish I hed a front winder to set to while I'm doin' on't," said she; but she patiently plied her scissors till dusk, only stopping for a short survey of the Mosely children. After days of steady work the pieces were put together again, this time the pink-rose calico in Mrs. Bliss's quilt. Martha Patch rolled the quilts up with a sigh of relief and a sense of virtuous triumph.

"I'll sort over the pieces that's left in the bags," said she, "then I'll take 'em over an' git my pay. I'm gittin' pretty short of vittles."

She began pulling the pieces out of the bed-ticking bag, laying them on her lap and smoothing them out, preparatory to doing them up in a neat, tight roll to take home—she was very methodical about everything she did. Suddenly she turned pale, and stared wildly at a tiny scrap of calico which she had just fished out of the bag.

"Massy sakes!" she cried; "it ain't, is it?" She clutched Mrs. Bliss's quilt from the table and laid the bit of calico beside the pink-rose squares.

"It's jest the same thing," she groaned, "an' it came out on Mis' Bennet's bag. Dear me suz! dear me suz!"

She dropped helplessly into her chair by the window, still holding the quilt and the telltale scrap of calico, and gazed out in a bewildered sort of way. Her poor old eyes looked dim and weak with tears.

"Thar's the Mosely children comin'," she said; "happy little gals, laughin' an' hollerin', goin' home to their mother to git a good dinner. Me a-settin' here's a lesson they ain't larned in their books yit; hope to goodness they never will; hope they won't ever hev to piece quilts fur a livin', without any front winder to set to. Thar's a dandelion blown out on that green spot. Reckon thar *is* somethin' buried thar. Lordy massy! *hev* I got to rip them two quilts to pieces agin an' sew 'em over?"

Finally she resolved to carry a bit of the pink-rose calico over to Mrs. Bennet's and find out, without betraying the dilemma she was in, if it were really hers.

Her poor old knees fairly shook under her when she entered Mrs. Bennet's sitting-room.

"Why, yes, Martha, it's mine," said Mrs. Bennet, in response to her agitated question. "Hattie had a dress like it, don't you remember? There was a lot of new pieces left, and I thought they would work into a quilt nice. But, for pity's sake, Martha, what is the matter? You look just as white as a sheet. You ain't sick, are you?"

"No," said Martha, with a feeble toss of her head, to keep up the deception; "I ain't sick, only kinder all gone with the warm weather. I reckon I'll hev to fix me up some thoroughwort tea. Thoroughwort's a great strengthener."

"I would," said Mrs. Bennet, sympathizingly; "and don't you work too hard on that quilt; I ain't in a bit of a hurry for it. I sha'n't want it before next winter anyway. I only thought I'd like to have it pieced and ready."

"I reckon I can't get it done afore another fortni't," said Martha, trembling.

"I don't care if you don't get it done for the next three months. Don't go yet, Martha; you ain't rested a minute, and it's a pretty long walk. Don't you want a bite of something before you go? Have a piece of cake? You look real faint."

"No, thanky," said Martha, and departed in spite of all friendly entreaties to tarry. Mrs. Bennet watched her moving slowly down the road, still holding the little pink calico rag in her brown, withered fingers.

"Martha Patch is failing; she ain't near so straight as she was," remarked Mrs. Bennet. "She looks real bent over to-day."

The little wiry springiness was, indeed, gone from her gait as she crept slowly along the sweet country road, and there was a helpless droop in her thin, narrow shoulders. It was a beautiful spring day; the fruit-trees were all in blossom. There were more orchards than houses on the way, and more blooming trees to pass than people.

Martha looked up at the white branches as she passed under them. "I kin smell the apple-blows," said she, "but somehow the goodness is all gone out on 'em. I'd jest as soon smell cabbage. Oh, dear me suz, kin I ever do them quilts over agin?"

When she got home, however, she rallied a little. There was a nervous force about this old woman which was not easily overcome even by an accumulation of misfortunes. She might bend a good deal, but she was almost sure to spring back again. She took off her hood and shawl, and straightened herself up. "Thar's no use puttin' it off; it's got to be done. I'll hev them quilts right ef it kills me!"

She tied on a purple calico apron and sat down at the window again, with a quilt and the scissors. Out came the pink roses. There she sat through the long afternoon, cutting the stitches which she had so laboriously put in—a little defiant old figure, its head, with a flat black lace cap on it, bobbing up and down in time with its hands. There were some purple bows on the cap, and they fluttered; quite a little wind blew in at the window.

The eight-day clock on the mantel ticked peacefully. It was a queer old timepiece, which had belonged to her grandmother Patch. A painting of a quaint female, with puffed hair and a bunch of roses, adorned the front of it, under the dial-plate. It was flanked on either side by tall, green vases.

There was a dull-colored rag-carpet of Martha's own manufacture on the floor of the room. Some wooden chairs stood around stiffly; an old, yellow map of Massachusetts and a portrait of George Washington hung on the walls. There was not a speck of dust anywhere, nor any disorder. Neatness was one of the comforts of Martha's life. Putting and keeping things in order was one of the interests which enlivened her dulness and made the world attractive to her.

The poor soul sat at the window, bending over the quilt, until dusk, and she sat there, bending over the quilt until dusk, many a day after.

It is a hard question to decide, whether there were any real merit in such finely strained honesty, or whether it were merely a case of morbid conscientiousness. Perhaps the old woman, inheriting very likely her father's scruples, had had them so intensified by age and childishness that they had become a little off the bias of reason.

Be that as it may, she thought it was the right course for her to make the quilts over, and, thinking so, it was all that she could do. She could never have been satisfied otherwise. It took her a considerable while longer to finish the quilts again, and this time she began to suffer from other causes than mere fatigue. Her stock of provisions commenced to run low, and her money was gone. At last she had nothing but a few potatoes in the house to eat. She contrived to dig some dandelion greens once or twice; these with the potatoes were all her diet. There was really no necessity for such a state of things; she was surrounded by kindly well-to-do people, who would have gone without themselves rather than let her suffer. But she had always been very reticent about her needs, and felt great pride about accepting anything for which she did not pay.

But she struggled along until the quilts were done, and no one knew. She set the last stitch quite late one evening; then she spread the quilts out and surveyed them. "Thar they air now, all right," said she; "the pink roses is in Mis' Bennet's, an' I ain't cheated nobody out on their caliker, an' I've airned my money. I'll take 'em hum in the mornin', an' then I'll buy somethin' to eat. I begin to feel a dreadful sinkin' at my stummuck."

She locked up the house carefully—she always felt a great responsibility when she had people's work on hand—and went to bed.

Next morning she woke up so faint and dizzy that she hardly knew herself. She crawled out into the kitchen, and sank down on the floor. She could not move another step.

"Lor sakes!" she moaned, "I reckon I'm 'bout done to!"

The quilts lay near her on the table; she stared up at them with feeble complacency. "Ef I'm goin' to die, I'm glad I got them quilts done right fust. Massy, how sinkin' I do feel! I wish I had a cup of tea."

There she lay, and the beautiful spring morning wore on. The sun shone in at the window, and moved nearer and nearer, until finally she lay in a sunbeam, a poor, shrivelled little old woman, whose resolute spirit had nearly been her death, in her scant nightgown and ruffled cap, a little shawl falling from her shoulders. She did not feel ill, only absolutely too weak and helpless to move. Her mind was just as active as ever, and her black eyes peered sharply out of her pinched face. She kept making efforts to rise, but she could not stir.

"Lor sakes!" she snapped out at length, "how long *hev* I got to lay here? I'm mad!"

She saw some dust on the black paint of a chair which stood in the sun, and she eyed that distressfully.

"Jest look at that dust on the runs of that cheer!" she muttered. "What if anybody come in! I wonder if I can't reach it!"

The chair was near her and she managed to stretch out her limp old hand and rub the dust off the rounds. Then she let it sink down, panting.

"I wonder ef I *ain't* goin' to die," she gasped. "I wonder ef I'm prepared. I never took nothin' that shouldn't belong to me that I knows on. Oh, dear me suz, I wish somebody would come!"

When her strained ears did catch the sound of footsteps outside, a sudden resolve sprang up in her heart.

"I won't let on to nobody how I've made them quilts over, an' how I hevn't had enough to eat—I won't."

When the door was tried she called out feebly, "Who is thar?"

The voice of Mrs. Peters, her next-door neighbor, came back in response: "It's me. What's the matter, Marthy?"

"I'm kinder used up; don't know how you'll git in; I can't git to the door to unlock it to save my life."

"Can't I get in at the window?"

"Mebbe you kin."

Mrs. Peters was a long-limbed, spare woman, and she got in through the window with considerable ease, it being quite low from the ground.

She turned pale when she saw Martha lying on the floor. "Why, Marthy, what is the matter? How long have you been laying there?"

"Ever since I got up. I was kinder dizzy, an' hed a dreadful sinkin' feelin'. It ain't much, I reckon. Ef I could hev a cup of tea it would set me right up. Thar's a spoonful left in the pantry. Ef you jest put a few kindlin's in the stove, Mis' Peters, an' set in the kettle an' made me a cup, I could git up, I know. I've got to go an' kerry them quilts hum to Mis' Bliss an' Mis' Bennet."

"I don't believe but what you've got all tired out over the quilts. You've been working too hard."

"No, I 'ain't, Mis' Peters; it's nothin' but play piecin' quilts. All I mind is not havin' a front winder to set to while I'm doin' on't."

Mrs. Peters was a quiet, sensible woman of few words; she insisted upon carrying Martha into the bedroom and putting her comfortably to bed. It was easily done; she was muscular, and the old woman a very light weight. Then she went into the pantry. She was beginning to suspect the state of affairs, and her suspicions were strengthened when she saw the bare shelves. She started the fire, put on the tea-kettle, and then slipped across the yard to her own house for further reinforcements.

Pretty soon Martha was drinking her cup of tea and eating her toast and a dropped egg. She had taken the food with some reluctance, half starved as she was. Finally she gave in—the sight of it was too much for her. "Well, I will borry it, Mis' Peters," said she; "an' I'll pay you jest as soon as I kin git up."

After she had eaten she felt stronger. Mrs. Peters had hard work to keep her quiet until afternoon; then she would get up and carry the quilts home. The two ladies were profuse in praises. Martha, proud and smiling. Mrs. Bennet noticed the pink roses at once. "How pretty that calico did work in," she remarked.

"Yes," assented Martha, between an inclination to chuckle and to cry.

"Ef I ain't thankful I did them quilts over," thought she, creeping slowly homeward, her hard-earned two dollars knotted into a corner of her handkerchief for security.

About sunset Mrs. Peters came in again. "Marthy," she said, after a while, "Sam says he's out of work just now, and he'll cut through a front window for you. He's got some old sash and glass that's been laying round in the barn ever since I can remember. It'll be a real charity for you to take it off his hands, and he'll like to do it. Sam's as uneasy as a fish out of water when he hasn't got any work."

Martha eyed her suspiciously. "Thanky; but I don't want nothin' done that I can't pay for," said she, with a stiff toss of her head.

"It would be pay enough, just letting Sam do it, Marthy; but, if you really feel set about it, I've got some sheets that need turning. You can do them some time this summer, and that will pay us for all it's worth."

The black eyes looked at her sharply. "Air you sure?"

"Yes; it's fully as much as it's worth," said Mrs. Peters. "I'm most afraid it's more. There's four sheets, and putting in a window is nothing more than putting in a patch—the old stuff ain't worth anything."

When Martha fully realized that she was going to have a front window, and that her pride might suffer it to be given to her and yet receive no insult, she was as delighted as a child.

"Lor sakes!" said she, "jest to think that I shall have a front winder to set to! I wish mother could ha' lived to see it. Mebbe you kinder wonder at it, Mis' Peters—you've allers had front winders; but you haven't any idea what a great thing it seems to me. It kinder makes me feel younger. Thar's the Mosely children; they're 'bout all I've ever seen pass *this* winder, Mis' Peters. Jest see that green spot out thar; it's been greener than the rest of the yard all the spring, an' now thar's lots of dandelions blowed out on it, an' some clover. I b'lieve the sun shines more on it, somehow. Law me, to think I'm going to hev a front winder!"

"Sarah was in this afternoon," said Mrs. Peters, further (Sarah was her married daughter), "and she says she wants same braided rugs right away. She'll send the rags over by Willie to-morrow."

"You don't say so! Well I'll be glad to do it; an' thar's one thing 'bout it, Mis' Peters—mebbe you'll think it queer for me to say so, but I'm kinder thankful it's rugs she wants. I'm kinder sick of bed-quilts somehow."

A Conflict Ended

In Acton there were two churches, a Congregational and a Baptist. They stood on opposite sides of the road, and the Baptist edifice was a little farther down than the other. On Sunday morning both bells were ringing. The Baptist bell was much larger, and followed quickly on the soft peal of the Congregational with a heavy brazen clang which vibrated a good while. The people went flocking through the street to the irregular jangle of the bells. It was a very hot day, and the sun beat down heavily; parasols were bobbing over all the ladies' heads.

More people went into the Baptist church, whose society was

much the larger of the two. It had been for the last ten years—
ever since the Congregational had settled a new minister. His
advent had divided the church, and a good third of the congregation had gone over to the Baptist brethren, with whom they
still remained.

It is probable that many of them passed their old sanctuary
to-day with the original stubborn animosity as active as ever in
their hearts, and led their families up the Baptist steps with the
same strong spiritual pull of indignation.

One old lady, who had made herself prominent on the opposition, trotted by this morning with the identical wiry vehemence
which she had manifested ten years ago. She wore a full black
silk skirt, which she held up inanely in front, and allowed to trail
in the dust in the rear.

Some of the stanch Congregational people glanced at her
amusedly. One fleshy, fair-faced girl in blue muslin said to her
companion, with a laugh: "See that old lady trailing her best
black silk by to the Baptist. Ain't it ridiculous how she keeps on
showing out? I heard some one talking about it yesterday."

"Yes."

The girl colored up confusedly. "Oh dear!" she thought to
herself. The lady with her had an unpleasant history connected
with this old church quarrel. She was a small, bony woman in a
shiny purple silk, which was strained very tightly across her
sharp shoulder-blades. Her bonnet was quite elaborate with flowers and plumes, as was also her companion's. In fact, she was
the village milliner, and the girl was her apprentice.

When the two went up the church steps, they passed a man
of about fifty, who was sitting thereon well to one side. He had a
singular face—a mild forehead, a gently curving mouth, and a
terrible chin, with a look of strength in it that might have abashed
mountains. He held his straw hat in his hand, and the sun was
shining full on his bald head.

The milliner half stopped, and gave an anxious glance at him;
then passed on. In the vestibule she stopped again.

"You go right in, Margy," she said to the girl. "I'll be along
in a minute."

"Where be you going, Miss Barney?"

"You go right in. I'll be there in a minute."

Margy entered the audience-room then, as if fairly brushed
in by the imperious wave of a little knotty hand, and Esther
Barney stood waiting until the rush of entering people was over.

Then she stepped swiftly back to the side of the man seated on the steps. She spread her large black parasol deliberately, and extended the handle towards him.

"No, no, Esther; I don't want it—I don't want it."

"If you're determined on setting out in this broiling sun, Marcus Woodman, you jest take this parasol of mine an' use it."

"I don't want your parasol, Esther. I—"

"Don't you say it over again. Take it."

"I won't—not if I don't want to."

"You'll get a sun-stroke."

"That's my own lookout."

"Marcus Woodman, you take it."

She threw all the force there was in her intense, nervous nature into her tone and look; but she failed in her attempt, because of the utter difference in quality between her own will and that with which she had to deal. They were on such different planes that hers slid by his with its own momentum; there could be no contact even of antagonism between them. He sat there rigid, every line of his face stiffened into an icy obstinacy. She held out the parasol towards him like a weapon.

Finally she let it drop at her side, her whole expression changed.

"Marcus," said she, "how's your mother?"

He started, "Pretty well, thank you, Esther."

"She's out to meeting, then?"

"Yes."

"I've been a-thinking—I ain't drove jest now—that maybe I'd come over an' see her some day this week."

He rose politely then. "Wish you would, Esther. Mother'd be real pleased, I know."

"Well, I'll see—Wednesday, p'rhaps, if I ain't too busy. I must go in now; they're 'most through singing."

"Esther—"

"I don't believe I can stop any longer, Marcus."

"About the parasol—thank you jest the same if I don't take it. Of course you know I can't set out here holding a parasol; folks would laugh. But I'm obliged to you all the same. Hope I didn't say anything to hurt your feelings?"

"Oh, no; why, no, Marcus. Of course I don't want to make you take it if you don't want it. I don't know but it would look kinder queer, come to think of it. Oh dear! they are through singing."

"Say, Esther, I don't know but I might as well take that parasol, if you'd jest as soon. The sun is pretty hot, an' I might get a headache. I forgot my umbrella, to tell the truth."

"I might have known better than to have gone at him the way I did," thought Esther to herself, when she was seated at last in the cool church beside Margy. "Seems as if I might have got used to Marcus Woodman by this time."

She did not see him when she came out of church; but a little boy in the vestibule handed her the parasol, with the remark, "Mr. Woodman said for me to give this to you."

She and Margy passed down the street towards home. Going by the Baptist church, they noticed a young man standing by the entrance. He stared hard at Margy.

She began to laugh after they had passed him. "Did you see that fellow stare?" said she. "Hope he'll know me next time."

"That's George Elliot; he's that old lady's son you was speaking about this morning."

"Well, that's enough for me."

"He's a real good, steady young man."

Margy sniffed.

"P'rhaps you'll change your mind some day."

She did, and speedily, too. That glimpse of Margy Wilson's pretty, new face—for she was a stranger in the town—had been too much for George Elliot. He obtained an introduction, and soon was a steady visitor at Esther Barney's house. Margy fell in love with him easily. She had never had much attention from the young men, and he was an engaging young fellow, small and bright-eyed, though with a nervous persistency like his mother's in his manner.

"I'm going to have it an understood thing," Margy told Esther, after her lover had become constant in his attentions, "that I'm going with George, and I ain't going with his mother. I can't bear that old woman."

But poor Margy found that it was not so easy to thrust determined old age off the stage, even when young Love was flying about so fast on his butterfly wings that he seemed to multiply himself, and there was no room for anything else, because the air was so full of Loves. That old mother, with her trailing black skirt and her wiry obstinacy, trotted as unwaveringly through the sweet stir as a ghost through a door.

One Monday morning Margy could not eat any breakfast, and there were tear stains around her blue eyes.

"Why, what's the matter, Margy?" asked Esther, eying her across the little kitchen-table.

"Nothing's the matter. I ain't hungry any to speak of, that's all. I guess I'll go right to work on Mis' Fuller's bonnet."

"I'd try an' eat something if I was you. Be sure you cut that velvet straight, if you go to work on it."

When the two were sitting together at their work in the little room back of the shop, Margy suddenly threw her scissors down. "There!" said she, "I've done it; I knew I would. I've cut this velvet bias. I knew I should cut everything bias I touched to-day."

There was a droll pucker on her mouth; then it began to quiver. She hid her face in her hands and sobbed. "Oh, dear, dear, dear!"

"Margy Wilson, what is the matter?"

"George and I—had a talk last night. We've broke the engagement, an' it's killing me. An' now I've cut this velvet bias. Oh, dear, dear, *dear,* dear!"

"For the land's sake, don't mind anything about the velvet. What's come betwixt you an' George?"

"His mother—horrid old thing! He said she'd got to live with us, and I said she shouldn't. Then he said he wouldn't marry any girl that wasn't willing to live with his mother, and I said he wouldn't ever marry me, then. If George Elliot thinks more of his mother than he does of me, he can have her. I don't care. I'll show him I can get along without him."

"Well, I don't know, Margy. I'm real sorry about it. George Elliot's a good, likely young man; but if you didn't want to live with his mother, it was better to say so right in the beginning. And I don't know as I blame you much: she's pretty set in her ways."

"I guess she is. I never could bear her. I guess he'll find out—"

Margy dried her eyes defiantly, and took up the velvet again. "I've spoilt this velvet. I don't see why being disappointed in love should affect a girl so's to make her cut bias."

There was a whimsical element in Margy which seemed to roll uppermost along with her grief.

Esther looked a little puzzled. "Never mind the velvet, child: it ain't much, anyway." She began tossing over some ribbons to cover her departure from her usual reticence. "I'm real sorry about it, Margy. Such things are hard to bear, but they can be lived through. I know something about it myself. You knew I'd had some of this kind of trouble, didn't you?"

"About Mr. Woodman, you mean?"

"Yes, about Marcus Woodman. I'll tell you what 'tis, Margy Wilson, you've got one thing to be thankful for, and that is that there ain't anything ridickerlous about this affair of yourn. That makes it the hardest of anything, according to my mind—when you know that everybody's laughing, and you can hardly help laughing yourself, though you feel 'most ready to die."

"Ain't that Mr. Woodman crazy?"

"No, he ain't crazy; he's got too much will for his common-sense, that's all, and the will teeters the sense a little too far into the air. I see all through it from the beginning. I could read Marcus Woodman jest like a book."

"I don't see how in the world you ever come to like such a man."

"Well, I s'pose love's the strongest when there ain't any good reason for it. They say it is. I can't say as I ever really admired Marcus Woodman much. I always see right through him; but that didn't hinder my thinking so much of him that I never felt as if I could marry any other man. And I've had chances, though I shouldn't want you to say so."

"You turned him off because he went to sitting on the church steps?"

"Course I did. Do you s'pose I was going to marry a man who made a laughing-stock of himself that way?"

"I don't see how he ever come to do it. It's the funniest thing I ever heard of."

"I know it. It seems so silly nobody 'd believe it. Well, all there is about it, Marcus Woodman's got so much mulishness in him it makes him almost miraculous. You see, he got up an' spoke in that church meeting when they had such a row about Mr. Morton's being settled here—Marcus was awful set again' him. I never could see any reason why, and I don't think he could. He said Mr. Morton wa'n't doctrinal; that was what they all said; but I don't believe half of 'em knew what doctrinal was. I never could see why Mr. Morton wa'n't as good as most ministers—enough sight better than them that treated him so, anyway. I always felt that they was really setting him in a pulpit high over their heads by using him the way they did, though they didn't know it.

"Well, Marcus spoke in that church meeting, an' he kept getting more and more set every word he said. He always had a way of saying things over and over, as if he was making steps out of 'em, an' raising of himself up on 'em, till there was no moving him at all. And he did that night. Finally, when he was up real high, he said, as for him, if Mr. Morton was settled over that church, he'd never go inside the door himself as long as he lived. Somebody spoke out then—I never quite knew who 'twas, though I suspected—an' says, 'You'll have to set on the steps, then, Brother Woodman.'

"Everybody laughed at that but Marcus. He didn't see nothing to laugh at. He spoke out awful set, kinder gritting his teeth, 'I will set on the steps fifty years before I'll go into this house if that man's settled here.'

"I couldn't believe he'd really do it. We were going to be married that spring, an' it did seem as if he might listen to me; but he wouldn't. The Sunday Mr. Morton begun to preach, he begun to set on them steps, an' he's set there ever since, in all kinds of weather. It's a wonder it 'ain't killed him; but I guess it's made him tough."

"Why, didn't he feel bad when you wouldn't marry him?"

"Feel bad? Of course he did. He took on terribly. But it didn't make any difference; he wouldn't give in a hair's breadth. I declare it did seem as if I should die. His mother felt awfully too—she's a real good woman. I don't know what Marcus would have done without her. He wants a sight of tending and waiting on; he's dreadful babyish in some ways, though you wouldn't think it.

"Well, it's all over now, as far as I'm concerned. I've got over it a good deal, though sometimes it makes me jest as mad as ever to see him setting there. But I try to be reconciled, and I get along jest as well, mebbe, as if I'd had him—I don't know. I fretted more at first than there was any sense in, and I hope you won't."

"I ain't going to fret at all, Miss Barney. I may cut bias for a while, but I sha'n't do anything worse."

"How you do talk, child!"

A good deal of it was talk with Margy; she had not as much courage as her words proclaimed. She was capable of a strong temporary resolution, but of no enduring one. She gradually weakened as the days without her lover went on, and one Saturday night she succumbed entirely. There was quite a rush of business, but through it all she caught a conversation between some customers—two pretty young girls.

"Who was that with you last night at the concert?"

"That—oh, that was George Elliot. Didn't you know him?"

"He's got another girl," thought Margy, with a great throb.

The next Sunday night, coming out of meeting with Miss Barney, she left her suddenly. George Elliot was one of a waiting line of young men in the vestibule. She went straight up to him. He looked at her in bewilderment, his dark face turning red.

"Good-evening, Miss Wilson," he stammered out, finally.

"Good-evening," she whispered, and stood looking up at him piteously. She was white and trembling.

At last he stepped forward suddenly and offered her his arm. In spite of his resentment, he could not put her to open shame before all his mates, who were staring curiously.

When they were out in the dark, cool street, he bent over her. "Why, Margy, what does all this mean?"

"Oh, George, let her live with us, please. I want her to. I know I can get along with her if I try. I'll do everything I can. Please let her live with us."

"Who's *her*?"

"Your mother."

"And I suppose *us* is you and I? I thought that was all over, Margy; ain't it?"

"Oh, George, I am sorry I treated you so."

"And you are willing to let mother live with us now?"

"I'll do anything. Oh, George!"

"Don't cry, Margy. There—nobody's looking—give us a kiss. It's been a long time; ain't it, dear? So you've made up your mind that you're willing to let mother live with us?"

"Yes."

"Well, I don't believe she ever will, Margy. She's about made up her mind to go and live with my brother Edward, whether or no. So you won't be troubled with her. I dare say she might have been a little of a trial as she grew older."

"You didn't tell me."

"I thought it was your place to give in, dear."

"Yes, it was, George."

"I'm mighty glad you did. I tell you what it is, dear, I don't know how you've felt, but I've been pretty miserable lately."

"Poor George!"

They passed Esther Barney's house, and strolled along half a mile farther. When they returned, and Margy stole softly into the house and up-stairs, it was quite late, and Esther had gone to bed. Margy saw the light was not out in her room, so she peeped in. She could not wait till morning to tell her.

"Where have you been?" said Esther, looking up at her out of the pillows.

"Oh, I went to walk a little way with George."

"Then you've made up?"

"Yes."

"Is his mother going to live with you?"

"No; I guess not. She's going to live with Edward. But I told him I was willing she should. I've about made up my mind it's a woman's place to give in mostly. I s'pose you think I'm an awful fool."

"No, I don't; no, I don't, Margy. I'm real glad it's all right betwixt you and George. I've seen you weren't very happy lately."

They talked a little longer; then Margy said "Good-night," going over to Esther and kissing her. Being so rich in love made her generous with it. She looked down sweetly into the older woman's thin, red-cheeked face. "I wish you were as happy as I," said she. "I wish you and Mr. Woodman could make up too."

"That's an entirely different matter. I couldn't give in in such a thing as that."

Margy looked at her; she was not subtle, but she had just come out triumphant through innocent love and submission, and used the wisdom she had gained thereby.

"Don't you believe," said she, "if you was to give in the way I did, that he would?"

Esther started up with an astonished air. That had never occurred to her before. "Oh, I don't believe he would. You don't know him; he's awful set. Besides, I don't know but I'm better off the way it is."

In spite of herself, however, she could not help thinking of Margy's suggestion. Would he give in? She was hardly disposed to run the risk. With her peculiar cast of mind, her feeling for the ludicrous so keen that it almost amounted to a special sense, and her sensitiveness to ridicule, it would have been easier for her to have married a man under the shadow of a crime than one who was the deserving target of gibes and jests. Besides, she told herself, it was possible that he had changed his mind, that he no longer cared for her. How could she make the first overtures? She had not Margy's impulsiveness and innocence of youth to excuse her.

Also, she was partly influenced by the reason which she had given Margy: she was not so very sure that it would be best for her to take any such step. She was more fixed in the peace and pride of her old maidenhood than she had realized, and was more shy of disturbing it. Her comfortable meals, her tidy house-keeping, and her prosperous work had become such sources of satisfaction to her that she was almost wedded to them, and jealous of any interference.

So it is doubtful if there would have been any change in the state of affairs if Marcus Woodman's mother had not died towards spring. Esther was greatly distressed about it.

"I don't see what Marcus is going to do," she told Margy. "He ain't any fitter to take care of himself than a baby, and he won't have any housekeeper, they say."

One evening, after Marcus's mother had been dead about three weeks, Esther went over there. Margy had gone out to walk with George, so nobody knew. When she reached the house —a white cottage on a hill—she saw a light in the kitchen window.

"He's there," said she. She knocked on the door softly. Marcus shuffled over to it—he was in his stocking feet—and opened it.

"Good-evening, Marcus," said she, speaking first.

"Good-evening."

"I hadn't anything special to do this evening, so I thought I'd look in a minute and see how you was getting along."

"I ain't getting along very well; but I'm glad to see you. Come right in."

When she was seated opposite him by the kitchen fire, she surveyed him and his surroundings pityingly. Everything had an abject air of forlornness; there was neither tidiness nor comfort. After a few words she rose energetically. "See here, Marcus," said she, "you jest fill up that tea-kettle, and I'm going to slick up here a little for you while I stay."

"Now, Esther, I don't feel as if—"

"Don't you say nothing. Here's the tea-kettle. I might jest as well be doing that as setting still."

He watched her, in a way that made her nervous, as she flew about putting things to rights; but she said to herself that this was easier than sitting still, and gradually leading up to the object for which she had come. She kept wondering if she could ever accomplish it. When the room was in order, finally, she sat down again, with a strained-up look in her face.

"Marcus," said she, "I might as well begin. There was something I wanted to say to you to-night."

He looked at her, and she went on:

"I've been thinking some lately about how matters used to be betwixt you an' me, and it's jest possible—I don't know—but I might have been a little more patient than I was. I don't know as I'd feel the same way now if—"

"Oh, Esther, what do you mean?"

"I ain't going to tell you, Marcus Woodman, if you can't find out. I've said full enough; more'n I ever thought I should."

He was an awkward man, but he rose and threw himself on his knees at her feet with all the grace of complete unconsciousness of action. "Oh, Esther, you don't mean, do you?—you don't mean that you'd be willing to—marry me?"

"No; not if you don't get up. You look ridickerlous."

"Esther, do you mean it?"

"Yes. Now get up."

"You ain't thinking—I can't give up what we had the trouble about, any more now than I could then."

"Ain't I said once that wouldn't make any difference?"

At that he put his head down on her knees and sobbed.

"Do, for mercy sake, stop. Somebody 'll be coming in. 'Tain't as if we was a young couple."

"I ain't going to till I've told you about it, Esther. You ain't never really understood. In the first of it, we was both mad; but we ain't now, and we can talk it over. Oh, Esther, I've had such an awful life! I've looked at you, and— Oh, dear, dear, dear!"

"Marcus, you scare me to death crying so."

"I won't. Esther, look here—it's the gospel truth: I ain't a thing again' Mr. Morton now."

"Then why on earth don't you go into the meeting-house and behave yourself?"

"Don't you suppose I would if I could? I can't, Esther—I can't."

"I don't know what you mean by can't."

"Do you s'pose I've took any comfort sitting there on them steps in the winter snows an' the summer suns? Do you s'pose I've took any comfort not marrying you? Don't you s'pose

I'd given all I was worth any time the last ten year to have got
up an' walked into the church with the rest of the folks?"

"Well, I'll own, Marcus, I don't see why you couldn't if you
wanted to."

"I ain't sure as I see myself, Esther. All I know is I can't make
myself give it up. I can't. I ain't made strong enough to."

"As near as I can make out, you've taken to sitting on the
church steps the way other men take to smoking and drinking."

"I don't know but you're right, Esther, though I hadn't
thought of it in that way before."

"Well, you must try to overcome it."

"I never can, Esther. It ain't right for me to let you think
I can."

"Well, we won't talk about it any more to-night. It's time I
was going home."

"Esther—did you mean it?"

"Mean what?"

"That you'd marry me any way?"

"Yes, I did. Now do get up. I do hate to see you looking so
silly."

Esther had a new pearl-colored silk gown, and a little mantle
like it, and a bonnet trimmed with roses and plumes, and she
and Marcus were married in June.

The Sunday on which she came out a bride they were late at
church; but late as it was, curious people were lingering by the
steps to watch them. What would they do? Would Marcus
Woodman enter that church door which his awful will had
guarded for him so long?

They walked slowly up the steps between the watching people.
When they came to the place where he was accustomed to sit,
Marcus stopped short and looked down at his wife with an
agonized face.

"Oh, Esther, I've—got—to stop."

"Well, we'll both sit down here, then."

"You?"

"Yes; I'm willing."

"No; you go in."

"No, Marcus; I sit with you on our wedding Sunday."

Her sharp, middle-aged face as she looked up at him was fairly
heroic. This was all that she could do: her last weapon was used.
If this failed, she would accept the chances with which she had

married, and before the eyes of all these tittering people she would sit down at his side on these church steps. She was determined, and she would not weaken.

He stood for a moment staring into her face. He trembled so that the bystanders noticed it. He actually leaned over towards his old seat as if wire ropes were pulling him down upon it. Then he stood up straight, like a man, and walked through the church door with his wife.

The people followed. Not one of them even smiled. They had felt the pathos in the comedy.

The sitters in the pews watched Marcus wonderingly as he went up the aisle with Esther. He looked strange to them; he had almost the grand mien of a conqueror.

Sister Liddy

There were no trees near the almshouse; it stood in its bare, sandy lot, and there were no leaves or branches to cast shadows on its walls. It seemed like the folks whom it sheltered, out in the full glare of day, without any little kindly shade between itself and the dull, unfeeling stare of curiosity. The almshouse stood upon rising ground, so one could see it for a long distance. It was a new building, Mansard-roofed and well painted. The village took pride in it: no town far or near had such a house for the poor. It was so fine and costly that the village did not feel able to give its insane paupers separate support in a regular asylum; so they lived in the almshouse with the sane paupers, and there was a padded cell in case they waxed too violent.

Around the almshouse lay the town fields. In summer they were green with corn and potatoes, now they showed ugly plough ridges sloping over the uneven ground, and yellow corn stubble. Beyond the field at the west of the almshouse was a little wood of elms and oaks and wild apple-trees. The yellow leaves had all fallen from the elms and the apple-trees, but most of the brown ones stayed on the oaks.

Polly Moss stood at the west window in the women's sitting-room and gazed over at the trees. "It's cur'us how them oak leaves hang on arter the others have all fell off," she remarked.

A tall old woman sitting beside the stove looked around suddenly. She had singular bright eyes, and a sardonic smile around her mouth. "It's a way they allers have," she returned, scornfully. "Guess there ain't nothin' very cur'us about it. When the oak leaves fall off an' the others hang on, then you can be lookin' for the end of the world; that's goin' to be one of the signs."

"Allers a-harpin' on the end of the world," growled another old woman, in a deep bass voice. "I've got jest about sick on't. Seems as if I should go crazy myself, hearin' on't the whole time." She was sewing a seam in coarse cloth, and she sat on a stool on the other side of the stove. She was short and stout, and she sat with a heavy settle as if she were stuffed with lead.

The tall old woman took no further notice. She sat rigidly straight, and fixed her bright eyes upon the top of the door, and her sardonic smile deepened.

The stout old woman gave an ugly look at her; then she sewed with more impetus. Now and then she muttered something in her deep voice.

There were, besides herself, three old women in the room—Polly Moss, the tall one, and a pretty one in a white cap and black dress. There was also a young woman; she sat in a rocking-chair and leaned her head back. She was handsome, but she kept her mouth parted miserably, and there were ghastly white streaks around it and her nostrils. She never spoke. Her pretty black hair was rough, and her dress sagged at the neck. She had been living out at a large farm, and had overworked. She had no friends or relatives to take her in; so she had come to the alms-house to rest and try to recover. She had no refuge but the alms-house or the hospital, and she had a terrible horror of a hospital. Dreadful visions arose in her ignorant childish mind whenever she thought of one. She had a lover, but he had not been to see her since she came to the almshouse, six weeks before; she wept most of the time over that and her physical misery.

Polly Moss stood at the window until a little boy trudged into the room, bringing his small feet down with a clapping noise. He went up to Polly and twitched her dress. She looked around at him. "Well, now, Tommy, what do ye want?"

"Come out-doors an' play hide an' coot wis me, Polly."

Tommy was a stout little boy. He wore a calico tier that sagged to his heels in the back, and showed in front his little calico trousers. His round face was pleasant and innocent and charming.

Polly put her arms around the boy and hugged him. "Tommy's a darlin'," she said; "can't he give poor Polly a kiss?"

Tommy put up his lips. "Come out-doors an' play hide an' coot wis me," he said again, breathing the words out with the kiss.

"Now, Tommy, jest look out of the winder. Don't he see that it's rainin', hey?"

The child shook his head stubbornly, although he was looking straight at the window, which revealed plainly enough that long sheets of rain were driving over the fields. "Come out-doors and play hide an' coot wis me, Polly."

"Now, Tommy, jest listen to Polly. Don't he know he can't go out-doors when it's rainin' this way? He'd get all wet, an' Polly too. But I'll tell you what Polly an' Tommy can do. We'll jest go out in the hall an' we'll roll the ball. Tommy go run quick an' get his ball."

Tommy raised a shout, and clapped out of the room; his sweet nature was easily diverted. Polly followed him. She had a twisting limp, and was so bent that she was not much taller than Tommy, her little pale triangular face seemed to look from the middle of her flat chest.

"The wust-lookin' objeck," growled the stout old woman when Polly was out of the room: "looks more like an old cat that's had to airn it's own livin' than a human bein'. It 'bout makes me sick to look at her." Her deep tones travelled far; Polly, out in the corridor waiting for Tommy, heard every word.

"She is a dretful-lookin' cretur," assented the pretty old woman. As she spoke she puckered her little red mouth daintily, and drew herself up with a genteel air.

The stout old woman surveyed her contemptuously. "Well, good looks don't amount to much, nohow," said she, "if folks ain't got common-sense to balance 'em. I'd enough sight ruther know a leetle somethin' than have a dolly-face myself."

"Seems to me she is about the dretfulest-lookin' cretur that I ever did see," repeated the pretty old woman, quite unmoved. Aspersions on her intellect never aroused her in the least.

The stout old woman looked baffled. "Jest turn your head a leetle that way, will you, Mis' Handy?" she said, presently.

The pretty old woman turned her head obediently. "What is it?" she inquired, with a conscious simper.

"Jest turn your head a leetle more. Yes, it's funny I ain't never noticed it afore. Your nose is a leetle grain crooked—ain't it, Mis' Handy?"

Mrs. Handy's face turned a deep pink—even her little ears and her delicate old neck were suffused; her blue eyes looked like an enraged bird's. "Crooked! H'm! I shouldn't think that folks that's got a nose like some folks had better say much about other folks' noses. There can't nobody tell me nothin' about my nose; I know all about it. Folks that wouldn't wipe their feet on some folks, nor look twice at 'em, has praised it. My nose ain't crooked an' never was, an' if anybody says so it's 'cause they're so spity, 'cause they're so mortal homely themselves. Guess I know." She drew breath, and paused for a return shot, but she got none. The stout old woman sewed and chuckled to herself, the tall one still fixed her eyes upon the top of the door, and the young woman leaned back with her lips parted, and her black eyes rolled.

The pretty old woman began again in defence of her nose; she talked fiercely, and kept feeling of it. Finally she arose and went out of the room with a flirt.

Then the stout old woman laughed. "She's gone to look at her nose in the lookin'-glass, an' make sure it ain't crooked: if it ain't a good joke!" she exclaimed, delightedly.

But she got no response. The young woman never stirred, and the tall old one lowered her gaze from the door to the stove, which she regarded disapprovingly. "I call it the devil's stove," she remarked, after a while.

The stout old woman gave a grunt and sewed her seam; she was done with talking to such an audience. The shouts of children out in the corridor could be heard. "Pesky young ones!" she muttered.

In the corridor Polly Moss played ball with the children. She never caught the ball, and she threw it with weak, aimless jerks; her back ached, but she was patient, and her face was full of simple childish smiles. There were two children besides Tommy —his sister and a little boy.

The corridor was long; doors in both sides led into the paupers' bedrooms. Suddenly one of the doors flew open, and a little figure shot out. She went down the corridor with a swift trot like a child. She had on nothing but a woolen petticoat and a calico waist; she held her head down, and her narrow shoulders worked as she ran; her mop of soft white hair flew out. The children looked around at her; she was a horrible caricature of themselves.

The stout old woman came pressing out of the sitting-room. She went directly to the room that the running figure had left, and peered in; then she looked around significantly. "I knowed it," she said; "it's tore all to pieces agin. I'd jest been thinkin' to myself that Sally was dretful still, and I'd bet she was pullin' her bed to pieces. There 'tis, an' made up jest as nice a few minutes ago! I'm goin' to see Mis' Arms."

Mrs. Arms was the matron. The old woman went off with an important air, and presently she returned with her. The matron was a large woman with a calm, benignant, and weary face.

Polly Moss continued to play ball, but several other old women had assembled, and they all talked volubly. They demonstrated that Sally had torn her bed to pieces, that it had been very nicely made, and that she should be punished.

The matron listened; she did not say much. Then she returned to the kitchen, where she was preparing dinner. Some of the paupers assisted her. An old man, with his baggy trousers hitched high, chopped something in a tray, an old woman peeled potatoes, and a young one washed pans at the sink. The young woman, as she washed, kept looking over her shoulder and rolling her dark eyes at the other people in the room. She was mindful of every motion behind her back.

Mrs. Arms herself worked and directed the others. When dinner was ready the old man clanged a bell in the corridor, and everybody flocked to the dining-room except the young woman at the kitchen sink; she still stood there washing dishes. The dinner was coarse and abundant. The paupers, with the exception of the sick young woman, ate with gusto. The children were all hearty, and although the world had lost all its savor for the hearts and minds of the old ones, it was still somewhat salt to their palates. Now that their thoughts had ceased reaching and grasping, they could still put out their tongues, for that primitive instinct of life with which they had been born still survived and gave them pleasure. In this world it is the child only that is immortal.

The old people and the children ate after the same manner. There was a loud smacking of lips and gurgling noises. The rain drove against the windows of the dining-room, with its bare floor, its board tables and benches, and rows of feeding paupers. The smooth yellow heads of the children seemed to catch all the light in the room. Once in a while they raised imperious clamors. The overseer sat at one end of the table and served the beef. He was stout, and had a handsome, heavy face.

The meal was nearly finished when there was a crash of breaking crockery, a door slammed, and there was a wild shriek out in the corridor. The overseer and one of the old men who was quite able-bodied sprang and rushed out of the room. The matron followed, and the children tagged at her heels. The others continued feeding as if nothing had happened. "That Agnes is wuss agin," remarked the stout old woman. "I've seed it a-comin' on fer a couple of days. They'd orter have put her in the cell yesterday; I told Mis' Arms so, but they're allers puttin' off, an' puttin' off."

"They air a-takin' on her up to the cell now," said the pretty old woman; and she brought around her knifeful of cabbage with a sidewise motion, and stretched her little red mouth to receive it.

Out in the corridor shriek followed shriek; there were loud voices and scuffling. The children were huddled in the doorway, peeping, but the old paupers continued to eat. The sick young woman laid down her knife and fork and wept.

Presently the shrieks and the scuffling grew faint in the distance; the children had followed on. Then, after a little, they all returned and the dinner was finished.

After dinner, when the women paupers had done their share of the clearing away, they were again assembled in their sitting-room. The windows were cloudy with fine mist; the rain continued to drive past them from over the yellow stubbly fields. There was a good fire in the stove, and the room was hot and close. The stout old woman sewed again on her coarse seam, the others were idle. There were now six old women present; one of them was the little creature whom they called Sally. She sat close to the stove, bent over and motionless. Her clothing hardly covered her. The sick young woman was absent; she was lying down on the lounge in the matron's room, and the children too were in there.

Polly Moss sat by the window. The old women began talking among themselves. The pretty old one had taken off her cap and had it in her lap, perking up the lace and straightening it. It was a flimsy rag, like a soiled cobweb. The stout old woman

Seacoast and Upland

cast a contemptuous glance at it. She raised her nose and her upper lip scornfully. "I don't see how you can wear that nasty thing nohow, Mis' Handy," said she.

Mrs. Handy flushed pink again. She bridled and began to speak, then she looked at the little soft soiled mass in her lap, and paused. She had not the force of character to proclaim black white while she was looking at it. Had the old cap been in the bureau drawer, or even on her head, she might have defended it to the death, but here before her eyes it silenced her.

But after her momentary subsidence she aroused herself; her blue eyes gleamed dimly at the stout old woman. "It was a handsome cap when it was new, anyhow!" said she; "better'n some folks ever had, I'll warrant. Folks that ain't got no caps at all can't afford to be flingin' at them that has, if they ain't quite so nice as they was. You'd orter have seen the cap I had when my daughter was married! All white wrought lace, an' bows of pink ribbon, an' long streamers, an' some artificial roses on't. I don't s'pose you ever see anythin' like it, Mis' Paine."

The stout woman was Mrs. Paine. "Mebbe I ain't," said she, sarcastically.

The tall old woman chimed in suddenly; her thin, nervous voice clanged after the others like a sharply struck bell. "I ain't never had any caps to speak of," she proclaimed; "never thought much of 'em, anyhow; heatin' things; an' I never heard that folks in heaven wore caps. But I have had some good clothes. I've got a piece of silk in my bureau drawer. That silk would stand alone. An' I had a good thibet; there was rows an' rows of velvet ribbon on it. I always had good clothes; my husband, he wanted I should, an' he got 'em fer me. I airned some myself, too. I 'ain't got any now, an' I dunno as I care if I ain't, fer the signs are increasin'."

"Allers a-harpin' on that," muttered the stout old woman.

"I had a handsome blue silk when I was marri'd," vouchsafed Mrs. Handy.

"I've seen the piece of it," returned the tall one; "it ain't near so thick as mine is."

The old woman who had not been present in the morning now spoke. She had been listening with a superior air. She was the only one in the company who had possessed considerable property, and had fallen from a widely differing estate. She was tall and dark and gaunt; she towered up next the pretty old woman like a scraggy old pine beside a faded lily. She was a single woman, and she had lost all her property through an injudicious male relative. "Well," she proclaimed, "everybody knows I've had things if I ain't got 'em now. There I had a whole house, with Brussels carpets on all the rooms except the kitchen, an' stuffed furniture, an' beddin' packed away in chists, an' bureau drawers full of things. An' I ruther think I've had silk dresses an' bunnits an' caps."

"I remember you had a real handsome blue bunnit once, but it warn't so becomin' as some you'd had, you was so dark-complected," remarked the pretty old woman, in a soft, spiteful voice. "I had a white one, drawn silk, an' white feathers on't, when I was married, and they all said it was real becomin'. I was allers real white myself. I had a white muslin dress with a flounce on it, once, too, an' a black silk spencer cape."

"I had a fitch tippet an' muff that cost twenty-five dollars," remarked the stout old woman, emphatically, *"an'* a cashmire shawl."

"I had two cashmire shawls, an' *my* tippet cost fifty dollars," retorted the dark old woman, with dignity.

"My fust baby had an elegant blue cashmire cloak, all worked with silk as deep as that," said Mrs. Handy. She now had the old cap on her head, and looked more assertive.

"Mine had a little wagon with a velvet cushion to ride in; an' I had a tea-set, real chiny, with a green sprig on't," said the stout old woman.

"I had a Brittany teapot," returned Mrs. Handy.

"I had gilt vases as tall as that on my parlor mantel-shelf," said the dark old woman.

"I had a chiny figger, a girl with a basket of flowers on her arm, once," rejoined the tall one; "it used to set side of the clock. An' when I was fust married I used to live in a white house, with a flower-garden to one side. I can smell them pinks an' roses now, an' I s'pose I allers shall, jest as far as I go."

"I had a pump in my kitchen sink, an' things real handy," said the stout old one; "an' I used to look as well as anybody, an' my husband too, when we went to meetin'. I remember one winter I had a new brown alpaca with velvet buttons, an' he had a new great-coat with a velvet collar."

Suddenly the little cowering Sally raised herself and gave testimony to her own little crumb of past comfort. Her wits were few and scattering, and had been all her days, but the conversation of the other women seemed to set some vibrating into momentary concord. She laughed, and her bleared blue eyes twinkled. "I had a pink caliker gownd once," she quavered out. "Mis' Thompson, she gin it me when I lived there."

"Do hear the poor cretur," said the pretty old woman, with an indulgent air.

Now everybody had spoken but Polly Moss. She sat by the misty window, and her little pale triangular face looked from her sunken chest at the others. This conversation was a usual one. Many and many an afternoon the almshouse old women sat together and bore witness to their past glories. Now they had nothing, but at one time or another they had had something over which to plume themselves and feel that precious pride of possession. Their present was to them a state of simple existence, they regarded their future with a vague resignation; they were none of them thinkers, and there was no case of rapturous piety among them. In their pasts alone they took real comfort, and they kept, as it were, feeling of them to see if they were not still warm with life.

The old women delighted in these inventories and comparing of notes. Polly Moss alone had never spoken. She alone had never had anything in which to take pride. She had been always deformed and poor and friendless. She had worked for scanty pay as long as she was able, and had then drifted and struck on the almshouse, where she had grown old. She had not even a right to the charity of this particular village: this was merely the place where her working powers had failed her; but no one could trace her back to her birthplace, or the town which was responsible for her support. Polly Moss herself did not know— she went humbly where she was told. All her life the world had seemed to her simply standing-ground; she had gotten little more out of it.

Every day, when the others talked, she listened admiringly, and searched her memory for some little past treasure of her own, but she could not remember any. The dim image of a certain delaine dress, with bright flowers scattered over it, which she had once owned, away back in her girlhood, sometimes floated before her eyes when they were talking, and she had a half-mind to mention that, but her heart would fail her. She feared that it was not worthy to be compared with the others' fine departed gowns; it paled before even Sally's pink calico. Polly's poor clothes, covering her pitiful crookedness, had never given her any firm stimulus to gratulation. So she was always silent, and the other old women had come to talk at her. Their conversation acquired a gusto from this listener who could not join in. When a new item of past property was given, there was always a side-glance in Polly's direction.

None of the old women expected to ever hear a word from Polly, but this afternoon, when they had all, down to Sally, testified, she spoke up:

"You'd orter have seen my sister Liddy," said she; her voice was very small, it sounded like the piping of a feeble bird in a bush.

There was a dead silence. The other old women looked at each other. "Didn't know you ever had a sister Liddy," the stout old woman blurted out, finally, with an amazed air.

"My sister Liddy was jest as handsome as a pictur'," Polly returned.

The pretty old woman flushed jealously. "Was she fair-complected?" she inquired.

"She was jest as fair as a lily—a good deal fairer than you ever was, Mis' Handy, an' she had long yaller curls a-hangin' clean down to her waist, an' her cheeks were jest as pink, an' she had the biggest blue eyes I ever see, an' the beautifulest leetle red mouth."

"Lor'!" ejaculated the stout old woman, and the pretty old woman sniffed.

But Polly went on; she was not to be daunted; she had been silent all this time; and now her category poured forth, not piecemeal, but in a flood, upon her astonished hearers.

"Liddy, she could sing the best of anybody anywheres around," she continued; "nobody ever heerd sech singin'. It was so dretful loud an' sweet that you could hear it 'way down the road when the winders was shut. She used to sing in the meetin'-house, she did, an' all the folks used to sit up an' look at her when she begun. She used to wear a black silk dress to meetin', an' a white cashmire shawl, an' a bunnit with a pink wreath around the face, an' she had white kid gloves. Folks used to go to that meetin'-house jest to hear Liddy sing an' see her. They thought 'nough sight more of that than they did of the preachin'.

"Liddy had a feather fan, an' she used to sit an' fan her when she wa'n't singin', an' she allers had scent on her handkercher. An' when meetin' was done in the evenin' all the young fellars used to be crowdin' 'round, an' pushin' and bowin' an' scrapin', a-tryin' to get a chance to see her home. But Liddy she wouldn't look at none of them; she married a real rich fellar from Bostown. He was jest as straight as an arrer, an' he had black eyes an' hair, an' he wore a beautiful coat an' a satin vest, an' he spoke jest as perlite.

"When Liddy was married she had a whole chistful of clothes, real fine cotton cloth, all tucks an' laid-work, an' she had a pair of silk stockin's, an' some white shoes. An' her weddin' dress was white satin, with a great long trail to it, an' she had a lace veil, an' she wore great long ear-drops that shone like everythin'. *An'* she come out bride in a blue silk dress, an' a black lace mantilly, an' a white bunnit trimmed with lutestring ribbon."

"Where did your sister Liddy live arter she was married?" inquired the pretty old woman, with a subdued air.

"She lived in Bostown, an' she had a great big house with a parlor an' settin'-room, an' a room to eat in besides the kitchen. An' she had real velvet carpets on all the floors down to the kitchen, an' great pictur's in gilt frames a-hangin' on all the walls. An' her furnitur' was all stuffed, an' kivered with red velvet, an' she had a pianner, an' great big marble images a-settin' on her mantel-shelf. An' she had a coach with lamps on the sides, an' blue satin cushings, to ride in, an' four horses to draw it, an' a man to drive. An' she allers had a hired girl in the kitchen. I never knowed Liddy to be without a hired girl.

"Liddy's husband, he thought everythin' of her; he never used to come home from his work without he brought her somethin', an' she used to run out to meet him. She was allers dretful lovin', an' had a good disposition. Liddy, she had the beautifulest baby you ever see, an' she had a cradle lined with blue silk to rock him in, an' he had a white silk cloak, an' a leetle lace cap—"

"I shouldn't think your beautiful sister Liddy an' her husband would let you come to the poor-house," interrupted the dark old woman.

"Liddy's dead, or she wouldn't."

"Are her husband an' the baby dead, too?"

"They're all dead," responded Polly Moss. She looked out of the window again, her face was a burning red, and there were tears in her eyes.

There was silence among the other old women. They were at once overawed and incredulous. Polly left the room before long, then they began to discuss the matter. "I dun know whether to believe it or not," said the dark old woman.

"Well, I dun know, neither; I never knowed her to tell any-thin' that wa'n't so," responded the stout old one, doubtfully.

The old women could not make up their minds whether to believe or disbelieve. The pretty one was the most incredulous of any. She said openly that she did not believe it possible that such a "homely cretur" as Polly Moss could have had such a handsome sister.

But, credulous or not, their interest and curiosity were lively. Every day Polly Moss was questioned and cross-examined concerning her sister Liddy. She rose to the occasion; she did not often contradict herself, and the glories of her sister were increased daily. Old Polly Moss, her little withered face gleaming with reckless enthusiasm, sang the praises of her sister Liddy as wildly and faithfully as any minnesinger his angel mistress, and the old women listened with ever-increasing bewilderment and awe.

It was two weeks before Polly Moss died with pneumonia that she first mentioned her sister Liddy, and there was not one afternoon until the day when she was taken ill that she did not relate the story, with new and startling additions, to the old women.

Polly was not ill long, she settled meekly down under the disease: her little distorted frame had no resistance in it. She died at three o'clock in the morning. The afternoon before, she seemed better; she was quite rational, and she told the matron that she wanted to see her comrades, the old women. "I've got somethin' to tell 'em, Mis' Arms," Polly whispered, and her eyes were piteous.

So the other old women came into the room. They stood around Polly's little iron bed and looked at her. "I—want to—tell you—somethin'," she began. But there was a soft rush, and the sick young woman entered. She pressed straight to the matron; she disregarded the others. Her wan face seemed a very lamp of life—to throw a light over and above all present darkness, even of the grave. She moved nimbly; she was so full of joy that her sickly body seemed permeated by it, and almost a spiritual one. She did not appear in the least feeble. She caught the matron's arm. "Charley has come, Mis' Arms!" she cried out. "Charley has come! He's got a house ready. He's goin' to marry me, an' take me home, an' take care of me till I get well. I'm goin' right away!"

The old women all turned away from Polly and stared at the radiant girl. The matron sent her away, with a promise to see her in a few minutes. "Polly's dyin'," she whispered, and the girl stole out with a hushed air, but the light in her face was not dimmed. What was death to her, when she had just stepped on a height of life where one can see beyond it?

"Tell them what you wanted to, now, Polly," said the matron.

"I—want to tell you—somethin'," Polly repeated. "I s'pose I've been dretful wicked, but I ain't never had nothin' in my whole life. I—s'pose the Lord orter have been enough, but it's dretful hard sometimes to keep holt of him, an' not look anywheres else, when you see other folks a-clawin' an' gettin' other things, an' actin' as if they was wuth havin'. I ain't never had nothin' as fur as them other things go; I don't want nothin' else now. I've—got past 'em. I see I don't want nothin' but the Lord. But I used to feel dretful bad an' wicked when I heerd you all talkin' 'bout things you'd had, an' I hadn't never had nothin', so—" Polly Moss stopped talking, and coughed. The matron supported her. The old women nudged each other; their awed, sympathetic, yet sharply inquiring eyes never left her face. The children were peeping in at the open door; old Sally trotted past —she had just torn her bed to pieces. As soon as she got breath enough, Polly Moss finished what she had to say. "I—s'pose I —was dretful wicked," she whispered; "but—I never had any sister Liddy."

A Poetess

The garden-patch at the right of the house was all a gay spangle with sweet-peas and red-flowering beans, and flanked with feathery asparagus. A woman in blue was moving about there. Another woman, in a black bonnet, stood at the front door of the house. She knocked and waited. She could not see from where she stood the blue-clad woman in the garden. The house was very close to the road, from which a tall evergreen hedge separated it, and the view to the side was in a measure cut off.

The front door was open; the woman had to reach to knock

on it, as it swung into the entry. She was a small woman and quite young, with a bright alertness about her which had almost the effect of prettiness. It was to her what greenness and crispness are to a plant. She poked her little face forward, and her sharp pretty eyes took in the entry and a room at the left, of which the door stood open. The entry was small and square and unfurnished, except for a well-rubbed old card-table against the back wall. The room was full of green light from the tall hedge, and bristling with grasses and flowers and asparagus stalks.

"Betsey, you there?" called the woman. When she spoke, a yellow canary, whose cage hung beside the front door, began to chirp and twitter.

"Betsey, you there?" the woman called again. The bird's chirps came in a quick volley; then he began to trill and sing.

"She ain't there," said the woman. She turned and went out of the yard through the gap in the hedge; then she looked around. She caught sight of the blue figure in the garden. "There she is," said she.

She went around the house to the garden. She wore a gay cashmere-patterned calico dress with her mourning bonnet, and she held it carefully away from the dewy grass and vines.

The other woman did not notice her until she was close to her and said, "Good-mornin', Betsey." Then she started and turned around.

"Why, Mis' Caxton! That you?" said she.

"Yes. I've been standin' at your door for the last half-hour. I was jest goin' away when I caught sight of you out here."

In spite of her brisk speech her manner was subdued. She drew down the corners of her mouth sadly.

"I declare I'm dreadful sorry you had to stan' there so long!" said the other woman.

She set a pan partly filled with beans on the ground, wiped her hands, which were damp and green from the wet vines, on her apron, then extended her right one with a solemn and sympathetic air.

"It don't make much odds, Betsey," replied Mrs. Caxton. "I ain't got much to take up my time nowadays." She sighed heavily as she shook hands, and the other echoed her.

"We'll go right in now. I'm dreadful sorry you stood there so long," said Betsey.

"You'd better finish pickin' your beans."

"No; I wa'n't goin' to pick any more. I was jest goin' in."

"I declare, Betsey Dole, I shouldn't think you'd got enough for a cat!" said Mrs. Caxton, eying the pan.

"I've got pretty near all there is. I guess I've got more flowerin' beans than eatin' ones, anyway."

"I should think you had," said Mrs. Caxton, surveying the row of bean-poles topped with swarms of delicate red flowers. "I should think they were pretty near all flowerin' ones. Had any peas?"

"I didn't have more'n three or four messes. I guess I planted sweet-peas mostly. I don't know hardly how I happened to."

"Had any summer squash?"

"Two or three. There's some more set, if they ever get ripe. I planted some gourds. I think they look real pretty on the kitchen shelf in the winter."

"I should think you'd got a sage bed big enough for the whole town."

"Well, I have got a pretty good-sized one. I always liked them blue sage-blows. You'd better hold up your dress real careful goin' through here, Mis' Caxton, or you'll get it wet."

The two women picked their way through the dewy grass, around a corner of the hedge, and Betsey ushered her visitor into the house.

"Set right down in the rockin-chair," said she. "I'll jest carry these beans out into the kitchen."

"I should think you'd better get another pan and string 'em, or you won't get 'em done for dinner."

"Well, mebbe I will, if you'll excuse it, Mis' Caxton. The beans had ought to boil quite a while; they're pretty old."

Betsey went into the kitchen and returned with a pan and an old knife. She seated herself opposite Mrs. Caxton, and began to string and cut the beans.

"If I was in your place I shouldn't feel as if I'd got enough to boil a kettle for," said Mrs. Caxton, eying the beans. "I should 'most have thought when you didn't have any more room for a garden than you've got that you'd planted more real beans and peas instead of so many flowerin' ones. I'd rather have a good mess of green peas boiled with a piece of salt pork than all the sweet-peas you could give me. I like flowers well enough, but I never set up for a butterfly, an' I want something else to live on." She looked at Betsey with pensive superiority.

Betsey was near-sighted; she had to bend low over the beans in order to string them. She was fifty years old, but she wore her streaky light hair in curls like a young girl. The curls hung over her faded cheeks and almost concealed them. Once in a while she flung them back with a childish gesture which sat strangely upon her.

"I dare say you're in the right of it," she said, meekly.

"I know I am. You folks that write poetry wouldn't have a single thing to eat growin' if they were left alone. And that brings to mind what I come for. I've been thinkin' about it ever since—our—little Willie—left us." Mrs. Caxton's manner was suddenly full of shamefaced dramatic fervor, her eyes reddened with tears.

Betsey looked up inquiringly, throwing back her curls. Her face took on unconsciously lines of grief so like the other woman's that she looked like her for the minute.

"I thought maybe," Mrs. Caxton went on, tremulously, "you'd be willin' to—write a few lines."

"O course I will, Mis' Caxton. I'll be glad to, if I can do 'em to suit you," Betsy said, tearfully.

"I thought jest a few—lines. You could mention how—handsome he was, and good, and I never had to punish him but once in his life, and how pleased he was with his little new suit, and what a sufferer he was, and—how we hope he is at rest—in a better land."

"I'll try, Mis' Caxton, I'll try," sobbed Betsey. The two women wept together for a few minutes.

"It seems as if—I couldn't have it so sometimes," Mrs. Caxton said, brokenly. "I keep thinkin' he's in the other—room. Every time I go back home when I've been away it's like—losin' him again. Oh, it don't seem as if I could go home and not find him there—it don't, it don't! Oh, you don't know anything about it, Betsey. You never had any children!"

"I don't s'pose I do, Mis' Caxton; I don't s'pose I do."

Presently Mrs. Caxton wiped her eyes. "I've been thinkin'," said she, keeping her mouth steady with an effort, "that it would be real pretty to have—some lines printed on some sheets of white paper with a neat black border. I'd like to send some to my folks, and one to the Perkinses in Brigham, and there's a good many others I thought would value 'em."

"I'll do jest the best I can, Mis' Caxton, an' be glad to. It's little enough anybody can do at such times."

Mrs. Caxton broke out weeping again. "Oh, it's true, it's true, Betsey!" she sobbed. "Nobody can do anything, and nothin' amounts to anything—poetry or anything else—when he's *gone*. Nothin' can bring him back. Oh, what shall I do, what shall I do?"

Mrs. Caxton dried her tears again, and arose to take leave. "Well, I must be goin', or Wilson won't have any dinner," she said, with an effort at self-control.

"Well, I'll do jest the best I can with the poetry," said Betsey. "I'll write it this afternoon." She had set down her pan of beans and was standing beside Mrs. Caxton. She reached up and straightened her black bonnet, which had slipped backward.

"I've got to get a pin," said Mrs. Caxton, tearfully. "I can't keep it anywheres. It drags right off my head, the veil is so heavy."

Betsey went to the door with her visitor. "It's dreadful dusty, ain't it?" she remarked, in that sad, contemptuous tone with which one speaks of discomforts in the presence of affliction.

"Terrible," replied Mrs. Caxton. "I wouldn't wear my black dress in it nohow; a black bonnet is bad enough. This dress is 'most too good. It's enough to spoil everything. Well, I'm much obliged to you, Betsey, for bein' willin' to do that."

"I'll do jest the best I can, Mis' Caxton."

After Betsey had watched her visitor out of the yard she returned to the sitting-room and took up the pan of beans. She looked doubtfully at the handful of beans all nicely strung and cut up. "I declare I don't know what to do," said she. "Seems as if I should kind of relish these, but it's goin' to take some time to cook 'em, tendin' the fire an' everything, an' I'd ought to go to work on that poetry. Then, there's another thing, if I have 'em to-day, I can't to-morrow. Mebbe I shall take more comfort thinkin' about 'em. I guess I'll leave 'em over till to-morrow."

Betsey carried the pan of beans out into the kitchen and set them away in the pantry. She stood scrutinizing the shelves like a veritable Mother Hubbard. There was a plate containing three or four potatoes and a slice of cold boiled pork, and a spoonful of red jelly in a tumbler; that was all the food in sight. Betsey stooped and lifted the lid from an earthen jar on the floor. She took out two slices of bread. "There!" said she. "I'll have this bread and that jelly this noon, an' to-night I'll have a kind of dinner-supper with them potatoes warmed up with the pork. An' then I can sit right down an' go to work on that poetry."

It was scarcely eleven o'clock, and not time for dinner. Betsey returned to the sitting-room, got an old black portfolio and pen and ink out of the chimney cupboard, and seated herself to work. She meditated, and wrote one line, then another. Now and then she read aloud what she had written with a solemn intonation. She sat there thinking and writing, and the time went on. The twelve-o'clock bell rang, but she never noticed it; she had quite forgotten the bread and jelly. The long curls drooped over her cheeks; her thin yellow hand, cramped around the pen, moved slowly and fitfully over the paper. The light in the room was dim and green, like the light in an arbor, from the tall hedge before the windows. Great plumy bunches of asparagus waved over the tops of the looking-glass; a framed sampler, a steel engraving of a female head taken from some old magazine, and sheaves of dried grasses hung on or were fastened to the walls; vases and tumblers of flowers stood on the shelf and table. The air was heavy and sweet.

Betsey in this room, bending over her portfolio, looked like the very genius of gentle, old-fashioned, sentimental poetry. It seemed as if one, given the premises of herself and the room, could easily deduce what she would write, and read without seeing those lines wherein flowers rhymed sweetly with vernal bowers, home with beyond the tomb, and heaven with even.

The summer afternoon wore on. It grew warmer and closer; the air was full of the rasping babble of insects, with the cicadas shrilling over them; now and then a team passed, and a dust cloud floated over the top of the hedge; the canary at the door chirped and trilled, and Betsey wrote poor little Willie Caxton's obituary poetry.

Tears stood in her pale blue eyes; occasionally they rolled down her cheeks, and she wiped them away. She kept her handkerchief in her lap with her portfolio. When she looked away from the paper she seemed to see two childish forms in the room —one purely human, a boy clad in his little girl petticoats, with a fair chubby face; the other in a little straight white night-gown, with long, shining wings, and the same face. Betsey had not enough imagination to change the face. Little Willie Caxton's angel was still himself to her, although decked in the paraphernalia of the resurrection.

"I s'pose I can't feel about it nor write about it anything the way I could if I'd had any children of my own an' lost 'em. I s'pose it *would* have come home to me different," Betsey murmured once, sniffing. A soft color flamed up under her curls at the thought. For a second the room seemed all aslant with white wings, and smiling with the faces of children that had never been. Betsey straightened herself as if she were trying to be dignified to her inner consciousness. "That's one trouble I've been clear of, anyhow," said she; "an' I guess I can enter into her feelin's considerable."

She glanced at a great pink shell on the shelf, and remembered how she had often given it to the dead child to play with when he had been in with his mother, and how he had put it to his ear to hear the sea.

"Dear little fellow!" she sobbed, and sat awhile with her handkerchief at her face.

Betsey wrote her poem upon backs of old letters and odd scraps of paper. She found it difficult to procure enough paper for fair copies of her poems when composed; she was forced to be very economical with the first draft. Her portfolio was piled with a loose litter of written papers when she at length arose and stretched her stiff limbs. It was near sunset; men with dinner-pails were tramping past the gate, going home from their work.

Betsey laid the portfolio on the table. "There! I've wrote sixteen verses," said she, "an' I guess I've got everything in. I guess she'll think that's enough. I can copy if off nice to-morrow. I can't see to-night to do it, anyhow."

There were red spots on Betsey's cheeks; her knees were unsteady when she walked. She went into the kitchen and made a fire, and set on the tea-kettle. "I guess I won't warm up them potatoes to-night," said she; "I'll have the bread an' jelly, an' save 'em for breakfast. Somehow I don't seem to feel so much like 'em as I did, an' fried potatoes is apt to lay heavy at night."

When the kettle boiled, Betsey drank her cup of tea and soaked her slice of bread in it; then she put away her cup and saucer and plate, and went out to water her garden. The weather was so dry and hot it had to be watered every night. Betsey had to carry the water from a neighbor's well; her own was dry. Back and forth she went in the deepening twilight, her slender body strained to one side with the heavy water-pail, until the garden-mould looked dark and wet. Then she took in the canary-bird, locked up her house, and soon her light went out. Often on these summer nights Betsey went to bed without lighting a lamp at all. There was no moon, but it was a beautiful starlight night. She lay awake nearly all night, thinking of her poem. She altered several lines in her mind.

She arose early, made herself a cup of tea, and warmed over

the potatoes, then sat down to copy the poem. She wrote it out on both sides of note-paper, in a neat, cramped hand. It was the middle of the afternoon before it was finished. She had been obliged to stop work and cook the beans for dinner, although she begrudged the time. When the poem was fairly copied, she rolled it neatly and tied it with a bit of black ribbon; then she made herself ready to carry it to Mrs. Caxton's.

It was a hot afternoon. Betsey went down the street in her thinnest dress—an old delaine, with delicate bunches of faded flowers on a faded green ground. There was a narrow green belt ribbon around her long waist. She wore a green barège bonnet, stiffened with rattans, scooping over her face, with her curls pushed forward over her thin cheeks in two bunches, and she carried a small green parasol with a jointed handle. Her costume was obsolete, even in the little country village where she lived. She had worn it every summer for the last twenty years. She made no more change in her attire than the old perennials in her garden. She had no money with which to buy new clothes, and the old satisfied her. She had come to regard them as being as unalterably a part of herself as her body.

Betsey went on, setting her slim, cloth-gaitered feet daintily in the hot sand of the road. She carried her roll of poetry in a black-mitted hand. She walked rather slowly. She was not very strong; there was a limp feeling in her knees; her face, under the green shade of her bonnet, was pale and moist with the heat.

She was glad to reach Mrs. Caxton's and sit down in her parlor, damp and cool and dark as twilight, for the blinds and curtains had been drawn all day. Not a breath of the fervid out-door air had penetrated it.

"Come right in this way; it's cooler than the sittin'-room," Mrs. Caxton said; and Betsey sank into the haircloth rocker and waved a palm-leaf fan.

Mrs. Caxton sat close to the window in the dim light, and read the poem. She took out her handkerchief and wiped her eyes as she read. "It's beautiful, beautiful," she said, tearfully, when she had finished. "It's jest as comfortin' as it can be, and you worked that in about his new suit so nice. I feel real obliged to you, Betsey, and you shall have one of the printed ones when they're done. I'm goin' to see to it right off."

Betsey flushed and smiled. It was to her as if her poem had been approved and accepted by one of the great magazines. She had the pride and self-wonderment of recognized genius. She went home buoyantly, under the wilting sun, after her call was done. When she reached home there was no one to whom she could tell her triumph, but the hot spicy breath of the evergreen hedge and the fervent sweetness of the sweet-peas seemed to greet her like the voices of friends.

She could scarcely wait for the printed poem. Mrs. Caxton brought it, and she inspected it, neatly printed in its black border. She was quite overcome with innocent pride.

"Well, I don't know but it does read pretty well," said she.

"It's beautiful," said Mrs. Caxton, fervently. "Mr. White said he never read anything any more touchin', when I carried it to him to print. I think folks are goin' to think a good deal of havin' it. I've had two dozen printed."

It was to Betsey like a large edition of a book. She had written obituary poems before, but never one had been printed in this sumptuous fashion. "I declare I think it would look pretty framed!" said she.

"Well, I don't know but it would," said Mrs. Caxton. "Anybody might have a neat little black frame, and it would look real appropriate."

"I wonder how much it would cost?" said Betsey.

After Mrs. Caxton had gone, she sat long, staring admiringly at the poem, and speculating as to the cost of a frame. "There ain't no use; I can't have it nohow, not if it don't cost more'n a quarter of a dollar," said she.

Then she put the poem away and got her supper. Nobody knew how frugal Betsey Dole's suppers and breakfasts and dinners were. Nearly all her food in the summer came from the scanty vegetables which flourished between the flowers in her garden. She ate scarcely more than her canary-bird, and sang as assiduously. Her income was almost infinitesimal: the interest at a low per cent. of a tiny sum in the village savings-bank, the remnant of her father's little hoard after his funeral expenses had been paid. Betsey had lived upon it for twenty years, and considered herself well-to-do. She had never received a cent for her poems; she had not thought of such a thing as possible. The appearance of this last in such shape was worth more to her than its words represented in as many dollars.

Betsey kept the poem pinned on the wall under the looking-glass; if any one came in, she tried with delicate hints to call attention to it. It was two weeks after she received it that the downfall of her innocent pride came.

One afternoon Mrs. Caxton called. It was raining hard. Betsey could scarcely believe it was she when she went to the door and found her standing there.

"Why, Mis' Caxton!" said she. "Ain't you wet to your skin?"

"Yes, I guess I be, pretty near. I s'pose I hadn't ought to come 'way down here in such a soak; but I went into Sarah Rogers's a minute after dinner, and something she said made me so mad, I made up my mind I'd come down here and tell you about it if I got drowned." Mrs. Caxton was out of breath; rain-drops trickled from her hair over her face; she stood in the door and shut her umbrella with a vicious shake to scatter the water from it. "I don't know what you're goin' to do with this," said she; "it's drippin'."

"I'll take it out an' put it in the kitchen sink."

"Well, I'll take off my shawl here too, and you can hang it out in the kitchen. I spread this shawl out. I thought it would keep the rain off me some. I know one thing, I'm goin' to have a water-proof if I live."

When the two women were seated in the sitting-room, Mrs. Caxton was quiet for a moment. There was a hesitating look on her face, fresh with the moist wind, with strands of wet hair clinging to the temples.

"I don't know as I had ought to tell you," she said, doubtfully.

"Why hadn't you ought to?"

"Well, I don't care; I'm goin' to, anyhow. I think you'd ought to know, an' it ain't so bad for you as it is for me. It don't begin to be. I put considerable money into 'em. I think Mr. White was pretty high, myself."

Betsey looked scared. "What is it?" she asked, in a weak voice.

"Sarah Rogers says that the minister told her Ida that that poetry you wrote was jest as poor as it could be, an' it was in dreadful bad taste to have it printed an' sent round that way. What do you think of that?"

Betsey did not reply. She sat looking at Mrs. Caxton as a victim whom the first blow had not killed might look at her executioner. Her face was like a pale wedge of ice between her curls.

Mrs. Caxton went on. "Yes, she said that right to my face, word for word. An' there was something else. She said the minister said that you had never wrote anything that could be called poetry, an' it was a dreadful waste of time. I don't s'pose he thought 'twas comin' back to you. You know he goes with Ida Rogers, an' I s'pose he said it to her kind of confidential when she showed him the poetry. There! I gave Sarah Rogers one of them nice printed ones, an' she acted glad enough to have it. Bad taste! H'm! If anybody wants to say anything against that beautiful poetry, printed with that nice black border, they can. I don't care if it's the minister, or who it is. I don't care if he does write poetry himself, an' has had some printed in a magazine. Maybe his ain't quite so fine as he thinks 'tis. Maybe them magazine folks jest took his for lack of something better. I'd like to have you send that poetry there. Bad taste! I jest got right up. 'Sarah Rogers,' says I, 'I hope you won't never do anything yourself in any worse taste.' I trembled so I could hardly speak, and I made up my mind I'd come right straight over here."

Mrs. Caxton went on and on. Betsey sat listening, and saying nothing. She looked ghastly. Just before Mrs. Caxton went home she noticed it. "Why, Betsey Dole," she cried, "you look as white as a sheet. You ain't takin' it to heart as much as all that comes to, I hope. Goodness, I wish I hadn't told you!"

"I'd a good deal ruther you told me," replied Betsey, with a certain dignity. She looked at Mrs. Caxton. Her back was as stiff as if she were bound to a stake.

"Well, I thought you would," said Mrs. Caxton, uneasily; "and you're dreadful silly if you take it to heart, Betsey, that's all I've got to say. Goodness, I guess I don't, and it's full as hard on me as 'tis on you!"

Mrs. Caxton arose to go. Betsey brought her shawl and umbrella from the kitchen, and helped her off. Mrs. Caxton turned on the door-step and looked back at Betsey's white face. "Now don't go to thinkin' about it any more," said she. "I ain't goin' to. It ain't worth mindin'. Everybody knows what Sarah Rogers is. Good-by."

"Good-by, Mis' Caxton," said Betsey. She went back into the sitting-room. It was a cold rain, and the room was gloomy and chilly. She stood looking out of the window, watching the rain pelt on the hedge. The bird-cage hung at the other window. The bird watched her with his head on one side; then he begun to chirp.

Suddenly Betsey faced about and began talking. It was not as if she were talking to herself; it seemed as if she recognized some other presence in the room. "I'd like to know if it's fair," said she. "I'd like to know if you think it's fair. Had I ought to have been born with the wantin' to write poetry if I couldn't write it—had I? Had I ought to have been let to write all my life, an' not know before there wa'n't any use in it? Would it be fair if that canary-bird there, that ain't never done anything but sing, should turn out not to be singin'? Would it, I'd like to know? S'pose them sweet-peas shouldn't be smellin' the right way? I ain't been dealt with as fair as they have, I'd like to know if I have."

The bird trilled and trilled. It was as if the golden down on his throat bubbled. Betsey went across the room to a cupboard beside the chimney. On the shelves were neatly stacked newspapers and little white rolls of writing-paper. Betsey began clearing the shelves. She took out the newspapers first, got the scissors, and cut a poem neatly out of the corner of each. Then she took up the clipped poems and the white rolls in her apron, and carried them into the kitchen. She cleaned out the stove carefully, removing every trace of ashes; then she put in the papers, and set them on fire. She stood watching them as their edges curled and blackened, then leaped into flame. Her face twisted as if the fire were curling over it also. Other women might have burned their lovers' letters in agony of heart. Betsey had never had any lover, but she was burning all the love-letters that had passed between her and life. When the flames died out she got a blue china sugarbowl from the pantry and dipped the ashes into it with one of her thin silver teaspoons; then she put on the cover and set it away in the sitting-room cupboard.

The bird, who had been silent while she was out, began chirping again. Betsey went back to the pantry and got a lump of sugar, which she stuck between the cage wires. She looked at the clock on the kitchen shelf as she went by. It was after six. "I guess I don't want any supper to-night," she muttered.

She sat down by the window again. The bird pecked at his sugar. Betsey shivered and coughed. She had coughed more or less for years. People said she had the old-fashioned consumption. She sat at the window until it was quite dark; then she went to bed in her little bedroom out of the sitting-room. She shivered so she could not hold herself upright crossing the room. She coughed a great deal in the night.

Betsey was always an early riser. She was up at five the next morning. The sun shone, but it was very cold for the season. The leaves showed white in a north wind, and the flowers looked brighter than usual, though they were bent with the rain of the day before. Betsey went out in the garden to straighten her sweet-peas.

Coming back, a neighbor passing in the street eyed her curiously. "Why, Betsey, you sick?" said she.

"No; I'm kinder chilly, that's all," replied Betsey.

But the woman went home and reported that Betsey Dole looked dreadfully, and she didn't believe she'd ever see another summer.

It was now late August. Before October it was quite generally recognized that Betsey Dole's life was nearly over. She had no relatives, and hired nurses were rare in this little village. Mrs. Caxton came voluntarily and took care of her, only going home to prepare her husband's meals. Betsey's bed was moved into the sitting-room, and the neighbors came every day to see her, and brought little delicacies. Betsey had talked very little all her life; she talked less now, and there was a reticence about her which somewhat intimidated the other women. They would look pityingly and solemnly at her, and whisper in the entry when they went out.

Betsey never complained; but she kept asking if the minister had got home. He had been called away by his mother's illness, and returned only a week before Betsey died.

He came over at once to see her. Mrs. Caxton ushered him in one afternoon.

"Here's Mr. Lang come to see you, Betsey," said she, in the tone she would have used towards a little child. She placed the rocking-chair for the minister, and was about to seat herself, when Betsey spoke:

"Would you mind goin' out in the kitchen jest a few minutes, Mis' Caxton?" said she.

Mrs. Caxton arose, and went out with an embarrassed trot. Then there was silence. The minister was a young man—a country boy who had worked his way through a country college. He was gaunt and awkward, but sturdy in his loose clothes. He had a homely, impetuous face, with a good forehead.

He looked at Betsey's gentle, wasted face, sunken in the pillow, framed by its clusters of curls; finally he began to speak in the stilted fashion, yet with a certain force by reason of his unpolished honesty, about her spiritual welfare. Betsey listened quietly; now and then she assented. She had been a church member for years. It seemed now to the young man that this elderly maiden, drawing near the end of her simple, innocent life, had indeed her lamp, which no strong winds of temptation had ever met, well trimmed and burning.

When he paused, Betsey spoke. "Will you go to the cupboard side of the chimney and bring me the blue sugar-bowl on the top shelf?" said she, feebly.

The young man stared at her a minute; then he went to the cupboard, and brought the sugar-bowl to her. He held it, and Betsey took off the lid with her weak hand. "Do you see what's in there?" said she.

"It looks like ashes."

"It's—the ashes of all—the poetry I—ever wrote."

"Why, what made you burn it, Miss Dole?"

"I found out it wa'n't worth nothin'."

The minister looked at her in a bewildered way. He began to question if she were not wandering in her mind. He did not once suspect his own connection with the matter.

Betsey fastened her eager, sunken eyes upon his face. "What I want to know is—if you'll 'tend to—havin' this—buried with me."

The minister recoiled. He thought to himself that she certainly was wandering.

"No, I ain't out of my head," said Betsey. "I know what I'm sayin'. Maybe it's queer soundin', but it's a notion I've took. If you'll—'tend to it, I shall be—much obliged. I don't know anybody else I can ask."

"Well, I'll attend to it, if you wish me to, Miss Dole," said the minister, in a serious, perplexed manner. She replaced the lid on the sugar-bowl, and left it in his hands.

"Well, I shall be much obliged if you will 'tend to it; an' now there's something else," said she.

"What is it, Miss Dole?"

She hesitated a moment. "You write poetry, don't you?"

The minister colored. "Why, yes; a little sometimes."

"It's good poetry, ain't it? They printed some in a magazine."

The minister laughed confusedly. "Well, Miss Dole, I don't know how good poetry it may be, but they did print some in a magazine."

Betsey lay looking at him. "I never wrote none that was—good," she whispered, presently; "but I've been thinkin'—if you would jest write a few—lines about me—afterward—I've been thinkin' that—mebbe my—dyin' was goin' to make me—a good subject for—poetry, if I never wrote none. If you would jest write a few lines."

The minister stood holding the sugar-bowl; he was quite pale with bewilderment and sympathy. "I'll—do the best I can, Miss Dole," he stammered.

"I'll be much obliged," said Betsey, as if the sense of grateful obligation was immortal like herself. She smiled, and the sweetness of the smile was as evident through the drawn lines of her mouth as the old red in the leaves of a withered rose. The sun was setting; a red beam flashed softly over the top of the hedge and lay along the opposite wall; then the bird in his cage began to chirp. He chirped faster and faster until he trilled into a triumphant song.

Old Woman Magoun

The hamlet of Barry's Ford is situated in a sort of high valley among the mountains. Below it the hills lie in moveless curves like a petrified ocean; above it they rise in green-cresting waves which never break. It is *Barry's* Ford because at one time the Barry family was the most important in the place; and *Ford* because just at the beginning of the hamlet the little turbulent Barry River is fordable. There is, however, now a rude bridge across the river.

Old Woman Magoun was largely instrumental in bringing the bridge to pass. She haunted the miserable little grocery, wherein whiskey and hands of tobacco were the most salient features of the stock in trade, and she talked much. She would elbow herself into the midst of a knot of idlers and talk.

"That bridge ought to be built this very summer," said Old Woman Magoun. She spread her strong arms like wings, and sent the loafers, half laughing, half angry, flying in every direction. "If I were a *man*," said she, "I'd go out this very minute and lay the fust log. If I were a passel of lazy men layin' round, I'd start up for once in my life, I would." The men cowered visibly—all except Nelson Barry; he swore under his breath and strode over to the counter.

Old Woman Magoun looked after him majestically. "You can cuss all you want to, Nelson Barry," said she; "I ain't afraid of you. I don't expect you to lay ary log of the bridge, but I'm goin' to have it built this very summer." She did. The weakness of the masculine element in Barry's Ford was laid low before such strenuous feminine assertion.

Old Woman Magoun and some other women planned a treat —two sucking pigs, and pies, and sweet cake—for a reward after the bridge should be finished. They even viewed leniently the increased consumption of ardent spirits.

"It seems queer to me," Old Woman Magoun said to Sally Jinks, "that men can't do nothin' without havin' to drink and chew to keep their sperits up. Lord! I've worked all my life and never done nuther."

"Men is different," said Sally Jinks.

"Yes, they be," assented Old Woman Magoun, with open contempt.

The two women sat on a bench in front of Old Woman Magoun's house, and little Lily Barry, her granddaughter, sat holding her doll on a small mossy stone near by. From where they sat they could see the men at work on the new bridge. It was the last day of the work.

Lily clasped her doll—a poor old rag thing—close to her childish bosom, like a little mother, and her face, round which curled her long yellow hair, was fixed upon the men at work. Little Lily had never been allowed to run with the other children of Barry's Ford. Her grandmother had taught her everything she knew—which was not much, but tending at least to a certain measure of spiritual growth—for she, as it were, poured the goodness of her own soul into this little receptive vase of another. Lily was firmly grounded in her knowledge that it was wrong to lie or steal or disobey her grandmother. She had also learned that one should be very industrious. It was seldom that Lily sat idly holding her doll-baby, but this was a holiday because of the bridge. She looked only a child, although she was nearly fourteen; her mother had been married at sixteen. That is, Old Woman Magoun said that her daughter, Lily's mother, had married at sixteen; there had been rumors, but no one had dared openly gainsay the old woman. She said that her daughter had married Nelson Barry, and he had deserted her. She had lived in her mother's house, and Lily had been born there, and she had died when the baby was only a week old. Lily's father, Nelson Barry, was the fairly dangerous degenerate of a good old family. Nelson's father before him had been bad. He was now the last of the family, with the exception of a sister of feeble intellect, with whom he lived in the old Barry house. He was a middle-aged man, still handsome. The shiftless population of Barry's Ford looked up to him as to an evil deity. They wondered how Old Woman Magoun dared brave him as she did. But Old Woman Magoun had within her a mighty sense of reliance upon herself as being on the right track in the midst of a maze of evil, which gave her courage. Nelson Barry had manifested no interest whatever in his daughter. Lily seldom saw her father. She did not often go to the store which was his favorite haunt. Her grandmother took care that she should not do so.

However, that afternoon she departed from her usual custom and sent Lily to the store.

She came in from the kitchen, whither she had been to baste the roasting pig. "There's no use talkin'," said she, "I've got to have some more salt. I've jest used the very last I had to dredge over that pig. I've got to go to the store."

Sally Jinks looked at Lily. "Why don't you send her?" she asked.

Old Woman Magoun gazed irresolutely at the girl. She was herself very tired. It did not seem to her that she could drag herself up the dusty hill to the store. She glanced with covert resentment at Sally Jinks. She thought that she might offer to go. But Sally Jinks said again, "Why don't you let her go?" and looked with a languid eye at Lily holding her doll on the stone.

Lily was watching the men at work on the bridge, with her childish delight in a spectacle of any kind, when her grandmother addressed her.

"Guess I'll let you go down to the store an' git some salt, Lily," said she.

The girl turned uncomprehending eyes upon her grandmother at the sound of her voice. She had been filled with one of the innocent reveries of childhood. Lily had in her the making of an artist or a poet. Her prolonged childhood went to prove it, and also her retrospective eyes, as clear and blue as blue light itself, which seemed to see past all that she looked upon. She had not come of the old Barry family for nothing. The best of the strain was in her, along with the splendid stanchness in humble lines which she had acquired from her grandmother.

"Put on your hat," said Old Woman Magoun; "the sun is hot, and you might git a headache." She called the girl to her, and put back the shower of fair curls under the rubber band which confined the hat. She gave Lily some money, and watched her knot it into a corner of her little cotton handkerchief. "Be careful you don't lose it," said she, "and don't stop to talk to anybody, for I am in a hurry for that salt. Of course, if anybody speaks to you answer them polite, and then come right along."

Lily started, her pocket-handkerchief weighted with the small silver dangling from one hand, and her rag doll carried over her shoulder like a baby. The absurd travesty of a face peeped forth from Lily's yellow curls. Sally Jinks looked after her with a sniff.

"She ain't goin' to carry that rag doll to the store?" said she.

"She likes to," replied Old Woman Magoun, in a half-shamed yet defiantly extenuating voice.

"Some girls at her age is thinkin' about beaux instead of rag dolls," said Sally Jinks.

The grandmother bristled, "Lily ain't big nor old for her age," said she. "I ain't in any hurry to have her git married. She ain't none too strong."

"She's got a good color," said Sally Jinks. She was crocheting white cotton lace, making her thick fingers fly. She really knew how to do scarcely anything except to crochet that coarse lace; somehow her heavy brain or her fingers had mastered that.

"I know she's got a beautiful color," replied Old Woman Magoun, with an odd mixture of pride and anxiety, "but it comes an' goes."

"I've heard that was a bad sign," remarked Sally Jinks, loosening some thread from her spool.

"Yes, it is," said the grandmother. "She's nothin' but a baby, though she's quicker than most to learn."

Lily Barry went on her way to the store. She was clad in a scanty short frock of blue cotton; her hat was tipped back, forming an oval frame for her innocent face. She was very small, and walked like a child, with the clap-clap of little feet of babyhood. She might have been considered, from her looks, under ten.

Presently she heard footsteps behind her; she turned around a little timidly to see who was coming. When she saw a handsome, well-dressed man, she felt reassured. The man came alongside and glanced down carelessly at first, then his look deepened. He smiled, and Lily saw he was very handsome indeed, and that his smile was not only reassuring but wonderfully sweet and compelling.

"Well, little one," said the man, "where are you bound, you and your dolly?"

"I am going to the store to buy some salt for grandma," replied Lily, in her sweet treble. She looked up in the man's face, and he fairly started at the revelation of its innocent beauty. He regulated his pace by hers, and the two went on together. The man did not speak again at once. Lily kept glancing timidly up at him, and every time that she did so the man smiled and her confidence increased. Presently when the man's hand grasped her little childish one hanging by her side, she felt a complete trust in him. Then she smiled up at him. She felt glad that this nice man had come along, for just here the road was lonely.

After a while the man spoke. "What is your name, little one?" he asked, caressingly.

"Lily Barry."

The man started. "What is your father's name?"

"Nelson Barry," replied Lily.

The man whistled. "Is your mother dead?"

"Yes, sir."

"How old are you, my dear?"

"Fourteen," replied Lily.

The man looked at her with surprise. "As old as that?"

Lily suddenly shrank from the man. She could not have told why. She pulled her little hand from his, and he let it go with no remonstrance. She clasped both her arms around her rag doll, in order that her hand should not be free for him to grasp again.

She walked a little farther away from the man, and he looked amused.

"You still play with your doll?" he said, in a soft voice.

"Yes, sir," replied Lily. She quickened her pace and reached the store.

When Lily entered the store, Hiram Gates, the owner, was behind the counter. The only man besides in the store was Nelson Barry. He sat tipping his chair back against the wall; he was half asleep, and his handsome face was bristling with a beard of several days' growth and darkly flushed. He opened his eyes when Lily entered, the strange man following. He brought his chair down on all fours, and he looked at the man—not noticing Lily at all—with a look compounded of defiance and uneasiness.

"Hullo, Jim!" he said.

"Hullo, old man!" returned the stranger.

Lily went over to the counter and asked for the salt, in her pretty little voice. When she had paid for it and was crossing the store, Nelson Barry was on his feet.

"Well, how are you, Lily? It is Lily, isn't it?" he said.

"Yes, sir," replied Lily, faintly.

Her father bent down and, for the first time in her life, kissed her, and the whiskey odor of his breath came into her face.

Lily involuntarily started, and shrank away from him. Then she rubbed her mouth violently with her little cotton handkerchief, which she held gathered up with the rag doll.

"Damn it all! I believe she is afraid of me," said Nelson Barry, in a thick voice.

"Looks a little like it," said the other man, laughing.

"It's that damned old woman," said Nelson Barry. Then he smiled again at Lily. "I didn't know what a pretty little daughter I was blessed with," said he, and he softly stroked Lily's pink cheek under her hat.

Now Lily did not shrink from him. Hereditary instincts and nature itself were asserting themselves in the child's innocent, receptive breast.

Nelson Barry looked curiously at Lily. "How old are you, anyway, child?" he asked.

"I'll be fourteen in September," replied Lily.

"But you still play with your doll?" said Barry, laughing kindly down at her.

Lily hugged her doll more tightly, in spite of her father's kind voice. "Yes, sir," she replied.

Nelson glanced across at some glass jars filled with sticks of candy. "See here, little Lily, do you like candy?" said he.

"Yes, sir."

"Wait a minute."

Lily waited while her father went over to the counter. Soon he returned with a package of the candy.

"I don't see how you are going to carry so much," he said, smiling. "Suppose you throw away your doll?"

Lily gazed at her father and hugged the doll tightly, and there was all at once in the child's expression something mature. It became the reproach of a woman. Nelson's face sobered.

"Oh, it's all right, Lily," he said; "keep your doll. Here, I guess you can carry this candy under your arm."

Lily could not resist the candy. She obeyed Nelson's instructions for carrying it, and left the store laden. The two men also left, and walked in the opposite direction, talking busily.

When Lily reached home, her grandmother, who was watching for her, spied at once the package of candy.

"What's that?" she asked, sharply.

"My father gave it to me," answered Lily, in a faltering voice. Sally regarded her with something like alertness.

"Your father?"

"Yes, ma'am."

"Where did you see him?"

"In the store."

"He gave you this candy?"

"Yes, ma'am."

"What did he say?"

"He asked me how old I was, and—"

"And what?"

"I don't know," replied Lily; and it really seemed to her that she did not know, she was so frightened and bewildered by it all, and, more than anything else, by her grandmother's face as she questioned her.

Old Woman Magoun's face was that of one upon whom a long-anticipated blow had fallen. Sally Jinks gazed at her with a sort of stupid alarm.

Old Woman Magoun continued to gaze at her grandchild with that look of terrible solicitude, as if she saw the girl in the clutch of a tiger. "You can't remember what else he said?" she asked, fiercely, and the child began to whimper softly.

"No, ma'am," she sobbed. "I—don't know, and—"

"And what? Answer me."

"There was another man there. A real handsome man."

"Did he speak to you?" asked Old Woman Magoun.

"Yes, ma'am; he walked along with me a piece," confessed Lily, with a sob of terror and bewilderment.

"What did *he* say to you?" asked Old Woman Magoun, with a sort of despair.

Lily told, in her little, faltering, frightened voice, all of the conversation which she could recall. It sounded harmless enough, but the look of the realization of a long-expected blow never left her grandmother's face.

The sun was getting low, and the bridge was nearing completion. Soon the workmen would be crowding into the cabin for their promised supper. There became visible in the distance, far up the road, the heavily plodding figure of another woman who

had agreed to come and help. Old Woman Magoun turned
again to Lily.

"You go right up-stairs to your own chamber now," said she.

"Good land! ain't you goin' to let that poor child stay up and
see the fun?" said Sally Jinks.

"You jest mind your own business," said Old Woman Magoun, forcibly, and Sally Jinks shrank. "You go right up there
now, Lily," said the grandmother, in a softer tone, "and grandma will bring you up a nice plate of supper."

"When be you goin' to let that girl grow up?" asked Sally
Jinks, when Lily had disappeared.

"She'll grow up in the Lord's good time," replied Old Woman
Magoun, and there was in her voice something both sad and
threatening. Sally Jinks again shrank a little.

Soon the workmen came flocking noisily into the house. Old
Woman Magoun and her two helpers served the bountiful supper. Most of the men had drunk as much as, and more than,
was good for them, and Old Woman Magoun had stipulated
that there was to be no drinking of anything except coffee during
supper.

"I'll git you as good a meal as I know how," she said, "but if
I see ary one of you drinkin' a drop, I'll run you all out. If you
want anything to drink, you can go up to the store afterward.
That's the place for you to go to, if you've got to make hogs
of yourselves. I ain't goin' to have no hogs in my house."

Old Woman Magoun was implicitly obeyed. She had a curious
authority over most people when she chose to exercise it. When
the supper was in full swing, she quietly stole up-stairs and carried some food to Lily. She found the girl, with the rag doll in
her arms, crouching by the window in her little rocking-chair—
a relic of her infancy, which she still used.

"What a noise they are makin', grandma!" she said, in a
terrified whisper, as her grandmother placed the plate before
her on a chair.

"They've 'most all of 'em been drinkin'. They air a passel of
hogs," replied the old woman.

"Is the man that was with—with my father down there?"
asked Lily, in a timid fashion. Then she fairly cowered before
the look in her grandmother's eyes.

"No, he ain't; and what's more, he never will be down there
if I can help it," said Old Woman Magoun, in a fierce whisper.
"I know who he is. They can't cheat me. He's one of them

Willises—that family the Barrys married into. They're worse than the Barrys, ef they *have* got money. Eat your supper, and put him out of your mind, child."

It was after Lily was asleep, when Old Woman Magoun was alone, clearing away her supper dishes, that Lily's father came. The door was closed, and he knocked, and the old woman knew at once who was there. The sound of that knock meant as much to her as the whir of a bomb to the defender of a fortress. She opened the door, and Nelson Barry stood there.

"Good-evening, Mrs. Magoun," he said.

Old Woman Magoun stood before him, filling up the doorway with her firm bulk.

"Good-evening, Mrs. Magoun," said Nelson Barry again.

"I ain't got no time to waste," replied the old woman, harshly. "I've got my supper dishes to clean up after them men."

She stood there and looked at him as she might have looked at a rebellious animal which she was trying to tame. The man laughed.

"It's no use," said he. "You know me of old. No human being can turn me from my way when I am once started in it. You may as well let me come in."

Old Woman Magoun entered the house, and Barry followed her.

Barry began without any preface. "Where is the child?" asked he.

"Up-stairs. She has gone to bed."

"She goes to bed early."

"Children ought to," returned the old woman, polishing a plate.

Barry laughed. "You are keeping her a child a long while," he remarked, in a soft voice which had a sting in it.

"She *is* a child," returned the old woman, defiantly.

"Her mother was only three years older when Lily was born."

The old woman made a sudden motion toward the man which seemed fairly menacing. Then she turned again to her dish-washing.

"I want her," said Barry.

"You can't have her," replied the old woman, in a still stern voice.

"I don't see how you can help yourself. You have always acknowledged that she was my child."

The old woman continued her task, but her strong back heaved. Barry regarded her with an entirely pitiless expression.

"I am going to have the girl, that is the long and short of it," he said, "and it is for her best good, too. You are a fool, or you would see it."

"Her best good?" muttered the old woman.

"Yes, her best good. What are you going to do with her, anyway? The girl is a beauty, and almost a woman grown, although you try to make out that she is a baby. You can't live forever."

"The Lord will take care of her," replied the old woman, and again she turned and faced him, and her expression was that of a prophetess.

"Very well, let Him," said Barry, easily. "All the same I'm going to have her, and I tell you it is for her best good. Jim Willis saw her this afternoon, and—"

Old Woman Magoun looked at him. "Jim Willis!" she fairly shrieked.

"Well, what of it?"

"One of them Willises!" repeated the old woman, and this time her voice was thick. It seemed almost as if she were stricken with paralysis. She did not enunciate clearly.

The man shrank a little. "Now what is the need of your making such a fuss?" he said. "I will take her, and Isabel will look out for her."

"Your half-witted sister?" said Old Woman Magoun.

"Yes, my half-witted sister. She knows more than you think."

"More wickedness."

"Perhaps. Well, a knowledge of evil is a useful thing. How are you going to avoid evil if you don't know what it is like? My sister and I will take care of my daughter."

The old woman continued to look at the man, but his eyes never fell. Suddenly her gaze grew inconceivably keen. It was as if she saw through all externals.

"I know what it is!" she cried. "You have been playing cards and you lost, and this is the way you will pay him."

Then the man's face reddened, and he swore under his breath.

"Oh, my God!" said the old woman; and she really spoke with her eyes aloft as if addressing something outside of them both. Then she turned again to her dish-washing.

The man cast a dogged look at her back. "Well, there is no use talking. I have made up my mind," said he, "and you know me and what that means. I am going to have the girl."

"When?" said the old woman, without turning around.

"Well, I am willing to give you a week. Put her clothes in good order before she comes."

The old woman made no reply. She continued washing dishes. She even handled them so carefully that they did not rattle.

"You understand," said Barry. "Have her ready a week from to-day."

"Yes," said Old Woman Magoun, "I understand."

Nelson Barry, going up the mountain road, reflected that Old Woman Magoun had a strong character, that she understood much better than her sex in general the futility of withstanding the inevitable.

"Well," he said to Jim Willis when he reached home, "the old woman did not make such a fuss as I expected."

"Are you going to have the girl?"

"Yes; a week from to-day. Look here, Jim; you've got to stick to your promise."

"All right," said Willis. "Go you one better."

The two were playing at cards in the old parlor, once magnificent, now squalid, of the Barry house. Isabel, the half-witted sister, entered, bringing some glasses on a tray. She had learned with her feeble intellect some tricks, like a dog. One of them was the mixing of sundry drinks. She set the tray on a little stand near the two men, and watched them with her silly simper.

"Clear out now and go to bed," her brother said to her, and she obeyed.

Early the next morning Old Woman Magoun went up to Lily's little sleeping-chamber, and watched her a second as she lay asleep, with her yellow locks spread over the pillow. Then she spoke. "Lily," said she—"Lily, wake up. I am going to Greenham across the new bridge, and you can go with me."

Lily immediately sat up in bed and smiled at her grandmother. Her eyes were still misty, but the light of awakening was in them.

"Get right up," said the old woman. "You can wear your new dress if you want to."

Lily gurgled with pleasure like a baby. "And my new hat?" asked she.

"I don't care."

Old Woman Magoun and Lily started for Greenham before Barry Ford, which kept late hours, was fairly awake. It was three miles to Greenham. The old woman said that, since the horse was a little lame, they would walk. It was a beautiful morning, with a diamond radiance of dew over everything. Her grandmother had curled Lily's hair more punctiliously than usual. The little face peeped like a rose out of two rows of golden spirals. Lily wore her new muslin dress with a pink sash, and her best hat of a fine white straw trimmed with a wreath of rosebuds; also the neatest black open-work stockings and pretty shoes. She even had white cotton gloves. When they set out, the old, heavily stepping woman, in her black gown and cape and bonnet, looked down at the little pink fluttering figure. Her face was full of the tenderest love and admiration, and yet there was something terrible about it. They crossed the new bridge—a primitive structure built of logs in a slovenly fashion. Old Woman Magoun pointed to a gap.

"Jest see that," said she. "That's the way men work."

"Men ain't very nice, be they?" said Lily, in her sweet little voice.

"No, they ain't, take them all together," replied her grandmother.

"That man that walked to the store with me was nicer than some, I guess," Lily said, in a wishful fashion. Her grandmother reached down and took the child's hand in its small cotton glove. "You hurt me, holding my hand so tight," Lily said presently, in a deprecatory little voice.

The old woman loosened her grasp. "Grandma didn't know how tight she was holding your hand," said she. "She wouldn't hurt you for nothin', except it was to save your life, or somethin' like that." She spoke with an undertone of tremendous meaning which the girl was too childish to grasp. They walked along the country road. Just before they reached Greenham they passed a stone wall overgrown with blackberry-vines, and, an unusual thing in that vicinity, a lusty spread of deadly nightshade full of berries.

"Those berries look good to eat, grandma," Lily said.

At that instant the old woman's face became something terrible to see. "You can't have any now," she said, and hurried Lily along.

"They look real nice," said Lily.

When they reached Greenham, Old Woman Magoun took her way straight to the most pretentious house there, the residence of the lawyer, whose name was Mason. Old Woman Magoun bade Lily wait in the yard for a few moments, and Lily ventured to seat herself on a bench beneath an oak-tree; then she watched with some wonder her grandmother enter the lawyer's office door at the right of the house. Presently the lawyer's wife came out and spoke to Lily under the tree. She had in her hand a little tray containing a plate of cake, a glass of milk, and an early apple. She spoke very kindly to Lily; she even kissed her, and offered her the tray of refreshments, which Lily accepted gratefully. She sat eating, with Mrs. Mason watching her, when Old Woman Magoun came out of the lawyer's office with a ghastly face.

"What are you eatin'?" she asked Lily, sharply. "Is that a sour apple?"

"I thought she might be hungry," said the lawyer's wife, with loving, melancholy eyes upon the girl.

Lily had almost finished the apple. "It's real sour, but I like it; it's real nice, grandma," she said.

"You ain't been drinkin' milk with a sour apple?"

"It was real nice milk, grandma."

"You ought never to have drunk milk and eat a sour apple," said her grandmother. "Your stomach was all out of order this mornin', an' sour apples and milk is always apt to hurt anybody."

"I don't know but they are," Mrs. Mason said, apologetically, as she stood on the green lawn with her lavender muslin sweeping around her. "I am real sorry, Mrs. Magoun. I ought to have thought. Let me get some soda for her."

"Soda never agrees with her," replied the old woman, in a harsh voice. "Come," she said to Lily, "it's time we were goin' home."

After Lily and her grandmother had disappeared down the road, Lawyer Mason came out of his office and joined his wife, who had seated herself on the bench beneath the tree. She was idle, and her face wore the expression of those who review joys forever past. She had lost a little girl, her only child, years ago, and her husband always knew when she was thinking about her. Lawyer Mason looked older than his wife; he had a dry, shrewd, slightly one-sided face.

"What do you think, Maria?" he said. "That old woman came to me with the most pressing entreaty to adopt that little girl."

"She is a beautiful little girl," said Mrs. Mason, in a slightly husky voice.

"Yes, she is a pretty child," assented the lawyer, looking pityingly at his wife; "but it is out of the question, my dear. Adopting a child is a serious measure, and in this case a child who comes from Barry's Ford."

"But the grandmother seems a very good woman," said Mrs. Mason.

"I rather think she is. I never heard a word against her. But the father! No, Maria, we cannot take a child with Barry blood in her veins. The stock has run out; it is vitiated physically and morally. It won't do, my dear."

"Her grandmother had her dressed up as pretty as a little girl could be," said Mrs. Mason, and this time the tears welled into her faithful, wistful eyes.

"Well, we can't help that," said the lawyer, as he went back to his office.

Old Woman Magoun and Lily returned, going slowly along the road to Barry's Ford. When they came to the stone wall where the blackberry-vines and the deadly nightshade grew, Lily said she was tired, and asked if she could not sit down for a few minutes. The strange look on her grandmother's face had deepened. Now and then Lily glanced at her and had a feeling as if she were looking at a stranger.

"Yes, you can set down if you want to," said Old Woman Magoun, deeply and harshly.

Lily started and looked at her, as if to make sure that it was her grandmother who spoke. Then she sat down on a stone which was comparatively free of the vines.

"Ain't you goin' to set down, grandma?" Lily asked, timidly.

"No; I don't want to get into that mess," replied her grandmother. "I ain't tired. I'll stand here."

Lily sat still; her delicate little face was flushed with heat. She extended her tiny feet in her best shoes and gazed at them. "My shoes are all over dust," said she.

"It will brush off," said her grandmother, still in that strange voice.

Lily looked around. An elm-tree in the field behind her cast a spray of branches over her head; a little cool puff of wind came on her face. She gazed at the low mountains on the horizon, in the midst of which she lived, and she sighed, for no reason that she knew. She began idly picking at the blackberry-vines; there were no berries on them; then she put her little fingers on the berries of the deadly nightshade. "These look like nice berries," she said.

Old Woman Magoun, standing stiff and straight in the road, said nothing.

"They look good to eat," said Lily.

Old Woman Magoun still said nothing, but she looked up into the ineffable blue of the sky, over which spread at intervals great white clouds shaped like wings.

Lily picked some of the deadly nightshade berries and ate them. "Why, they are real sweet," said she. "They are nice." She picked some more and ate them.

Presently her grandmother spoke. "Come," she said, "it is time we were going. I guess you have set long enough."

Lily was still eating the berries when she slipped down from the wall and followed her grandmother obediently up the road.

Before they reached home, Lily complained of being very thirsty. She stopped and made a little cup of a leaf and drank long at a mountain brook. "I am dreadful dry, but it hurts me to swallow," she said to her grandmother when she stopped drinking and joined the old woman waiting for her in the road. Her grandmother's face seemed strangely dim to her. She took hold of Lily's hand as they went on. "My stomach burns," said Lily, presently. "I want some more water."

"There is another brook a little farther on," said Old Woman Magoun, in a dull voice.

When they reached that brook, Lily stopped and drank again, but she whimpered a little over her difficulty in swallowing. "My stomach burns, too," she said, walking on, "and my throat is so dry, grandma." Old Woman Magoun held Lily's hand more tightly. "You hurt me holding my hand so tight, grandma," said Lily, looking up at her grandmother, whose face she seemed to see through a mist, and the old woman loosened her grasp.

When at last they reached home, Lily was very ill. Old Woman Magoun put her on her own bed in the little bedroom out of the kitchen. Lily lay there and moaned, and Sally Jinks came in.

"Why, what ails her?" she asked. "She looks feverish."

Lily unexpectedly answered for herself. "I ate some sour apples and drank some milk," she moaned.

"Sour apples and milk are dreadful apt to hurt anybody," said Sally Jinks. She told several people on her way home that Old Woman Magoun was dreadful careless to let Lily eat such things.

Meanwhile Lily grew worse. She suffered cruelly from the burning in her stomach, the vertigo, and the deadly nausea. "I am so sick, I am so sick, grandma," she kept moaning. She could no longer see her grandmother as she bent over her, but she could hear her talk.

Old Woman Magoun talked as Lily had never heard her talk before, as nobody had ever heard her talk before. She spoke from the depths of her soul; her voice was as tender as the coo of a dove, and it was grand and exalted. "You'll feel better very soon, little Lily," said she.

"I am so sick, grandma."

"You will feel better very soon, and then—"

"I am sick."

"You shall go to a beautiful place."

Lily moaned.

"You shall go to a beautiful place," the old woman went on.

"Where?" asked Lily, groping feebly with her cold little hands. Then she moaned again.

"A beautiful place, where the flowers grow tall."

"What color? Oh, grandma, I am so sick."

"A blue color," replied the old woman. Blue was Lily's favorite color. "A beautiful blue color, and as tall as your knees, and the flowers always stay there, and they never fade."

"Not if you pick them, grandma? Oh!"

"No, not if you pick them; they never fade, and they are so sweet you can smell them a mile off; and there are birds that sing, and all the roads have gold stones in them, and the stone walls are made of gold."

"Like the ring grandpa gave you? I am so sick, grandma."

"Yes, gold like that. And all the houses are built of silver and gold, and the people all have wings, so when they get tired walking they can fly, and—"

"I am so sick, grandma."

"And all the dolls are alive," said Old Woman Magoun. "Dolls like yours can run, and talk, and love you back again."

Lily had her poor old rag doll in bed with her, clasped close to her agonized little heart. She tried very hard with her eyes, whose pupils were so dilated that they looked black, to see her grandmother's face when she said that, but she could not. "It is dark," she moaned, feebly.

"There where you are going it is always light," said the grandmother, "and the commonest things shine like that breastpin Mrs. Lawyer Mason had on to-day."

Lily moaned pitifully, and said something incoherent. Delirium was commencing. Presently she sat straight up in bed and raved; but even then her grandmother's wonderful compelling voice had an influence over her.

"You will come to a gate with all the colors of the rainbow," said her grandmother; "and it will open, and you will go right in and walk up the gold street, and cross the field where the blue flowers come up to your knees, until you find your mother, and she will take you home where you are going to live. She has a little white room all ready for you, white curtains at the windows, and a little white looking-glass, and when you look in it you will see—"

"What will I see? I am so sick, grandma."

"You will see a face like yours, only it's an angel's; and there will be a little white bed, and you can lay down an' rest."

"Won't I be sick, grandma?" asked Lily. Then she moaned and babbled wildly, although she seemed to understand through it all what her grandmother said.

"No, you will never be sick any more. Talkin' about sickness won't mean anything to you."

It continued. Lily talked on wildly, and her grandmother's great voice of soothing never ceased, until the child fell into a deep sleep, or what resembled sleep; but she lay stiffly in that sleep, and a candle flashed before her eyes made no impression on them.

Then it was that Nelson Barry came. Jim Willis waited outside the door. When Nelson entered he found Old Woman Magoun on her knees beside the bed, weeping with dry eyes and a might of agony which fairly shook Nelson Barry, the degenerate of a fine old race.

"Is she sick?" he asked, in a hushed voice.

Old Woman Magoun gave another terrible sob, which sounded like the gasp of one dying.

"Sally Jinks said that Lily was sick from eating milk and sour apples," said Barry, in a tremulous voice. "I remember that her mother was very sick once from eating them."

Lily lay still, and her grandmother on her knees shook with her terrible sobs.

Suddenly Nelson Barry started. "I guess I had better go to Greenham for a doctor if she's as bad as that," he said. He went close to the bed and looked at the sick child. He gave a great start. Then he felt of her hands and reached down under the bedclothes for her little feet. "Her hands and feet are like ice," he cried out. "Good God! why didn't you send for some one—for me—before? Why, she's dying; she's almost gone!"

Barry rushed out and spoke to Jim Willis, who turned pale and came in and stood by the bedside.

"She's almost gone," he said, in a hushed whisper.

"There's no use going for the doctor; she'd be dead before he got here," said Nelson, and he stood regarding the passing child with a strange, sad face—unutterably sad, because of his incapability of the truest sadness.

"Poor little thing, she's past suffering, anyhow," said the other man, and his own face also was sad with a puzzled, mystified sadness.

Lily died that night. There was quite a commotion in Barry's Ford until after the funeral, it was all so sudden, and then everything went on as usual. Old Woman Magoun continued to live as she had done before. She supported herself by the produce of her tiny farm; she was very industrious, but people said that she was a trifle touched, since every time she went over the log bridge with her eggs or her garden vegetables to sell in Greenham, she carried with her, as one might have carried an infant, Lily's old rag doll.

Alice Brown

Alice Brown (1857-1948) was born and brought up on her family's farm in Hampton Falls, New Hampshire, a few miles from Exeter. Her early schooling took place in the district school that she so lyrically describes in "Number Five." Unlike Mary E. Wilkins Freeman, she dwelt mainly upon the attractive, peaceful, and joyous aspects of rural life. A true Wordsworthian, she usually presents her characters as living in harmony with a lovely environment and deriving spiritual strength from it. Her best stories are collected in Meadow-Grass *(1895), from which both the selections that follow are taken, and in* Tiverton Tales *(1899).*

Number Five

We who are Tiverton born, though false ambition may have ridden us to market, or the world's voice incited us to kindred clamoring, have a way of shutting our eyes, now and then, to present changes, and seeing things as they were once, as they are still, in a certain sleepy yet altogether individual corner of country life. And especially do we delight in one bit of fine mental tracery, etched carelessly, yet for all time, so far as our own short span is concerned, by the unerring stylus of youth: the outline of a little red schoolhouse, distinguished from the other similar structures within Tiverton bounds by "District No. V.," painted on a shingle, in primitive black letters, and nailed

aloft over the door. Up to the very hollow which made its playground and weedy garden, the road was elm-bordered and lined
with fair meadows, skirted in the background by shadowy pines,
so soft they did not even wave; they only seemed to breathe.
The treasures of the road! On either side, the way was plumed
and paved with beauties so rare that now, disheartened dwellers
in city streets, we covetously con over in memory that roaming
walk to school and home again. We know it now for what it was,
a daily progress of delight. We see again the old watering-
trough, decayed into the mellow loveliness of gray lichen and
greenest moss. Here beside the ditch whence the water flowed,
grew the pale forget-me-not and sticky, star-blossomed cleavers.
A step farther, beyond the nook where the spring bubbled first,
were the riches of the common roadway; and over the gray,
lichen-bearded fence, the growth of stubbly upland pasture.
Everywhere, in road and pasture too, thronged milkweed, odor-
ous haunt of the bee and those frailest butterflies of the year,
born of one family with drifting blossoms; and straightly tall,
the solitary mullein, dust-covered but crowned with a gold softer
and more to be desired than the pride of kings. Perhaps the
carriage folk from the outer world, who sometimes penetrate
Tiverton's leafy quiet, may wonder at the queer little enclosures
of sticks and pebbles on many a bare, tree-shaded slope along
the road. "Left there from some game!" they say to one another,
and drive on, satisfied. But these are no mere discarded playthings, dear ignorant travellers! They are tokens of the mimic
earnest with which child-life is ever seeking to sober itself, and
rushing unsummoned into the workaday fields of an aimlessly
frantic world. They are houses, and the stone boundaries are
walls. This tree stump is an armchair, this board a velvet sofa.
Not more truly is "this thorn-bush, my thorn-bush; and this dog,
my dog."

Across the road, at easy running distance from the schoolhouse
at noontime or recess, crawled the little river, with its inevitable
"hole," which each mother's son was warned to avoid in swimming, lest he be seized with cramp there where the pool was
bottomless. What eerie wonders lurked within the mirror of
those shallow brown waters! Long black hairs cleaved and clung
in their limpid flowing. To this day, I know not whether they
were horse-hairs, far from home, or swaying willow roots; the
boys said they were "truly" hairs of the kind destined to become
snakes in their last estate; and the girls, listening, shivered with

all Mother Eve's premonitory thrill along the backbone. Wish-bugs, too, were here, skimming and darting. The peculiarity of a wish-bug is that he will bestow upon you your heart's desire, if only you hold him in the hand and wish. But the impossible premise defeats the conclusion. You never do hold him long enough, simply because you can't catch him in the first place. Yet the fascinating possibility is like a taste for drink, or the glamour of cards. Does the committee-man drive past to Sudleigh market, suggesting the prospect of a leisurely return that afternoon, and consequent dropping in to hear the geography class? Then do the laziest and most optimistic boys betake them hastily from their dinner-pails to the river, and spend their precious nooning in quest of the potent bug, through whose spell the unwelcome visit may be averted. The time so squandered in riotous gaming might have fixed the afternoon's "North Poles and Equators" triumphantly in mind, to the everlasting defiance of all alien questioning; but no! for human delight lies ever in the unattainable. The committee-man comes like Nemesis, *æquo pede,* the lesson is unlearned, and the stern-fibred little teacher orders out the rack known as staying after school. But what durance beyond hours in the indescribably desolate schoolroom ever taught mortal boy to shun the delusive insect created for his special undoing? So long as the heart has woes of its own breeding, so long also will it dodge the discipline of labor, and grasp at the flicker of an easy success.

On either side the little bridge (over which horses pounded with an ominous thunder and a rain of dust on the head of him who lingered beneath the sleepers, in a fearsome joy), the meadows were pranked with purple iris and whispering rushes, mingling each its sweetness with the good, rank smell of mud below. Here were the treasures of the water-course, close hidden, or blowing in the light of day. The pale, golden-hearted arrow-head neighbored the homespun pickerel-weed, and—oh, mysterious glory from an oozy bed!—luscious, sun-golden cow-lilies rose sturdily triumphant, dripping with color, glowing in sheen. The button-bush hung out her balls, and white alder painted the air with faint perfume; willow-herb built her bowery arches, and the flags were ever glancing like swords of roistering knights. These flags, be it known to such as have grown up in grievous ignorance of the lore inseparable from "deestrick school," hold the most practical significance in the mind of boy and girl; for they bring forth (I know we thought for our delight alone!)

a delicacy known as flag-buds, everlastingly dear to the childish palate. These were devoured by the wholesale in their season, and little mouths grew oozy-green as those of happy beasties in June, from much champing and chewing. Did we lose our appetite for the delectable dinner-pail through such literal going to pasture? I think not. Tastes were elastic, in those days; and Nature, so bullied, durst seldom revolt.

On one side, the nearest neighbor to the school lived at least a mile away; but on the other, the first house of all owned treasures manifold for the little squad who, though the day were wet or dry, fair or frowning, trotted thither at noon. Here were trees under which lay, in happy season, over-ripe Bartlett pears; here, too, was one mulberry-tree, whereof the suggestion was strange and wonderful, and the fruit less appealing to taste than to a mystical fancy. But outside the bank wall grew the balm-of-Gileads, in a stately, benevolent row,—trees of healing, of fragrance and romantic charm. No child ever sought the old home to beg pears and mulberries, or to fill the school-house pail at its dark-bosomed well, without bearing away a few of the leaves in a covetous grasp. Sweet treasure-trove these, to be pressed to fresh young faces, and held and patted in hot little palms, till they grew flabby but evermore fragrant, still diffusing over the dusty schoolroom that warm odor, whispering to those who read no corner but their own New England, of the myrrh and balsams of the East.

We knew everything in those days, we aimless knights-errant with dinner-pail and slate; the dry, frosty hollow where gentians bloom when the pride of the field is over, the woody slopes of the hepatica's awakening, under coverlet of withered leaves, and the sunny banks where violets love to live with their good gossip, the trembling anemone. At noon, we roved abroad into solitudes so deep that even our unsuspecting hearts sometimes quaked with fear of dark and lonesomeness; and then we came trooping back at the sound of the bell, untamed, happy little savages, ready to settle, with a long breath, to the afternoon's drowsy routine. Arrant nonsense that! the boundary of British America and the conjugation of the verb *to be!* Who that might loll away the hours upon a bank in silken ease, needed aught even of computation or the tongues? He alone had inherited the earth.

All the little figures flitting through those tranquil early dramas are so sharply drawn, so brightly colored still! I meet Melissa Crane sometimes nowadays, a prosperous matron with space enough on her broad back for the very largest plaid ever woven; but her present identity is hazy and unreal. I see instead, with a sudden throb of memory, the little Melissa, who, one recess, accepted a sugared doughnut from me, and said, with a quaint imitation of old folks' manner,—

"I think your mother will be a real good cook, if she lives!"

I hear of Susie Marden, who went out West, married, and grew up with the country in great magnificence; but to me she is and ever will be the little girl who made seventy pies, one Thanksgiving time, thereby earning the somewhat stinted admiration of those among us who could not cook. Many a great deed, tacitly promised in that springtime, never came to pass; many a brilliant career ingloriously ended. There was Sam Marshall. He could do sums to the admiration of class and teacher, and, Cuvier-like, evolve an entire flock from Colburn's two geese and a half. His memory was prodigious. He could name the Presidents, bound the States and Territories, and rattle off the list of prepositions so fast that you could almost see the spark-shower from his rushing wheels of thought. It was an understood thing among us, when Sam was in his teens, that he should at least enter the Senate; perhaps he would even be President, and scatter offices, like halfpence, among his scampering townsmen. But to-day he patiently does his haying—by hand! and "goes sleddin'" in the winter. The Senate is as far from him as the Polar Star, and I question whether he could even bear the crucial test of two geese and a half. Yet I still look upon him with a thrill of awe, as the man selected by the popular vote to represent us in fame's Valhalla, and mysteriously defeated by some unexpected move of the "unseen hand at the game."

There were a couple of boys such good comrades as never to be happy save when together. They cared only for the games made for two; all their goods were tacitly held in common, and a tradition still lives that David, when a new teacher asked his exact age, claimed his comrade's birthday, and then wondered why everybody laughed. They had a way of wandering off together to the woods, on Saturday mornings, when the routine of chores could be hurried through, and always they bore with them a store of eggs, apples, or sweet corn, to be cooked in happy seclusion. All this raw material was stolen from the respective haylofts and gardens at home, though, as the fathers owned, with an appreciative grin, the boys might have taken it openly for the asking. That, however, would so have alloyed the charm of gypsying that it was not to be thought of for a moment; and they crept about on their foraging expeditions with all the caution of a hostile tribe. Blessed fathers and mothers to wink at the escapade, and happy boys, wise chiefly in their longing to be free! We had a theory that Jonathan and David would go into business together. Perhaps we thought of them in the same country store, their chairs tilted on either side of the air-tight stove, telling stories, in the intervals of custom, as they apparently did in their earlier estate. For, shy as they were in general company, they chatted together with an intense earnestness all day long; and it was one of the stock questions in our neighborhood, when the social light burned low,—

"What under the sun do you s'pose Dave and Jont find to talk about?"

Alas! again the world had builded foolishly; for with early manhood, they fell in love with the same round-cheeked schoolteacher. Jonathan married her, after what wrench of feeling I know not; and the other fled to the town, whence he never returned save for the briefest visit at Thanksgiving or Christmas time. The stay-at-home lad is a warm farmer, and the little school-teacher a mother whose unlined face shows the record of a placid life; but David cannot know even this, save by hearsay, for he never sees them. He is a moneyed man, and not a year ago, gave the town a new library. But is he happy? Or does the old wound still show a ragged edge? For that may be, they tell us, even "when you come to forty year."

Then, clad in brighter vestments of memory, there was the lad who earned unto himself much renown, even among his disapproving relatives, by running away from home, in quest of gold and glory. True, he was brought back at the end of three days, footsore and muddy, and with noble appetite for the griddle-cakes his mother cooked him in lieu of the traditional veal,—but all undaunted. He never tried it again, yet people say he has thrown away all his chances of a thrifty living by perpetual wandering in the woods with gun and fishing-rod, and that he is cursed with a deplorable indifference to the state of his fences and potato-patch. No one could call him an admirable citizen, but I am not sure that he has chosen the worser part; for who is so jovial and sympathetic on a winter evening, when the apples are passed, and even the shining cat purrs content before the blaze, or in the wood solitudes, familiar to him as his own house door?

"Pa'tridges' nests?" he said, one spring, with a cock of his eye calculated to show at once a humorous recognition of his genius and his delinquencies. "Sartain! I wish I was as sure where I keep my scythe sned!"

He has learned all the lore of the woods, the ways of "wild critters," and the most efficacious means both to woo and kill them. Prim spinsters eye him acridly, as a man given over to "shif'less" ways, and wives set him up, like a lurid guidepost, before husbands prone to lapse from domestic thrift; but the dogs smile at him, and children, for whom he is ever ready to make kite or dory, though all his hay should mildew, or to string thimbleberries on a grass spear while supper cools within, tumble merrily at his heels. Such as he should never assume domestic relations, to be fettered with requirements of time and place. Let them rather claim maintenance from a grateful public, and live, like troubadours of old, ministrant to the general joy.

Not all the memories of that early day are quite unspotted by remorse. Although we wore the mask of jocund faces and straightforward glance, we little people repeatedly proclaimed ourselves the victims of Adam's fall. Even then we needed to pray for deliverance from those passions which have since pursued us. There was the little bound girl who lived with a "selec'man's" wife, a woman with children of her own, but a hard taskmistress to the stranger within her gates. Poor little Polly! her clothes, made over from those of her mistress, were of dark, rough flannel, often in uncouth plaids and appalling stripes. Her petticoats were dyed of a sickly hue known as cudbar, and she wore heavy woollen stockings of the same shade. Polly got up early, to milk and drive the cows; she set the table, washed milkpans, and ran hither and thither on her sturdy cudbar legs, always willing, sometimes singing, and often with a mute, questioning look on her little freckled face, as if she had already begun to wonder why it has pleased God to set so many boundary lines over which the feeble may not pass. The selec'man's son— a heavy-faced, greedy boy—was a bully, and Polly became his butt; she did his tasks, hectored by him in private, and with a child's strange reticence, she never told even us how unbearable he made her life. We could see it, however; for not much remains hidden in that communistic atmosphere of the country neighborhood. But sometimes Polly revolted; her temper blazed up, a harmless flash in the pan, and then, it was said, Mis' Jeremiah took her to the shed-chamber and trounced her soundly. I myself have seen her sitting at the little low window, when I trotted by, in the pride of young life, to "borry some emptin's," or the recipe for a new cake. Often she waved a timid hand to me; and I am glad to remember a certain sunny morning, illuminated now because I tossed her up a bright hollyhock in return. It was little to give out of a full and happy day; but Polly had nothing. Once she came near great good fortune—and missed it! For a lady, who boarded a few weeks in the neighborhood, took a fancy to Polly, and was stirred to outspoken wrath by our tales of the severity of her life. She gave her a pretty pink cambric dress, and Polly wore it on "last day," at the end of the summer term. She was evidently absorbed in love of it, and sat smoothing its shiny surface with her little cracked hand, so oblivious to the requirements of the occasion that she only looked up dazed when the teacher told her to describe the Amazon River, and unregretfully let the question pass. The lady meant to take Polly away with her, but she fell sick with erysipelas in the face, and was hurried off to the city to be nursed, "a sight to behold," as everybody said. And whether she died, or whether she got well and forgot Polly, none of us ever heard. We only knew she did not return, bringing the odor of violets and the rustle of starched petticoats into our placid lives.

But all these thoughts of Polly would be less wearing, when they come in the night-time knocking at the heart, if I could only remember her as glowing under the sympathy and loving-kindness of her little mates. Alas! it was not so. We were senseless little brutes, who, never having learned the taste of misery ourselves, had no pity for the misfortunes of others. She was, indeed, ill-treated; but what were we, to translate the phrase? She was an under dog, and we had no mercy on her. We "plagued" her, God forgive us! And what the word means, in its full horror, only a child can compass. We laughed at her cudbar petticoats, her little "chopped hands"; and when she stumbled over the arithmetic lesson, because she had been up at four o'clock every morning since the first bluebirds came, we laughed at that. Life in general seems to have treated Polly in somewhat the same way. I hear that she did not marry well, and that her children had begun to "turn out bad," when she died, prematurely bent and old, not many weeks ago. But when I think of what we might have given and what we did withhold, when I realize that one drop of water from each of us would have filled her little cup to overflowing, there is one compensating thought, and I murmur, conscience-smitten, "I'm glad she had the pink dress!"

And now the little school is ever present with us, ours still for counsel or reproof. Its long-closed sessions are open, by day and night; and I suppose, as time goes on, and we drop into the estate of those who sit by the fireside, oblivious to present scenes, yet acutely awake to such as

> Flash upon that inward eye
> Which is the bliss of solitude,

it will grow more and more lifelike and more near. Beside it, live all the joys of memory and many a long-past pain. For we who have walked in country ways, walk in them always, and with no divided love, even though brick pavements have been our chosen road this many a year. We follow the market, we buy and sell, and even run across the sea, to fit us with new armor for the soul, to guard it from the hurts of years; but ever do we keep the calendar of this one spring of life. Some unheard angelus summons us to days of feast and mourning; it may be the joy of the fresh-springing willow, or the nameless pain responsive to the croaking of frogs, in the month when twilights are misty, and waves of world-sorrow flood in upon the heart, we know not why. All those trembling half-thoughts of the sleep of the year and its awakening,—we have not escaped them by leaving the routine that brought them forth. We know when the first violets are blowing in the woods, and we paint for ourselves the tasselling of the alder and the red of maple-buds. We taste still the sting of checkerberry and woodsy flavor of the fragrant birch. When fields of corn are shimmering in the sun, we know exactly how it would seem to run through those dusty aisles, swept by that silken drapery, and counselled in whispers from the plumy tops so far above our heads. The ground-sparrow's nest is not strange to us; no, nor the partridge's hidden treasure within the wood. We can make pudding-bags of live-forever, dolls' bonnets, "trimmed up to the nines," out of the velvet mullein leaf, and from the ox-eyed daisies, round, cap-begirt faces, smiling as the sun. All the homely secrets of rural life are ours: the taste of pie, cinnamon-flavored, from the dinner-pails at noon; the smell of "pears a-b'ilin'," at that happiest hour when, in the early dusk, we tumble into the kitchen, to find the table set and the stove redolent of warmth and savor. "What you got for supper?" we cry,—question to be paralleled in the summer days by "What'd you have for dinner?" as, famished little bears, we rush to the dairy-wheel, to feed ravenously on the cold, delicious fragments of the meal eaten without us.

If time ever stood still, if we were condemned to the blank solitude of hospital nights or becalmed, mid-ocean days, and had hours for fruitless dreaming, I wonder what viands we should choose, in setting forth a banquet from that ambrosial past! Foods unknown to poetry and song: "cold b'iled dish," pandowdy, or rye drop-cakes dripping with butter! For these do we taste, in moments of retrospect; and perhaps we dwell the more on their homely savor because we dare not think what hands prepared them for our use, or, when the board was set, what faces smiled. We are too wise, with the cunning prudence of the years, to penetrate over-far beyond the rosy boundary of youth, lest we find also that bitter pool which is not Lethe, but the waters of a vain regret.

Farmer Eli's Vacation

"It don't seem as if we 'd really got round to it, does it, father?" asked Mrs. Pike.

The west was paling, and the August insects stirred the air with their crooning chirp. Eli and his wife sat together on the washing-bench outside the back door, waiting for the milk to cool before it should be strained. She was a large, comfortable woman, with an unlined face, and smooth, fine auburn hair; he was spare and somewhat bent, with curly iron-gray locks, growing thin, and crow's-feet about his deep-set gray eyes. He had been smoking the pipe of twilight contentment, but now he took it out and laid it on the bench beside him, uncrossing his legs and straightening himself, with the air of a man to whom it falls, after long pondering, to take some decisive step.

"No; it don't seem as if 'twas goin' to happen," he owned. "It looked pretty dark to me, all last week. It 's a good deal of an undertakin', come to think it all over. I dunno 's I care about goin'."

"Why, father! After you 've thought about it so many years, an' Sereno 's got the tents strapped up, an' all! You must be crazy!"

"Well," said the farmer, gently, as he rose and went to carry the milk-pails into the pantry, calling coaxingly, as he did so, "Kitty! kitty! You had your milk? Don't you joggle, now!" For one eager tabby rose on her hind legs, in purring haste, and hit her nose against the foaming saucer.

Mrs. Pike came ponderously to her feet, and followed, with the heavy, swaying motion of one grown fleshy and rheumatic. She was not in the least concerned about Eli's change of mood. He was a gentle soul, and she had always been able to guide him in paths of her own choosing. Moreover, the present undertaking was one involving his own good fortune, and she meant to tolerate no foolish scruples which might interfere with its result. For Eli, though he had lived all his life within easy driving distance of the ocean, had never seen it, and ever since his boyhood he had cherished one darling plan,—some day he would go to the shore, and camp out there for a week. This, in his starved imagination, was like a dream of the Acropolis to an artist stricken blind, or as mountain outlines to the dweller in a lonely plain. But the years had flitted past, and the dream never seemed nearer completion. There were always planting, haying, and harvesting to be considered; and though he was fairly prosperous, excursions were foreign to his simple habit of life. But at last, his wife had stepped into the van, and organized an expedition, with all the valor of a Francis Drake.

"Now, don't you say one word, father," she had said. "We 're goin' down to the beach, Sereno, an' Hattie, an' you an' me, an' we 're goin' to camp out. It 'll do us all good."

For days before the date of the excursion, Eli had been solemn and tremulous, as with joy; but now, on the eve of the great event, he shrank back from it, with an undefined notion that it was like death, and that he was not prepared. Next morning, however, when they all rose and took their early breakfast, preparatory to starting at five, he showed no sign of indecision, and even went about his outdoor tasks with an alacrity calculated, as his wife approvingly remarked, to "for'ard the v'y'ge." He had at last begun to see his way clear, and he looked well satisfied when his daughter Hattie and Sereno, her husband, drove into the yard, in a wagon cheerfully suggestive of a wandering life. The tents and a small hair-trunk were stored in the back, and the horse's pail swung below.

"Well, father," called Hattie, her rosy face like a flower under the large shade-hat she had trimmed for the occasion, "guess we 're goin' to have a good day!"

He nodded from the window, where he was patiently holding

his head high and undergoing strangulation, while his wife, breathing huskily with haste and importance, put on his stock.

"You come in, Hattie, an' help pack the doughnuts into that lard-pail on the table," she called. "I guess you 'll have to take two pails. They ain't very big."

At length, the two teams were ready, and Eli mounted to his place, where he looked very slender beside his towering mate. The hired man stood leaning on the pump, chewing a bit of straw, and the cats rubbed against his legs, with tails like banners; they were all impressed by a sense of the unusual.

"Well, good-by, Luke," Mrs. Pike called, over her shoulder; and Eli gave the man a solemn nod, gathered up the reins, and drove out of the yard. Just outside the gate, he pulled up.

"Whoa!" he called, and Luke lounged forward. "Don't you forgit them cats! Git up, Doll!" And this time, they were gone.

For the first ten miles of the way, familiar in being the road to market, Eli was placidly cheerful. The sense that he was going to do some strange deed, to step into an unknown country, dropped away from him, and he chatted, in his intermittent, serious fashion, of the crops and the lay of the land.

"Pretty bad job up along here, ain't it, father?" called Sereno, as they passed a sterile pasture where two plodding men and a yoke of oxen were redeeming the soil from its rocky fetters.

"There 's a good deal o' pastur', in some places, that ain't fit for nothin' but to hold the world together," returned Eli; and then he was silent, his eyes fixed on Doll's eloquent ears, his mouth working a little. For this progress through a less desirable stratum of life caused him to cast a backward glance over his own smooth, middle-aged road.

"We 've prospered, 'ain't we, Maria?" he said, at last; and his wife, unconsciously following his thoughts, in the manner of those who have lived long together, stroked her black silk *visite,* and answered, with a well-satisfied nod:

"I guess we 'ain't got no cause to complain."

The roadside was parched under an August sun; tansy was dust-covered, and ferns had grown ragged and gray. The jogging horses left behind their lazy feet a suffocating cloud.

"My land!" cried Mrs. Pike, "if that ain't goldenrod! I do b'lieve it comes earlier every year, or else the seasons are changin'. See them elderberries! Ain't they purple! You jest remember that bush, an' when we go back, we 'll fill some pails. I dunno when I 've made elderberry wine."

Like her husband, she was vaguely excited; she began to feel as if life would be all holidays. At noon, they stopped under the shadow of an elm-tree which, from its foothold in a field, completely arched the road; and there they ate a lunch of pie and doughnuts, while the horses, freed from their headstalls, placidly munched a generous feed of oats, near by. Hattie and her mother accepted this picnicking with an air of apologetic amusement; and when one or two passers-by looked at them, they smiled a little at vacancy, with the air of wishing it understood that they were by no means accustomed to such irregularities.

"I guess they think we 're gypsies," said Hattie, as one carriage rolled past.

"Well, they needn't trouble themselves," returned her mother, rising with difficulty to brush the crumbs from her capacious lap. "I guest I 've got as good an extension-table to home as any on 'em."

But Eli ate sparingly, and with a preoccupied and solemn look.

"Land, father!" exclaimed his wife, "you 'ain't eat no more'n a bird!"

"I guess I'll go over to that well," said he, "an' git a drink o' water. I drink more'n I eat, if I ain't workin'." But when he came back, carefully bearing a tin pail brimming with cool, clear water, his face expressed strong disapprobation, and he smacked his lips scornfully.

"Terrible flat water!" he announced. "Tastes as if it come out o' the cistern." But the others could find no fault with it, and Sereno drained the pail.

"Pretty good, I call it," he said; and Mrs. Pike rejoined,—

"You always was pretty particular about water, father."

But Eli still shook his head, and ejaculated, "Brackish, brackish!" as he began to put the bit in Doll's patient mouth. He was thinking, with a passion of loyalty, of the clear, ice-cold water at home, which had never been shut out, by a pump, from the purifying airs of heaven, but lay where the splashing bucket and chain broke, every day, the image of moss and fern. His throat grew parched and dry with longing.

When they were within three miles of the sea, it seemed to them that they could taste the saltness of the incoming breeze; the road was ankle-deep in dust; the garden flowers were glaring in their brightness. It was a new world. And when at last they emerged from the marsh-bordered road upon a ridge of sand, and turned a sudden corner, Mrs. Pike faced her husband in triumph.

"There, father!" she cried. "There 'tis!"

But Eli's eyes were fixed on the dashboard in front of him. He looked pale.

"Why, father," said she, impatiently, "ain't you goin' to look? It 's the sea!"

"Yes, yes," said Eli, quietly; "byme-by. I 'm goin' to put the horses up fust."

"Well, I never!" said Mrs. Pike; and as they drew up on the sandy tract where Sereno had previously arranged a place for their tents, she added, almost fretfully, turning to Hattie, "I dunno what 's come over your father. There 's the water, an' he won't even cast his eyes at it."

But Hattie understood her father, by some intuition of love, though not of likeness.

"Don't you bother him, ma," she said. "He 'll make up his mind to it pretty soon. Here, le's lift out these little things, while they 're unharnessin', and then they can get at the tents."

Mrs. Pike's mind was diverted by the exigencies of labor, and she said no more; but after the horses had been put up at a neighboring house, and Sereno, red-faced with exertion, had superintended the tent-raising, Hattie slipped her arm through her father's, and led him away.

"Come, pa," she said, in a whisper; "le's you and me climb over on them rocks."

Eli went; and when they had picked their way over sand and pools to a headland where the water thundered below, and salt spray dashed up in mist to their feet, he turned and looked at the sea. He faced it as a soul might face Almighty Greatness, only to be stricken blind thereafter; for his eyes filled painfully with slow, hot tears. Hattie did not look at him, but after a while she shouted in his ear, above the outcry of the surf,—

"Here, pa, take my handkerchief. I don't know how 'tis about you, but this spray gets in my eyes."

Eli took it obediently, but he did not speak; he only looked at the sea. The two sat there, chilled and quite content, until six o'clock, when Mrs. Pike came calling to them from the beach, with dramatic shouts, emphasized by the waving of her ample apron,—

"Supper 's ready! Sereno 's built a burn-fire, an' I 've made some tea!"

Then they slowly made their way back to the tents, and sat down to the evening meal. Sereno seemed content, and Mrs. Pike was bustling and triumphant; the familiar act of preparing food had given her the feeling of home.

"Well, father, what think?" she asked, smiling exuberantly, as she passed him his mug of tea. "Does it come up to what you expected?"

Eli turned upon her his mild, dazed eyes.

"I guess it does," he said, gently.

That night, they sat upon the shore while the moon rose and laid in the water her majestic pathway of light. Eli was the last to leave the rocks, and he lay down on his hard couch in the tent, without speaking.

"I wouldn't say much to father," whispered Hattie to her mother, as they parted for the night. "He feels it more 'n we do."

"Well, I s'pose he is some tired," said Mrs. Pike, acquiescing, after a brief look of surprise. "It 's a good deal of a jaunt, but I dunno but I feel paid a'ready. Should you take out your hairpins, Hattie?"

She slept soundly and vocally, but her husband did not close his eyes. He looked, though he could see nothing, through the opening in the tent, in the direction where lay the sea, solemnly clamorous, eternally responsive to some infinite whisper from without his world. The tension of the hour was almost more than he could bear; he longed for morning, in sharp suspense, with a faint hope that the light might bring relief. Just as the stars faded, and one luminous line pencilled the east, he rose, smoothed his hair, and stepped softly out upon the beach. There he saw two shadowy figures, Sereno and Hattie. She hurried forward to meet him.

"You goin' to see the sunrise, too, father?" she asked. "I made Sereno come. He 's awful mad at bein' waked up."

Eli grasped her arm.

"Hattie," he said, in a whisper, "don't you tell. I jest come out to see how 'twas here, before I go. I'm goin' home,—I'm goin' *now!*"

"Why, father!" said Hattie; but she peered more closely into his face, and her tone changed. "All right," she added, cheerfully. "Sereno 'll go and harness up."

"No; I 'm goin' to walk."

"But, father—"

"I don't mean to break up your stayin' here, nor your mother's. You tell her how 'twas. I 'm goin' to walk."

Hattie turned and whispered to her husband for a moment. Then she took her father's hand.

"I 'll slip into the tent and put you up somethin' for your breakfast and luncheon," she said. "Sereno 's gone to harness; for, pa, you must take one horse, and you can send Luke back with it Friday, so 's we can get the things home. What do we want of two horses down here, at two and ninepence a day? I guess I know!"

So Eli yielded; but before his wife appeared, he had turned his back on the sea, where the rose of dawn was fast unfolding. As he jogged homeward, the dusty roadsides bloomed with flowers of paradise, and the insects' dry chirp thrilled like the song of angels. He drove into the yard just at the turning of the day, when the fragrant smoke of many a crackling fire curls cheerily upward, in promise of the evening meal.

"What's busted?" asked Luke, swinging himself down from his load of fodder-corn, and beginning to unharness Doll.

"Oh, nothin'," said Eli, leaping from the wagon as if twenty years had been taken from his bones. "I guess I 'm too old for such jaunts. I hope you didn't forgit them cats."

Edwin Arlington Robinson

Until his thirtieth year, Edwin Arlington Robinson (1869-1935) lived in Gardiner, Maine, on the Kennebec River. Like many New England towns of that period, Gardiner—named Tilbury Town in Robinson's poems—was suffering from economic, social, and spiritual demoralization and was thus a spawning ground for damaged lives. In the poems included here, the miserly and misanthropic Aaron Stark, the hypersensitive Reuben Bright, and the frustrated Aunt Imogen, who in lieu of a family of her own finds she must make do with temporary borrowings of the love and charm of her married sister's children, are predictable products of the time and place. The feelings of depression, mystery, and even terror evoked by scenes of decay and desertion in the town and surrounding countryside are transmitted in "The Dead Village," "The House on the Hill," and "The Tavern." The sonnet "Boston" conveys the contrasting sense of exhilarating escape that even a "counterfeit" metropolis provided for one, like Robinson, too long immersed in the northern gloom.

*Robinson is, of course, of far more than merely regional importance. Like Emily Dickinson and Robert Frost, he is among America's most famous and most universally appealing poets. The inclusion of a few of his poems in this collection serves (as do the selections by Frost and Emily Dickinson) to demonstrate the high potential for literary greatness in the tradition of rural New England writing. The foundation of Robinson's achievement was laid in his first three books—*The Torrent and the Night Before *(1896),* The Children of the Night *(1897), and* Captain Craig *(1902)—all of which drew primarily from his Gardiner experience. The poems that follow are chosen from these early volumes.*

Seven Poems

AARON STARK

Withal a meagre man was Aaron Stark,—
Cursed and unkempt, shrewd, shrivelled, and morose.
A miser was he, with a miser's nose,
And eyes like little dollars in the dark.
His thin, pinched mouth was nothing but a mark;
And when he spoke there came like sullen blows
Through scattered fangs a few snarled words and close,
As if a cur were chary of its bark.

Glad for the murmur of his hard renown,
Year after year he shambled through the town,—
A loveless exile moving with a staff;
And oftentimes there crept into his ears
A sound of alien pity, touched with tears,—
And then (and only then) did Aaron laugh.

THE DEAD VILLAGE

Here there is death. But even here, they say,—
Here where the dull sun shines this afternoon
As desolate as ever the dead moon
Did glimmer on dead Sardis,—men were gay;
And there were little children here to play,
With small soft hands that once did keep in tune
The strings that stretch from heaven, till too soon
The change came, and the music passed away.

Now there is nothing but the ghosts of things,—

No life, no love, no children, and no men;
And over the forgotten place there clings
The strange and unrememberable light
That is in dreams. The music failed, and then
God frowned, and shut the village from His sight.

THE HOUSE ON THE HILL

They are all gone away,
   The House is shut and still,
There is nothing more to say.

Through broken walls and gray
   The winds blow bleak and shrill:
They are all gone away.

Nor is there one to-day
   To speak them good or ill:
There is nothing more to say.

Why is it then we stray
   Around that sunken sill?
They are all gone away,

And our poor fancy-play
   For them is wasted skill:
There is nothing more to say.

There is ruin and decay
   In the House on the Hill:
They are all gone away,
There is nothing more to say.

BOSTON

My northern pines are good enough for me,
But there's a town my memory uprears—
A town that always like a friend appears,
And always in the sunrise by the sea.
And over it, somehow, there seems to be

A downward flash of something new and fierce,
That ever strives to clear, but never clears
The dimness of a charmed antiquity.

I know my Boston is a counterfeit,—
A frameless imitation, all bereft
Of living nearness, noise, and common speech;
But I am glad for every glimpse of it,—
And there it is, plain as a name that's left
In letters by warm hands I cannot reach.

REUBEN BRIGHT

Because he was a butcher and thereby
Did earn an honest living (and did right),
I would not have you think that Reuben Bright
Was any more a brute than you or I;
For when they told him that his wife must die,
He stared at them, and shook with grief and fright,
And cried like a great baby half that night,
And made the women cry to see him cry.

And after she was dead, and he had paid
The singers and the sexton and the rest,
He packed a lot of things that she had made
Most mournfully away in an old chest
Of hers, and put some chopped-up cedar boughs
In with them, and tore down the slaughter-house.

THE TAVERN

Whenever I go by there nowadays
And look at the rank weeds and the strange grass,
The torn blue curtains and the broken glass,
I seem to be afraid of the old place;
And something stiffens up and down my face,
For all the world as if I saw the ghost
Of old Ham Amory, the murdered host,
With his dead eyes turned on me all aglaze.

The Tavern has a story, but no man
Can tell us what it is. We only know
That once long after midnight, years ago,
A stranger galloped up from Tilbury Town,
Who brushed, and scared, and all but overran
That skirt-crazed reprobate, John Evereldown.

AUNT IMOGEN

Aunt Imogen was coming, and therefore
The children—Jane, Sylvester, and Young George—
Were eyes and ears; for there was only one
Aunt Imogen to them in the whole world,
And she was in it only for four weeks
In fifty-two. But those great bites of time
Made all September a Queen's Festival;
And they would strive, informally, to make
The most of them.—The mother understood,
And wisely stepped away. Aunt Imogen
Was there for only one month in the year,
While she, the mother,—she was always there;
And that was what made all the difference.
She knew it must be so, for Jane had once
Expounded it to her so learnedly
That she had looked away from the child's eyes
And thought; and she had thought of many things.

There was a demonstration every time
Aunt Imogen appeared, and there was more
Than one this time. And she was at a loss
Just how to name the meaning of it all:
It puzzled her to think that she could be
So much to any crazy things alive—
Even to her sister's little savages
Who knew no better than to be themselves;
But in the midst of her glad wonderment
She found herself besieged and overcome
By two tight arms and one tumultuous head,
And therewith half bewildered and half pained
By the joy she felt and by the sudden love

That proved itself in childhood's honest noise.
Jane, by the wings of sex, had reached her first;
And while she strangled her, approvingly,
Sylvester thumped his drum and Young George howled.—
But finally, when all was rectified,
And she had stilled the clamor of Young George
By letting him go "pig-back" through the hall,
They went together into the old room
That looked across the fields; and Imogen
Gazed out with a girl's gladness in her eyes,
Happy to know that she was back once more
Where there were those who knew her, and at last
Had gloriously got away again
From cabs and clattered asphalt for a while;
And there she sat and talked and looked and laughed
And made the mother and the children laugh.
Aunt Imogen made everybody laugh.

There was the feminine paradox—that she
Who had so little sunshine for herself
Should have so much for others. How it was
That she could make, and feel for making it,
So much of joy for them, and all along
Be covering, like a scar, the while she smiled,
That hungering incompleteness and regret—
That passionate ache for something of her own,
For something of herself—she never knew.
She knew that she could seem to make them all
Believe there was no other part of her
Than her persistent happiness; but the why
And how she did not know. Still none of them
Could have a thought that she was living down—
Almost as if regret were criminal,
So proud it was and yet so profitless—
The penance of a dream, and that was good:
Even her big bewhiskered brother Giles
Had called her in his letter, not long since,
A superannuated pretty girl;
And she, to do the thing most adequate
Had posted back sarcastic sheets enough
To keep the beast in humor for a month.

But her sister Jane—the mother of little Jane,
Sylvester, and Young George—may, after all,
Have known; for she was—well, she was a woman.

Young George, however, did not yield himself
To nourish the false hunger of a ghost
That made no good return. He saw too much;
The accumulated wisdom of his years
Had so conclusively made plain to him
The permanent profusion of a world
Where everybody might have everything
To do, and almost everything to eat,
That he was jubilantly satisfied
And all unthwarted by adversity.
Young George knew things. The world, he had found out,
Was a good place, and life was a good game—
Particularly when Aunt Imogen
Was in it. And one day it came to pass—
One rainy day when she was holding him
And rocking him—that he, in his own right,
Took it upon himself to tell her so;
And something in his way of telling it—
The language, or the tone, or something else—
Gripped like a baby's fingers on her throat,
And then went feeling through as if to make
A plaything of her heart. Such undeserved
And unsophisticated confidence
Went mercilessly home; and had she sat
Before a looking glass, the deeps of it
Could not have shown more clearly to her then
Than one thought-mirrored little glimpse had shown
The pang that wrenched her face and filled her eyes
With anguish and intolerable mist.
The blow that she had vaguely thrust aside
Like fright so many times had found her now:
Clean-thrust and final it had come to her
From a child's lips at last, as it had come
Never before, and as it might be felt
Never again. Some grief, like some delight,
Stings hard but once: to custom after that
The rapture or the pain submits itself,
And we are wiser than we were before.

And Imogen was wiser; though at first
Her dream-defeating wisdom was indeed
A thankless heritage: there was no sweet,
No bitter now; nor was there anything
To make a daily meaning for her life—
Till truth, like Harlequin, leapt out somehow
From ambush and threw sudden savor to it—
But the blank taste of time. There were no dreams,
No phantoms in her future any more:
One clinching revelation of what was,
One by-flash of irrevocable chance,
Had acridly but honestly foretold
The mystical fulfillment of a life
That might have once . . . But that was all gone by:
There was no need of reaching back for that:
The triumph was not hers: there was no love
Save borrowed love: there was no might have been.

But there was yet Young George—and he had gone
Conveniently to sleep, like a good boy;
And there was yet Sylvester with his drum,
And there was frowzle-headed little Jane;
And there was Jane the sister, and the mother,—
Her sister, and the mother of them all.
They were not hers, not even one of them:
She was not born to be so much as that,
For she was born to be Aunt Imogen.
Now she could see the truth and look at it;
Now she could make stars out where once had palled
A future's emptiness; now she could share
With others—ah, the others!—to the end
The largess of a woman who could smile;
Now it was hers to dance the folly down,
And all the murmuring; now it was hers
To be Aunt Imogen.—So, when Young George
Woke up and blinked at her with his big eyes,
And smiled to see the way she blinked at him,
'T was only in old concord with the stars
That she took hold of him and held him close,
Close to herself, aund crushed him till he laughed.

Robert Frost

Robert Frost (1874–1963) is too well known to need an introduction here. During his writing lifetime he was the uncrowned poet laureate of New England, in which he passed most of his adult years. The two poems reprinted here originally appeared in North of Boston *(1914), a volume in which Frost's sensitivity to the rural New England scene and the strengths and weaknesses of its inhabitants reached its fullest expression. "The Black Cottage" celebrates one of the strengths seen in nostalgic retrospect. Blackened by age and weather, the unpainted cottage evokes memories of a steadfast and unadorned faith by which a deceased woman and her generation lived. On the other hand, "A Servant to Servants," one of Frost's greatest dramatic poems, records the undermining effects of residual Calvinistic fatalism and conscience on a countrywoman who might have stepped from the pages of Mary E. Wilkins Freeman. But in this poem Frost has surpassed the prose regionalists in that he has added the dimension of tragedy. The text of the poems as reprinted here is from* The Poetry of Robert Frost *(1969).*

Two Dramatic Poems

THE BLACK COTTAGE

We chanced in passing by that afternoon
To catch it in a sort of special picture

Among tar-banded ancient cherry trees,
Set well back from the road in rank lodged grass,
The little cottage we were speaking of,
A front with just a door between two windows,
Fresh painted by the shower a velvet black.
We paused, the minister and I, to look.
He made as if to hold it at arm's length
Or put the leaves aside that framed it in.
"Pretty," he said. "Come in. No one will care."
The path was a vague parting in the grass
That led us to a weathered windowsill.
We pressed our faces to the pane. "You see," he said,
"Everything's as she left it when she died.
Her sons won't sell the house or the things in it.
They say they mean to come and summer here
Where they were boys. They haven't come this year.
They live so far away—one is out West—
It will be hard for them to keep their word.
Anyway they won't have the place disturbed."
A buttoned haircloth lounge spread scrolling arms
Under a crayon portrait on the wall,
Done sadly from an old daguerreotype.
"That was the father as he went to war.
She always, when she talked about the war,
Sooner or later came and leaned, half knelt,
Against the lounge beside it, though I doubt
If such unlifelike lines kept power to stir
Anything in her after all the years.
He fell at Gettysburg or Fredericksburg,
I ought to know—it makes a difference which:
Fredericksburg wasn't Gettysburg, of course.
But what I'm getting to is how forsaken
A little cottage this has always seemed;
Since she went, more than ever, but before—
I don't mean altogether by the lives
That had gone out of it, the father first,
Then the two sons, till she was left alone.
(Nothing could draw her after those two sons.
She valued the considerate neglect
She had at some cost taught them after years.)
I mean by the world's having passed it by—
As we almost got by this afternoon.

It always seems to me a sort of mark
To measure how far fifty years have brought us.
Why not sit down if you are in no haste?
These doorsteps seldom have a visitor.
The warping boards pull out their own old nails
With none to tread and put them in their place.
She had her own idea of things, the old lady.
And she liked talk. She had seen Garrison
And Whittier, and had her story of them.
One wasn't long in learning that she thought,
Whatever else the Civil War was for,
It wasn't just to keep the States together,
Nor just to free the slaves, though it did both.
She wouldn't have believed those ends enough
To have given outright for them all she gave.
Her giving somehow touched the principle
That all men are created free and equal.
And to hear her quaint phrases—so removed
From the world's view today of all those things.
That's a hard mystery of Jefferson's.
What did he mean? Of course the easy way
Is to decide it simply isn't true.
It may not be. I heard a fellow say so.
But never mind, the Welshman got it planted
Where it will trouble us a thousand years.
Each age will have to reconsider it.
You couldn't tell her what the West was saying,
And what the South, to her serene belief.
She had some art of hearing and yet not
Hearing the latter wisdom of the world.
White was the only race she ever knew.
Black she had scarcely seen, and yellow never.
But how could they be made so very unlike
By the same hand working in the same stuff?
She had supposed the war decided that.
What are you going to do with such a person?
Strange how such innocence gets its own way.
I shouldn't be surprised if in this world
It were the force that would at last prevail.
Do you know but for her there was a time
When, to please younger members of the church,
Or rather say non-members in the church,

Whom we all have to think of nowadays,
I would have changed the Creed a very little?
Not that she ever had to ask me not to;
It never got so far as that; but the bare thought
Of her old tremulous bonnet in the pew,
And of her half asleep, was too much for me.
Why, I might wake her up and startle her.
It was the words 'descended into Hades'
That seemed too pagan to our liberal youth.
You know they suffered from a general onslaught.
And well, if they weren't true why keep right on
Saying them like the heathen? We could drop them.
Only—there was the bonnet in the pew.
Such a phrase couldn't have meant much to her.
But suppose she had missed it from the Creed,
As a child misses the unsaid Good-night
And falls asleep with heartache—how should *I* feel?
I'm just as glad she made me keep hands off,
For, dear me, why abandon a belief
Merely because it ceases to be true.
Cling to it long enough, and not a doubt
It will turn true again, for so it goes.
Most of the change we think we see in life
Is due to truths being in and out of favor.
As I sit here, and oftentimes, I wish
I could be monarch of a desert land
I could devote and dedicate forever
To the truths we keep coming back and back to.
So desert it would have to be, so walled
By mountain ranges half in summer snow,
No one would covet it or think it worth
The pains of conquering to force change on.
Scattered oases where men dwelt, but mostly
Sand dunes held loosely in tamarisk
Blown over and over themselves in idleness.
Sand grains should sugar in the natal dew
The babe born to the desert, the sandstorm
Retard mid-waste my cowering caravans—

"There are bees in this wall." He struck the clapboards,
Fierce heads looked out; small bodies pivoted.
We rose to go. Sunset blazed on the windows.

A SERVANT TO SERVANTS

I didn't make you know how glad I was
To have you come and camp here on our land.
I promised myself to get down some day
And see the way you lived, but I don't know!
With a houseful of hungry men to feed
I guess you'd find. . . . It seems to me
I can't express my feelings, any more
Than I can raise my voice or want to lift
My hand (oh, I can lift it when I have to).
Did ever you feel so? I hope you never.
It's got so I don't even know for sure
Whether I *am* glad, sorry, or anything.
There's nothing but a voice-like left inside
That seems to tell me how I ought to feel,
And would feel if I wasn't all gone wrong.
You take the lake. I look and look at it.
I see it's a fair, pretty sheet of water.
I stand and make myself repeat out loud
The advantages it has, so long and narrow,
Like a deep piece of some old running river
Cut short off at both ends. It lies five miles
Straightaway through the mountain notch
From the sink window where I wash the plates,
And all our storms come up toward the house,
Drawing the slow waves whiter and whiter and whiter.
It took my mind off doughnuts and soda biscuit
To step outdoors and take the water dazzle
A sunny morning, or take the rising wind
About my face and body and through my wrapper,
When a storm threatened from the Dragon's Den,
And a cold chill shivered across the lake.
I see it's a fair, pretty sheet of water,
Our Willoughby! How did you hear of it?
I expect, though, everyone's heard of it.
In a book about ferns? Listen to that!
You let things more like feathers regulate
Your going and coming. And you like it here?
I can see how you might. But I don't know!
It would be different if more people came,

For then there would be business. As it is,
The cottages Len built, sometimes we rent them,
Sometimes we don't. We've a good piece of shore
That ought to be worth something, and may yet.
But I don't count on it as much as Len.
He looks on the bright side of everything,
Including me. He thinks I'll be all right
With doctoring. But it's not medicine—
Lowe is the only doctor's dared to say so—
It's rest I want—there, I have said it out—
From cooking meals for hungry hired men
And washing dishes after them—from doing
Things over and over that just won't stay done.
By good rights I ought not to have so much
Put on me, but there seems no other way.
Len says one steady pull more ought to do it.
He says the best way out is always through.
And I agree to that, or in so far
As that I can see no way out but through—
Leastways for me—and then they'll be convinced.
It's not that Len don't want the best for me.
It was his plan our moving over in
Beside the lake from where that day I showed you
We used to live—ten miles from anywhere.
We didn't change without some sacrifice,
But Len went at it to make up the loss.
His work's a man's, of course, from sun to sun,
But he works when he works as hard as I do—
Though there's small profit in comparisons.
(Women and men will make them all the same.)
But work ain't all. Len undertakes too much.
He's into everything in town. This year
It's highways, and he's got too many men
Around him to look after that make waste.
They take advantage of him shamefully,
And proud, too, of themselves for doing so.
We have four here to board, great good-for-nothings,
Sprawling about the kitchen with their talk
While I fry their bacon. Much they care!
No more put out in what they do or say
Than if I wasn't in the room at all.
Coming and going all the time, they are:

I don't learn what their names are, let alone
Their characters, or whether they are safe
To have inside the house with doors unlocked.
I'm not afraid of them, though, if they're not
Afraid of me. There's two can play at that.
I have my fancies: it runs in the family.
My father's brother wasn't right. They kept him
Locked up for years back there at the old farm.
I've been away once—yes, I've been away.
The State Asylum. I was prejudiced;
I wouldn't have sent anyone of mine there;
You know the old idea—the only asylum
Was the poorhouse, and those who could afford,
Rather than send their folks to such a place,
Kept them at home; and it does seem more human.
But it's not so: the place is the asylum.
There they have every means proper to do with,
And you aren't darkening other people's lives—
Worse than no good to them, and they no good
To you in your condition; you can't know
Affection or the want of it in that state.
I've heard too much of the old-fashioned way.
My father's brother, he went mad quite young.
Some thought he had been bitten by a dog
Because his violence took on the form
Of carrying his pillow in his teeth;
But it's more likely he was crossed in love,
Or so the story goes. It was some girl.
Anyway all he talked about was love.
They soon saw he would do someone a mischief
If he wa'n't kept strict watch of, and it ended
In father's building him a sort of cage,
Or room within a room, of hickory poles,
Like stanchions in the barn, from floor to ceiling—
A narrow passage all the way around.
Anything they put in for furniture
He'd tear to pieces, even a bed to lie on.
So they made the place comfortable with straw,
Like a beast's stall, to ease their consciences.
Of course they had to feed him without dishes.
They tried to keep him clothed, but he paraded
With his clothes on his arm—all of his clothes.

Cruel—it sounds. I s'pose they did the best
They knew. And just when he was at the height,
Father and mother married, and mother came,
A bride, to help take care of such a creature,
And accommodate her young life to his.
That was what marrying father meant to her.
She had to lie and hear love things made dreadful
By his shouts in the night. He'd shout and shout
Until the strength was shouted out of him,
And his voice died down slowly from exhaustion.
He'd pull his bars apart like bow and bowstring,
And let them go and make them twang, until
His hands had worn them smooth as any oxbow.
And then he'd crow as if he thought that child's play—
The only fun he had. I've heard them say, though,
They found a way to put a stop to it.
He was before my time—I never saw him;
But the pen stayed exactly as it was,
There in the upper chamber in the ell,
A sort of catchall full of attic clutter.
I often think of the smooth hickory bars.
It got so I would say—you know, half fooling—
"It's time I took my turn upstairs in jail"—
Just as you will till it becomes a habit.
No wonder I was glad to get away.
Mind you, I waited till Len said the word.
I didn't want the blame if things went wrong.
I was glad though, no end, when we moved out,
And I looked to be happy, and I was,
As I said, for a while—but I don't know!
Somehow the change wore out like a prescription.
And there's more to it than just window views
And living by a lake. I'm past such help—
Unless Len took the notion, which he won't,
And I won't ask him—it's not sure enough.
I s'pose I've got to go the road I'm going:
Other folks have to, and why shouldn't I?
I almost think if I could do like you,
Drop everything and live out on the ground—
But it might be, come night, I shouldn't like it,
Or a long rain. I should soon get enough,
And be glad of a good roof overhead.

I've lain awake thinking of you, I'll warrant,
More than you have yourself, some of these nights.
The wonder was the tents weren't snatched away
From over you as you lay in your beds.
I haven't courage for a risk like that.
Bless you, of course you're keeping me from work,
But the thing of it is, I need to *be* kept.
There's work enough to do—there's always that;
But behind's behind. The worst that you can do
Is set me back a little more behind.
I shan't catch up in this world, anyway.
I'd *rather* you'd not go unless you must.

Dorothy Canfield Fisher

Dorothy Canfield [Fisher] (1879–1958), though born in Kansas, was descended from early settlers in Arlington, Vermont, where she resided in her ancestral home from 1907 to her death. The New England way of life never had a more ardent supporter, as is evidenced in her Vermont Tradition *(1953), a state history. Most of her writing was fiction, mainly novels, frequently but not always with Vermont subjects and settings. "Old Man Warner," from* Raw Material *(1923), a collection of vignettes and stories of Arlington and its vicinity, illustrates the basic sense of community in a New England township of the post-Puritan period and the pride of the inhabitants in a man who can maintain his independence against grave handicaps.*

Old Man Warner

I must warn you at the outset that unless you or some of your folks came from Vermont, it is hardly worth your while to read about Old Man Warner. You will not be able to see anything in his story except, as we say in Vermont, a "gape and swallow" about nothing. Well, I don't claim much dramatic action for the story of old man Warner, but I am setting it down on the chance that it may fall into the hands of some one brought up on Vermont stories as I was. I know that for him there will be something in Old Man Warner's life, something of Vermont, something we feel and cannot express, as we feel the incommunicable aura of a personality.

The old man has been a weight on the collective mind of our town ever since I was a little girl, and that is a long time ago. He was an old man even then. Year after year, as our Board of Selectmen planned the year's town budget they had this worry about Old Man Warner, and what to do with him. It was not that old Mr. Warner was a dangerous character, or anything but strictly honest and law-abiding. But he had his own way of bothering his fellow citizens.

In his young days he had inherited a farm from his father, back up in Arnold Hollow, where at that time, about 1850, there was a cozy little settlement of five or six farms with big families. He settled there, cultivated the farm, married, and brought up a family of three sons. When the Civil War came, he volunteered together with his oldest boy, and went off to fight in the second year of the war. He came back alone in 1864, the son having fallen in the Battle of the Wilderness. And he went back up to Arnold Hollow to live and there he stayed, although the rest of his world broke up and rearranged itself in a different pattern, mostly centering about the new railroad track in the main valley.

Only the older men returned to the Arnold Hollow settlement to go on cultivating their steep, rocky farms. The younger ones set off for the West, the two remaining Warner boys with the others. Their father and mother stayed, the man hardly ever leaving the farm now even to go to town. His wife said once he seemed to feel as though he never could get caught up on the years he had missed during the war. She said he always had thought the world of his own home.

The boys did pretty well out in Iowa, had the usual ups and downs of pioneer farmers, and by 1898, when their mother died, leaving their father alone at seventy-one, they were men of forty-eight and forty-six, who had comfortable homes to which to invite him to pass his old age.

Everybody in our town began to lay plans about what they would buy at the auction, when Old Man Warner would sell off his things, as the other Arnold Hollow families had. By this time, for one reason or another, the Warners were the only people left up there. The Selectmen planned to cut out the road up into Arnold Hollow, and put the tidy little sum saved from its upkeep into improvements on the main valley thoroughfare. But old Mr. Warner wrote his sons and told the Selectmen that he saw no reason for leaving his home to go and live in a strange place and be a burden to his children, with whom, having seen

them at the rarest intervals during the last thirty years, he did
not feel very well acquainted. And he always had liked his own
home. Why should he leave it? It was pretty late in the day for
him to get used to western ways. He'd just be a bother to his
boys. He didn't want to be a bother to anybody, and he didn't
propose to be!

There were a good many protests all round, but of course the
Selectmen had not the faintest authority over him, and as quite
probably his sons were at heart relieved, nothing was done. The
town very grudgingly voted the money to keep up the Arnold
Hollow road, but consoled itself by saying freely that the old
cuss never had been so very bright and was worse now, evidently
had no idea what he was trying to do, and would soon get tired
of living alone and "doing for himself."

That was twenty-two years ago. Selectmen who were then
vigorous and middle-aged, grew old, decrepit, died, and were
buried. Boys who were learning their letters then, grew up, married, had children, and became Selectmen in their turn. Old
Man Warner's sons grew old and died, and the names of most
of his grand-children, scattered all over the West, were unknown
to us. And still the old man lived alone in his home and "did
for himself."

Every spring, when road work began, the Selectmen groaned
over having to keep up the Arnold Hollow road, and every autumn they tried their best to persuade the old man to come down
to a settlement where he could be taken care of. Our town is
very poor, and taxes are a heavy item in our calculations. It is
just all we can do to keep our schools and roads going, and we
grudge every penny we are forced to spend on tramps, paupers,
or the indigent sick. Selectmen in whose régime town expenses
were high, are not only never reëlected to town office, but their
name is a by-word and a reproach for years afterwards. We
elect them, among other things, to see to it that town expenses
are not high, and to lay their plans accordingly.

Decades of Selectmen, heavy with this responsibility, tried
to lay their plans accordingly in regard to Old Man Warner,
and ran their heads into a stone wall. One Board of Selectmen
after another knew exactly what would happen; the old dumb-
head would get a stroke of paralysis, or palsy, or softening of
the brain, or something, and the town Treasury would bleed

at every pore for expensive medical service, maybe an operation at a hospital, and after that, somebody paid to take care of him. If they could only ship him off to his family! One of the granddaughters, now a middle-aged woman, kept up a tenuous connection with the old man, and answered, after long intervals, anxious communications from the Selectmen. Or if not that, if only they could get him down out of there in the winter, so they would not be saddled with the perpetual worry about what was happening to him, with the perpetual need to break out the snow in the road and go up there to see that he was all right.

But Old Man Warner was still not bright enough to see any reason why he should lie down on his own folks, or why he should not live in his own home. When gentle expostulations were tried, he always answered mildly that he guessed he'd rather go on living the way he was for a while longer; and when blustering was tried, he straightened up, looked the blusterer in the eye, and said he guessed there wasn't no law in Vermont to turn a man off his own farm, s'long's he paid his debts, and he didn't owe any that he knew of.

That was the fact, too. He paid spot cash for what he bought in his semi-yearly trips to the village to "do trading," as our phrase goes. He bought very little, a couple of pairs of overalls a year, a bag apiece of sugar, and coffee, and rice, and salt, and flour, some raisins, and pepper. And once or twice during the long period of his hermit life, an overcoat and a new pair of trousers. What he brought down from his farm was more than enough to pay for such purchases, for he continued to cultivate his land, less and less of it, of course, each year, but still enough to feed his horse and cow and pig and hens, and to provide him with corn and potatoes and onions. He salted down and smoked a hog every fall and ate his hens when they got too old to lay.

And, of course, as long as he was actually economically independent, the town, groaning with apprehension over the danger to its treasury though it was, could not lay a finger on the cranky old codger. And yet, of course, his economic independence couldn't last! From one day to the next, something was bound to happen to him, something that would cost the town money.

Each year the Selectmen planning the town expenditures with the concentrated prudence born of hard necessity, cast an uneasy mental glance up Arnold Hollow way, and scringed at the thought that perhaps this was the year when money would have to be taken away from the road or the school fund to pay for

Old Man Warner's doctoring and nursing; and finally for his burial, because as the years went by, even the tenuous western granddaughter vanished: died, or moved, or something. Old Man Warner was now entirely alone in the world.

All during my childhood and youth he was a legendary figure of "sot" obstinacy and queerness. We children used to be sent up once in a while, to take our turn in seeing that the old man was all right. It was an expedition like no other. You turned off the main road and went up the steep, stony winding mountain road, dense with the shade of sugar-maples and oaks. At the top, when your blown horse stopped to rest, you saw before you the grassy lane leading across the little upland plateau where the Arnold Hollow settlement had been. The older people said they could almost hear faint echoes of whetting scythes, and barking dogs, and cheerful homely noises, as there had been in the old days. But for us children there was nothing but a breathlessly hushed, sunny glade of lush meadows, oppressively silent and spooky, with a few eyeless old wrecks of abandoned farm houses, drooping and gray. You went past the creepy place as fast as your horse could gallop, and clattered into the thicket of shivering white birches which grew close to the road like a screen; and then—there was no sensation in my childhood quite like the coming out into the ordered, inhabited, humanized little clearing, in front of Old Man Warner's home. There were portly hens crooning around on the close-cropped grass, and a pig grunting sociably from his pen at you, and shining milk-pans lying in the sun tilted against the white birch sticks of the wood-pile, and Old Man Warner, himself, infinitely aged and stooped, in his faded, clean overalls, emerging from the barn-door to peer at you out of his bright old eyes and to give you a hearty, "Well, you're quite a long ways from home, don't you know it? Git off your horse, can't ye? I've got a new calf in here." Or perhaps if it were a Sunday, he sat in the sun on the front porch, with a clean shirt on, reading the weekly edition of the *New York Tribune*. He drove two miles every Saturday afternoon, down to his R. F. D. mail-box on the main road, to get this.

You heard so much talk about him down in the valley, so much fussing and stewing about his being so "sot," and so queer, that it always surprised you when you saw him, to find he was just like anybody else. You saw his calf, and had a drink of milk in his clean, well-scrubbed kitchen, and played with the latest kitten, and then you said good-by for that time, and got on

your horse and went back through the birch thicket into the
ghostly decay of the abandoned farms, back down the long, stony
road to the valley where everybody was so cross with the unreasonable old man for causing them so much worry.

"How *could* he expect to go along like that, when other old
folks, so much younger than he, gave up and acted like other
people, and settled down where you could take care of them! The
house might burn down over his head, and he with it; or he
might fall and break his hip and be there for days, yelling and
fainting away till somebody happened to go by; or a cow might
get ugly and hook him, and nobody to send for help." All these
frightening possibilities and many others had been repeatedly
presented to the old man himself with the elaborations and detail
which came from heart-felt alarm about him. But he continued
to say mildly that he guessed he'd go on living the way he was
for a while yet.

"A *while!*" He was ninety years old.

And then he was ninety-one, and then ninety-two; and we
were surer and surer he would "come on the town," before each
fiscal year was over. At the beginning of last winter our Selectmen went up in a body to try to bully or coax the shrunken,
wizened old man, now only half his former size, to go down to
the valley. He remarked that he "guessed there wasn't no law
in Vermont" and so forth, just as he had to their fathers. He
was so old, that he could no longer straighten up as he said it,
for his back was helplessly bent with rheumatism, and for lack
of teeth he whistled and clucked and lisped a good deal as he
pronounced his formula. But his meaning was as clear as it had
been thirty years ago. They came sulkily away without him,
knowing that they would both be laughed at and blamed, in the
valley, because the cussed old crab had got the best of them,
again.

Last February, a couple of men, crossing over to a lumber-job
on Hemlock Mountain, by way of the Arnold Hollow road, saw
no smoke coming out of the chimney, knocked at the door, and,
getting no answer, opened it and stepped in. There lay Old
Man Warner, dead on his kitchen floor in front of his well-
blacked cook-stove. The tiny, crooked, old body was fully
dressed, even to a fur cap and mittens, and in one hand was his
sharp, well-ground ax. One stove-lid was off, and a charred stick
of wood lay half in and half out of the fire box. Evidently the
old man had stepped to the fire to put in a stick of wood before

he went out to split some more, and had been stricken instantly, before he could move a step. His cold, white old face was composed and quiet, just as it had always been in life.

The two lumbermen fed the half-starved pig and hens and turned back to the valley with the news, driving the old man's cow and horse in front of them; and in a couple of hours we all knew that Old Man Warner had died, all alone, in his own kitchen.

Well, what do you think! We were as stirred up about it—! We turned out and gave him one of the best funerals the town ever saw. And we put up a good marble tombstone that told all about how he had lived. We found we were proud of him, as proud as could be, the darned old bull-dog, who had stuck it out all alone, in spite of us. We brag now about his single-handed victory over old age and loneliness, and we keep talking about him to the children, just as we brag about our grandfather's victories in the Civil War, and talk to the children about the doings of the Green Mountain Boys. Old Man Warner has become history. We take as much satisfaction in the old fellow's spunk, as though he had been our own grandfather, and we spare our listeners no detail of his story: ". . . And there he stuck year after year, with the whole town plaguing at him to quit. And he earned his own living, and chopped his own wood, and kept himself and the house just as decent, and never got queer and frowzy and half-cracked, but stayed just like anybody, as nice an old man as ever you saw—all alone, all stark alone—beholden to nobody—asking no odds of anybody—yes, sir, and died with his boots on, at ninety-three, on a kitchen floor you could have et off of, 'twas so clean."

Mary Ellen Chase

Mary Ellen Chase (1887–　) is a native of Blue Hill on the Maine coast east of Penobscot Bay. The daughter of a lawyer, she grew up there and attended the local academy. For most of her life she has been a teacher, beginning in a one-room school not far from Blue Hill and eventually becoming a professor of English, especially of the Bible as literature, at Smith College. Her novels on Maine include Mary Peters *(1934),* Silas Crockett *(1935), and* The Edge of Darkness *(1957), from which last the excerpt in this volume is taken. These three novels comprise a comprehensive social history of the Maine coast. The* Edge of Darkness *recounts the events in a coastal town and the feelings of its inhabitants on the death of its oldest and most revered citizen, Mrs. Holt, who had become a symbol of a lost heritage. The section included here presents us with the sorry spectacle of religion gone to seed and village pettiness at its worst, though the latter is temporarily suspended in honor of Mrs. Holt.*

Hannah and Benjamin Stevens

In the earliest years of the present century, before he embraced the fisherman's life, Benjamin Stevens had been a lighthouse keeper. This calling, always an honored one and often handed down from father to son before the Coast Guard took over the maintenance and service of light-stations, had been in the Stevens family for three generations. Ben was born and reared on less than an acre of rock, which, rising from the open sea seven miles from the mainland, marked one of the most dangerous of channels. His open-air playground as a boy had been a precarious one, and his paternal roof-tree a small gray house attached to the light-shaft which rose a hundred feet above it.

From his childhood he had climbed with his father the narrow, winding iron stairs which went up and up to the lantern-room and watched the trimming, cleaning, and filling of the great oil lamp, which was raised and lowered every four hours from twilight to clear dawn. Not an especially sensitive or imaginative child and knowing little or nothing of the activities of other children with which to compare his own, he took his singular background and experiences very much for granted. It was annoying, but not particularly strange to him to be securely tethered at high tide to an iron rung of the outside ladder which mounted the tower, until his mother decided that he was old enough to take his chances.

At low tide, when his playground, at least on fair days, extended some twenty feet on all sides, he found plenty to do. He could scare the great flocks of terns, cormorants, and gulls from their perches and enjoy their raucous, angry cries; watch the seals, which with slow, muscular writhings pulled their sleek bodies awkwardly from the sea to the crests of the ledges and boulders to lie there in the sun; search among the olive-green masses of kelp and seaweed at the water's edge for drift cast up by the tides, lobster traps and buoys, cork floats, clear glass toggles, lengths of tangled rope; and explore the deep fissures which the pounding, gigantic seas had cut among the high, jagged shores. At any time, except on the worst days, he could fish from the end of the slip leading from the boat-shed; and he always relished the excitement of the unannounced visits of the Government cutter, loaded with oil and other supplies and bent on inspection. During the summer, when the sea allowed a landing at the slip for the tenders of sloops and launches, visitors sometimes came to climb the many stairs to the top of the tower, see the workings of the great lantern, look out over the wide view of islands and of distant coastline, and exclaim over the desolation of such a life. As he grew older, he set a few traps off the sloping ledges on the west side of the station and caught some lobsters for the family table or even for his father to carry on his infrequent trips to the mainland after mail and more supplies. His only playmate was his sister, five years younger than he, whom his mother worried about and who was often an annoying hindrance to his plans and projects.

His schooling was scanty enough, confined to the little help his mother could offer with books lent by the nearest mainland school and to the fortnight once or twice a year when the Seacoast Mission boat brought the light-teacher, a dauntless young woman, who for eleven months out of the twelve was carried from lighthouse to lighthouse where there were children and taught whatever she could in that brief space of time. Her school-room with them was the circular entrance to the shaft, a tiny room furnished at these intervals with two small desks and chairs and a pine table for the teacher, whom his little sister always welcomed with far more eagerness than he did. When he was twelve, his father left him on the mainland with relatives there for three or four terms of school. He did not like books any better there and felt out-of-place in the unfamiliar surroundings.

He grew to be a big young man, tall and heavy with powerful muscles and great strength in his hands, though he was quick and even agile in all his movements. He was handsome, too, after a rough, masterful manner, with a kind of arrogance assumed to disguise his uncouthness. He took it for granted that he also would tend a light, probably the same one, when his father was through and had gone to the mainland to retire after his ceaseless struggle to keep the channel safe for passing ships of every sort, whether fishing-boats, lumber schooners, coastwise steamers, or pleasure craft.

2

As he grew older and began to feel uneasy stirrings within him and to think, slowly and practically, about other necessary details concerning his future, he now and again, when tides and winds permitted, crossed by himself to small mainland towns to see the sights, and to take in a dance, once he had summoned up the courage. Sometimes he met there the son of a neighboring light-keeper in an equally dangerous stretch of sea some ten miles away. The two of them not infrequently picked up an argument or even a fight with mainland boys, in which encounters they easily came off victorious and at the same time established a reputation for both brawn and prowess.

On one of these trips and at the close of such a combat he met a girl named Hannah Alley. Her father owned a clam-factory and was a man both of parts and of money in their coast village. Hannah was a slight, pretty girl, who danced well, was willing to tolerate his stumbling, uncertain steps and even to guide them, and who quite clearly admired him. She wore nice clothes which she had actually bought in Boston during her yearly journeys there with one of her friends. She was a good girl, too, everyone said, cheerfully worked for her father in his factory, and played the organ in the Baptist church. Her parents did not much favor her dancing; but, as young Benjamin early concluded, she held the upper hand over them both. He had never been admired by a girl before; and since things were as they were and his certain future required stability and assistance, he rather roughly one evening asked Hannah to marry him. To his immense relief and satisfaction, she said that she would. He was twenty-one at the time, and Hannah was going on twenty-four.

Things worked out admirably for them both, he often thought rather ruthlessly, though that manner of his thinking never entered his mind. His father at fifty was stiff from rheumatism and found the inescapable stairs to the lantern-room more and more difficult; and his mother, deprived from her girlhood of mainland ways, longed to recapture them and live for the rest of her life away from impenetrable fogs, tumultuous seas, constant anxiety, and the lonely screaming of gulls. His sister, far more advanced than he in their uncertain, slender opportunities for study, could now go to high school as she had long dreamed. What could be more fortunate for all than that Ben should take over the rocky reef? He would be the third of his stock to do so. Government inspectors and officials had long since learned that family tradition and upbringing were safe qualities to depend upon for the guarding and guiding of vessels.

After a year on the light-station, when the admiration of her friends had worn as threadbare as her own earlier sense of adventure and daring, even of heroism, Hannah became unhappy and homesick. She was often petulant and demanding, wanting more trips to the mainland than Benjamin, knowing the unpredictable ways of the Government cutter and honestly feeling his new responsibility, felt safe or fair to make. She was afraid in storms, and superstitious over sudden ominous happenings, Northern Lights, shooting-stars, sun-dogs, strange rings around the moon. When her baby was coming and she felt lumpish and unwieldly in her small kitchen, which with the rest of the house must be kept immaculate, every dish shining and in place, every brass doorknob polished, no matter how she might feel, she insisted upon being taken well ahead of time to her father's home. She would not depend, she said, on any doctor reaching the station in time, even if weather conditions were possible to fetch him as they often were not. If the wives of other light-keepers chose to wait out their time in such frightening solitude, they were quite welcome to do so.

Their sojourn at the light-station turned out to be a brief one. Hannah found it no place for a baby and a perilous one for an irresponsible, restive child. She hated tying her little girl out of reach of danger and was forever expostulating against it to her husband, who grew steadily more impatient of her complaining discontent. One spring day, while he was busy about the shore and boat-shed and she was setting things to rights within the house, the child, then three years old, fell into a deep fissure in the rocks. They did not find her until an hour later, after the tide had turned. Whether she had been killed by the fall or drowned in the rising waters, they never knew.

Just as soon as another keeper could be found, Benjamin Stevens joined Hannah on the mainland. Not many months afterward he became a lobster fisherman in the settlement at the cove. For several years they were haunted by the memory of the child, although they rarely mentioned it to each other and never to anyone else. Hannah felt precisely as though a jagged rock lay somewhere deep within her, turning restlessly from time to time as rocks are turned about by the incoming tide. When a son was born to her, she felt better able to forget the restless jagged rock which had for so long torn at her and weighted her down.

But it had never forgotten her.

3

From the beginning of their life in the fishing-village they maintained more interests outside it than did their neighbors. Ben, Hannah said, welcomed a change once in a while and surely warranted it with all his hard work. He was a steady, careful fisherman, although never an adventuresome one. He did not invest his hard-earned money in a herring weir to supplement his lobster traps, partly because he did not like working with anyone in the association which a weir almost demanded, largely because he was wary of any investment which in the beginning was likely to require capital from one or another of the large fish-packing concerns eastward. He preferred to stick to lobsters and even to sink his traps in relatively quiet waters. But with the death of Hannah's father and her considerable share in the profits which he left behind him, they found themselves, some ten years after they had come to the cove, in comfortable circumstances. Long before Joel Norton had saved enough money to buy his truck, Benjamin and Hannah were amply able to afford a car. They used this, especially on Sundays, to escape their humdrum existence and to see something of the world outside it.

To them this world outside meant primarily a small church some twenty miles inland at the head of the Tidal River. It belonged to none of those sects common to New England coast regions, but was instead a somewhat lonely outpost of extreme evangelism. Its rather diminutive congregation consisted of ardent, anxious people who adhered unquestioningly to the inspired Word of God as revealed to His prophets and to His apostles. In their minds every sentence of this Word to its utmost syllable had been dictated by God Himself and proclaimed once and for all time by His Son. Their theology, if their simple tenets could be dignified by such a term, was extremely tangible. It demanded an entire recognition of sin, past and present; humble repentance and public acknowledgment; and total immersion in the cold waters of some bay or estuary in the sight of brethren and sisters, after which salvation was unconditionally guaranteed. In comparison with its unrelenting demands, even the rigid doctrines and practices of Hannah's earlier Baptist faith were expansive. Indeed, upon her entrance into this newer communion of saints, she had been made so conscious of guilt and remorse that she had submitted not only willingly, but eagerly to a second baptism.

Benjamin's conversion came some twenty years after he had settled down as a fisherman. At first he had taken Hannah to church on Sundays, and occasionally to the frequent evening prayer-circles because things went decidedly better at home if he allowed her these satisfactions. But gradually the sense of belonging somewhere, of having something to hang on to, began to stir some unsatisfied need within him also. Perhaps the sentiment often uttered by minister and congregation, that, just as the Lord had chosen fishermen in the beginning to carry on His work, so now He needed them above all others to conclude it at a time which all signs proved to be close at hand, had its part in his slow awakening. He had a good and true bass voice and, after some time of uneasy embarrassment, began to sing on Sunday mornings with the others, while Hannah, pumping the small organ with her feet and pressing the often recalcitrant keys, sent him glances of encouragement from the platform to the right of the pulpit. The grateful, admiring comments of his new neighbors at the close of the morning service began to sound sweet in his ears. All these influences were, in fact, far more powerful than Hannah's anxious warnings about the Ultimate Future when families would be either ruthlessly and justly separated for eternity or reunited to live in bliss, all earthly imperfections blotted out, all sins forgotten. When at last during one of the frequent revival seasons he summoned up the courage to walk forward to the mercy-seat, his great head and shoulders towering above the few weeping, shuffling figures of other penitents, he felt relieved and settled in his mind, even without that strange inner peace which the preacher had so eloquently promised him.

He was never a power in the church like Hannah, who, from her entrance into it, had begun to mould its destinies. Her position as organist and as superintendent of the tiny Sunday-school in themselves gave her prominence; but these were but outward and visible signs of her strength and influence. When Ben had left at dawn to haul his traps, she always sat down at her kitchen table for another cup of coffee over her daily Bible reading. It was then that she pondered over less obvious church problems, stealing into their intricacies like some black otter making its way into hidden crevices among the rocks and ledges of the shore. Secure in the Scriptural decrees that each is responsible for the sins and shortcomings of his brethren and that unworthy branches of the tree must be hacked down, cast into the fire, and burned, she carefully considered those human beings who together made up the congregation, weighed each in her self-constructed balance, and frequently found several wanting. Then, later on in the day, as she wove the tight meshes of her husband's bait-bags and trap-heads, her mind set to work to see what best could, and, indeed, must be done for the good of all.

When she was not employed in her religious employments and maneuverings, Hannah was a kind neighbor. She was a natural and excellent nurse and would willingly spend hours in caring for anyone who was ill or had been hurt, often driving miles to do so. A superlative housekeeper and cook, she loved bestowing products of her culinary art upon all her fellow housewives, not alone on those less gifted than she. She rarely imposed her religious convictions upon others in her immediate neighborhood, largely because her easily embarrassed husband had forbidden her to do so.

"Keep your mouth shut!" he said. "Let them all fry in Hell if that's what they want to do."

Although such a summary injunction seemed on the most cursory examination directly opposed both in word and in spirit to that missionary zeal encouraged every Sunday by the shepherd of their flock, Hannah wisely concluded to follow it.

4

On the day of old Mrs. Holt's funeral, when she went to keep the store during Lucy Norton's morning absence from it, she took with her in the bottom of her work-basket some sheets of paper upon which to write a letter. The paper was placed within the pages of her Bible which she also carried, both because she felt more secure with it close at hand and also because she might well wish to quote from it. The letter must be written with the utmost circumspection and care; and although for many days she had been composing it in her mind, she had not yet arrived at the wisest and most effective manner of its expression. She had decided upon the store as the best possible place for its composition since there could be no trade to speak of with everybody hauling traps and even the children safely, or unsafely, out of the way, and since for some completely inexplicable and vaguely troublesome reason, she could not seem to get it down on paper among the familiar sights of home.

For all her correspondence Hannah used stationery printed at the top with Scriptural messages and warnings. These sheets were purchased at the church, the profits from their sale going to increase the slender funds for missionary work. *For God so loved the world that He gave His Only Begotten Son,* one said. *Come unto me all ye that labor and are heavy laden,* pleaded another. And a third, *Though your sins be as scarlet, they shall be as white as snow; though they be red like crimson, they shall be as wool.*

This letter, which had to do with the present minister of her church, was addressed to the head of some Home Missionary

Board in Boston, a board which presided over the placing of those pastors dedicated to the obscure and zealous sect, here represented by the Tidal River congregation. Hannah had already spent several weeks in earnest thought over the minister's works and ways and a lesser time in what, she had convinced herself, was equally earnest prayer for guidance. It was difficult to write the letter, for only a few months previously she had reported, as church clerk, to the same Board that all were pleased with young Mr. Simpson, his wife and three small children, that souls were being miraculously saved under his inspired preaching, and that the parish was on the point of raising his meager salary after his four years of devoted service among them. Now that she had a far different report to make, she must seek carefully and prayerfully both for right words and for valid reasons which would bear weight with the Board in Boston.

Mr. Simpson was an earnest, fervent, ungrammatical young man of twenty-eight, who had early been converted in a Gospel Tent, raised along some remote Damascus Road among the mountains of Kentucky. At about the same time and under the same circumstances he had found his wife, a shy, frightened girl, who looked upon him as a veritable major prophet and pathetically wanted only to contribute her all, which was little enough, to his advancement. He honestly and quite humbly believed that he had been specifically chosen to rescue his fellow men from the perils of sin; and once he had discovered a struggling training-school which cared less for learning than for zeal and was in sad need of recruits, he had spent two years in the study of the Bible and in the revivalistic methods of its interpretation. The congregation at the head of the Tidal River was his first parish; and he and his wife had transported their few shabby possessions with a pride and pleasure which, he sometimes feared, competed dangerously, perhaps even wickedly, with the purposes of God for him.

From the beginning of his ministry and even, so far as he was aware, until now, Hannah Stevens had been his bulwark, the strong, defended wall and tower of the ancient prophet. She had manned his Sunday-school, played his organ, suggested subjects for his sermons, over which he laboriously struggled, and ferreted out needy souls in a dozen isolated hamlets. She had encouraged his wife with confidence and new recipes, replenished their depleted larder, and clothed their children. He had, it is true, felt somewhat diffident with her husband, whose very size and strength were overpowering. Still, Benjamin Stevens was conspicuously generous with his Sunday morning offerings; and once, on a Saturday afternoon, he had taken the whole Simpson family on a sail in his fishing-boat, an experience which so excited them all that they had found it difficult on their return home to compose themselves for family prayers. The minister thanked God daily for Hannah, who was in truth his Dorcas, Priscilla, Lois, and Eunice combined in one woman; and he prayed almost desperately that he might be allowed to remain permanently in this particular vineyard where the compensations were so many and the need, likewise, so great.

Hannah, in her turn, as she strove now to write her letter, recalled uncomfortably these more pleasant aspects of Mr. Simpson's stay among them. She strove, too, to rid her mind of other tenacious memories: of the reckless ruin of her petunia bed by the oldest of his children; of the able substitution of little Mrs. Simpson at the organ when snow had made the long road impassable for Benjamin and her. Yet these, she told herself with ever-growing conviction, had nothing to do with her real and honest conclusion that the congregation needed a change in pastors. It was, of course, undeniably true that a minister's children should be an example rather than a warning and that a minister's wife should not be apparently eager to take over duties so well performed by others. Yet these were only straws in the wind, and she would not for a moment allow them to influence those indisputable facts supporting Mr. Simpson's incompetency, facts which she, sitting behind the counter in the store, was striving to assemble in her mind and to write down on her paper.

She decided finally that she might well begin with his lack of courage in dealing with intemperance, alas! so common an evil in homes quite within his reach, now that the church had provided him with a second-hand car. She remembered that there were fortunately among her sheets of note-paper some appropriately headed: *Look not thou upon the wine when it is red. At the last it biteth like a serpent, and stingeth like an adder.* Just then, when she had barely determined upon her opening words, the Randall child came in for ten cents' worth of licorice, the other children standing in a silent group outside. Once she had put the ten sticks in a paper bag before the child's frightened stare and called from the porch a warning to her grandchildren not to forget for one moment what she had told them at breakfast, she returned to her letter.

"Rev. Sir," she wrote on a piece of tablet paper with a pencil, for the letter must be composed to her satisfaction before it was transferred in ink upon the proper sheets.

"Rev. Sir:

As clerk of our church, and organist for ten years, and Supt. of our Sunday School for many more years, I feel it is my painful duty as a Christian to set before you . . ."

5

Even while she was setting down the first words, she saw the children trailing up the hill in search of flowers for old Mrs. Holt. Why the sight of them setting forth should so interpose itself between her and her task, she could not see, and she felt suddenly flushed and irritated. Then, when she had banished the children from her mind, she recalled the disturbing fact that she had not been asked to help in performing the last duties for Sarah Holt as she had been asked to do in numberless similar situations and in far more important communities than this one. She thought of Ben out there hauling his traps and of what he might say unless she could keep her letter concealed from his knowledge. She even recalled, in spite of herself, the surprised and delighted exclamations of the minister's wife over cakes and pies she had made for her in the recent past, one cake identical with that which she had baked this morning in an effort to quiet the resentment and suspicion which nagged at her from more than one quarter. And behind and through all these unwelcome images and recollections which seemed maliciously bent on tormenting her, lay the face of the dead woman, which she had purposely not gone over to look upon.

Lucy Norton's clock on the shelf above the stove ticked away the two hours upon which she had counted for her letter. There was still no question in her mind that it must and would be written; but today was clearly not the day for it. When she saw Lucy coming down the road, she put away the sheets of paper in her Bible and concealed both in the bottom of her workbasket before she went out on the porch.

Perry D. Westbrook

Perry D. Westbrook (1916–   ), the editor of this anthology, has written a number of books on New England subjects: Acres of Flint: Writers of Rural New England, 1870–1900 *(1951),* Biography of an Island *(1958),* Mary Ellen Chase *(1965), and* Mary Wilkins Freeman *(1967). The selection included here is the final chapter of* Biography of an Island, *a study of the Maine fishing community of Swans Island, where such foundation institutions of New England as the town meeting are still alive and reasonably healthy. There are three hamlets (known as "sides" in local parlance) in the township—Atlantic, Minturn, and Swans Island Village.*

Town Meeting

I

A milky sun, slashed by the saw teeth of the spruces, rises across the harbor on which a film of ice awaits dissolution by the tide and the morning breezes. A motorboat, "going outside" to haul lobster traps, rocks tentatively on the swell at the harbor mouth. But many boats are still at their moorings, where in the changing winds they will pivot all day. This is town meeting day, and already a curl of smoke unwinds from the chimney of the towering Oddfellows' Hall a half mile up from the shore. Soon the selectmen will gather there to "correct the list of voters." At ten o'clock the meeting itself will begin, the 120th in the island's history.

Since 1834 the island has had yearly meetings to elect officers, to levy taxes, to establish schools, and to lay out roads. In 1897 the community was made a town, with added responsibilities particularly in regard to the support of the poor. The plantation meeting of 1896 had rejected by a vote of eighty-two to fifty-nine this town status as provided by special action of the state legislature, for taxes are usually higher in a town than in a plantation. But the next year the legislature passed a mandatory bill, and willy-nilly the island assumed its larger role of self-government and self-support.

On this first day of March, 1954, the townspeople are assembling to consider commitments and enterprises greater than any ever placed before them. In 1839, the first year for which records are extant, the voters "raised" only $265: $90 for schools, $150 for roads, and $25 for administrative expenses. In 1897, the first year of town status, they raised $2,135: $735 for schools, $500 for roads, $200 for support of the poor, and $700 for administration of the government. In 1954 they were to vote $12,001.75 for schools, $1,733 for roads, $500 for support of the poor, $2,400 for a doctor's subsidy, and other sums for such purposes as "advertising the recreational resources of the island" and cleaning up the town dump. The total was to be $24,584.75 for a community of four hundred and fifty persons, or eighty-nine times that of 1839, when the population was about two hundred and fifty, and eleven times that of 1898, when the population was seven hundred and fifty.

This hazy, springlike March morning, as the cars converge on the Oddfellows' Hall, the occupants are unconcerned at the great sum the public weal has come to cost. This is to be largely a young peoples' meeting, though by no means all the young people attend. The fine weather has lured some outside to haul. Lobsters have been scarce and money scarcer. Only fifty or sixty of the town's total of three hundred voters appear. Many of the young, even among those who are present, are indifferent, but most numerous among the stay-aways are the older people, who have been left behind by the race of events in the past ten years and have lost whatever control they have had on local affairs. Recently, according to them, the island has parted its mooring and is adrift in shoal water. They point to the debt of about one hundred and fifty thousand to the R.E.A. for their power plant and to the debt of thirty-three thousand to the state for their new school building. Such obligations are a heavy burden on a hundred or so fishermen. And, though they seldom speak of it, at the back of their minds is the spectre of a failure of the lobster supply. Thus many of the old folks sit at home and complain that the town is run by two or three irresponsibles and that the meetings are not fit places for level-headed citizens who believe in paying their bills.

Everybody is acquained in detail with what has been going on. In each box in the three island post offices has been placed a copy of the "Annual Report of the Municipal Officers," printed at a cost of two hundred dollars at Stonington for distribution to the voters. In its thirty-two pages they have read a complete history of town affairs during the past year: the names of the officers, the valuation of real estate and personal property, with tables giving the numbers of such taxable possessions as boats, radios, musical instruments, horses, oxen, sheep, and cows; the town appropriations at the last meeting with an itemized account of how they were spent; lists of tax delinquents during the past ten years; and a report by the school superintendent, containing a census of scholars, an accounting of the year's expenditures, and an estimate of what next year's budget will be. At the end of the report is a copy of the warrant, duly posted by a constable, and listing the fifty-four articles on which the meeting will have to act.

The islanders save their reports from year to year and build up files of them which they study occasionally in their spare time, with the result that they become expert in town finances and politics. They discuss abatements, overlays, and negotiable notes. By studying the names of those who have been paid for services to the town they can spot favoritism and nepotism. Yet though they see with such a knowing eye, they are reluctant to act on their knowledge and to attend town meeting and oppose measures and practices that they consider harmful.

2

When the meeting opens sometime after ten only thirty-five or so voters are present. Some of these are seated in a little island of rickety chairs in the center of the large second-floor room. Others sit or stand along the walls. Directly before the stage—for this room is the scene of dances and cowboy shows—is a table where sit the three selectmen and the town clerk with his leather-bound record book. On the open floor children run and play and shout. The door at the back is constantly banging as citizens come and go.

The first selectman, a carpenter of benign countenance getting on in years, rises and speaks into a microphone connected with a squawky amplifier, which lifts the voices of the speakers above the din of children playing Indians and women gossiping. Matter-of-factly he calls the meeting to order and requests the nomination of a moderator. At once the moderator of the previous years is elected. He is a young lobster fisherman, a married man with several children who are at present running about with the other youngsters on the floor. He is a man noted for his courtesy, presence of mind, and quiet forcefulness. He doesn't lose his temper even when, during a discussion as to the disposal of the old schoolhouse, some wag suggests putting a match to the building and someone else is silly enough to second the motion. He merely insists on a sensible motion. "You can't burn a public building, even if you aren't going to use it any more." And a sensible motion is soon forthcoming when a young man who owns a truck offers to dismantle the school and cart away the materials if he can have them for his own use free of charge.

The first part of the meeting is given over to the election of officers. First a town clerk is chosen, for he will have to record the minutes. Fifteen or twenty voters scribble a name on scraps of paper and walk with them to the front of the room, where they drop them into a cigar box on the moderator's table. As everyone expects, the man who has been clerk for years is reelected. He is the most energetic man of affairs in the town— a holder of many offices. In addition to being town clerk, he is chairman of the schoolboard, a tireless worker for the better education of the children over the whining and sometimes snarling opposition of the taxpayers. He is also deputy sheriff, collector of excise taxes, assistant sexton, a notary public, a mail carrier, and a member of the school-planning committee, the budget committee, and the public-health and sanitation committee. In private life he used to be one of the two partners controlling the granite quarry and is now half-owner, treasurer, and chief linesman of the Swans Island Telephone and Telegraph Company. He occasionally is the town barber. In his spare time he is a lobster fisherman.

After the moderator and town clerk have been elected, the officers of the past year present their reports, as printed in the booklet previously distributed to every voter. The elections then continue with the choice of a board of selectmen, who will also serve as assessors and as overseers of the poor. The

moderator explains that it is customary to elect one selectman from each of the three "sides." The same principle of
"one from each side" obtains in the choosing of a school committee and constables. This year the previous selectmen are
retained, but their compensations are increased. The first selectman will now make ten dollars a day; the second, nine; and
the third, eight. The year before each worked about fifty days
on town affairs.

Next the attractive young wife of a local storekeeper is
elected town treasurer, a position in which she has already
served for four years. She is the first woman in the town's
history to hold an important office. Since she was first elected,
there has been a woman tax collector, and several women have
sat on various committees. The town has yet to elect a select-
woman, but the possibility is no longer discounted. Until now
the men have monopolized law enforcement and politics. The
holders of important positions—selectmen, town clerk, treasurer, head of the school board—have tended to become fix-
tures. Twenty or thirty years for one man in such an office
are not unusual. The only major position to change hands
often is that of road commissioner. The "road patrol," as he
is called, is paid well, but he is open to criticism. Imperfections
in road surfaces are more noticeable than those in fiscal or
school policy.

The election hits a snag, at this meeting, when the time
comes to choose constables. Since law enforcement is almost
entirely relegated to the deputy sheriff, the most exciting thing
a constable does is to tack up warrants of town meetings in
the three post offices. As for wages, he is lucky if he makes
ten dollars a year. Consequently, the first to be elected from
the Atlantic side declines the honor. He is a lobsterman with
four-hundred traps out. He is about to start a lobster-buying
business of his own. He clearly will have no time even for
the limited duties of a constable. Next a man who is not
present is elected. A willing candidate is found for Minturn,
but since no one from the village of Swans Island is available,
a tradition is broken by the election of a second man from
Atlantic, with the understanding that he is to represent the
other village.

Other dignitaries are chosen—two sextons, a collector of
excise taxes, a surveyor of wood and lumber, and a fire warden.
As each officer is picked, the town clerk swears him in on the

spot. Only a half dozen or so vote for some of these positions. In the election of the fire warden, only one vote is cast, but on being asked by the moderator, the assembly declares itself satisfied. The election of the collector of personal and real estate taxes fills the last political office. Of the past year's taxes $1,876.32 remain ungathered, so that a new collector seems desirable. A man who has held the job in the past with great efficiency is finally chosen. He acknowledges the honor and announces that if the fishermen have any money next fall he will get the taxes. His terms are three percent, part of which he will turn over to the school fund. The previous collector turned over all her percentage to the school.

Taxes, of course, are a sore point throughout the meeting. One irate citizen says that the owner—or previous owner—of a house on which there has been a tax lien has been renting an apartment in it and keeping the rent. The selectmen reluctantly admit that this had been so. They had winked at the situation because they thought the owner "could use the money." They promise not to make a practice of that sort of thing. A special motion is then passed authorizing the selectmen "to sell and dispose of any real estate acquired by the town for non-payment of taxes thereon and to execute quitclaim deeds for such property." It is also voted that the town will collect 6 percent on taxes not paid by October 1—a date chosen because usually at that time of year the lobsters "are coming well" and the fishermen have as much money as they ever have.

At noon the meeting adjourns for an hour. The last piece of morning business was to "raise" $8,603 for school expenses—teachers' and superintendent's pay, supplies, and textbooks. The people have already started to straggle downstairs where for one dollar a plate the Rebeccahs have prepared a dinner of beans, brown bread, salad, macaroni, coffee and pie. There have been no hard words upstairs, and there won't be. Anyone who wished to say something—even if he was not a legal voter—has had his chance to speak. Most, in fact, have said nothing but have participated by voting for officers on slips of paper or by show of hands on the issues brought up. Now all sit together at the long tables and eat, but only after the minister has said grace. A separate table has been spread for the children, for school has been closed so that the teachers may attend the meeting in their own home town on the mainland.

3

The meal is leisurely. Nothing in the day's proceedings is done with haste. But by quarter past one the officers are again at their places upstairs and the townspeople have begun to drift up. The afternoon's work will be almost entirely the appropriating of money. The men are more alert now. A shrewd, shifty look creeps over the faces of some of them. They gaze at the floor and glance out of the corners of their eyes as each sum is mentioned: funds for hot lunches at the school, $1,285 towards the payment on the school building, two hundred dollars for a garage for the town truck and school bus, eight hundred for town roads and bridges. Someone wants to know why this last sum is so high. Various people speak, among them a woman from a shanty at the North, who says that there is no longer any road out her way. The moderator corroborates her; the road, in fact, was dug up and, as gravel, taken elsewhere for fill. On the strength of such evidence the sum of eight hundred dollars stands.

The recommended appropriations have all been figured out ahead of time by a budget committee of five from each side, and their recommendations are followed without demur in the meeting. The town clerk is proud of this device, which saves much time and argument. What wrangles do occur are good-natured ones over small matters. For example, the question of the public wharf—formerly the steamboat landing—consumes almost an hour. The wharf was bought by the town three or four years ago for the sum of two thousand dollars, but nothing has been done to keep it in repair. Large-sized draggers coming into the harbor for the night tied up to the spilings and gradually broke them loose. The wharf, in a state of dangerous delapidation, is now used by a half dozen lobstermen as a storage place for their traps. At the town meeting someone fears that if one of these men falls through the rotten planking and breaks a leg, he will sue the town. The moderator asks if that wouldn't be a pretty cheap thing for anyone to do who is getting his facilities free, but the meeting decides that the selectmen should place a sign on the wharf disclaiming any legal responsibility. As for mending the wharf, no one wants the town to put out any money on it. Someone suggests that the town charge rent for its use, but the question of who would collect the rent is unsolvable. Finally it is voted that if the six present users wish to make some repairs at their own expense and risk, the town would place no obstacles in their way. Also a certain man who wishes to establish a fish-buying business on the island may build a shack on the wharf and make other improvements, if he so desires. Several citizens hope that Mr. Bousfield of the Maine Sea Coast Mission will take over the wharf as a place for the Mission boat to tie up. He would keep it in good repair and, of course, permit anyone else to use it.

Another discussion develops over the town dump. The present one has been condemned as unsightly and a breeder of rats. One hundred dollars are needed—and voted—to clear it up. But some other site must be found. The moderator speaks sternly of the litter made by people dumping their trash on the beaches, particularly near the homes of some of the older summer people. "It is disgraceful that that should be done to people who have been coming here so long and admire Swans Island the way they do." No one takes issue with his remarks. These are lovers of neatness, the possessors of spotless kitchens and boats. The indiscriminate disposal of garbage offends them more deeply than it does the summer people. Finally, a committee is appointed to study the matter and make some recommendations.

The meeting draws on towards the fifty-fourth and last article on the warrant. There has been little talking for the sake of talking. Yet anyone may speak. At no time does the moderator attempt to railroad an issue through. Always he is saying, "It's your decision. What do you think?" The only tense moment during the day was when someone questioned how the town could spend $876 removing two light falls of snow from 12.85 miles of road. The answer is that the state contributes sixty-five dollars per mile of road for snow removal; it would be folly not to use it.

The last article on the warrant now comes up: "To see if the town will vote to change the name of Finney (Phinney) Island, so-called, to Asa's Island as requested by Asa Phillips, Jr." The moderator's eyelids narrow as he reads the proposition. This island, an acre or so in size, is just north of the main island—named after an enterprising Irish citizen of the last century. But, the moderator explains, it is a hobby among yachtsmen to have an island namesake. Grins form on the lips of the townspeople and someone mutters the cliché, "These summer people do the craziest things." Mr. Asa

Phillips, the moderator continues, is a prominent lawyer. His attorney approached some island dignitaries concerning the change of name. They had been non-committal; they had said that the islanders always try to be obliging. But they thought that Mr. Phillips might be interested to know that the town was currently under heavy expense in building a school and everything wasn't covered by the state loan. Mr. Phillips is a public-spirited man and not one to receive favors without proper show of gratitude. "Now," the moderator went on, "we've received nothing yet, but neither have we given anything. For my part, I see no reason why we need to call the island anything but Finney ourselves. But if we put this through, the name will be Asa on the charts when they are reprinted." For the town, the moderator saw in the proposition a sum well in three figures. The vote is unanimously in the affirmative.

A few other items of business not on the warrant are discussed and the meeting adjourns. During the afternoon a mist has crept in, and a keen wind has begun to blow off the ocean to the eastward. In the twilight the people drive home hoping that lobsters will become more numerous before the tax deadline next October 1. But they have a feeling of fulfillment, of a job done to the best of their abilities and in accordance with the tradition of their island and race. There are no flamboyant mouthings about democracy any more than there was talk for the sake of talk in the meeting itself. Nor is there any smug condescension and regret over those who stayed at home out of inertia or spite. Compulsory attendance at town meetings has never been a part of the tradition.